WHY JESUS CHRIST WOULD NEVER, EVER VOTE REPUBLICAN

By
Richard John Siviur

Ranking the Presidents

A 1995 survey by 168 noted historians:

1. Franklin D. Roosevelt.	21. William H. Taft
2. Abraham Lincoln	22. Martin Van Buren
3. Theodore Roosevelt	23. Richard Nixon
4. George Washington	24. Rutherford B. Hayes
5. Thomas Jefferson	25. Jimmy Carter
6. Woodrow Wilson	26. Chester Arthur
7. Harry Truman	27. James Garfield
8. Dwight Eisenhower	28. William H. Harrison
9. James Madison	29. Herbert Hoover
10. John Kennedy	30. Benjamin Harrison
11. Andrew Jackson	31. George Bush
12. John Adams	32. Gerald Ford
13. Lyndon Johnson	33. Zachary Taylor
14. James Polk	34. John Tyler
15. James Monroe	35. Millard Fillmore
16. Bill Clinton	36. Calvin Coolidge
17. John Quincy Adams	37. Franklin Pierce
18. William McKinley	38. Ulysses S. Grant
19. Grover Cleveland	39. James Buchanan
20. Ronald Reagan	40. Andrew Johnson

41. Warren G. Harding

WHY JESUS CHRIST WOULD
NEVER, EVER VOTE REPUBLICAN

*****

CHAPTER I

This book, a labor of both toil and pleasure, constitutes a surgical dissection of the George Walker Bush Administration, together with the Republican Party past and present. Consider the party's first president, Abraham Lincoln, elected in 1860 and compare him to the current occupant of the White House, George Walker Bush, selected by the Supreme Court, one hundred and forty years later in 2000. Kindly pay close attention to that revealing phrase "current occupant" because at no point in this work is he referred to as president. Bush is and shall ever remain the Grand Larcenist, the candidate who in November, 2000, purposefully purloined the presidential office. A more appropriate title might be Thief-In-Chief. That infamous chapter will be dealt with in great detail further along in this disquisition.

In the 1860 presidential campaign, Abraham Lincoln had three other well-known opponents. But, even though he did not receive a single vote from Southern states, he still garnered 40% of the total, and carried eighteen states. His closest opponent, Stephen A. Douglas, like Abe from Illinois as well but a Democrat, netted 29% of the total but carried only one state, Missouri. Lincoln's two remaining contestants triumphed in fourteen states of which eleven would form the Confederacy in the forthcoming Civil War.

In the 2000 election, Bush's opponent, Vice President Al Gore, had a plurality of 540,000 votes but due to massive, and I do mean massive, fraud in Florida, where his brother Jeb was governor, and the worst decision by the U.S. Supreme Court in its entire history, Bush wound up in the White House.

Lincoln, having won his office honorably and convincingly in the most tumultuous election in the nation's history, was instantly confronted with an undeclared war even before assuming office. Seven Southern states met a month before his inauguration and voted to secede from the Union and form the Confederate States of America. They would shortly be joined by four others and these eleven states would, by firing on Fort Sumter, a federal fort in Charleston, S.C., harbor on April 12, 1861, officially launch the horrific civil war. The new president would guide our badly divided country, now ripped asunder by a bloody conflict, with unimaginable leadership skills, not merely as a politician at the head of state, but as a military tactician directing the army and navy. Simply put, he was absolutely majestic at both functions.

In so doing he manifested prodigious quantities of honesty, humility and most assuredly, integrity. Not long into his presidency, he came to be known as "Honest Abe." By comparison, can you possibly imagine anyone referring to George Walker Bush as Honest George? Well, perhaps his wife, Laura, and his mother Barbara might do so together with a scant but diminishing cadre of close relatives plus devoted sycophants that comprise his administration.

I would like to confess that "Honest Abe" is my favorite president from the standpoint of depth of character and likeability but understandably second only to the incomparable Franklin Delano Roosevelt, Democrat, elected in 1932.

And may I also dispose of the twin deceptions the Republicans frequently employ, one that they are the Party of Lincoln? An even more palpable attempt at deception is that they represent the Big Tent. The idea that the GOP is representative of many diverse elements is frankly hilarious. Overwhelmingly they are the POBB, the Party of Big Business. Most emphatically they are the Party of the White Male. One only has to scan their roster in Congress, and the list of governors, to establish the palpable absurdity of the Big Tent. In the current House of Representatives, part of the 110th Congress, there are 43 Black Americans. Due to a highly unusual alignment of sociological factors, all 43 are Democrats. In the Senate there is one Black American, a very famous one by now Barack Obama, and by an equally improbable situation, he too is Democratic. And, he too is from Illinois, just like "Honest Abe." Of the fifty governors, only one is black, Devall Patrick, of Massachusetts. Now this is becoming difficult to believe but Governor Devall Patrick is also Democratic. My, that's not much in the way of a Big Tent, is it? Now, let's complete the count. The House is comprised of 435 members. There are an even 100 in the Senate. Now, add the 50 governors and the total comes to 585 elected officials. That's 585 *of the highest elected politicians in the land.* The Republicans, the Party of the Big Tent lack a single black member. Let's count women in office. In the House there are 53 Democrats, 22 Republicans; in the Senate 11 Democrats and five Republicans. Among governors, six Democrats and three Republicans. Total 70 – 30. So, combining the 45 black Democrats, as opposed to zero Republicans and 70 Democratic women with 30 Republicans, we have 115 to 30 – almost a four to one ratio.

BLACKS

House	43 Democrats	zero Republican
Senate	one Democrat	zero "
Governors	one Democrat	zero "

WOMEN IN OFFICE

	Democrats	Republicans
House	53 Democrats	22 Republicans
Senate	11 "	5 "
Governors	6 "	3 "
Total	70 Democrats	30 Republicans
Blacks	45 "	0 "
Grand Total	115 "	30 "

"Well, we are the 'Party of Lincoln'," they boast. Suppose we examine the hollowness of that boast.

If Abraham Lincoln were to be transported back to the America of today, he would find himself comfortable in a niche somewhat to the left of center in today's Democratic Party. More to the point, he would view with absolute horror the guiding philosophy of today's Republican Congress and especially all the members of the Bush Administration. To validate that assertion, permit me to use his own writings and his lifelong political and economic philosophy. "The legitimate object of government," Honest Abe famously said, "is to do for a community of people whatever they need to have done, but cannot do at all, or cannot do so well for themselves in their separate and individual capacities." His concept of government's relationship to the economic welfare of the working class bears absolutely no consonance with that of the reactionary Republicans who controlled Congress until January, 2007, or to the Bushes' still in control of the White House.

Lincoln was elected four consecutive times to the Illinois Legislature from 1834 to 1840 as a member of the Whig Party. The Republican Party then was only a distant concept. During his eight years in office, he along with nearly all his fellow Whigs concentrated on passing progressive legislation to finance an elaborate program of roads, bridges, canals and railroads. All of these measures were to be funded either by the federal government or have the federal government guarantee state bonds.

Illinois at that early period in the nation's history still had a very small population and most parts of it were in dire need of a vastly expanded infrastructure. Everything produced by farms, factories and mines required transportation to move those products from the point of origin to the consumer. Still, the specter of what many conservatives considered to be socialism frightened them away from governmental assistance. Passionately wedded to the religion of *laissez-faire* economic theory, they demanded that private enterprise, and only private enterprise, undertake all of these improvements. Let business build toll-roads and toll-bridges or provide ferry boats to cross rivers and streams, they proclaimed. They had the identical attitude toward canals and railroads.

The financial Panic of 1837 short-circuited all the proposed legislation and none of it was undertaken. Still, Lincoln had established his credentials as a liberal, one firmly committed to governmental involvement in improving the lives of the people. He most emphatically was not in favor of *laissez-faire* economics, a term no longer used in politics today. Its new version is 'supply-side economics.' "These capitalists," he told his audience, "generally act harmoniously, and in concert, to fleece the people."

It is important to understand that Abraham Lincoln had been subjected to hard physical labor all his life until the age of twenty-four when, in May of 1833 he was appointed to the position of Postmaster in Salem, Illinois. (Parenthetically, I might add, George W. Bush has scarcely performed an honest day's work in his entire life.) Hence it is only natural that Lincoln would voice this attitude toward hard work. "Labor in this country is independent and proud. Capital is the only fruit of labor, and would never have existed if labor had not first existed. Labor is the superior of capital and deserves much more the higher consideration."

He would be more emphatic with this utterance, "As labor is the common burden of our race, so the effort of some to shift the burden onto the shoulders of others is the great doable curse of our race."

Honest Abe is the diametric opposite of the current occupant of the White House in nearly every aspect, but most emphatically in his position on economic thought. Lincoln's every action and statement forcefully demonstrates how liberal he was. In stark contrast, Bush ranks at the very top of reactionary Republicans who have reached the White House. William McKinley, first elected in 1896, was easily the most reactionary of 19th century Republican presidents. Ronald Reagan achieved that honor in the 20th century. Bush is their equal. So the idea today, that the Republican Party is the 'Party of Lincoln', is as laughable as the nonsense about the Big Tent.

But Lincoln and his fellow Illinois legislators unquestionably were influenced in their attitude toward governmental initiatives in the enhancement of the infrastructure, and improving transportation, by what had occurred in New York State earlier in the century. Beginning in 1817, Governor DeWitt Clinton persuaded the state legislature to fund a project that would soon attain international renown, the Erie Canal. Governor Clinton (and please note that name, Clinton) early on saw the fantastic potential in a canal from Albany, the state capital, to Buffalo, a major city on the eastern shore of Lake Erie. Albany was located on the upper reaches of the broad, navigable Hudson River. The canal would then link New York City with its enormous Atlantic Ocean traffic, to that of the trans-Allegheny region of Lake Erie together with the four other Great Lakes. The cost would be $7 million, a gargantuan sum of money in those days, probably the equivalent of $3 billion in today's dollars. The proposed canal would be 363 miles long, forty-four feet wide and four feet deep.

This project required more than eight years to track through the wilderness area from Albany to Buffalo. Roads didn't exist to accommodate the needs of both horsepower and man's efforts so they had to be built. There was a 500-foot rise in elevation crossing the Allegheny Mountains so that eighty- two locks had to be constructed. A stupendous amount of solid rock had to be removed enroute to Lake Erie.

The canal finally opened on October 25, 1825, when Abraham Lincoln was sixteen years old. The result was nearly unimaginable except perhaps for Governor Clinton, its originator. New York City simply exploded with commercial activity. A virtual tsunami of immigrants and settlers flowed westward into the burgeoning areas of Ohio, Indiana, Illinois and Michigan. Towns along the route such as Schenectady, Syracuse, Rochester, and, of course, Buffalo expanded tremendously.

Transportation costs from New York City to Buffalo were slashed by 90%, from $100 to $10 a ton. In only nine years the canal paid for itself and by 1882, transportation on it was free. Of equal importance, the canal soon funded the construction of several smaller canals that fed into Erie. Over the course of some years, this marvelous mode of transportation was widened, deepened and had automatic locks installed.

None of this, of course, had any significance to the worshipers of *laissez-faire* economics. Translated from the French it means, "let people do as they please." What it translated into for right-wing types was, "let business get away with as much as it can." What enraged these pirates was the government's encroaching onto the sacred province of private business, an arena which must be preserved for all eternity for individual entrepreneurs. They were venomous in denouncing any governmental entity tackling these desperately needed improvements. But waiting for private capital to finance the insatiable need for internal improvements would slow the pace of construction to a glacial rate.

CHAPTER II

Abraham Lincoln's political career was indeed modest before he captured the Republican Party's nomination for the presidency in 1860. He had served four consecutive terms in the Illinois State Legislature, beginning in 1834 when he was but twenty-five years old .He immediately tried for Congress in1844, was defeated but two years later he was elected. In his two years in the House of Representatives he accomplished little of merit. An unwritten agreement existed between the various contestants limiting their service in the House to one term. He spent the next eleven years expanding his career as an attorney and by 1858 he had become one of the most successful lawyers in the state.

How did Abe pull this off with the multitude of formidable handicaps confronting him? First off, he had but one year of so-called formal education. One year, mind you! And that over a period of far more than one year, and under different itinerant teachers, and some with less than exemplary educational backgrounds. Finally, all of it in a one-room schoolhouse! His first mother, although beloved of him, was illiterate and died when he was but nine-years old. His next mother could neither read nor write, nor could his father.

Abe was extremely tall and grew to be six feet, four inches, a most unusual height for that era. He had enormous hands and moved somewhat awkwardly. He had spent his entire youth in crude log shacks, lacking any amenities. One entire winter he lived in a structure open to the elements at the entrance. Course material was used for his clothing which, in addition, was roughly made and always fit him poorly. Without exception his hands and feet extended inches from the ends of his sleeves and pants legs.

Yet, young Mr. Lincoln possessed two absolutely priceless characteristics that would enable him to crawl out of these wretched circumstances and become such a transcendental figure in our nation's history. His family's genes bequeathed to him an inordinately high IQ, one that permits me to say he was our country's most intelligent president. The other ingredient, and probably just as important, was his memory which suggested near total recall.

A close examination of that intellect persuades Mario M. Cuomo in his book, *Why Lincoln Matters*, to announce, "We are dazzled by the dimensions of his intelligence and the strength of his will." He would then add, "the breadth, width and depth of his wisdom penetrate through the surface of many temporal issues into the heart of matters modern and seemingly insoluble."

As Governor of New York, Mr. Cuomo continued the glorious tradition of the two Roosevelts: Theodore in the 19th century, and cousin Franklin Delano in the 20th. In his book which is an absolute delight to read, Governor Cuomo continues his appraisal of Honest Abe. "His high intelligence, powerful sense of practicality, elegant speeches and writings, and his general deportment which created an implosion of rock-solid honesty, integrity and strength wrapped in a charming persona, added to his attractiveness."

We have already compared President Lincoln with Bush on the matter of honesty, so now let us approach the area of intelligence. Dubya is a member of the species *Homo sapiens,* a Latin form usually translated as "thinking man." But just as nobody other than a select few of his relatives, and a comparative number of his inner circle, would refer to him as Honest George, only a similar number would unite "intelligent" with "George W. Bush." Many years of slavish devotion to various forms of alcohol have seriously eroded what native cognitive ability he once possessed. Combine that with his well- known affinity for cocaine and the result is a tragically diminished capacity for any type of leadership, much less leading the free world.

One other matter deserves our attention. In Abraham Lincoln we have a president with the least formal education of all our chief executives and yet he effortlessly surpasses all others in his oratorical ability. Most of our presidents in the 20th Century had a team of speech writers, yet Lincoln alone authored all of his speeches. Biographers refer to his astonishing oratory; they praise his 'haunting poetry'; they speak in awe of the lyricism of his phrases and discuss in learned fashion how those phrases approached the metered cadences of poetry. Terms like 'musical rhythms' are often employed.

His first truly notable speech was delivered to a tough audience of fifteen hundred smart, well-educated New Yorkers on February 27, 1860. Lincoln had attracted a modest national reputation following a series of seven debates with Senator Stephen A. Douglas of Illinois, in a contest for the senatorial seat in the 1858 election. Douglas was one of the best known political figures in the nation whereas Lincoln had a following largely confined to Illinois. But, those debates gradually attracted a nationwide audience as they were reproduced in many of the country's leading newspapers. Our-boy-Abe more than held his own with the polished Douglas as they discussed the matter of slavery and its possible expansion into the new territories. Senatorial elections were decided by the state legislatures, as they would continue to be until 1913 so, in 1858, the Illinois group unfairly awarded the seat to Douglas.

Lincoln had won a coveted invitation to speak to this crowd at Cooper Union, a New York City College. By that date, in 1860, he had become one of the sharpest attorneys in Illinois and had established a handsome legal practice. He could now afford to purchase appropriate clothing and indeed he did invest in a new suit for the occasion but it still fit him badly. As he rose to speak he was acutely aware that he was altogether different from the members of the audience. Not only was he much taller than anybody else but he spoke with a rural twang and had mannerisms which identified him as an unsophisticated Midwesterner. Also, that brand new suit was badly rumpled from the long trip.

As soon as he began his speech, these minor faults were overlooked and he rapidly gained the confidence of the group. His initial remarks were for the benefit of Southerners who were agitating for secession from the Union and were more than willing to go to war if necessary. Lincoln appealed to them to look upon the North not as their enemy, but as fellow countrymen who were entirely willing to allow slavery to continue in The South.

Next he addressed the Republicans in the audience by vigorously defending his new party. He insisted that peace must be preserved. "Let us do nothing through passion and ill-temper. Even though the southern people will not so much as listen to us, let us calmly consider their demands, and yield to them if, in our deliberate view of our duty, we possibly can."

But he also insisted that slavery must be contained and never allowed to contaminate the new territories. In a highly charged closing, he admonished them, "Let us have faith that right makes might, and in that faith, let us to the end, dare to do our duty as we understand it."

The moment he finished the audience sprang to its feet, motivated by the intensity both of the speaker and his message. Large numbers of them hurried to the speaker's platform, anxious to shake Lincoln's hand. It was almost unheard of for a newcomer to the area to have so forceful an impact on a large, worldly group as this Cooper Union crowd.

The following morning the New York Tribune published a story on its editorial page glorifying Lincoln's speech. Horace Greeley, the nationally known founder and editor of the paper declared, "The speech of Abraham Lincoln at the Cooper Union last evening was one of the happiest and most convincing political arguments ever made in this city to a crowded and appreciating audience. Mr. Lincoln is one of the nation's orators, using his rare powers solely and effectively to convince, though their inevitable effect is to delight and electrify as well. No man ever before made such an impression in his first appeal to a New York audience."

The author of these remarks was very likely the most renowned newspaper figure in America and had almost single-handedly built the New York Tribune into a powerhouse of publishing with a paid circulation of 216,000. It was widely read in nearby states like Pennsylvania, Illinois and Ohio. Greeley had jumped on the bandwagon of the New Republican Party right from its inception because both he and the party were militantly opposed to slavery. The other three New York papers also printed his speech in its entirety.

Lincoln's political prospects bounded forward at an astonishing rate immediately following his epochal oration. Invitations poured in for him to address fellow Republicans particularly throughout New England. Very quickly he embarked on an ambitious tour of Rhode Island, Connecticut and New Hampshire. Prominent state politicians flocked to join his cavalcade. He was even introduced as the nation's next president. This extensive circuit rapidly became an unimaginable triumph as Republicans began to cherish this new face on the presidential horizon. In a matter of a few weeks, Lincoln had risen from near total obscurity to one of shining prominence.

Back home in Illinois his Republican admirers also began regarding him in this new light – that of a presidential hopeful. They began more openly to discuss his positive worthiness for that high office. Because of his newly acquired popularity, Lincoln soon acquired a sense of self-assurance. What's more he now openly admitted that he might have a shot at the Republican nomination. When confronted by an old acquaintance he coyly admitted, "the taste is in my mouth a little."

Good fortune of course hadn't descended upon him completely by chance. He had crafted the now famous speech, working alone over a period of six days. He had no cadre of speech writers struggling in his behalf. No indeed, he labored in a painstaking manner, working and manipulating the phrases and sentences. In the process he was carefully unifying the artistic skills necessary to becoming the consummate architect of speech craft that was his goal. With his simple and touching eloquence he fashioned an impressive structure that was marvelously effective in its imaginative power and soaring grandeur. The 1500 members of the audience at Cooper Union were spellbound.

Books were treasured objects for young Abe. He had access to but a few, but he did more than read them, he nearly devoured them. He remembered five that greatly influenced his formative years: *The Life of George Washington, Aesop's Fables, Pilgrim's Progress, Robinson Crusoe,* and *A History of the United States.* His biographers emphasize how he would eagerly walk for miles to gain access to a book and then shortly return it to its owner. There is no record of his parents owning such a valued commodity.

Reading books was not considered a valuable way in which to expend time for George Bush. A painful distinction must be made between the two men. Dubya was 180° separated from Lincoln when the subject of intellectual curiosity arose. That becomes readily apparent in listening to him deliver a speech. Within a sentence or two he quickly puts to flight any possible thought of oratorical greatness. Worse, the content of those remarks is invariably pedestrian, unbecoming the current occupant of the White House.

CHAPTER III

It can be said with complete justification that in the human brain the evolutionary process arrived at its apogee. No part of any mammal, as indeed we *Homo sapiens* are also mammals, can possibly compare with the perfection that is our brain. Evolution toiled for a handful of millions of years –advancing, regressing– producing in turn *Homo habilis, Homo erectus, Neanderthal man,* then *Cro-Magnon man,* and finally, our species. In searching for a definitive description of the human brain, we should turn to Hippocrates, the ancient Greek regarded as the true father of medicine. Born in the year 460 B.C., he is easily medicine's most venerated figure. He bequeathed to mankind an enchanting description of that glob of grey matter located between our ears. "Not only our pleasure, our joy and our laughter but also our sorrow, pain, grief and fears arise from the brain, and the brain alone. With it we think and understand, see and hear, and we discriminate between the ugly and beautiful, between what is pleasant and what is unpleasant, and between good and evil."

With a kindly assist from Evolution, George Herbert Walker Bush and Barbara Bush would produce George Walker Bush on July 6, 1946 in New Haven, Connecticut. The three Bushes would reside there for two more years before venturing forth to Odessa, Texas. In so doing, the family moved from a profoundly blue state, that is, a decidedly liberal one, to a frighteningly backward red state, one moving inexorably toward a reactionary entity.

For the first seven years of his educational life, little George attended public schools, but the following year saw him at the exclusive, private Kinkaid in Houston. Next would be the even more private, exclusive Phillips Academy in Andover, Massachusetts. There he was confronted with a tough schedule, not designed for average students who wanted only to stroll through its curriculum.

In a deeply discerning review of George W. and the entire Bush clan, *Fortunate Son* by J.H. Hatfield, we learn how, at this stage of his life, "The new student at Phillips had a badly compromised comprehension of English, his native tongue." For his first English assignment –an essay on an emotional experience—Dubya looked up the word "tears" in a thesaurus his mother had given him. He then proceeded to hand in a paper which read, "Lacerates ran down my cheeks." Mr. Hatfield continues, "This prompted his professor to give him a big fat zero and called Junior's paper disgraceful." At this juncture, the young student was extremely worried about flunking out of school.

Mr. Hatfield's biography is a splendidly amusing read for anybody who views Bush as a disgrace to our nation's history and considers him the worst chief executive of all time.

As Mr. Hatfield recounts, "In his final year at Andover, the school dean asked George where he planned to attend college. When Bush replied that he was considering Yale, the school administrator quickly informed him that there was no way he could gain admission there and suggested he consider an alternative school".

The dean, of course, was absolutely correct. Had the student's name been George Walker he and Yale would never have had any association. But, as we will repeatedly observe, where George Walker Bush is concerned wondrous happenings occur, and indeed, one would take place shortly. His father, George Herbert Walker Bush, was a graduate of Yale, as was his grandfather, Prescott, who also was a United States senator from Connecticut. In addition, George had uncles who too were alumni of the university.

With the swelling chorus of those voices importuning the Admissions Office to admit little Georgie, you can readily understand how Yale's beckoning arms would soon embrace the Pampered Parasite, also known as the P.P. As his home while at Yale, he would naturally select the nationally famous, fatuous fraternity of Delta Kappa Epsilon, justifiably celebrated across the land as campus party animals. He fit in with his fellow frat members like a hand in a custom-made glove.

Majoring in downing alcohol and scoring with sorority girls, he breezed through Yale in a glorious haze. The latter was the result of not infrequent bouts with cocaine and marijuana. Throughout his political life he has never denied his association with the two mind-altering drugs (although I have long suspected there was not much there to alter). With all these elements in mind, he graduated *summa cum laude*, at the absolute pinnacle of his class, that is within the narrow ranks of the frat animals.

Years later when he began his political career in Texas, and was forced to defend the profligacy of his college years he would say, "When I was young and irresponsible, I behaved young and irresponsible." I suppose that is a modest improvement over "Lacerates ran down my cheeks," but I can't believe that Yale is proud of his English grammar.

After enduring this rigorous educational trial for four years, he then applied to the University of Texas Law School for admittance. The dean, Page Keeton, was rather unimpressed with the Yalie's academic credentials. When one of the P.P's family friends recommended him for acceptance, the dean replied: "I am sure young Mr. Bush has all the many amiable qualities you describe, and so will find a place at one of the many fine institutions around the country. But not at the University of Texas." I am indebted for that quote to the late Molly Ivins who embedded that gem in her fascinating study, "Shrub," published in 2000, but before the presidential elections of that year.

Dismissing his humiliation, however momentary, Dubya would not remain downcast for long since Harvard Business School extended an invitation to him. In later life he would loudly condemn those of his critics who had the temerity to suggest that his acceptance into Yale and Harvard was due to political and monetary intervention. He would point out rather testily that just because two generations of Bushes had graduated from Yale is totally irrelevant. The further point that Grandfather Bush was a U.S. Senator from Connecticut was simply unimportant.

It is indeed interesting to note that while in Harvard for those two years, the Pampered Parasite would appear on campus wearing cowboy boots, chewing a wad of tobacco and carrying in hand a small plastic cup for the excretions. He also prominently displayed a large Confederate flag in his fraternity room.

In May of 1968, our MBA from Harvard, together with millions of young American men were becoming acutely concerned with the intense level of military conflict taking place in Southeast Asia, with particular reference to a long, thin country called Vietnam. They were even more sensitive to the fact that a universal draft for young American men was in effect. Television and newspapers informed them in an exceedingly graphic manner that unacceptable numbers of draftees were being killed and maimed on a daily basis in that undeclared war.

Meanwhile rock-ribbed Republicans, conservatives and reactionaries alike, steadfastly believed that Vietnam was where the deadly advance of Communism must be stopped in its tracks. The domino theory, a highly charged issue in those circles, was in play. They passionately believed if that country fell, then Communistic hordes would roll unchecked throughout the region. When it came time to stopping Communism in its tracks however, they didn't intend for their sons and nephews to do the stopping. No, that would be the work of other people's sons and nephews. Accordingly those rock-ribbed Republicans adopted evasive stratagems such as enrolling their offspring in divinity schools or joining National Guard units or having the family physician stoutfastly maintain, in a letter to the young man's draft board, that he had a bum knee or a bad back which simply must preclude him from service. Numerous members of today's Congress benefited from such a letter. To this day I find it near miraculous how, after the conflict ended the knees and backs responded to treatment and the spared recruit managed a providential recovery.

Naturally the idea of escaping combat in that dreadful, tropical country would appeal to the P.P. Enlisting in the Texas Air National Guard suddenly had enormous merit, both in his and his family's eyes. A considerable problem existed however. Tens of thousands of other young men in Texas, with just the same goal in mind, had already signed up. Dubya was too far down the list to avoid that damned draft.

But wait! Remember the peculiar circumstance of his gaining acceptance into Yale? Well, several more of these strange coincidences were about to unfold. An underground railroad system was in effect in Texas and it would move our boy George to the front of the line ahead of those thousands of young Texas men. In all fairness it must be pointed out that the underground railroad didn't exist for the exclusive benefit of the fortunate son. Numerous members of the Dallas Cowboys football team, plus the sons of bigshot Texas politicians also took advantage of this equal opportunity. The offspring of former Senator Lloyd Bentson and former Governor John Connally, both Democrats, benefited from the fast forwarding to the Guard.

Colin Powell, Secretary of State in the first Bush Administration, and former Chief of Staff of the Army of the United States, had this acerbic comment in his autobiography: "I am angry that so many of the sons of the powerful and well-placed managed to wangle slots in Reserve and National Guard units. Of the many tragedies in Vietnam, this new class discrimination strikes me as the most damaging to the ideal that all Americans are created equal."

Dick Cheney, who helped purloin the White House in 2000, also benefited from this class distinction. On five separate occasions he successfully fought off his draft board's efforts to outfit him in an army uniform. I really believe it was in this period that he and Bush evolved their highly successful "cut-and-run" strategy which they so artfully employed against the Democrats after the Grand Larceny. Dubya would cut while Cheney would run, then Cheney would cut while Bush did the running. It worked beautifully.

The further we venture into Dubya's military adventure, the sleazier it becomes. As a newly accepted member of the Texas Air National Guard he entered with the bottom rank of private, an undesirable status for a man of his accustomed level of gentility. He had only to wait a few months and more opportunity would come his way. He received his second lieutenant rank in what could only be described as an immaculate ascension, one of the fastest promotions in American military history. Numerous qualifications were necessary to gain officer status and he lacked every one of them. For example, a year and a half of prior military service plus six months of active duty. He didn't have a day of prior service. Then it was mandatory that officer training be completed. He fails there, also.

The rapid ascent of the Pampered Parasite in the Guard most emphatically was not the result of a series of fortuitous events; oh no, it came after four strategically placed phone calls. The first of these was from his father, George Herbert Walker Bush, then a Congressman representing Houston, and it was directed to a family friend and an influential businessman in Texas. This friend, Sidney Adger, next made a call to Ben Barnes, the Speaker of the Texas House of Representatives. The third call came from Mr. Barnes to the Commanding Officer of the Texas National Guard, Brigadier General James Rose. Only one last telephone call was necessary and that from the General to the Commanding Officer of the 147th Fighter Group, Lieutenant Colonel Buck Staudt.

Now a Lieutenant Colonel quickly perceives what's on the mind of a Brigadier General, two grades of command higher and if he wishes someday to become a Brigadier General he immediately acquiesces to the chain of command. Our boy George was now a member of the 147th Fighter Group, also known as the "Champagne Group" since it contained all the young men who rode in on the underground railroad.

According to the "pampered one", under no circumstances were these unbelievably providential breaks the result of intervention on the part of his father. "They just happened," he would say, adding, "I think they just needed pilots."

Why on earth would the officers running the Texas Air National Guard select an applicant whose score was at the very bottom of those qualifying for admission? Consuming unwholesome amounts of alcohol and snorting unhealthy doses of cocaine doesn't sharpen the rapid response needed to pilot a jet. Somehow the P.P. never bothered to address that problem.

Dubya's father was equally assertive in maintaining this elaborate falsehood that he never used his influence to obtain a highly desirable slot for his son. Both Bushes have evolved into enormously skillful artists at duplicity and political cunning; at plausible deniability they are world class.

Permit me to insert a priceless joke told by Senator John McCain who contested Bush in the 2000 Republican primary. The Senator related that, as a prisoner of war for five long years and as an actual combat pilot, he was enormously heartened by the knowledge that his opponent was sweeping the skies of Texas free of any Viet Cong aircraft. Nonetheless the T.B.s, the True Believers, the faithful pimps on right wing talk shows, together with George's resolute buddies on Fox News, the fair and balanced network, are ever ready to vouchsafe that his service in the Texas Air National Guard "has been fully documented" and everything was in order. When you add the contribution of the sickening sycophants from the Wall Street Journal editorial page, one becomes aware of the powerful tidal wave available to the RRRs, the Rotten Reactionary Republicans.

Consider the difference between Dubya and his 2000 presidential opponent, Vice President Al Gore. Albert Gore was the sole member of his Harvard graduating class to volunteer for duty in Vietnam. He actually spent six months in that wretched country as a combat photographer but the lunatics on the far right denigrated his service to the nation by a shameful degree. According to one version, young Mr. Gore had fifteen bodyguards escorting him. Count them, fifteen bodyguards! Now his father, a former Senator from Tennessee, could have began making phone calls a la Dubya's dad. Instead his son volunteered for service in Vietnam at about the same time Dubya was running around like a terrified bunny rabbit to ensure that he never embarked upon a boat headed for Southeast Asia.

It would be interesting to determine the source of the fifteen bodyguard rumor. Just possibly it might have been the fair-and-balanced Rush Limbaugh or the pristinely non-partisan Karl Rove, widely believed to be "Bush's Brain." With Bush's cognitive failings, he needs one.

Our boy's Texas Guard misadventure was an obscene joke. It was virtually a continuation of his college career which consisted of idling through life, doing nothing of any merit, downing heroic quantities of alcohol while punctuating these episodes with not infrequent indulgences in narcotics. He had only entered the Guard on May 27, 1968 but by September of that year he was able to go on inactive duty to help promote the candidacy of Edward Gurney, running as a Republican in the Florida Senate race. Gurney would campaign against LeRoy Collins, the former governor of Florida. Governor Collins had the distinction of being the first politician of any stature in any of the former slave states to inveigh against segregation, calling it both "unfair and morally wrong." Gurney seized upon this and, being a contemptuous racist, tarred Collins as "Liberal LeRoy."

I lived in St. Petersburg at the time and looked upon Gurney as a near worthless scoundrel. (Very likely any scoundrel, by definition, is near worthless.) Nevertheless he coasted to an easy victory, with a winning margin of 300,000 votes. Contributing mightily to that plurality were the voters from rural and small town Florida, the Bible Belt Boobs or BBBs. Their voting habits haven't changed noticeably since the early 19th century.

Few citizens of Florida today remember Gurney, since he was a one-term Senator, whereas LeRoy Collins commands outstanding respect as the best politician the state ever produced. But, our boy George witnessed the unfolding event close-up and quickly realized that the "Southern Strategy" initially espoused by Barry Goldwater in 1964 and quickly adopted by Richard Nixon in 1968, had an abundance of political merit. Nixon limped to victory that year over Hubert Humphrey and to this day I regard that win of "Tricky Dick" to have been a political catastrophe for the nation and the office of the presidency. To liberals, Tricky Dick already had several coats of slime affixed to him and would prove to be a dishonorable crook doomed to impeachment. His running mate, Spiro Agnew was himself a crook but conducted activities on a much lower level. He was forced to resign his office nearly a year before Nixon was quite literally kicked out of office in August, 1974.

In making comparisons of presidential/vice-presidential tandems, the absolute nadir was reached by the duo of Warren Gamaliel Harding, President, and his running mate Calvin Coolidge, both reactionary Republicans. A review of the rank of presidents at the beginning of this book shows that Harding is the least meritorious of all presidents. Our boy George, the Pampered Parasite, has already supplanted him and will be number forty-two.

Obviously, with Harding in the lowest position and Coolidge outdistancing all but a handful to reside at number-36, they are well deserving of their place in history. Clearly Nixon and Agnew are the runners-up, that is, before Bush/Cheney are counted. Both Tricky Dick and Agnew were intelligent men but possessed a malignant strain of dishonesty and mendacity which caused their downfall. During the 1974 impeachment hearings, for Nixon, the House of Representatives approved of three articles: Obstruction of justice; abuse of power; and finally, failure to comply with congressional subpoenas. On August 9, 1974, knowing that the Senate was in a near unanimous desire to convict him, Richard Milhous Nixon very reluctantly quit his office.

We now turn to Spiro T. Agnew, holder of the all-time record of felony counts charged to either a president or vice president. His political fate was sealed when the brother of a former Republican Senator from Maryland was assigned to lead a team of investigators looking into allegations of bribery in the Maryland governor's office. The governor being pursued was a Democrat who immediately preceded Agnew. It is with a particularly delicious irony that we find the person responsible for launching the investigation was President Richard Nixon. He was supremely confident that large mounds of Democratic dirt would be unearthed in the ensuing inquiry. Instead, the trail toward iniquity quickly led to Nixon's Vice-President, old Spiro. This was a disquieting turn of events for all concerned – the investigators, the President of the United States and, of course, Agnew who, it was overwhelmingly disclosed, had been on the take as county executive in Baltimore and then as governor. What was worse, it soon became distressingly obvious that he was unwilling to end a good thing with his election to the vice-presidency and had continued to accept bribes throughout his first term in that office.

Agnew's election to Governor of Maryland was an absolute fluke, a point which we won't pursue here. Nixon then selected him for his running mate because it appeared he would carry less unfavorable baggage than any other candidate.

Back in Maryland, the Nixon appointed inquisitors originally decided to charge Agnew with fifty-seven counts of felony. My goodness, nearly five dozen! In another case of delectable irony, had the Watergate scenario not been brought to light, and that required innumerable interventions of good fortune, felonious Spiro might have become the next president in the 1976 election. Before the twin devastations of the Agnew problem and Watergate, he was the putative Republican candidate for the nomination that year. Trailing him well in the rear was Ronald Reagan, then Governor of California.

With the combined total of their favorable ratings at considerably less than 50%, Bush and Cheney will plummet to the bottom of the heap, given that the total is far more likely to decline than rise. I remain supremely confident in that prediction, what with their inimitable ability to do nothing right. President Clinton's rating meanwhile remains comfortably around 65%.

Now, back to the Texas Air National Guard. Dubya graduated from training school, went on to Tyndall Air Force Base in Florida where he also completed his mission. However, during that year of 1970 he spent a notable amount of time working for his father's U.S. Senatorial campaign against Senator Ralph Yarborough of Texas. The senior Bush did not win. Shortly thereafter we find Dubya attached to the staff of Winston "Red" Blount who resigned his post as Postmaster General in the Nixon Administration to challenge the Senator from Alabama, John Sparkman. Nixon, running for reelection, carried Alabama with 72% of the vote, while Blount came in with exactly half that amount. During the race, the familiar Republican themes of race were introduced by the Blount faction. This pernicious feature would play a significant role in future Bush family campaigns. By way of illustration, the TV ads which Bush Senior employed in the 1988 presidential run against Governor Dukakis of Massachusetts are still considered paradigms of wretched, vicious campaigning. Dubya would employ these tactics with savage effectiveness, first in his 2000 presidential primary race against Senator John McCain in South Carolina and then against Senator John Kerry in the 2004 presidential contest. The Bushes are fast learners and recognize a good thing when they see it.

Our hero was now in a status called "obligated reservist" which mandated that he must pursue his Guard training. He next made application to transfer from Texas to Alabama but his application was rejected since the Alabama National Guard had no planes and hence did no flying. A critic of Bush might sardonically suggest that this was the overriding reason for his request. As a consequence, during the months of May through August, while by law he was required to travel back to Houston to pursue his Guard duties there, he simply did nothing. Worse than that, he was now confronted with a major dilemma – he was keenly aware he could not resume flying until he took and passed the annual physical, and he knew he couldn't pass that dreaded test due to his preferred life style.

Once again intercession from a powerful source eased his passage to a non-flying status – he was transferred to the 187th Tactical Reconnaissance Group in Montgomery, Alabama. Ordered to report to Lieutenant Colonel William Turnipseed, the P.P. never bothered to show up.

During the 2000 presidential campaign, Col. Turnipseed appeared before the public and strongly asserted that if a first lieutenant from Texas by the name of Bush had appeared he would easily have remembered it. No such person ever showed up!

During the protracted and senseless war in Vietnam, 58,209 American military were killed in combat, while 153,000 were wounded. Huge numbers of these were maimed for life, shorn of a limb or eye. One statistic that has endlessly eluded me is how many additional veterans from that war have taken their own life after service. I believe it is in the thousands! Altogether about two and a half million men and women saw service in 'Nam'. But not, of course, Bush or Cheney. In addition to those two, fluffy types like Karl Rove, Richard Perle, Paul Wolfowitz and others perfected the technique of the cut-and-run to remain comfortably out of reach of their draft boards. It's probably just as well – militarily speaking, they would have had the combat capabilities of fighting field mice.

The reference to mice calls to mind a famous poem by Robert Burns, the National Poet of Scotland who departed from this earth in 1796, after only a very brief stay. The poem is "To A Mouse" and contains several of the most widely quoted lines in all of poetdom. Bobby Burns owned a small farm in Scotland and during the spring plowing season unearthed the burrowed nest of a mother mouse. The poet very much regretted the incident:

"But, mousie, thou art no thy lane,
In proving foresight may be vain:
The best laid schemes o' mice and men

Gang aft a-gley
An' leave us naught but grief and pain.
For promised joy."

The quintet of Bushes' cited above toiled ceaselessly to stampede the nation into a war with Iraq by trumpeting the enormous benefits to be obtained. Those 'best laid schemes' would lead to a quick and painless victory, they promised, and even further assured us that flowers would be strewn in the paths of our conquering troops. Alas, all of the Bushes' lacked the vision to see that their plans would ultimately leave 'naught but grief and pain for promised joy.'

Several lines later, Burns casts his eye 'on prospects drear.' Regrettably that is what American eyes will behold in the coming year.

A little known and almost secretive program was undertaken during the Vietnam War called Project 100,000, a truly pernicious application of the draft. In order to compensate for all the white, affluent chaps who were able to cut-and-run, this project was inaugurated in 1966. Its aim was to select 100,000 mostly indigent, poorly educated men each year and "rehabilitate them for induction material." These lads had previously failed to pass minimum qualifications. Simply by lowering the qualifying score, it became easier to be eligible for draft material. The project came to be known as the "Moron Squad." In this manner all those marvelous student deferments and bloated National Guard units could be maintained.

In 1970, the Defense Department released a study which found that 41% of the group were black soldiers, compared to 12% in the regular draft. 40% of the project's members were trained for combat compared to 25%. An earlier report in 1969 revealed that the project's combat fatalities were nearly twice the rate of the other draftees. The Bush Administration has seen fit to promote a similar gambit to keep the Army ranks filled. According to a New York Times editorial on February 20, 2007, "the Army has had to keep lowering its expectations. Diluting educational, aptitude and medical standards has not been enough. Nor have larger enlistment bonuses plugged the gap. So the Army has found itself recklessly expanding the granting of "moral waivers" which let people convicted of serious misdemeanors and even felonies enlist in its ranks."

The editorial continues by pointing out that in the past three years, "more than 125,000 moral waivers have been granted by America's four military services." Most of them were for serious misdemeanors – we're not talking small bore stuff here. No, "more like aggravated assault, robbery, burglary and vehicular homicide." Also, around 900 were for felonies. Just look at what our cut-and-run experts can do when they set their minds to the task.

Permit me to turn for a moment to Dubya's 2000 presidential campaign, painful as that episode is. During the race his numerous and highly vociferous defenders boldly asserted that every aspect of his Guard service "was fully documented" and "his performance was in compliance with the Guard regulations; further more, the subject should be closed." Many of these same voices tried to crucify Bill Clinton when he ran in 1992 against Bush Senior. Funny thing. President Clinton's record, while not reflecting the finest traditions of patriotic performance was never closed. The RRRs, the Rotten Reactionary Republicans, hounded him throughout the election process. Actually, they tore into him starting back in 1991. But Bill Clinton didn't have a father who was a Congressman, or a grandfather who had been a U.S. Senator. His father had died in an auto accident months before his birth. His mother was compelled to leave him in the care of her mother while she completed nursing school. Young Bill had nobody to call the Speaker of the House of Representative in Arkansas, or to intercede for him with the Commanding Officer of the Arkansas National Guard. Young Bill made no effort to join a bogus National Guard unit.

When his draft status came up for review, Bill Clinton was a Rhodes Scholar in England. This is a highly elevated educational status which reflects a brain functioning at a spectacular level. I would wager serious money that in a Mensa administered IQ test the former president could spot the current occupant of the White House 50-points and still easily beat him. Instead of a Rhodes Scholar, Dubya could more appropriately be called a Rogue Scholar.

Returning to the States, the Rhodes Scholar easily qualified for the very prestigious Yale Law School. Recall that Dubya's candidacy for the University of Texas Law School was rejected by the law dean, Page Keeton, with more than a little disdain. That law school is not widely celebrated for its high degree of merit whereas the Yale Law School is at the very pinnacle of excellence. From time to time I might be forced to point out differences between the two men.

CHAPTER IV

We now need to peer into the P.P.'s career in the oil business which is a resounding litany of abysmal failures, making his academic years appear scintillating by contrast. His initial foray into entrepreneurship began when he cobbled together a company called Arbusto. See, George speaks Spanish, although not nearly as well as he speaks English, and he thought that Arbusto means Bush. Actually, it means shrub. A more realistic spelling might have been ArBusto since the company devoured several millions of stockholder dollars before it went bust. None of those dollars ever belonged to the P.P., of course. He was, I might point out, rather adroit at separating people from their money, which he did when he sold stock to the investors. His very rich Uncle Jonathan Bush smoothed the way immeasurably by making phone calls on behalf of his nephew and the new enterprise. CEOs of large corporations would invest a modest $100,000 or so and before long our budding capitalist had accumulated $4.7 million. The only tangible assets that any of these investors retrieved from this venture was a tax deduction, which was not inconsiderable.

By 1981, George Bush senior had become Vice-President of the United States and with that the family name could bring in real money or –it could cause a white knight on horseback to appear. Sure enough, a knight appeared in the person of Phillip Uzielli who would pay Dubya a cool $1 million for a measly 10% of Arbusto. What is so strange about this transaction is that the book value of Arbusto was $382,376. Now, I'm not accustomed to dealing with large monetary sums but paying $1 million for only $38,237 doesn't make much sense. But, by now we've observed how strange coincidences continually appear on the P.P.s horizon. That same year our hero elected to rename the organization since caustic critics were taking liberty with the firm name Arbusto. The new venture was entitled "Bush Explorations," but lamentably was no more successful than its predecessor. But, did Dubya worry? Why should he when he was certain that more mounted knights would appear? In some type of arcane maneuver he found himself a large stock holder in yet another oil corporation, this one called "Spectrum 7." This too would provide no cause for celebration for its investors and would soon founder; George still persisted. Now, his father was president of these United States and both he and his father had the first name of George and, of course, an entire squadron of white knights were ever-ready to help.

This might prove hard to believe but Dubya received $500,000 in stock plus a bountiful annual consulting fee for his share of stock in "Spectrum 7." The fact that the company was virtually worthless appeared to be immaterial. "Spectrum 7" was spun off into a new company named Harken, and it would prove to be a bonanza for our hero, but a near zero for its other investors. He would sell off a considerable portion of this newly acquired stock just days before news of the company's woeful financial condition was made public.

The background on this period of Bush's business career is readily available in a number of splendid books delving into his life. One of the very best at detailing this unusually ignoble episode is *"The Book on Bush"* by Eric Alterman and Mark Green. A close reading of their examination of the manner in which the Pampered Parasite sold his stock illustrates why he should have received a stiff prison sentence. Numerous financiers who acted in the same manner as did the current occupant of the White House are now clothed in ill-fitting garb and are spending their days in a prison cell, usually for five or more years.

Bush finally sold his stock on June 22, 1990. "On May 17, 1990, Bush attended a board meeting in which he was told that Harken was three days away from running out of cash." The authors would continue, "Following the May 22nd announcement, Bush asked Harken for advice on selling his stock." Harken's law firm, Haynes and Boone, would inform Bush in the most unambiguous terms that "the act of trading, particularly if close in time to the receipt of the inside information, is strong evidence that the insider's investment decision was based on the inside information... Unless the favorable facts clearly are more important than the unfavorable, the insider should be advised *not to sell*."

Mind you, in addition to this most emphatic directive not to sell, he also sat on the audit committee of Harken, where it was evident that the company was unable to unearth any further source for loans. Since his father was president of the country, Dubya felt secure in the knowledge that the laws of probability and chance didn't apply to him, so he sold his stock. The value of it plummeted within a few days. The Securities & Exchange Commission required him to file notice of his sale at once. It took him eight months to do so.

The inevitable SEC investigation, of course, would follow. Of the five commissioners, four of them had been appointed by his dad, so you have every reason to believe the group went into exhaustive detail in their search for the truth. Lending further credence for this "investigation," the commission's general counsel was James Doty who would represent the P.P. when he ventured into the professional baseball business (we will explore that venture shortly). In the meantime, isn't it simply marvelous how these fortuitous coincidences continue to entwine themselves with our hero?

Dubya was forever denying that his father's political status had anything to do with his free ride through life. In an interview with the Dallas Morning

News a few years later, he would insist that his "success" in the oil business and his later "success" in the world of baseball were due solely to "hard work, skillful investments, the ability to read an environment that was ever changing at times and react quickly." Tell that to his investors in the oil patch.

Before leaving the Harken scandal, several additional areas must be looked into. In 1989, now that his father was president, Dubya's salary was inflated to $120,000 a year. Next, the Harken board of directors, of which George was a member, very generously loaned him $180,375 at a low, low 5% interest rate which he instantly used to buy more company stock. Not wishing to appear niggardly, the board granted him the right to purchase more company stock at a 40% discounted rate. In that same year, Harken lost at least $12 million, so it was exceedingly generous to the son of the president. While this was taking place, Harken's largest creditors were seriously considering foreclosure but the Harken board contained seasoned old manipulators and apparent con artists, so the company stayed afloat.

Even more illuminating is the fact that some of these board members had connections to a bank that would shortly achieve worldwide notoriety. The bank was known by the initials, "BCCI," but its full title was "Bank of Credit and Commerce, International." The U.S. Justice Department would also refer to it as the Bank of Crooks and Criminals. A few years later it would be forced to close its doors, having defrauded investors of $10 billion, the largest bank fraud in all history. The bank specialized in unusually sleazy transactions, chief among them money laundering for despicable thugs. Our boy George was associating with some world class crooks.

We need now to turn to Dick Cheney, the other half of the tandem that perpetrated the widely celebrated Grand Larceny election in 2000. For this material I am once again indebted to "The Book on Bush." From 1995 to 2000, Cheney served as the CEO and Chairman of Halliburton which at the time was an energy-services company with headquarters in Texas. Like Bush, Cheney sold stock before bad financial news regarding his company was made public. In August, 2000, Cheney made $18.5 million profit from stock sales…Two months later, Halliburton released news that its engineering and construction business would not meet revenue expectation and that the company was under investigation for over-billing the government. Cheney sold his shares at Halliburton's all-time peak of $52.00 per share, by the end of the year it had fallen to $35.00 and by January, 2002, it was down to $10.00. There has been no investigation of Cheney's sales, and there won't be one in the future.

Back in the 1930s, a professional boxer out of Brooklyn, New York, achieved some level of prominence. His name was Al Davis but he quickly acquired the sobriquet of "Bummy." Now, in a sport not well known for its adherence to sportsman-like tactics, acquiring a nickname like "Bummy" meant the fighter had some distinguishing characteristics such as hitting below the belt, punching after the bell ending the round, hitting on the break, just to name several. Might I suggest we refer to George Walker Bush as "Bummy Bush!" It has a nice authoritative ring to it, don't you think?

If by now the reader has concluded that our hero doesn't shrink from continual wrongdoing, just be patient. There's a whole lot more awaiting development. As "Bummy" wrapped up his sparkling performance in the oil business, the world of professional baseball management was dawning.

The fact that he had absolutely no experience in that field meant nothing; after all, he had no background drilling for oil and look what he accomplished!

The Texas Rangers, based in Arlington was up for sale and the P.P. was soon to become involved in its purchase. Bill DeWitt, Jr., whose father once owned the Cincinnati Reds and who was, like Bush, a Yale grad with an MBA degree from Harvard as well, contacted Bush and strongly urged that he join a small group of investors in buying the club. Dubya, of course, was to be purely a front man, a figurehead. This same DeWitt had bailed him out of the Arbusto/Bush Exploration fiasco and merged that into Spectrum-7, which as you recall also failed. When that morphed into Harken, Bush really struck it rich, not from finding oil but in finding stock virtually for nothing. His profits from the purchase and sale of the Rangers would far exceed the illicit gains from Harken.

First he would need to invest a wee dab in this new enterprise. To do so, he obtained a loan of $500,000 from a local bank where he had been a director. As collateral he put up some of his Harken stock. Now he was in position to buy into the franchise, paying $640,000 for a 2% ownership position. By provisions in the owner's contract that 2% could quickly rise to 11% if certain events transpired. With Dubya in on the deal we can be assured that those events would transpire.

What follows now is a series of sordid, shameless financial maneuvers that would quickly make the Rangers a fabulously profitable investment for the investors, but only the investors. The townspeople of Arlington would be the victims of a nasty shell game. If readers are not certain what a shell game involves, a brief explanation is in order. It probably was initially perpetrated during the Depression Era and involved a fast-talking dealer in a large city working with a small folding table and keeping his eye out for the local patrolman. On the table were three empty walnut shells, face down. Under one of the shells was an individual pea. The suckers would bet which shell hid the pea. After the bets were made the dealer would hurriedly swirl the shells around but in the process would ever so deftly remove the pea. Of course, there were no winners; everybody except the dealer lost. That would be the fate of the Arlington taxpayers – they all lost. That group did not include Bummy Bush. He would emerge with a $14.5 million increase on his original investment of $640,000.

The process is abundantly clear – with this transaction he could purchase, with the purloined profits, his luxurious estate in Crawford, Texas. Not a dollar of these gains was righteously earned, nor honestly obtained.

The new owners were to pay $30 million as a down payment while the taxpayers were obligated for $135 million to construct the new stadium. Here is where we observe the first application of the shell game. The new owners didn't put up a single dollar. Customers attending the games in the new stadium would be charged an extra dollar per head until the $30 million was accumulated. Then another phase of the shell game was introduced. As part of the contract, these nifty rip-off artists had only to pay an additional $5 million a year for a mere twelve years at which time they would own the stadium free and clear. It pays to remember Harken Oil and the BCCI, the Bank of Crooks and Criminals. Some of the same players from those operations were swirling the empty walnut shells around in Arlington, Texas, and Bummy Bush would participate in the profits.

At this juncture the name of Richard Greene needs to be introduced. I should also mention how indebted I am to *Big Lies*, a definitive biography of Bummy written by Joe Conason. In it Mr. Conason details how Greene, the Mayor of Arlington, signed the contract for the city which guaranteed $135 million toward the stadium's estimated price of $190 million. This in itself was an outrage – an usually high level of Grand Larceny by the investors. But the contact ventured much further into iniquity when it also rewarded the purchasing group with "an additional 270 acres of valuable land … that legislation represented crony capitalism at its worst. Never before had a municipal authority in Texas been given license to seize the property of a private citizen for the benefit of other private citizens."

Now, it would be manifestly unfair to call Mayor Greene a "two-bit crook." No, that modest indictment severely underestimates his proclivity for larcenist transgressions. To quote further from "Big Lies": "When Mayor Greene signed on to this give-away deal, he was simultaneously negotiating with federal authorities to settle a massive lawsuit against him. In yet another savings-and-loan bust, Greene had formerly been president of the Arlington branch of Sunbelt Savings Association, characterized by a prominent Texas newspaper as "one of the most notorious failures of the S&L scandal." Mr. Conason proceeds with the lurid tale of still another Bush associate. "Sunbelt had lost an estimated $2 billion and cleaning up the mess cost the feds about $297 million."

"With the stadium being readied to open the following spring, Bush announced in November, 1993 that he would be running for governor. He didn't blush when he proclaimed that his campaign theme would promote self-reliance and personal responsibility rather than dependence on government." Yes sir, self reliance and personal responsibility must be highlighted at every stage of the Preposterous Imposter's improbable rise to stardom. It's difficult to single out the most salient episode. Perhaps it was admittance to Yale or Harvard Graduate School. Surely the scintillating scenario of his heroic adventures in the Texas Air National Guard, sweeping the skies above Texas free from those malicious North Vietnam aircraft, merit our approval. Many of his most ardent supporters would single out his stellar performance in the Oil Patch, while others with equal pride could point to his baseball career where he delivered a sparkling new $195 million baseball stadium to the suffering souls in Arlington. And this is the crucial point—without, mind you, any involvement from government. We need to be emphatic here. There was *no dependence on government*. Well, maybe just a teenie bit on the part of Mayor Greene.

What happened to the mayor after negotiating this gigantic swindle acting as its super salesman? Readers will be pleased to learn that upon Bush gaining the White House, the subject in question was appointed Administrator for the Environmental Protection Agency, the EPA. After all, he had protected the good folks in Arlington so why not have him spread his beneficence throughout the nation? The occupant of the White House likes to reward good deeds.

CHAPTER V

Friends of the Preposterous Imposter began to position him for the 1994 Texas Governor's race. They naturally pointed to his illustrious background in the Texas Air National Guard, in the oil business and now his executive status with the Texas Rangers in Arlington. They wanted a candidate with strong family values, one with a firm hold on integrity and honesty. In the eyes of state Republicans, who was better positioned than George Walker Bush?

To best inform us of this episode of his illustrious background we need to turn to *"Shrub,"* an extremely revealing yet often hilarious scrutiny of Bummy's life. This biography, one of a dozen or more I have perused, was written by the late Molly Ivins, who became a cancer victim in March of 2007. Her death created a period of mourning and unfeigned sorrow within the family of liberal columnists. When they penned her obituary, it was entirely obvious that they viewed her with unconcealed affection combined with awe at her journalistic skills.

Bush's opponent would be the incumbent governor, Ann Richards. When polls were conducted after Labor Day, she maintained a commanding lead, around 60%. As Molly relates it, "Crime was down, school scores were up, the economy was humming; there were no new taxes. Nine weeks later she was out of office. The simple explanation is God, gays and guns." The previous year she had vetoed a concealed-weapon bill, a bill permitting Texans to walk around with a fully loaded but concealed gun. In her veto message she pointed out that, "there's not a woman in this state who could find a weapon in her handbag." The National Rifle Association took violent exception to this act and poured heroic amounts of effort and money into their effort to defeat her. The good ol' boys across the state rallied to that cause. She had also appointed to various state boards a mere handful of either gays or lesbians, well under 1%. This infuriated the Bible Belt Boobs, the BBBs, who closed ranks and became part of the gun carrying, gay bashing crusade against the governor. The Evangelical Christian movement was growing at an inordinate rate both in strength and fervor.

Not to be overlooked in Bush's conclusive victory was the addition of Karl Rove as one of his campaign counselors. Rove was pleased to refer to himself as "a diehard Nixonite." It's well beyond difficult for me to believe that anyone would admit to being a Nixonite, never mind one that's a diehard. Nixon was a sleazy crook in every sense of the word. He lied, cheated and stole; and those are some of his better qualities. His entire presidency was shrouded in larceny, paranoia and secrecy. His most unforgivable utterance was referring to the combined administrations of Franklin Delano Roosevelt and Harry S. Truman as "twenty years of treason." FDR remains our greatest President while his Vice President, Mr. Truman is positioned at number seven in our list of greatest presidents.

On April 12, 1945, the day that FDR succumbed to a cerebral hemorrhage, the entire nation was stricken with grief; citizens by the millions felt as though a valued friend had been snatched from their midst. On that day, I was stationed at an Air Force Base in Germany; I cried as did a few million of my fellow GIs all over the world. To many of us he was the only president we had ever known. And then, scarcely seven years later, in the election year of 1952, to hear Tricky Dick Nixon mouth such a dastardly lie represented a tragically low point in politicking.

Returning once again to Karl Rove, it's easy to understand why he would feel a powerful attraction to Nixon. He attended high school in Utah, then briefly, very briefly, went to classes at the University of Utah. Many liberal Americans look upon that state as the most reactionary as well as the most un-American of any of our fifty states. Reactionary and un-American are adjectives that can honorably be associated with Rove. He has become "Bush's Brain" but I view him as a malignant politico who would be in the employ of only somebody like Bummy Bush. No Democratic candidate would place such a political assassin on his or her staff.

Bush and Rove immediately formed an especially tight political bond. It's obvious why Dubya was drawn to this reptilian creature that possesses an infinitude of low animal cunning. One Bummy would naturally embrace another kindred soul.

We must recall how George W, during his draft evasion days when he was employing his cut-and-run strategy, had witnessed character assassination close up, first with Edward Gurney in Florida. Gurney coasted to victory over an infinitely superior candidate by hanging the label "Liberal LeRoy" around the neck of Governor LeRoy Collins. The BBBs in Florida considered that a reprehensible term and voted for Gurney. When the P.P. joined his father's staff in the 1988 presidential contest he saw the masterful Lee Atwater at work, guiding his candidate to a huge win. Of course, Atwater was masterful only in that he did not hesitate to put into play a destructive, treacherous venality to achieve his political goals. Atwater also became the mentor for Karl Rove. Scruples were burdensome afflictions never really considered. Just win, baby! And win he and his candidate would. Together he and Bush Senior demolished the candidacy of Michael Dukakis, the highly regarded governor of Massachusetts. In the opinion polls taken after the Democratic National Convention, the governor held a 17% edge over George G.W. Bush. But then he decided to go on vacation for a month.

Atwater however remained on the job and opened the spigot for an outpouring of venomous charges against Dukakis. Rarely did he concentrate on Bush's virtues as a contestant. Instead we saw such serious violence to the truth employed in the campaign process that even today it is still regarded as a paradigm of electioneering dishonesty and trickery.

As his contribution to the campaign, Dubya was heard shouting this neighborly message to Al Hunt, a highly regarded columnist for the Wall Street Journal. "You fucking son-of-a-bitch, I saw what you wrote. We're not going to forget this." Mr. Hunt was standing with his wife and two small children as this dispatch was hurled his way. At this stage of his life, Dubya was forty-two years old and had already undergone the cleansing process necessary to become "a born again Christian." We can only speculate what he might have retorted had he not been born again.

Dubya had a front seat to this scenario and would put this lesson to effective use six years later. With Karl Rove, his nasty election counselor at his side, adding to the cache of political skullduggery available to them, they proceeded to demolish Governor Richards. Once again Molly Ivins weighs in. "... Bush, a rather unlikely source of moral authority, preaches the solid middle-class virtues of thrift, sobriety, and personal responsibility." She analyzes Rove with precision, "For years Rove was regarded as a junkyard dog of campaign consulting, no holds barred." She in effect calls him a moral maggot.

With Rove at his side, Bummy preached the arrant hypocrisy at which he is so dexterous. The Republican Party platform in Texas that year was massively Christian in its application: a newly found love affair for more prisons, longer sentences, less welfare, eliminating the minimum wage and speeding up executions. The Evangelical Christians who by now had veered to the far right on these matters didn't want to listen to any twaddle about what would Jesus say; to hell with the 2000 year old tradition of turning the other cheek. In his speech to the Texas Convention Bush accepted every plank with no reservations. He most emphatically embraced the call for more jails to be constructed together with longer sentences. He particularly stressed the need for longer drug sentences, presenting his case with an intensity of feeling. Under the existing Texas law, what he had been guilty of when he was young and foolish (that is until he was forty years old) would have landed him in the slammer for many years.

It's particularly instructive to note how on this problem the well of his compassion had been wrung dry. With the added wisdom that accrues from many years spent breaking the law, he wanted that law to be still more punitive, even though it already was one of the most forbidding in the land. Had he been apprehended under the new and more repellant regulation he might not have lived to see freedom.

In addition to his troubling record of inadequacy, mendacity and outright failure at every juncture in his life, with not a single salient event that could be pointed to with pride, we must now review his record on capital punishment. The newly installed governor soon set about to thin the ranks of the huge number of prisoners housed on the death row, overwhelmingly Black and Latino. In the "Bush-Haters Handbook" by Jack Huberman, we are presented with a gruesome spectacle of wholesale executions unrivaled by any governor in this country's history. That record manifests a blood lust that approaches psychopathic status.

As governor of Texas, Bush signed death warrants for 152 executions – an average of one every two weeks—making him (in just one and a half terms) the deadliest governor in U.S. history, and making Texas a more prolific executioner by far not just from any other state but any other country in the Western world. From 1982 until Bush became governor in 1995, Texas had carried out eighteen executions. Bush achieved 152 in just six years. Attempting to justify this wanton taking of life, Bush would say, "I do not believe we've put a guilty – I mean innocent person to death in the state of Texas." Mr. Huberman counters that in this manner, "Well, nationwide, from 1976 to 2002, more than eighty-two people who were sentenced to death, or one-in-seven on death row, were released from prison after being fully exonerated:… There is every reason to believe Texas's record –under Bush—is much worse."

The Texas appellate courts never found reason to overturn even one of those death warrants. The manner in which many of these victims were convicted was a positive atrocity; actually the entire Texas judicial and penal system is an atrocity. It leads the nation in the percentage of citizens who are imprisoned. It has the worst record in the nation for providing its accused with legal counsel. More than a few of the attorneys appointed to represent a man on trial for his life deserved imprisonment themselves. Some were drug addicts, hopeless drunks or wretched racists who cared little if their black client was convicted of a capital crime. A few had been disbarred but had been reinstated by the Texas Bar Association.

At every turn Bummy Bush managed to make this savage atmosphere even worse. He vetoed a bill by the Legislature to provide better counsel for indigents, saying he "liked the way the law is now."

In discussing this situation, I am reminded of the late Al Capp, the creator of Li'l Abner and Daisy Mae in Dogpatch, in my opinion the most hilarious segment ever published in the "funny papers." Al endowed all of humanity with a "goodness gland," which bestowed on mankind a large measure of charity, compassion and most emphatically, generosity of spirit. With the Pampered Parasite the goodness gland has completely withered away and no residue remains. In his case, all that church attending and Bible study has proved to be an enormous waste of energy and time. The same can be said for the overwhelming majority of his RRRs in Congress and in his administration.

The famous Supreme Court case of Gideon v. Wainwright was decided in 1963 when an indigent was arrested on a simple breaking and entering charge in Panama City, Florida. His name was Clarence Earl Gideon. Many older readers will recall a spell-binding movie about the case called "Gideon's Trumpet," starring Henry Fonda as Gideon. The movie attained nationwide celebrity. Since Gideon had pauper status he requested the local court to provide counsel for him. The miserable perp of a judge naturally denied this request, so Gideon was forced to conduct his own defense. It should come as no surprise that he was quickly found guilty and given a harsh sentence.

Studies have proven very conclusively that defendants who are tried without counsel are found guilty in a hideously high percentage of cases. Gideon, an untutored middle aged man, filed a handwritten habeas corpus petition with the Florida Supreme Court. Since the court consisted of nine white men, middle-aged to elderly, it gave no credence to this crude request. He next filed another petition, also handwritten, an "informa pauperis" type with the United States Supreme Court, then under the guidance of perhaps the nation's greatest chief justice, Earl Warren. He had been the Republican governor of California, a man with considerable status. Further, he had been a legitimate contender for the 1952 Republican presidential nomination.

Playing a key role in derailing his nomination was the Republican Senator from California, our old friend, Richard Milhous Nixon. Even though Nixon was pledged to support his governor, as was the entire California delegation, Nixon, in a typically treacherous maneuver, worked for the nomination of Dwight David Eisenhower. (Why do you think he was called Tricky Dick?)

When Governor Warren realized that victory had eluded him, he threw his support to General Eisenhower but only after receiving a guarantee that the General would then nominate him to the Supreme Court, to fill the first vacancy.

Professor of journalism at the University of Southern California, Ed Cray, has written a biography of Earl Warren that makes for most pleasurable reading. "The governor was, in the eyes of the conservatives, a traitor to Republican tenets. He favored big government, particularly on social issues, and expanding international entanglements. …He would propose measures to expand schools, parks, highways and other public services necessary to serve a population doubling every twenty years. He would advocate a clutch of social welfare programs – health insurance, enhanced disability benefits, child care centers, fair employment laws, among others …"

In the battle for the Republican nomination, the list of contenders finally was winnowed down to Eisenhower and Robert Taft, a noxious, far-right, anti-labor senator from Ohio. Taft managed to be on the wrong side of most of the important issues in his senatorial career. He was uncooperative in helping Franklin Delano Roosevelt rebuild the nation's woeful military capabilities in the 1930s and 1940s. He had voted against renewing the lend-lease program in 1940 which was propping up England, then battling against Nazi Germany. Without the prodigious aid of the program, which mainly consisted of naval destroyers, artillery, rifles and ammunition, the beleaguered Brits might not have survived. Taft would also vote to prevent this country from joining NATO, the North American Treaty Organization. This was a military alliance consisting of Western European countries fighting against the encroachment of the Soviet Union. The U.S. would play a heroic role in that treaty. By contrast, a vote against it would display a cretinish understanding of foreign policy. The same could be said of his appreciation of this country's role in the looming World War II. That the Republican Party could seriously entertain having such a colossal simpleton as Taft as its president standard bearer is evidence of its badly flawed nature.

Eisenhower prevailed in the nominating process, won the general election against Adlai Stevenson and was soon confronted with a vacancy on the Supreme Court – Chief Justice Frederick Vinson had died. Now, the new president was presented with a problem. While he was willing to appoint a progressive like Earl Warren to the court, he was exceedingly reluctant to make him the Chief Justice. Alas, none of the other justices possessed the judicial temperament to take over as chief, so holding his presidential nose in disdain, he did the unthinkable for him, and appointed the governor to the position of Chief Justice.

Several years later Eisenhower was asked to assess this selection –he grumbled it was "the worst damn fool appointment I ever made." A verdict differing far from Eisenhower's has been reached by the entire legal community. Law professors, defense counsels, judges, police departments, even prosecuting attorneys view the majestic decisions of the Warren Court, from 1953—1969 as a political and moral revolution. At a minimum, they forced the recalcitrant Southern legal system to observe the Constitution of the United States and the laws passed by Congress. The justice system of the all-white male was finally defeated.

Returning again to *"Chief Justice,"* the delightful biography of Earl Warren by law professor Ed Cray – "Any estimate of Warren's career will mark him as one of the seminal figures not only of his time, but of the years that followed his death. As chief justice, Warren ranks among the smallest handful of men to have served on the Supreme Court, second in greatness only to John Marshall himself in the eyes of most impartial students of the Court as well as the Court's critics."

We once again return to Clarence Earl Gideon, after this interminable digression. Dame Fortune bestowed one of her most benevolent smiles upon him when his "informa pauperis" petition, hand written as it was, came to rest upon the desk of the new Chief Justice. Had it been directed to the Court of the blatantly racist William Rehnquist, recently deceased, or his successor, Chief Justice Roberts, a Bush appointee, it would have settled into the nearest wastebasket.

Another smile graced Gideon's countenance when the court appointed Abe Fortas to argue the case. The prosecutorial hacks in that small town of Panama City didn't have a legitimate case to begin with. Gideon had been railroaded to a conviction by perjured evidence but under the brilliant defense of Mr. Fortas, the verdict was never in doubt. Fortas would become a Supreme Court justice within a few years. An overriding consideration behind this case was overturning Betts v. Brady. Betts had ruled that counsel would be provided only in felony cases and only in special circumstances. In most areas the special circumstances never applied. The established law under Betts was overridden, and the right to counsel meant the *right to effective counsel* and for misdemeanor cases as well as felonies where defendants couldn't afford private attorneys. In the large majority of major cities in the U.S., this new law is in effect but still not universally applied.

You can be certain it wasn't applied in Texas where Bummy Bush, the compassionate conservative, vetoed a bill passed by the state Legislature that indeed did provide funds for defendants who were indigent. In a typical display of merciless conduct, his veto message referred to the legislation as "a threat to public safety."

In his 1998 reelection effort, Dubya would win an overwhelming victory after absolutely fracturing all previous Texas fund-raising efforts by amassing $25 million. The polls had scarcely closed when he and Rove began planning for the 2000 presidential race. By now he had completely captivated the Evangelical Christians who, it must be pointed out, were dominantly Republicans. It wasn't necessary for him or his campaign to make any overtures toward them. As a born-again Christian he was one of them and both had the same objective – to be one with Jesus.

With the Bummer soaking up huge amounts of available campaign funds, one by one his primary opponents began dropping out of the race. Finally, only Senator John McCain of Arizona was left standing.

At the beginning our boy went to heroic lengths to proclaim the virtue of his candidacy. Not for him would be attack ads. He would eschew nasty tactics and more to the point solemnly swear not to engage in name-calling. He deplored the uncivil nature of the methods employed by other of his fellow politicians and most assuredly would not attack a fellow Republican. Accordingly, both he and the Senator shook hands and promised an honest, decent level of discourse.

However, on February 1, 2000, McCain committed an unpardonable impropriety as far as Bush and Rove were concerned, when he trounced Bush in the New Hampshire primary by 49% to 31%. Up to that point, Dubya was convinced there was a level of inevitability about his victory, not only in the primary but in the general election as well. Suddenly, all those solemn promises about the nature of the contest were cast aside. Every syllable the P.P. had uttered about that nonsense went out the window.

Now was the time to utilize his malignant character assassin, Karl Rove, and start wading into the political sewer. The next primary state was South Carolina. If Bush failed there his campaign was finished. At once, an intense barrage of lies, distortions and virulent rumors began flowing from Karl Rove, i.e. Bush's Brain. The first was that Senator McCain was gay; following that in a kind of sexual contradiction, McCain was cheating on his wife. The most telling lie came next, particularly in a still very racist state, the only one in the South where the Rebel flag still flutters every day on the Capitol grounds.

A few years earlier, McCain and his wife, Cindy, had adopted a young child from Bangladesh. Now the political rumors started that the little girl was the product of a sexual relationship between the Senator and a black prostitute. Bush made no effort to renounce any of these vicious canards. Instead he asserted that they were in retaliation for his opponent's ads. Actually the senator had observed all the fair play rules originally agreed to. The P.P. was only doing what he had always done – lie and cheat.

He won the South Carolina primary convincingly. Now, happy Republicans around the country, concluding they had a candidate possessing the sterling qualities of integrity, honesty and decency, awarded him the nomination as the Republican presidential candidate.

In the general election he told his audience that he was "a uniter, not a divider"; he only wanted to be "the president of all the people." Oh yes, he was also a "Compassionate Conservative." In all of these and like statements he was remarkably faithless to the truth.

Al Gore should have whipped Bush resoundingly, actually did defeat him by any honest measurement. On the popular vote he polled 540,000 more than his opponent. In the critical state of Florida Bummy won by 537 votes and its twenty-five electoral just barely provided for his victory. The Governor of Florida was Jeb Bush, the younger brother of the Grand Larcenist, who unquestionably was responsible for denying Gore tens of thousands of votes. We shall devote much space to that theft a little later.

CHAPTER VI

Why did George Bush even come close to defeating the Vice President instead of being swamped by a far superior human being? Al Franken in his hilarious but incisive work, *"Lies and the Lying Liars that tell them,"* points to the amazingly duplicitous role that the American press played in the campaign. Even the New York Times, a paper I've subscribed to for some years and one that I consider the greatest newspaper in the entire world, piled on. It printed almost twice as many pro-Bush stories as pro-Gore stories on its front page.

Mr. Franken refers to the Pew Charitable Trust -- "Their Project for Excellence in Journalism ... as one of the few media research organizations without a political axe to grind." The project made "a comprehensive study examining 1,149 stories from seventeen leading new sources ... on media coverage during the 2000 election." In this comprehensive study, Gore received a "positive coverage 13% of the time" while Bummy Bush was the recipient of 24% positive coverage. On negative coverage, Gore took a hit 56% of the times while the P.P .had a far lesser figure of 48%. The author went on, "Somewhere along the line, the pack decided that Gore was a sanctimonious, graspy exaggerator running against a likeable if dim-witted goof-off. Instead of covering the issues and how they might affect average Americans, the media looked for little scraps of evidence to support its story line of Gore the Exaggerator."

There are at least two books published detailing how the Preposterous Imposter mangles the English language. Mr. Franken highlights a few actual quotes uttered during the election campaign that were particularly egregious.

1) More and more of our imports are coming from overseas.

2) I know how hard it is for you to put food on your family.

3) I will have a foreign-handed foreign policy.

4) I know the human being and fish can coexist peacefully.

5) Families is where our nation finds hope, where our wings take dream.

6) Rarely is the question asked, "Is our children learning?"

These were not statements "taken out of context" – every one of these, and dozens more, were faithfully recorded and preserved for posterity.

In addition to the miserable press and mindless creatures on TV who preferred Bush as a drinking buddy, Dubya could also count on his loyal "base". These are the Evangelical Christians or the Bible Belt Boobs who turn out to vote for him in heroic numbers. They were whipped into a rage about abortion, gay marriage, homosexuality, gun control, flag burnings and like matters. In their burning zeal they were passionately determined to elect Bush no matter what his short comings might be. They seized upon every tiny flaw they could unearth in the Vice President, but closed their eyes to the revolting magnitude of their darling's imperfections.

The fact that Gore had volunteered for service in Vietnam, the only member of his Harvard graduating class to do so, was passed by without comment. Bush's frantic, evasive maneuvers to elude the draft were met with unconditional denial. The unforgivable pimps on reactionary talk shows, always ready to denigrate Gore, were quick to conceal the P.P.'s evasions and miraculous vault into officer status with the "fully documented" routine.

Though he did poorly in the three debates between the two candidates, the mere fact that he didn't drool or come across as a complete idiot was sufficient for them. Bush had said that "I got into politics initially because I wanted to help change the culture." And he has been most successful in that quest, one of the very few areas where he has been true to his word. He has transformed our culture to an almost unrecognizable degree. As a great consequence, there exists in his 110th Congress only the faintest wisp of bipartisan consensus. Most votes reflect the make-up of each body. As of this writing, the Republicans have 202 members in the House. Of that number, upwards of 99% will vote with the administration. In the Senate the GOP has 49 members. On occasion two or three senators may break rank and side with the Democrats; otherwise it's a straight party vote.

Contributing enormously to this hostility and dishonest discourse are the overwhelming majority of Republicans in the eleven former Confederate States, those that I prefer to regard as the ex-slave states. They are Alabama, Arkansas, Florida, Georgia, Louisiana, Mississippi, North Carolina, South Carolina, Tennessee, Texas and Virginia. In both the 2000 and 2004 contests they unanimously cast their electoral votes for Bush. Of their twenty-two senators, all but five are Republicans, most of them still convulsed in hatred for Bill Clinton. The goal of that batch is to "end the long nightmare of the Clinton years." Let's first review the dismal years under Republican administrations before Mr. Clinton took office. In each and every year of the Nixon-Ford presidency, the federal Treasury Department suffered a significant loss.

When MCI Reagan (Mild Cognitive Impairment) ran against President Jimmy Carter in 1980, he immediately vilified the President for running up a modest $70 billion deficit for the previous fiscal year. Reagan was outraged about this reckless extravagance and stoutly maintained that any corporate CEO would be fired if he performed in such a shameless manner. The total federal debt when he took office was just a mite under $1 trillion. Reagan solemnly assured the voters he would balance the budget within four years and that, mind you, after cutting taxes and increasing military appropriations.

Of course he did no such thing. Oh, he did cut taxes and boost spending in the Pentagon to a profligate degree, but the deficits skyrocketed into outer space. After the twelve year reign of Reagan and Bush Senior, the deficit had grown to $3.2 trillion. The average annual deficit for those twelve years was $185 billion. Today a huge majority of the RRRs in the Bush Administration and in Congress have nearly deified Reagan and view him as the paragon with whom ordinary presidents must be compared.

A contrary opinion is held by most of his biographers, nearly all of whom treat him as our most overrated president. A number of them were highly regarded journalists or TV personalities who were able, over a period of many years, and often within feet of him, to view him in a rational manner, unfettered by political prejudice. He could still read the script from his teleprompter and do so in a highly professional manner. But on those infrequent episodes where he was subject to questions from the journalist and TV newsmen, his eroding cognitive ability came into evidence.

By the end of his first term he was seventy-two years old, older by far than any serving president. His problem was that he had a brain that hadn't been tenderly nurtured. One wag insisted that the president owned more horses than books. There will be more on MCI Reagan.

CHAPTER VII

With the passage of years I no longer scrutinize the 2000 election with the stomach-churning effect it had so often produced, but it still invokes a deeply disturbing feeling. It required thirty-six days between November 7 and December 13, before Al Gore finally conceded the election to the Grand Larcenist. The Thief-in-Chief was sworn into office by Chief Justice William H. Rehnquist, appointed to the office by our only criminal president, Richard Nixon. He was next elevated to the status of Chief Justice by Reagan. How had Gore been cheated out of his victory? Let me cite the ways.

The official vote count had given Gore a plurality of 539,900 votes. Holding it at that level required the vote count in Florida to be tampered with, or manipulated at every turn, always to the election thief's advantage. The governor of the state was Jeb Bush, the far more intelligent son in the family. The Secretary of State was Katherine Harris, a Republican ideologue appointed to office by Jeb Bush. She and the governor went to heroic lengths to cheat, steal or deny the Vice President every vote possible. Bush had eked out a tiny, tiny margin of 537 votes. Upwards of 60,000 mostly black voters were stricken from the rosters of registered voters by openly fraudulent means. Some of these were convicted felons but once they had completed their sentences their names should have been added to the list. They weren't. Next, Theresa Le Pore, the supervisor of elections of Palm Beach County had to place the candidates of ten different political parties on the ballot. As a long time resident of Florida, and an ardent political junkie, I had never heard of most of them —either the party or the contestant. Still Ms. LePore, a Democrat, treated each of them equally. The result was an extremely confusing butterfly ballot.

Voting procedure in use that year required voters to punch in the circle opposite the candidate's name. The circle, or dot, for a man I still regard as utterly despicable, Patrick J. Buchanan, was higher on the ballot than that for Gore. Buchanan had been a speech writer for the openly criminal Richard Nixon, and to this day is an unrepentant apologist for that man. The Palm Beach Post discovered that 5,330 voters punched in both Gore and Buchanan thereby invalidating their vote. That particular precinct was heavily Jewish and one such lady voter was widely quoted as proclaiming: "I would rather have a colonoscopy than vote for that son-of-a-bitch Buchanan."

I cannot allow this opportunity to pass without commenting on how frequently Buchanan is caught in a flagrantly anti-Semitic utterance only to quickly deny that he is an anti-Semite. (Nixon's tape recordings reveal the frequency with which he, Nixon, defiled Jews.) In one of Buchanan's numerous books he definitely seems to be an apologist for Adolph Hitler, a position which cost him much chastisement.

In addition to that loss, 2,908 voters punched a hole for both Gore and a Socialist known only to his immediate family. Bush lost a scant 1631 votes when his slot and Buchanan's were punched but the net loss for the Vice-President was 6607, about twelve times the tiny majority of 537 votes that awarded the state to Bush.

The further we venture into this miserable thicket, the more corrupt and dishonest it becomes. Florida and the rest of the country were now introduced to the realm of "hanging chads." A "hanging chad" was a ballot which had not been punched through completely but was still hanging by a small or even tiny fraction. Some of the machines hadn't been cleaned for years and it could be somewhat difficult for elderly voters to notice that the hole for Gore had not been punched through entirely. In both Miami-Dade and Palm Beach Counties, voters were 60% to 70% Democrats so that not counting those hanging chads worked against Democratic candidates. Florida law was very clear on the subject. The Legislature had decreed that "no vote shall be declared invalid or void if there is a clear indication of the intent of the voter as determined by the Canvassing Board." Yet in the final determination, the five Republican Supreme Court justices who gave the P.P. the election ignored this long established law and ruled that a ballot that is imperfect for whatever reason is invalid even though the voter's inclination was abundantly clear. Another 9,000 votes with hanging chads were thrown out, the clear majority of which should have counted for the Vice-President.

Now finally we must thrust ourselves into the lethal Supreme Court ruling which stole the election from Al Gore and awarded it to his Fraudulency, Bummy Bush. Five right-wing justices, each appointed by Republican presidents whom I deeply despise, allowed their personal and highly partisan judgment to overcome the historical interpretation of the Constitution. By so doing their decision in Bush v. Gore has become unequivocally the worst verdict ever handed down by the Supreme Court in the nation's entire history. So decreed upwards of 700 law professors across the land —men and women; Democrats and Republicans. Initially this evaluation was presented in a full page advertisement in the New York Times signed by 534 of these law professors. Subsequently the petition was signed by the remainder who wished to add their name to the list.

What had set the standard previously as the most blatant example of judicial venality? There were two cases actually, both in the nineteenth century and both involving civil rights for black Americans. The first was the Dred Scott case, officially known as *Scott v. Sandford*. This litigation proved to be a veritable bomb shell and quite literally propelled the nation down the path to our Civil War in 1861. Dred Scott was a black slave who, because his master took him onto free soil to live, decided to look for relief and freedom through the courts. Chief Justice Roger B. Taney, together with four other slave-loving justices, ruled in 1857 that Negro slaves were held to be of such inferior stock "that they had no rights which the white man was bound to respect." As a consequence, since Scott was not deemed to be a citizen, he had no legal standing on which to sue. Taney therefore dismissed the case.

Had he stopped there, the possibility existed that an overt break between the North and South might have been averted. Instead Taney lurched into uncharted and highly forbidding areas. The five justices were, besides being Southerners, fixed in their desire to shape public opinion to protect slavery, and, much worse, to strangle all threats to its place in society and moreover to foster its expansion. The decision manifested a recklessness that was truly repugnant. The court, in a 7 -2 decision, advanced the argument that black slaves, in addition to being inferior, "were unfit to associate with the white race either in social or political relations."

This *Scott v. Sanford* case unleashed vehement reaction from multiple sources within the North. From newspapers, from Congress and from large religious groups came a tidal wave of condemnation while in the South could be heard pleased justification. Those opposed to slavery, and especially the fierce Abolitionists were aghast by what they regarded as another move to promote slavery in the new territories.

This turmoil caused the Court to be assailed with a ferocity previously unrecorded in the nation's history, and in turn eroded its credibility and prestige. By blundering into the slavery question much of the judiciary, both state and federal came to the conclusion that the North and South were on a fatal course towards war.

With near unanimity the legal courts, law professors and constitutional scholars regard this case as the worst ever handed down by the Supreme Court.

In 1896, the U.S. Supreme Court handed down a second monstrous judicial opinion in the case of *Plessy v. Ferguson*. Here, the State of Louisiana had passed a statute mandating that railroads within the state provide "equal but separate accommodations to the white and colored races" and bar the races from being in each other's cars. In this case the Supreme Court upheld this witless law and by so doing entrenched and expanded segregation throughout the South. The same brutal sociopaths that trumpeted the virtues of slavery: the politicians, the newspaper editors and finally the preachers of evangelical religions could now be heard braying about the advantages of segregation. They would continue doing so even after new Supreme Court rulings and Congressional Legislation outlawed the barbarous and unspeakably cruel tradition. In the Deep South, bitter hostility and militant opposition towards the Civil Rights Acts of 1964 and 1965 remained in place well into the 1970s.

Re-immersing myself in the Bush v. Gore case means a painful bath in treacherous Republican tactics, not merely political but judicial as well. There was not a single instance where any of their involvement in the case was anything but dishonest and reckless partisanship. Here was Bummy Bush at his best, or his worst, depending upon your political perspective.

First, let's examine the background of the five rightwing Republicans who comprised the bare majority which ushered Bush into the Oval Office. Singling out one as the prize perp is too difficult since three of them represent a triumvirate of reactionary, partisan political opinion. They are William Rehnquist, lately deceased, Antonin Scalia and Clarence Thomas. Rehnquist was appointed to the Court in 1972 by my favorite criminal president, Richard Nixon. Then in 1986 MCI Reagan would elevate him to the role of Chief Justice. For a stunning example of his judicial temperament we find that in 1953, when clerking for a Supreme Court Justice, Rehnquist argued in favor of upholding the separate but equal doctrine of *Plessy v. Ferguson*. He was a confirmed racist and was known to challenge black voters waiting in line and question their eligibility to vote. In Arizona politics he streaked past a mere conservative position until he reached reactionary territory. Naturally these sterling qualities would appeal to Tricky Dick Nixon.

Next comes Antonin Scalia who has waded even further into uncharted right wing country. Among his numerous failings was scathing criticism of his fellow justices, a practice considered an unpardonable breach of etiquette where the aura of brotherhood contributes to the Court's mystique. Early on in his Supreme Court career he manifested an intolerable arrogance in his opinions. He rarely viewed a civil rights case with favor and similarly dismissed any opportunity to assist the working class. In his effort to improve America's future, he sired nine children, never mind that overpopulation is the worst nightmare of this nation and most of the world.

We now turn to Clarence Thomas who first viewed life in Pin Point, a hopelessly poverty stricken village in Georgia, exclusively black. At every critical turning point in his life, the Justice was ably assisted by helping hands devoted to raising poor blacks out of their forlorn condition. No sooner had he attained a position where he could help his fellow blacks than he abruptly turned his back on them, actually scorning to be of any help. He was unable to find a suitable black woman for marriage so he selected a white woman, one who is in the employ of the far right wing Heritage Foundation. It would be difficult to find another famous black man who is viewed by the black community with such contempt as he is.

Further to the point, Thomas is the polar opposite of the first black Justice of the Supreme Court, the man he replaced, Thurgood Marshall. Lyndon Johnson appointed Marshall to the Court while George Bush Senior promoted Thomas to that rank. Johnson is easily the greatest civil right president we have ever had, whereas Bush viewed those rights with suspicion, not caring to be identified with them. Republican presidents since Abe Lincoln, with the single exception of Theodore Roosevelt, have scarcely raised a finger to assist minorities. The current Bush managed only 5% of the black vote in Texas in the 2000 contest.

I can argue with complete conviction that Thurgood Marshall did more to assist his fellow blacks than even Martin Luther King. Hurriedly I wish to state that I hold Doctor King in the very highest regard and am most pleased that we now have a national holiday to keep alive his memory. But, and this is a very significant but, Thurgood Marshall almost single-handedly was responsible for ringing up twenty-nine Supreme Court victories. As special counsel to the National Association of Colored Peoples, the NAACP, he bent the Court to his persuasion in numerous landmark cases. Undoubtedly the most important of these was Brown v. Board of Education in 1954 which began the task of ridding the nation of the hideous doctrine established by *Plessy v. Ferguson*. We have already seen where Rehnquist had advised that Plessy be retained.

Justice Marshall graced the Supreme Court with his presence from 1967 to 1991. In matters of civil rights and equal protection for minorities, he weighed in with powerful dissenting opinions. Initially the full Court did not accept his dissents but over a period of time these consistent criticisms moved the court to less rigidity and more flexibility.

Clarence Thomas, Marshall's successor, does not deserve to be on the U.S. Supreme Court. He has been subjected to the most vigorous censure of any Justice in my lifetime. This reproach strongly suggested that he as a black man is consumed with self-loathing. One famous cartoon showed him as a puppet sitting on Scalia's lap and responding, "Yassuh Boss" to a Scalia directive. The Senior Bush made a number of ill-advised decisions that have proved harmful to the nation. This was one of the worst.

Sandra Day O'Conner is next to be reviewed. She was nothing if not a hard right Republican political animal. She spent her entire adult life active in the Arizona Republican Party, and got her feet immersed in that style of politics during Barry Goldwater's vain run for the presidency in 1964. Goldwater had voted against the 1964 Civil Rights Act which essentially divided the bigots, the haters and Southern Segregationists from those with a clear, moral compass. He maintained his vote was a matter of principle. It was not. It was a matter of unprincipled racism.

I observed early in my high school years that the girls with the least principle earned the most interest from randy boys. Barry earned an unhealthy amount of interest from the Southern Segs and managed to carry five of the ex-slave states: Alabama, Georgia, Louisiana, Mississippi and South Carolina, in addition of course to the then reactionary and racist state of Arizona. Before being nominated by my favorite Alzheimer's president, Ronald Reagan, Sandra Day O'Conner was recommended by Kenneth Starr who commanded the impeachment seeking legions that nearly crucified President William Jefferson Clinton.

That leaves the fifth Republican, Anthony Kennedy, who more than a few times voted as an impartial jurist, not a partisan ideologue such as the four just mentioned. Whatever his motives, when he voted in the 5 -4 decision to seat Bush, and steal the election from Gore, he participated in the most corrupt decision any Supreme Court has made in our country's history. Such are the five shameless shills for the Republican Party who sold our country down the river to elect a Pampered Parasite to the highest office in the land.

Reviewing this 2000 decision is a steep descent into judicial wrongdoing that is nearly as vexatious now as it was more than seven years ago. One observation by Justice Stephen Breyer, among the four dissenting justices noted that "in this highly politicized matter, the appearance of a split decision, and badly split, runs the risk of undermining the public's confidence in the Court itself…We risk a self-inflicted wound — a wound that may harm not just the Court, but the nation". An additional dissent from Justice John Paul Stevens warned us that the five judge's opinion "can only lend credence to the most cynical appraisal of the work of judges throughout the land."

Traditionally, the power of our Supreme Court is limited both by the federal Constitution and federal statutes. It should not decide issues involving purely state law. Moreover, the Supreme Court of each state should be the final arbiter in state matters, lacking a federal interest. *Bush v. Gore* involved the vote count in Florida which is hardly of federal interest.

Let us now turn to a riveting, deeply penetrating study of this case –"*Supreme Injustice,*" by Alan M. Dershowitz written in 2001. For this work a little background information is in order. He was initially appointed to the Harvard Law School faculty whereupon he vaulted to a full professorship by the tender age of twenty-eight, the youngest in the school's history. When we mention the Harvard Law School we are speaking of the premier law school in the land, not to be mistaken for the Texas Law School, which as you will recall rejected Bummy Bush's application.

Professor Dershowitz brilliantly outlines the corrupt path chosen by the Supreme Court to hijack the election process. The majority of the Florida Supreme Court ordered "an immediate hand tabulation of the approximately 9,000 Miami-Dade ballots which the machine registered as non-votes but which had never been manually reviewed. And it ordered all counties that have not conducted a manual recount or tabulation of the undervotes in this election to do forthwith."

This famous Florida Supreme Court verdict was distributed to an awaiting press and public late Friday afternoon on December 8. The counting in the individual counties could begin. But in less than twenty-four hours the rancid U. S. Supreme Court, in another 5-4 ruling, permitted a Bush application for a stay to take effect. As Professor Dershowitz points out, this "stopped the counting. That decision effectively ended the election and gave it to Bush."

In explaining why he voted for the stay, Scalia, in an unusual opinion, wrote: "The counting of votes that are of questionable legality does in my view, threaten irreparable harm to petitioner [Bush] and to the country by casting a cloud upon what he claims to be the legality of his election. Count first, and rule upon legality afterwards, is not a recipe for producing election results that have the public acceptance democratic stability requires." Borrowing once more from "Supreme Injustice," we find more priceless quotes. "Scalia's stay was the single most disingenuous opinion I have ever read." Disingenuous opinion hell! It mirrors that of the old reprobate Roger Taney who ruled in the 1857 case, *Scot v. Sandford*, that the slave, Scott, in addition to being inferior "was unfit to associate with the white race either in social or political relations." Mary McGory, one of my all time favorite journalists added her conviction, "Antonin Scalia might as well have been wearing a Bush button on his robe." Mary, sadly, has departed our planet.

The petitioner, George Walker Bush, was according to Scalia, the alleged victim. But he was not a citizen of Florida and hence "did not have any valid claim to the votes of any specific category of voters. The law cannot presume that the votes not counted by machine in any particular county belong to one candidate or the other. The right to have votes counted belongs to the *voter*, not the candidate. There was no claim of systematic discrimination against Bush voters."

The five justices participating in this Judicial Grand Larceny quite artfully, "never identified the victim of its claimed equal-protection violation...yes, there was an equal- protection violation in this case: the one produced the U. S.

Supreme Court's decision disenfranchising *thousands of voters* who cast ballots under Florida law, thus enhancing the value of the voters who also cast valid ballots."

The five election thieves based their decision "not on general principals applicable in all cases, but on a principal that has never been recognized by any court and that will never again be recognized by this court." In so thoroughly demolishing the artful contrivance hastily assembled by the gang of five, Professor Dershowitz introduces a delightful tidbit – a judgment rendered by Scalia in the case of United States v. Virginia in which Scalia wrote: "The Supreme Court of the United States does not sit to announce unique dispositions. Its principal function is to establish precedent – that is, to set forth principles of law that every court in America must follow."

CHAPTER VIII

Sooner or later we must address the contribution made to the 2000 campaign by Ralph Nader. Prior to that race he was considered one of the most admired Americans, most particularly among liberal Democrats. I certainly counted myself in that huge group. Here was a man who had contributed immeasurably to the improvement of corporate responsibility and standards.

Beginning around January of 2001, after the White House had been purloined beyond redemption, I began referring to him as Rotten Ralphie or Nader the Nadir. The word nadir means 'the lowest point.' That's where he had sunken in the political landscape. The important groups which had all aligned themselves with him, environmentalists, labor unions, liberal groups plus every women's rights organization felt completely betrayed by him.

During the campaign Rotten Ralphie headed up the Green Party and bleated incessantly that "there isn't a dime's worth of difference between the two parties." I wouldn't have been so infuriated at him if he had employed an equal division of his bile. That is, why not attack both candidates on an equivalent basis? But no, he had to savage Gore at every opportunity while almost never hurling any blasts at Bush.

He knew that this was a dishonest attack. After all the Democrats were better, much, much better at protecting the American consumer and the environment, at supporting Labor, raising minimum wages and advancing the rights of women, minorities and grays. His candidacy was an exercise in arrogance and was completely short sighted. It was a cynical tactic to fashion a defeat for Gore to the hope of forcing reform on his terms.

Typical of the vehement assaults on Nader the Nadir was from Kate Michelman, strongly linked to abortion rights for women groups. Nader, she said, "pursued blindly his own goals without regard to the risks it posed for those of us who have struggled long and hard for rights that now are in jeopardy." Bush's two nominees to the court are typical hard right Republicans, Alito and Roberts. Both voted this year to deny women the right to have a third term abortion in yet another 5-4 vote. Every woman in America who wishes to retain the right to an abortion has ample reason to be fearful of a Republican in the White House.

Addressing the inherent insanity of there not being a dime's worth of difference between the two parties: Knowledgeable authorities on fiscal matters have repeatedly emphasized that the difference already in 2007 has surpassed an estimated one trillion dollars and is growing by the day. That figure takes into account the mountainous cost of caring for the more than 35,000 of our wounded military for decades, perhaps numerous decades, as a consequence of the P.P.'s unfathomable decision to invade Iraq. That decision ranks at the identical level as the one that caused us to venture into Vietnam four decades ago. Neither country posed the slightest threat to our security unless viewed through the distorted lens of totally irrational leaders and advisors. Unfortunately for our country, this is an apt description of those in power in the 1960s and in 2003.

Rotten Ralphie's feckless forays into Florida netted him 97,000 votes in that state. Since these votes were from thinking, caring citizens few of them would have cast their ballot for Bush. You will recall that the Supreme Court stopped the balloting process when Bummy's winning margin was a miniscule 537 votes. But this was enough to give him Florida's twenty-five electoral votes, and inched his total electoral vote to 271 while Gore ended up with 266 (one Gore vote was never cast).

It is truly breathtaking to realize the audacity of the *coup d'etat* fashioned by the five Supreme Court judges, judges appointed by three inferior right-wing Republican presidents.

We must now turn to Bush's choice for his vice-president, Dick Cheney. Earlier in the campaign, Cheney had been appointed by the Bush team to conduct an exhaustive search for a suitable running mate for the Pampered Parasite. After an unrelenting quest for this candidate, Cheney modestly nominated himself and so became Bush's running mate. The new selection had been a six term House of Representatives member from Wyoming – that state has only one member in the House. While serving for those twelve years, he easily distinguished himself as that body's most reactionary member. On the three occasions where there was a bill to fund the Head Start program he voted against it. Now, the Head Start initiative was designed to grant small children from badly deprived settings an opportunity to catch up a little. In those three votes he revealed himself to be a remorseless monster. In the Senate, presidential candidate John McCain, voted in a like manner.

Cheney viewed every environmental bill presented in Congress with total abhorrence. He was militantly opposed to school lunch programs which for many youngsters was their first meal of the day. Not wanting to be perceived as a bleeding-heart-liberal, he also voted against childhood vaccinations.

Many in the Bush Administration were, and still are, eager to point out any dereliction among other members when it comes to the Bible. "Missed you in Bible study today" was a charge that might be directed to a wayward soul who hadn't been in attendance at the morning meeting. So it is with great pleasure that I quote from Paul's *First Epistle to the Corinthians*, one of the most famous maxims in the Bible. "Though I speak with the tongues of men and angels and have not charity, I am become as a sounding brass or a tinkling symbol.

And although I have the gift of prophesy and understand all mysteries and all knowledge and though I have faith, so that I could remove mountains and have not charity, I am nothing." Here on the unimpeachable words of the Bible, we have established that *Cheney is nothing.*

And what of Bush? Surely consigning 152 Texas inmates to their deaths has to be an utter abandonment of every semblance of charity. So then, <u>Bush</u> <u>too</u> is <u>nothing</u>. Well, we already knew that! Bush and Cheney are entirely capable of curdling the milk of human kindness even from a considerable distance.

CHAPTER IX

It is with a high degree of amusement that I now turn to the 2000 Republican National Convention. At the minimum it could truthfully be called an extravagant exercise in hypocrisy. First of all the delegates in the audience were 83% white, while only 4% were Black and 3% Hispanic. To open festivities an Afro-American lady sang the National Anthem. Next followed mostly black and female speakers. Following them on the stage was a parade of gospel singers, blues singers and break dancers, 100% black in what could only be called a Minstrel Show. I surely thought we would see a video of Martin Luther King giving his inspirational speech, "We Shall Overcome." At times it appeared there were more black faces on the stage than in the audience.

While closely observing this travesty on the stage, I couldn't help but wonder why any of the black delegates would belong to the Republican Party, a party which has been so cruel and uncharitable to the black race. In the 2000 election only 5% of black voters in Texas would mark Bush's slate. Let's examine the case of Colin Powell, the most famous black in the Bush Administration. During the first Gulf War he had been the Army Chief of Staff, the highest ranking officer in the army. In this capacity he served under President George Herbert Walker Bush.

For the general, this fortuitous state of affairs was the result of the actions of two Democratic Administrations. In 1947, President Harry S. Truman desegregated all branches of the military. Prior to that time the army had resolutely clung to its tradition of segregation, but after repeated muscular prodding by President Truman, it reversed roles and became a model of color-blind performance. Truman's successor, General Dwight Eisenhower, had been the highest ranking officer in Europe during WWII and now continued the desegregating process, even though he was an avowed, but not militant, racist.

Except for this slight bow to civil rights, one can look in vain for any White House activity from the next five Republican presidents. Thus it wasn't until the Jimmy Carter years that the movement was furthered along. Clifford Alexander was his Secretary of the Army and soon found no black colonels on a list of proposed promotions to the rank of Brigadier General. By army tradition, an officer must be promoted to general rank after a given period in service, or his army career is terminated. Suspicious, Secretary Alexander ordered the review boards to examine the early records of the eligible black colonels to see if their ratings in past years had been influenced by the racist prejudices of the white officers doing the rating. When the reviews were completed, a number of black colonels with superior records appeared.

Colonel Colin Powell was among that list so he was immediately promoted to Brigadier General. Had this action not been taken by a Democratic administration scarcely anybody in America would ever have heard of Colin Powell.

Immediately the question pops up in my mind – what in the world is General Powell doing in the Republican ranks? While he was on stage speaking at the 1996 Republican Convention he was booed with some enthusiasm. Prior to that, was he blind to the outrageous problems the Republican Party presented to his fellow blacks?

Had he forgotten the 1964 election campaign when the Republican candidate for the presidency, Barry Goldwater, promoted his infamous Southern Strategy? Goldwater, as previously mentioned, had voted against the 1964 Civil Rights Act and had clearly enunciated a calculated plan to reverse the rights of black people. By doing so he began the conversion of numerous Southern Democrats to the welcoming folds of the Republican Party. The first of these was the venomous old toad Strom Thurmond, the Senator from South Carolina. Thurmond was the most implacable foe of all black people, but most emphatically those living in the South.

Midway into the summer of 1964 an event that would prove to be of epic proportions was underway in the vile, small town of Philadelphia, Mississippi, which seemed to be a collection of wretched humanity. On Sunday, June 21, three civil rights workers who volunteered to improve the lot of black inhabitants had vanished. The three were young men in their early 20s –one was black, James Chaney; the other two, Michael Schwerner and Andrew Goodman, were Jewish.

For some highly instructive comments on the political climate in Mississippi that summer it is most profitable to turn to *"My Soul is a Witness"* - a chronology of the Civil Rights Era 1954-1965, written by Bettye Collier-Thomas and V.P. Franklin. "During the summer of 1964, Southern Nonviolent Coordinating Committee (SNCC) and Congress of Racial Equality (CORE) members, Council of Federated Organizations workers, and black and white supporters in Mississippi were subject to at least one thousand arrests, over forty shooting incidents, numerous beatings and six known murders. Between June and September, eleven churches were burned to the ground in McComb, Mississippi alone. Additionally, homes, businesses and freedom schools were targeted for tear gas grenades, fire bombing, dynamiting, shotgun blasts and Molotov cocktails; and civil rights workers and their supporters regularly received terroristic threats in McComb...Meridian, Vicksburg, and Jackson."

"Non-violent direct action protests were being met with violence in many places; however, in 1964, Mississippi was undoubtedly the most deadly place a black person could be."

For a still deeper immersion into the mind-set of the locals, we are indebted to a truly noble history of the period, *"Pillar of Fire,"* a Pulitzer Prize winner and New York Times bestseller by Taylor Branch. This is the first of three volumes which constitutes "a magisterial history of one of the most tumultuous periods in postwar America," quoted from a book review in Newsweek.

"Meanwhile, a civic-minded local woman named Florence Mars stopped by to ask the editor of the 'Neshoba Democrat' if it could be true that Klansmen had burned the nearby Mount Zion AME church the previous Tuesday night, as reported in her out-of-state newspaper. The editor replied that he was withholding the story as untrustworthy, because he was finding Negro members who were so deeply troubled by the idea of civil rights work at Mount Zion that they might have destroyed their own church in protest. Crazy things were happening, he told the skeptical Ms. Mars, informing her of the fresh kidnapping rumors that could be no more than a fund-raising hoax."

At nearly the same time as this conversation was concluding, Neshoba County Sheriff Lawrence Rainey and his deputy, Cecil Price, were holding a press conference for national reporters who were beginning to infiltrate the town. The two admitted that they had held the three young men for six hours on a speeding charge but then had released them about ten-thirty the previous evening. "If they are missing," said Rainey, they just hid somewhere trying to get a lot of publicity out of it, I figure."

That these two could stand before the reporters from big time, big city newspapers and issue this stream of unspeakable lies attests to the depths of their depravity. The bodies of Chaney, Goodman and Schwerner were already buried beneath tons of freshly moved earth on the Olen Burrage farm, about five miles southwest of Philadelphia. This had been the work of the local Ku Klux Klan to whom killings such as this, or torture or intimidation of black people was routine conduct. Sheriff Rainey and his deputy, Cecil Price, were highly regarded members of the Philadelphia Klavern. That these two and the newspaper editor across the street could deceive with self-possession and aplomb is vivid testimony to their complete departure from civilized behavior.

Many of the residents of this sordid dwelling place had some association with the Klan. This cluster of humanity gathered unto its bosom the ignorant, the intolerant, the rabid and the virulent haters. They abhorred people unlike themselves. The blacks were first on the list and they were referred to in polite society as negras but the more familiar term was niggers, about as pejorative a term as they knew. The next group that aroused their ill-will was the Jews and that in spite of the fact they rarely encountered any. No Jew would come close to a place like Philadelphia. Catholics also rated high on their list of undesirables. That the town's citizenry could maintain such an elevated level of contempt for these other groups is truly astonishing given their own degree of degradation.

The case of the three missing civil rights workers was rapidly gathering momentum across the nation. J. Edgar Hoover, director of the FBI, was being goaded into action by both President Lyndon Johnson and his Attorney General, Robert Kennedy, brother of the recently slain president, John Fitzgerald Kennedy. Hoover was one of the most virulent racists in the North. Mississippi was the only state with no FBI office, a fact that was rapidly becoming an inconvenient truth for Hoover, since it was also home to far more civil rights violence than any other. There had been some forty black churches burned to the ground and not a single culprit had been apprehended. Worse, there didn't appear to be any effort within the state even to investigate this organized arson. Seldom in the long and storied annals of Christianity had so many Christians burned so many Christian Churches.

And so it was that with a Bible in one hand and a can of gasoline in the other, many devoted white Mississippians were determined to right some kind of wrong. And it must be stressed that these same folks were passionate in their devotion to religion. After all, the local Klan chapter had an official chaplain, Delmar Dennis. (That would be the equivalent of Bush and Cheney appointing a truth commission to evaluate their comments.) It is indeed likely that their local preachers, for they were numerous in the town, had referred on occasion to Christ's Sermon on the Mount, one of the most revered guides to moral conduct found in the Bible.

"And seeing the crowds, he went up into the mountains. And when he was seated his disciples came to him. And opening his mouth he taught them, saying, "Blessed are the poor in spirit, for theirs is the kingdom of heaven. Blessed are the meek, for they shall possess the earth. Blessed are they who mourn, for they shall be comforted. Blessed are those who hunger and thirst for justice, for they shall obtain mercy. Blessed are the clean of heart, for they shall see God.

"Blessed are the peacemakers, for they shall be called children of God. Blessed are they who suffer persecution for justice's sake, for theirs is the kingdom of heaven.

"Therefore whoever does away with any of these commandments, and so teaches men, shall be called least in the kingdom of heaven.

"You have heard that it was said to the ancients: 'Thou shall not kill. And that whoever shall kill shall be liable to judgments'." Those dedicated Christians in Philadelphia, Mississippi, regarded this last imprecation as being subject to interpretation – killings didn't apply to the local negras.

Accompanying the swelling interest in the case was the attitude of James Eastland, the Senator from Mississippi who was the state's counterpart of Strom Thurmond in South Carolina. President Johnson was on the phone with him and sought his advice. Eastland, dripping with skepticism about the disappearance of the three, replied, "Why, I don't think there is a damn thing to it. That's why I think it's a publicity stunt." He further assured the President that no Klan chapter existed in Neshoba County.

Somewhat later, in a speech to the Senate, he charged "that integrationists had such glaring character defects that they were not above concocting the Neshoba County murders as a hoax." In *"Pillar of Fire,"* Taylor Branch quotes the Senator. "Many people in our state assert that there is just as much evidence, as of today, that they are voluntarily missing as there is that they have been abducted."

Contrariwise, many of the FBI agents working to solve the case, were by now positive that the missing young men were indeed murdered and they might have asserted that knowledge of the killings extended far, far beyond Philadelphia and might have reached Washington and perhaps into the Senate Chambers.

Joseph Sullivan, an FBI inspector, had been appointed to head up the investigation. Not far into the inquiry he included Sheriff Rainey and at least a dozen more locals as suspects in the disappearance. As July turned towards August, "Inspector Sullivan's agents loosed a whirlwind of gossip in Philadelphia. His rumor blitz was designed not to stimulate the flow of information but to conceal the identity of one informant who had talked already. For $30,000, contingent upon positive identification, Sullivan had just bought precious information that the three bodies lay beneath a fresh earthen dam on the Olen Burrage farm."

And from whom did he buy the precise information? Well, it was from Delmar Dennis, the chaplain to the Klan! Burrowing into the treasure trove of evidence brought to his fortunate reader, Taylor Branch explains, "When Dennis agreed to risk his life for an informant's fee of a hundred dollars a week, FBI agents John Martin and Tom Van Ripper took forty pages of notes." Meanwhile a young, rookie FBI agent, Roy Mitchell, had been able to "turn" a local police officer who began to despair of the increasing violence. When this officer, Wallace Miller, confirmed every thing Delmar Dennis was telling his handlers, this "gave the agents a new veneer of omniscience in psychological warfare."

One quick example of the deeply pervasive criminal nature of the town: "All that week, on leads developed by the FBI task force under Inspector Sullivan, Justice Department attorneys began hauling one hundred subpoenaed witnesses before a U.S. grand jury in Biloxi, whereupon a state grand jury in Neshoba County instantly called most of the same witnesses to ask what they were telling the feds. The two grand juries dueled. Judge O. H. Barnett introduced to the state grand jury as its investigative leader, Lawrence Rainey, whom the judge assured the jury, was the most *courageous* sheriff in all America."

Had the judge substituted "murderous" or "homicidal" for courageous he would have been absolutely correct. That level of judicial contamination, may never have occurred before or since in America. Judge Barnett was openly conducting a widespread criminal conspiracy which under normal circumstances would have resulted in a lengthy prison sentence.

In McComb, scene of the burnings of 14 black churches, local law enforcement officials had obviously suffered a considerable amount of mental derangement. The justice department reported to President Johnson that McComb's "local officials are publicly claiming that negroes are bombing their own homes and have responded to the latest bombings by arresting a number of negroes."

Three McComb klansmen arrested in this period on bomb charges, a crime which carried a considerable prison sentence, "were soon released to probation on suspended charges by state judge William Watkins, who told the defendants that because they were unduly provoked by outsiders of low morality and unhygienic (those were the judge's words) he had decided to make their punishment light and hoped they would appreciate it."

On this same day, McComb police arrested thirteen civil rights workers "on charges of sharing meals without a food license."

On Sunday August 2nd, the FBI arranged to secure a search warrant and then hired out-of-town earth moving equipment. On Tuesday, August 4, the Caterpillar dragline operator was ordered "to cease excavations and the FBI agents, using handheld garden tools began carefully chipping away the dirt. Soon they had uncovered a shirtless man pitched face down behind outstretched arms, like a diver. From his left rear pocket they pulled out Mickey Schwerner's draft card."

The Encyclopaedia of Civil Rights, Volume II, casts further light on the loathsome state of Mississippi. "The FBI by now had confessions from three different sources within the local klavern. One was from Horace Doyle Barnette. Based on his signed statement, the FBI arrested a number of suspects mostly from local law enforcement members." A few days later at a preliminary hearing, U.S. Mississippi Commissioner Esther Carter dismissed the charges. Carter deemed Barnette's confession hearsay because only one other person had been in the room to hear his confession. Although the FBI also had a sworn statement, the Justice Department dropped the case rather than reveal too much evidence and the defendants walked free. Fears that the men might go unpunished increased."

The FBI and the entire Justice Department were quickly learning that nearly all of the Mississippi judiciary might as well have been duly inducted members of the Klan. However, Inspector Sullivan was not going to allow this rebuff to spoil his case. At dawn on December 4th, dozens of his agents struck and arrested twenty-one targeted suspects, including Sheriff Rainey and Deputy Price.

"In January federal officials won indictments from *a federal grand jury.* United States v. Price commenced in Meridian on October 7, 1966. A Justice Department Attorney from Washington supervised the prosecution and faced twelve defense attorneys. On October 20th, the jury returned guilty verdicts against Price and six others. Their sentences ranged from three to 10 years. All of the prisoners were paroled well before serving their full term." It should be noted that the defendants were not indicted for the three murders, but for the far lesser charge of violating the victim's civil rights. After all, this was still Mississippi in the 1960s.

Sheriff Rainey actually considered a run for the governor's office in the next election and in fact received more than a little encouragement. Considering the level of professional quality of many of the past governors of the state, that wasn't as far fetched as one might think.

Meanwhile in that pivotal year of 1964, Barry Goldwater and his lusty hordes of intolerant enthusiasts were nailing down the Republican presidential nomination. Dr. Martin Luther King Jr., who had already been awarded the Nobel Peace Prize for 1964 was deadly accurate when he made this observation: "While not himself a racist, Mr. Goldwater articulates a philosophy which gives aid and comfort to the racist. His candidacy and philosophy will serve as an umbrella under which extremists of all stripes will stand."

Goldwater may not have been a racist but he approached that stance of intolerance and hatred much too closely for comfort. He never found a civil rights bill he would even come near. Instead he energized the flow of hard right Democrats and, of course, worthless segregationists to the Republican Party which eagerly welcomed them. He would win five former confederate states in the 1964 race: Alabama, Georgia, Louisiana, our old friend Mississippi, and South Carolina plus his home state of Arizona. This flow was a tiny trickle but with each presidential election it would grow to an engulfing torrent. Bummy Bush would carry all eleven "confederate states" in both 2000 and 2004.

Not a single Republican President since Theodore Roosevelt, who left office in 1909, could honestly be said to have actually promoted civil rights. Eisenhower was the only one who actually did *anything* that was even a nod in that direction and that was a mere continuance of Harry Truman's courageous act of desegregating the armed forces, already alluded to. Barry Goldwater, while not a president, in reality did his best to suppress the forward momentum of Black American rights. Nixon did little better. Now we must address the role played by Ronald Wilson Reagan in this matter.

In 1980 my favorite cognitively impaired president would begin his successful run for the White House. Now the burning question is – In what abhorrent, murderous, unchristian little town in Mississippi would Ronald Wilson Reagan select to kick off his presidential campaign? Surely you say, and with a look of horror, it can't be Philadelphia. Not that Philadelphia! Only a bare few miles from where the large band of sickening psychopaths buried the brutalized bodies of Chaney, Goodman and Schwerner?

Had I been forced to drive through that horrible hamlet, I'm sure I would have suffered more than a little physical distress and apprehension. Yet, here was presidential aspirant Ronnie Reagan, all smiles and bonhomie, doing his gig before a record crowd of white Republicans, who wildly cheered his every reference to the hallowed precept of 'States Rights'. Ronnie knew what States Rights meant to these folks and he was only too willing to employ wretched racism to gather votes. States Rights meant the same as it had when Goldwater used it in 1964 and it meant the same as when Strom Thurman used it in 1948 running on the Dixiecrat Party ticket and it meant the same as it had in 1861 when eleven Confederate States forced the nation into our gruesome Civil War.

Reagan opposed every civil rights initiative advanced during his presidency and either slowed or stopped enforcement of existing civil rights laws. "You can't guarantee someone's freedom by imposing it on someone else's," he would tell the nation.

That typified Reagan's philosophy on the subject and hence it isn't unfair to suggest he was joined at the hip with those unspeakable brutes in Philadelphia, Mississippi. Oh, to be sure, he wouldn't participate in any killings or burnings of black churches, but by merely showing up in Neshoba County, addressing jubilant audiences and proclaiming the virtues of States Rights, he revealed where his heart resided. Nor is it unfair to inquire why Colin Powell's heart could be found among Republican ranks, after all these developments.

Reagan would triumph in the 1980 election, defeating President Carter, who has to be the unluckiest chief executive this nation has ever seen. In that year Jimmy Carter was besieged with an overload of tumult, what with the Iranian hostage situation, gas prices rocketing to over $1 a gallon (the first time in our history), calamitous gas shortages (again the first time for our nation) plus ruinous inflation.

Ronald Reagan, the Master Illusionist, easily the most overrated president in all history, would retire and leave behind a legacy never likely to be approached, let alone equaled.

Let's begin with federal deficits. On the day when Reagan set up shop in the Oval Office, January 20, 1981, the total national indebtedness was just a wee bit under $1 trillion. That sum embodied every dime we had rung up beginning with the Revolutionary War in 1775. It included the cost of the War of 1812, the Mexican-American War, the Civil War, the Spanish-American War, World War I and the nearly unimaginable cost of World War II. Calculated into the debt was the frightful amount needed to battle out of the Republican induced Depression. Finally, financing the fiasco in Vietnam had to be reckoned with.

All during the election campaign Reagan had brutally denounced Jimmy Carter for running up a $60 billion deficit for fiscal year 1980. "If a corporate CEO would perform in this manner," he would ventilate, "he would be fired quickly." He was particularly acute in lambasting the Carter administration for permitting waste and fraud. Under a Reagan government, he would prophesize endlessly, waste and fraud would be banished. Continuing with this vein of optimism, he predicted that Carter's $60 billion shortfall would be cut in his first year alone to $45 billion and to $23 billion after two years. Moreover, he guaranteed a surplus by the end of his third year in office.

At the conclusion of his first fiscal year the budget deficit had actually ballooned to $100 billion, possibly because of all the hot air coming from the Oval Office. Alas, that would be his best year, fiscally speaking. In three out of the next four years the annual deficit would exceed $200 billion and that of course after eliminating those twin evils of waste and fraud. After eight years of the Reagan disaster the federal debt had doubled to slightly more than $2 trillion. The Treasury Department has been, since 1989, paying interest on those extra trillion dollars and what with the compounded interest, the Reagan debt is now easily two trillion.

But this was not the worst injury inflicted on our suffering nation. "The Great Communicator," as his silly sycophants loved to call him, was soon revealed as "The Great Prevaricator." Towards the end of his presidency, "*The Reagan Reign of Error*" was published and in 173 exquisitely delineated pages the authors,

Mark Green and Gail MacColl, unmasked the sitting president as a WCL – a World Class Liar – and a veritable Prince of Ignorance." I even manufactured a new word for his follies -- 'inexactitudes', which roughly translated means 'well, not exactly.' Reagan was a fraud the public could believe in. "Many in the media didn't pursue Reagan's misstatements because few of them wanted to believe that the leader of the free world was either a chronic liar or an amiable dunce." Actually, the leader of the free world was a WCL with MCI.

Mark Green came tantalizingly close to winning the post of New York City's mayor, right after 9/11, only to lose to Michael Bloomberg who more or less purchased the office by spending countless millions of his own dollars.

For an insider's look at Reagan we are privileged to turn to Edmond Morris who authored "*Dutch: A Memoir of Ronald Reagan*" in 1999. The book was a nationwide best seller. Mr. Morris describes Reagan as "shatteringly banal, a cultural yahoo and vacuous." It's extraordinarily unlikely that any biographer of a U.S., President has ever described his subject in so denigrating a manner and Edmond Morris was no ordinary biographer. He had previously given an expression vastly different to his subject when he wrote "*The Rise of Theodore Roosevelt*," a Pulitzer Prize winner. He followed that up several years later with "*Theodore Rex*," a continuation of the life of the first Roosevelt to become president.

Reagan, in an interview with Fortune magazine, said that the ideal way to govern was to "surround yourself with the best people you can find, delegate authority and don't interfere." Had he followed that sage advice, he might easily have slipped through his eight years in office without incident. Unfortunately both for him and the country, he surrounded himself with a batch of hacks that produced a continuing stream of humiliating disasters for him. One that stood out from the start was the Housing and Urban Development Secretary, Samuel R. Pierce, who gained everlasting fame when he was called before a Congressional Investigating Committee and immediately resorted to the Fifth Amendment to avoid having to testify. (That has never happened, not even once, in a Democratic Administration.) From that point on he became known as Silent Sam. One of his principal associates was a comely young woman, Deborah Gore Dean, whose previous occupation before being thrust into this position of power, was a bartender in a Washington bistro.

Having surrounded himself with the best people he could find, President Reagan began to find himself surrounded with administrative headaches. Let's begin with his Attorney General, Edwin Meese III. This A.G. was under almost continual investigation during his seven-and-a-half-years with the administration. He was found to have far more money in a stock market account than belonged there. As early as 1985 the Office of Government Ethics charged that he was violating conflict-of-interest regulations. In 1988 the assistant attorney general of the criminal division, William Weld, resigned because of Meese. When he managed a confrontation with Reagan after his resignation, Weld told the president that if it was his decision, he would fire Meese.

After more than a year of investigation, an independent prosecutor, James McKay, charged in 1988 that Meese had "probably violated the criminal code on at least four occasions but no prosecution would continue because there is no evidence that Mr. Meese acted from motivation for personal gain."

In 1989 a report by the Justice Department Office of Professional Responsibility said that Meese had engaged in "conduct which should not be tolerated of any government employee, especially not the Attorney General." In 1987, after he was being targeted by a number of state and federal inquiries, the Attorney General hit upon the ideal solution. He appointed an independent council to investigate himself! That may have happened to some beleaguered A.G. in our past history, but a fairly exhaustive search failed to point to one.

As we shall shortly discover, the Republicans have maintained an absolute monopoly on presidential scandals. The first was during the eight year term of Ulysses S. Grant from 1869-1877. In that span, administrative wrong-doing became routine; a future Vice President and a future President were caught in various corruptions but escaped sanction. That was followed by the "Teapot Dome" misadventure under President Harding which featured two suicides, three prison sentences and an Attorney General, Harry Daugherty, twice indicted, but twice able to elude justice. All of this occurred following the death in office of Warren Gamaliel Harding, easily the lousiest president we've ever endured. (That is, until Bummy Bush.)

Tricky Dick Nixon was directly responsible for filling up a sizeable number of prison cells, all with members of his administration. His Attorney General, John Mitchell, occupied one of those cells. That brings us back to Reagan and Meese. No A.G. in our history more richly deserved a lengthy stay in the slammer than Meese, although Harry Daugherty competed for that honor.

Two other members of Reagan's close, inner circle were indicted and convicted, Michael Deaver and Lyn Nofziger. Deaver, in a number of respects, revealed near genius capabilities by adding to the mystique of the Reagan presidency. One has only to review Reagan's press conferences to admire the abundant cunning concealed in Deaver's masterful handling of his client. These scarce public appearances were rigidly controlled down to the last movement, the last practiced phrase of His Airheadedness. Always hovering over the horizon was the near panic that Reagan would give utterance to another of his mindless irrelevancies. Deaver and a tight band of zealous disciples such as Patrick Buchanan, the speech writer and Larry Speakes, the presidential spokesman, were extremely devoted to the president but lacked confidence in him. When the president was turned loose on his own and unscripted, they were in a constant state of trepidation because now they could not protect Reagan from the danger of his being Reagan.

Under ideal conditions the Great American Illusionist was a political virtuoso able to cast a mystical spell over the public. No other president, before or since, has been able to enunciate such an enchanting message of rose-colored optimism and fervent patriotism. Who else could articulate a joyous sentiment to rival "There's morning in America," and sell it with conviction? That was a favorite. Another was, "The Shining City on the hill," the location of which he never disclosed.

There was one rather small segment of the federal bureaucracy where Reagan was unable to cast any of that mystical spell. Before he left office, the Justice Department deemed it fitting and proper to single out 138 of his administrative family for official sanctions: convictions, indictments or investigation for gross misconduct. The Master Illusionist would leave behind a mark never likely to be approached much less equaled.

In our nation's total history there have been four administrations that attained mammoth levels of corruption. Additionally, there have been two involving egregious examples of election theft. I am saddened to state that all six were Republican. A review of these scandals is certainly in order. Starting with George Washington's presidency, in 1789, until Ulysses S. Grant assumed office in 1869, there had never been so much as a hint of inappropriate presidential conduct. But within just a few months of the start of Grant's presidency, misconduct came to the surface in a scheme to corner the gold market. Grant, the immensely successful Civil War general, contributed to the speculation by allowing himself to be entertained aboard the luxurious yachts of some of the perpetrators. He was never involved in any of this sordid affair, nor any of the subsequent scandals, but his flirtation with the high life was unacceptable.

Soon after came the calamitous Credit Mobilier, which involved cheating the federal government out of enormous sums of money. When the government financed the growth of the Union Pacific Railroad from the Mississippi River to California immediately after the Civil War ended in 1865, unacceptably large profits were skimmed by the holding company. In a vain effort to prevent an official investigation of the scheme, huge bribes were made in the form of very large discounts of company stock to members of Congress. (We earlier saw how George W. Bush profited from this chicanery in the Harken Oil deal.) Caught with both hands in the cookie jar was the Speaker of the House, Schuyler Colfax, who not long after became the Vice-President of our fair nation. Another culprit was Congressman James A. Garfield, who was elected *President* in 1880. Both of these distinguished Republicans suffered the equivalent of the gentlest tap on the wrist as punishment.

Poor Honest Abe Lincoln would have performed profuse pirouettes in his grave had he gained knowledge of the multitudinous affronts to the dignity of the presidential office that were taking place under Grant. In just one of these outbreaks of corruption, the Whiskey Ring, 110 conspirators were convicted. In this case, the officials responsible for collecting liquor taxes forgot to forward the proceeds to the tax office. There were several other instances of government employees involved in chicanery.

Following the scandal-splattered tenure of Grant, the 1876 election featured Rutherford B. Hayes, the Republican governor of Ohio, against Samuel J. Tilden, the Democratic governor of New York. Hayes and his managers launched into highly disreputable campaign tactics. The party slogan was "Rum, Romanism, Rebellion." Rum represented prohibition against alcohol, a sentiment which enjoyed more than a little currency among Republican voters; Romanism was a blatant appeal to anti-Catholic bigotry; finally, Rebellion reminded voters that the Democrats were the party of treason, responsible for the Civil War.

Tilden won the popular vote and was ahead in the electoral count; even Hayes thought the contest was lost. The Republicans, however, manufactured sufficient question about this conclusion and refused to admit defeat.

The issue came down to the electoral votes of three Southern States: Florida, Louisiana and South Carolina. The Republicans still controlled the election boards in those states and by adroitly disqualifying enough unfavorable votes managed to throw the outcome of the race into the hands of a commission.

At this juncture, Tilden had 184 electoral votes, Hayes was second with 165. There were twenty votes still undecided. The Republicans had to nail down every one of them to win.

The commission consisted of eight Republicans and seven Democrats. In an example of outstanding judicial impartiality, the eight Republicans voted to award Hayes every one of the twenty votes. As a result, Rutherford B. Hayes was declared the winner with the 185 electoral votes. Tilden finished second with 184 votes.

With the speed of lightning, Democratic critics amended the Rutherford in Hayes' name to Rutherfraud. The election was deemed the Fraud of the Century. Hayes soon declared that he would not be a candidate in the next election and so it was said of him, "he came in with a margin of one but left by unanimous consent."

The result of the race eerily forecast the 2000 election in which the outcome was decided by five partisan Supreme Court justices awarding the election to the Grand Larcenist.

Another Republican presidential descent into the depths of malfeasance took place while Warren Gamaliel Harding occupied the Oval Office from March, 1921, until August, 1923. An elevated blood pressure and an enlarged heart caused a fatal heart attack at age 58. This sorry excuse for a chief executive has long been regarded by American historians as our worst president (that rung on the presidential ladder will absolutely be changed in January of 2009.) Swept into office as his Vice-President was Calvin Coolidge, a priceless nincompoop.

Harding's selection of Harry Daugherty as his Attorney General should have inspired caution from Congress. Here was a man with absolutely no legal experience or credentials acting as the chief law enforcement officer of the land. Before long he was under indictment for a conspiracy to cheat the federal government out of its share of revenue. Not once but twice he eluded a prison sentence when his trials ended in a hung jury. He narrowly escaped impeachment on yet another charge. None of this mattered to Harding who continued to manifest confidence in his embattled Attorney General.

Albert B. Fall was Secretary of the Interior, and he too would draw the wrath of Congress and the Justice Department. In one case he was accused of accepting bribes of $308,000 from the Mammoth Oil Company in the widely celebrated "Teapot Dome" scandal. For this he would serve ten months in custody. Another member of his administration, Charles Forbes, drew two years in prison. Two lesser figures would commit suicide.

One other appointment made by Harding deserves mention – that of Daniel R. Crissinger, named as Chairman of the important Federal Reserve Board. This appointee's sole credential was his position as counsel to the Marion Steam Shovel Company of Marion, Ohio, which was Harding's home town.

John Kenneth Galbraith authored a book, "*The Great Crash-1929*," which was so popular it underwent innumerable printings. It is one of my all-time favorite works on American history. With impeccable grace and wit, he outlined the flamboyant period leading up to the Great Depression.

"The Federal Reserve Board in Washington was the policy-making body which guided and directed the twelve Federal Reserve Banks ... the Board in those times *was a body of startling incompetence*." Crissinger "was regarded as a hack politician from Ohio. His colleagues on the Board were among the more commonplace of Harding-Coolidge appointees." Herbert Hoover, elected president in 1928, "conservatively described them as mediocrities."

Before allowing Harding to pass from the scene we need to review his Supreme Court Justice selections and how their decisions would raise such havoc on the American working force and most particularly the young children in that working force. In his two-and-a-half years in office he would appoint four new members to the Court. Jimmy Carter, a Democrat in his four year term as president didn't have an opportunity to appoint even one. Bill Clinton, another Democrat, in eight years was able to select but two. Yet, fate permitted our lousiest leader to select in two-and-a-half years twice as many justices as presidents Carter and Clinton did in twelve years. And what shockingly bad nominees they were. They lacked judicial temperament and were besotted with the strict construction doctrine that reactionary Republicans adore. In their decisions regarding any aspect of the labor union moment, whether it is the right to form a union, the right to strike or to picket, they might as well have declared war on American labor. In his third month in office, Harding chose William Howard Taft, who was defeated for reelection in the presidential race of 1912. Moreover, he elevated him to Chief Justice. Acting quickly in his first year on the bench, Taft would strike down a portion of a bill that prevented the courts from issuing injunctions against men on strike from picketing the strike scene. In a truly tortured ruling, Taft wrote that picketing is in violation of the fourteenth Amendment because it might result in financial loss to a company. What followed the next year was a judicial atrocity that still fills me with rage whenever I see reference to it. In March of 1922, the Supreme Court, now under Taft's tutelage, decided in the infamous case of Bailey v. Drexel furniture. Congress in 1919 went to considerable lengths to protect children from being exploited in the work place and passed, by near unanimous margin in both houses, the Child Labor Tax Law. This act was a sincere effort to discourage the employment of underage children by imposing an excise tax on any products manufactured by them and sold through interstate commerce.

Going back a step into this battle between a progressive Congress and an obsessively reactionary Supreme Court, we need to review the previous Court ruling on child labor in the case of *Hammer v. Dagenhart* decided on June 3, 1918. In this rather famous case, the court in a five to four decision overruled the Keating-Owens Child Labor Act, passed in 1916, which mandated that any goods produced by children be banned from interstate commerce. Congress was passionate in its belief that underage children were being exploited, often in a vicious manner, by factory owners and mine operators, and quite frequently under dangerous working conditions. Accordingly, it passed legislation to put a stop to this practice.

In an opinion by Justice William Rufus Day, the Court ruled that if Congress was not stopped, then, "all freedom of commerce will be at an end and thus our system of government be practically destroyed." What Justice Doofus Day actually ruled, of course, was the right of manufacturers and mine owners to put little kids to work for pennies an hour which permitted the employers to make obscene profits. The idea of all commerce being at an end was mindless illusion. Darwinian conditions were being enforced – rich people deserved to be rich while poor people deserved their fate.

Now four years later, in Bailey v. Drexel Furniture, Chief Justice Taft and the Court ruled that he and it were in complete accord with the 1918 ruling on child labor, iniquitous though it was. By doing so he kept in place horrendous working conditions for youngsters, some of whom were already suffering from malnutrition. Republican presidents and rotten, uncaring Republican Congresses would maintain that position until the advent of the Franklin Delano Roosevelt Administration of 1933. Under his direction a whole new ballgame would be put into play and this nation would finally see the end of child labor. The child labor factor was enormously illuminated since it revealed the shocking callousness, the inhumanity, of the entire Republican faction during the twelve year span between Democratic presidents Wilson and FDR. The total absence of even a tiny dram of compassion for these small victims highlights in a most dramatic manner how devoid of feeling these monsters were. These children should have been in elementary schools; instead, their parents were forced to put them in the work place in order for the family to survive. I still harbor more than a little conviction that given an opportunity to rule on child labor, Scalia and Thomas would find in it something of judicial merit.

The Taft Court was rapidly shaping up as a bastion of white males who viewed *laissez-faire* economics with adoring eyes. It was strongly oriented toward allowing business to regulate itself while simultaneously displaying a marked hostility to anything suggestive of governmental regulation. Looking at the Court as soon as he was appointed, Taft would view with favor three of its members: Willis Van DeVanter whom he had appointed. James C. McReynolds, the nominee of President Wilson who had mistakenly singled him out as a moderate. This was one of Mr. Wilson's most glaring lapses of judgment. McReynolds would be on the bench from 1914 to 1941, endlessly polluting the Court in each of these years. Next, Justice Pitney who would prove to be astonishingly hostile to labor and a confirmed right-winger. Taft would further exert a powerful influence over Harding and persuade him to appoint a trio of proven conservatives. George Sutherland and Pierce Butler were added to the Court in 1922, both of whom were infected with right-wing malignancy. Finally, in Edward Sanford, Harding would make his last selection and he too would fit comfortably into the group. It's highly questionable that there ever were a quartet of judges that took such extremely conservative positions as Van DeVanter, McReynolds, Sutherland and Butler and who were seated on the same court. When you toss in Taft you have a quintet of malicious malefactors. The first four would contaminate the Court throughout the balance of the Harding Administration, next the five plus years of Coolidge, the four years of Hoover and into the fifth year of FDR before any of them would resign.

The Court was merely one aspect of the frightening faction that was mismanaging the economy and political sector. The threesome of Republican presidents starting with Harding, then continuing with Coolidge and culminating with Hoover would add to the mighty blows being administered to the farm sector, which constituted about forty percent of the populace; then add the huge laboring class and finally the blacks. In important aspects these blows amount to governmental misfeasance which deliberately inflicted harm upon others. By "others" I mean an enormous majority of the people being governed by a narrow spectrum of wealthy white businessmen who could control elections of important offices. Warren Harding didn't propel us into a tragic war in the mid-East but he did provide an administration infected with unhealthy amounts of corruption and incompetence. All three of these uncaring creatures had quite large majorities of RRRs to work with in Congress, Rotten Reactionary Republicans dedicated to the principle of staying in office.

From the initial onslaught of White House scandals during the Grant presidency, through the outrages committed during Harding's tenure and then onto Nixon and the Watergate crimes, the period took over 100 years. In many ways, and to many people, the felonies attributed to the regime of Richard Milhous Nixon constituted the most flagrant assault on presidential honor, dignity and prestige ever in our nation's history.

It can be stated without fear of contradiction that Nixon was the nation's only paranoid president — that is, of course, in addition to being the only crook ever to occupy the Oval Office. He gathered around him a cluster of unstable types whose actions only strengthened his suspicions. He mistrusted all but a tiny few of his inner circle and displayed a willingness to stretch presidential license to its extreme limits. This involved committing repeated felonies and engaging in numerous criminal conspiracies.

Two of the most outrageous crimes involved break-ins. On January 17, 1971 17, the New York Times published the Pentagon Papers which constituted a lengthy summary of the history of the war in Vietnam, assembled by Daniel Ellsberg. Since these papers did not present the case involving the Nixon White House in a favorable light, this naturally enough enraged Nixon and his entire staff whereupon they immediately went to court to stop further publications of this extended history. The case eventually rose to the U.S. Supreme Court level which ruled in favor of The Times.

Infuriated, this collection of misfits decided to create a collateral group of misfits called "the plumbers", whose task it would be to stop further damaging leaks to the press. One of the most animated of the group had an inspirational plan – they would break into the office of Daniel Ellsberg's psychiatrist located in Los Angeles. The idea was to conduct a surgical strike – a clean entry, photocopy any material that could be damaging to Ellsberg, then a clean exit.

Instead, the burglars blundered into the office with force, threw patient's files around, found nothing and returned back to base. This deplorable effort would eventually cost the freedom of Nixon's two closest aides, Robin Haldeman and John Ehrlichman for engaging in a conspiracy to commit a felony. These were easily the two most reviled members of Nixon's inner circle, absolutely detested by Nixon's Cabinet members, the White House press and even other members of his administration for their displays of arrogance. They soon acquired titles such as 'The Nazis,' or 'Hans and Fritz' or the most offensive form, 'The Dobermans.'

This caper was a mere trifle compared to the *pièce de résistance:* The Watergate break-in that followed. To this day it isn't clear why the headquarters of the Democratic National Headquarters, located in the Watergate complex in the capital, was selected to burglarize. Following a plan assiduously assembled by E. Gordon Liddy, frequently regarded by many of his fellow Nixonites as 'a loose cannon,' a team of five break-in experts were employed to do the dirty work. These operations were financed by the Committee to Reelect the President, also known as CREEP. In the early hours of June 17, 1972, the five men, well trained in illegal entry, quickly found themselves inside the Democratic Party office. Across the street in a hotel room facing the Watergate, was an accomplice ready to warn them if the police should arrive. Now began a series of unbelievable blunders committed by the 'experts'.

First, they taped the latch on the lock at the entrance to the suite so that it would not snap shut. Why they would be guilty of such an amateurish maneuver is still difficult to understand. The security guard making his rounds soon discovered the taped door, conducted a routine search of the suite and finding nothing amiss, removed the tape and continued his nightly routine. The five men inside had quickly concealed themselves. Some time later, he returned to the suite entrance and once more found the lock taped over.

He immediately called the police who arrived in a very brief time. At this point the accomplice across the street, seeing the police, tried to summon the experts by phone. Wouldn't you know? The radio had been turned off because it made loud squeaky noises. The police entered the suite, found the burglars and arrested them.

CREEP was awash with campaign contributions and could easily have purchased the finest two-way radios which didn't make unwanted noises. The Nixon miscreants might have selected a leader to perform the needed 'dirty tricks' with a firmer grasp of rationality than E. Gordon Liddy. The burglars had on their persons a considerable amount of identification and incriminating material that should have been left elsewhere. In their wallets were large amounts of cash, most of it in $100 bills, *in numerical sequence*.

Could have! Might have! When the voters elect a president perched on the edge of a psychotic world, and he gathers about him similar types who not only permit, but encourage, widespread wire tapping of fellow workers, and when he and those associates develop a formidable 'enemies list' compiled to harass their opponents by a variety of illicit actions, and then permits still another group of emotionally compromised associates to act as plumbers, bad things are going to happen. These actions firmly positioned a powder keg awaiting only a small stimulus to set it off. The powder keg exploded in the early morning hours of June 17, 1972.

For all its monumental consequences, the flow of events that brought down the vaunted edifice of the Nixon regime started out at a lethargic pace. The Washington Post acted as a lonely advocate while it carried out its investigative articles. The nation's press and media largely ignored the event.

Practiced prevaricators from the Nixon ranks, and of course Richard Milhous himself, would go into denial of any knowledge of the illegal entry.

John Mitchell, who had just recently resigned as the U.S. Attorney general, and now Nixon's campaign manager, commented the next day. It had already been determined that one of the burglars, James McCord, was the Security Coordinator for the very committee which Mitchell headed. Speaking with easy aplomb, Mitchell solemnly assured the reporters, "that this man and the other people involved were not operating on either our behalf or with our consent. There is no place in our campaign or in the electoral process for this type of activity and we will not permit or condone it."

That statement is a delightful example of what I call an inexactitude. Earlier in the year, on January 27th, and while still the Attorney General, Mitchell had entertained three Nixon associates in his office — John Dean, special counsel to the president; E. Gordon Liddy, whom we have already met and a third associate. Liddy presented his strategy for the Republican Convention: kidnapping suspected radical demonstrators, wire tapping Democrats at their Watergate office and, when the Democrats met in Miami at *their* convention, attempt to compromise them with the classy call girls. Now this, mind you, was in the office of the Attorney General of the United States. It is particularly ironic that the legend over the entrance to the Justice building proclaims: "No free government can survive that is not based on the supremacy of law."

Mitchell's reaction was to inform his fellow conspirators that this operation was far too costly and insisted that they return with a slightly less grandiose scheme. At this juncture, the Attorney General had already taken part in a conspiracy to commit multiple felonies – this is a serious breach of both state and federal penal codes and if indicted and convicted can result in numerous months in a House of Corrections. In less than two years Mitchell would be on trial, would be convicted, and then would serve 19 months.

Easily the most nimble at the craft of concealing the truth was Ronald L. Ziegler, Nixon's press secretary. With seeming effortless ease he could pour out statements laden with scorn for the Washington Post and its two rookie reporters. He delighted in referring to the entire Watergate episode as "a third rate burglary."

The two reporters, Carl Bernstein and Bob Woodward, knew from the first day on the assignment that this was no third rate burglary. One of the arrested burglars, James W. McCord Jr., quickly revealed at the initial hearing that he was a recently retired member of the CIA. Two of the other burglars had on their person the name E. Howard Hunt. Hunt, it soon developed, had two items of interest associated with him: He was a consultant to CREEP and he too had been associated with the CIA. Men associated with the CIA rarely are involved in third rate burglaries.

Armed with this knowledge, plus a bulldog determination, the two reporters would play a most decisive role in cracking the united front of the Nixon regime. Confronting them was the grim phalanx of the powerful, cocky Nixon White House, a place where truth no longer resided.

Comprising that clique were a member of men, never any women, who in addition to superior intelligence had no identity with a conscience. Robin Haldeman comes to mind – he was Nixon's Chief of Staff and perhaps the smartest of the entire administration. Close behind was John Ehrlichman, in charge of domestic affairs. They also were readily hated for their unbearable arrogance. Amongst other names they frequently were referred to as Nixon's Nazis. They didn't earn the president's approbation and become his closest aides by projecting Christian forbearance. Turning the other cheek was not a part of their daily conduct.

Then there was Charles W. Colson, Special Counsel to the President. His favorite aphorism, expressed in Latin, was the ultimate in ruthless tactics: *"Orchides forum trahite, cordes et mentes veniant."* Grab them by the balls, their hearts and minds will follow. Bernstein and Woodward would eventually refer to this attitude as the switchblade mentality of the president's men. Later the two would jointly author a wildly successful book called *"All the President's Men."*

During the balance of 1972, the nation paid little heed to what was regarded as a mild uproar in Washington. Nixon's trip to China in February had almost certainly guaranteed his election in November. (That's why the effort to wiretap the Democratic headquarters appears so mindless.) The Washington Post often seemed to be the only newspaper pursuing the case, except for occasional articles in the New York Times or the Los Angeles Times. The Wall Street Journal rarely sullied its pages with unfavorable news about one of its favorite Republican presidents.

Nixon would win a smashing victory in the November election, losing only in Massachusetts and the District of Columbia. But instead of that decision producing elation, the resident feeling within the White House on election night was dejection, mingled with one of impending imprisonment. The formerly impressive front of defiance was being chipped away, bit by bit.

By the end of March, 1973, both John Dean, counsel to the president and Jeb Magruder, deputy campaign director, began discussing their involvement in the case with their respective attorneys. By April 2nd, John Dean and his attorney would enter into a lengthy negotiating session with the prosecutors.

Shelves full of books have been written about the Nixon Presidency, almost all of which I have read, and few of them treat their subject with kindliness and respect. *"The Breach of Faith – The Fall of Richard Nixon,"* by Theodore White is typical and highly recommended. In three other works Teddy, as he was popularly known, applied his considerable journalistic skills – one each for Nixon's three presidential efforts in 1960, 1968, and 1972. In "The Breach" he ridicules the efforts of this misanthropic troop, "The cover-up was grotesquely mismanaged, hilariously ineffective, his white collar managers proving themselves hideously incompetent at what Mafiosi could do skillfully."

His scorn for the embattled president rises to an elevated level. "From mid-April of 1973 to his end in 1974, the President lied; lied again; continued to lie; and his lying not only fueled the anger of those who were on his trail, but slowly, irreversibly, corroded the faith of Americans in that President's honor."

In yet another poignant sentence, he would summarize the Nixon White House and in so doing perfectly describe George Bush and his group of hapless loyalists. "Because they felt their purpose was high and necessary and the purpose of their enemies dangerous or immoral, he and his men believed that the laws did not bind them –or that the laws could legitimately be bent."

CHAPTER X

The lengthy span of time between April 30, 1973 and August 9, 1974 was a period of unrelieved anguish for Nixon. Across the nation there was also an increased awareness that something was amiss with the Nixon administration, something that was distinctly un-presidential. To be sure, this was still a minority opinion but as events continued to unfold that small portion of the population would enlarge with each succeeding month.

The April date in 1973 was a bitter and most humiliating one for Nixon. He went up to the presidential retreat at Camp David and was forced by unwelcome developments to ask the 'Nazis", Robin Haldeman and John Ehrlichman, his two closest aides, to resign. He broke down and cried, an act utterly un-Nixonian. He also fired John Dean the same day. Forever after he would refer to his former special counsel as "that son-of-a-bitch Dean" for going to the federal prosecutors and confessing everything he knew about Watergate. Dean, in his own defense, was certain that Nixon and his inner circle were trying to frame him and make him the fall guy.

A rapid acceleration of events was under way. A new Attorney General, Elliot Richardson, had been appointed by Nixon, and he had accepted the post only after being assured by Nixon there was no presidential complicity in the scandal. The Attorney General's first official act was to appoint a Special Prosecutor, Archibald Cox, to investigate the blossoming Watergate Problem. At nearly the same time a predicament of frightful proportions was presented to Nixon. Federal prosecutors had irrefutable evidence that Vice-President Spiro Agnew had been pocketing substantial amounts of cash from contractors back in Maryland in the form of bribes. This had been going on for some years and included his entire term as Vice-President.

Nixon was now assailed from a new and unexpected quarter. As evidence began to accumulate pointing to his involvement in the Watergate scandal he was being forced to make another and even more painful decision. Agnew, an extremely popular figure in Republican Circles, would have to resign his office. The V.P., supremely confident he could survive the ordeal, would not even discuss the matter. He wasn't going to walk away from all this power and these enchanting perquisites of office.

The newly appointed Special Prosecutor was something quite unusual among Nixon hirelings. He was _not_ a faithful party hack. Burrowing into the frightful mess that was the administration, Cox soon learned that the president had secretly installed an elaborate tape recording system in the Oval Office. He now demanded that the White House surrender nine tapes that appeared to be of special interest.

Knowing how gravely the tapes would incriminate him, Nixon had no choice but to refuse Cox's demand. The True-Believers surrounding the president advised him, in the strongest possible terms, that his only course was to direct Cox to resign. Cox wasn't about to do that. Instead he seized the initiative and held a huge press conference in which he told the audience that he would continue to seek the tapes.

Nixon and his advisors realized that Cox had to be removed from office. The only person in the government that could legally do that was his boss, the Attorney General. Accordingly, Richardson was ordered to fire the insubordinate Special Prosecutor, but even when he was ordered to do so by the president, addressing him in person, the Attorney General refused. He instantly became the former Attorney General and his assistant, William Ruckelshaus, the Deputy General replaced him. His tenure as the chief law enforcement officer in the country lasted not a matter of minutes, but of seconds. When given a direct order to fire Cox, he too refused.

The Solicitor General, Robert Bork, was now drafted to fire the culprit and he obliged. Within a remarkably short period of time, the press spokesman, Ron Ziegler, trotted out to the briefing room and made the expected announcement. What wasn't anticipated by any of the press was his next sentence, "The office of the Watergate Special Prosecution Force has been abolished."

The entire episode beginning with Richardson lasted only a little more than three hours. It instantly acquired the status of an imperishable event officially known as The Saturday Night Massacre. The date was October 20, 1973.

What had been a mere whirlwind of events swirling around in Washington, and engulfing a completely bewildered populace, was now moving toward hurricane status. By firing Cox, the president had scarcely purchased any surcease from the agony of new developments. John Sirica, the judge presiding over the investigation, continued to hound the White House for the nine tapes requested by Cox.

Nixon refused this order, citing executive privilege, so the case advanced to the next level, the U.S. Court of Appeals. Within a bare few weeks, more quickly than Nixon appreciated, the decision of the lower court was upheld. Nixon was being forced into an ever shrinking corner.

Surely no other president in the nation's history ever came remotely close to the tribulations which confronted this president. Certainly Abe Lincoln during the Civil War, and Franklin Delano Roosevelt during WWII, had lengthy periods of unrelieved turmoil, but both saw victory emerging. Not so with Nixon.

We know from the tapes that within a few days of the Watergate break-in, on June 17, Nixon, Haldeman, Ehrlichman, Dean, Mitchell, Colson, Magruder and lesser lights were enmeshing themselves in the coils of conspiracy laws. Up to this point there was nothing flagrant. But as the weeks slipped into history the president and his men continued to tippy-toe further into the cover-up, and further into the conspiracy trap.

In September of 1972 the five burglars plus Liddy and Hunt were indicted. In January they were tried and convicted. In March, John Sirica, the presiding judge sentenced Hunt to thirty-five years, the burglars to forty! He hadn't earned the feared nickname "Maximum John" because of a history of leniency toward convicted felons. Judge Sirica felt offended by the conduct of the prisoners and their attorneys. He made it clear that these were provisional sentences. "I expect you to cooperate absolutely, completely and entirely." Furthermore, he admonished them, "Whosoever it is who interrogates you, you will openly and honestly testify."

Previous to the sentencing, James McCord, one of the burglars, he of the CIA background and the affiliation with CREEP, had sent the judge a letter. In it he explained how the White House had been importuning them to remain steadfast and not divulge any association with the Reelection Committee and dirty tricks. Howard Hunt, viewing that horrid prison sentence, began to demand hush money to the tune of $130,000, of which $60,000 was for his attorney.

A major problem now existed for the White House klutzes – CREEP had no more money left! Already $425,500 had been shelled out to purchase silence from the feckless seven. Now they were faced with these extortionate requests which needed quick resolution. Nixon, when informed of this new development, seemed unconcerned, and told Dean the money would be raised. $75,000 *in cash of course* was soon on its way. Nixon found the money.

Beginning in May of 1973, the Watergate scandal became front page news for all the major papers across the land. The New York Times would feature it on page one. All during May, June and July, every TV network was engrossed with minutiae about events and individual players in the drama. Almost without exception, *Time* and *Newsweek* displayed one of the participants on its front cover.

The Senate Watergate Committee was authorized by a unanimous vote in the Senate in February to begin public hearings in May. These were dutifully covered on TV, but the first ten witnesses, mostly lower level administration types, failed to spark much interest. Then the next player to pop up on the TV screen, Jeb Magruder, who had already pleaded guilty to the prosecutors, stoked the bonfire into much greater intensity when he directly implicated John

Mitchell. This was Nixon's Attorney General who had resigned to become the reelection campaign manager.

It certainly is worth a momentary digression to review the activities of four Attorney's General and how each of them thoroughly disgraced that high office. We have already touched on President Harding's A.G. – Harry Daugherty, who twice was indicted, twice tried on serious charges. Twice by virtue of hung juries he managed to slither free from justice. Then in the Nixon regime, we view with complete distaste John Mitchell, who because of his wanton abuse of power graced a federal slammer for 19 months. Next we turn to Reagan's A.G., the distinguished Edwin Meese III who was even more eel-like in eluding the penal system. Finally we are forced to consider George Bush's contribution to Attorney General greatness, "Alberto Gonzales". Who amongst us can forget "Blood Thirsty Alberto" who approved of Bush's executions in Texas? All, four to be sure, were Republicans.

Now, what a distinction can be drawn from the Democratic Attorney's General! Search the history books exhaustively and no parallel can be found. Not a single A.G. from the Democratic Party has ever become entangled with indictments; not even a serious question about honor and integrity.

We should feel free to add this segment to the Republican pretentiousness about the Big Tent and the Party of Lincoln.

Following Magruder's block buster testimony involving Mitchell's culpability in the growing scandal, John Dean would be the next important witness. He made his appearance Monday morning, July 11, and would continue his testimony the entire week. Perhaps never in the history of American television has a news program, during daylight hours, so totally mesmerized a nation as did this one, and this witness.

Beginning his riveting performance, Dean started to read his 245 page opening statement. He would spend the entire day doing so, barely finishing it in time for adjournment. The next four days would be taken up by questions, first from the two opposing attorneys, one for the Democrats and the other for the Republicans. Next the seven senators on the panel, four Democrats and three Republicans would have an opportunity for detailed interrogations. The Democrats generally looked favorably upon Dean's testimony, never making any serious efforts to entrap him in misstatements or contradictions. Making a sharp distinction, the Republicans, who were upset by this ruinous testimony about their president, were continually trying to trip him up. The worst of these was Edward Gurney, aptly described as Nixon's lackey. We encountered him earlier when he ran for office in Florida, aided by the efforts of George Bush, and revealed himself to be a typical Southern racist. Gurney's efforts were completely unavailing.

Dean's testimony, while on the surface utterly destructive of the president's insistence that he was unaware of the enlarging scandal, by no means convinced the majority of Americans that he was guilty. Most of the nation still wanted to believe in their commander-in-chief. After all, it was still Dean's word against the president's. By the following Monday an even more incriminating element was introduced. Alexander Butterfield testified before the same Committee and told the Senators and all of America that Richard Nixon had installed a highly sophisticated taping system in the White House and that all of his meetings with staff had been recorded.

Nixon, always obsessively secretive and paranoid, allowed no one other than Haldeman to know about the system. Dean began to suspect that Nixon was speaking into a microphone because of his strange mannerisms, when the two of them were talking, but lacked any way of proving it. Now, with Butterfield's testimony, conclusive proof existed to validate Dean's public assertions.

Dean had appeared several days earlier before the House Judiciary Committee, meeting in closed session, and exploring proposed impeachment charges against the president. In this session, he would be interrogated by White House Attorney, James St. Clair, who it was widely believed, would demolish Dean's testimony. St. Clair brought with him an aura of invincibility as a cross-examiner. Dean was much younger, had no courtroom experience, so the White House group looked forward to this encounter.

St. Clair began his line of questioning presumptuous in his ability to triumph over his youthful adversary. It quickly became apparent however that he was over-confident and under-prepared. This engagement is delightfully illustrated in Bernstein and Woodward's follow-up book on Watergate. Their first, *"All the President's Men"* had documented the dogged pursuit of the White House scandals. In *"The Final Days"* they pursue the narrative to its conclusion. In this segment St. Clair is grilling his subject. The questioning proceeded. "Dean continued to demonstrate his superior knowledge and understanding of the record. Several times he corrected St. Clair on dates or names. At one point, St. Clair asked Dean about a question John Mitchell had raised with the President. "Well," Dean corrected, "I testified that *Mr. Ehrlichman* raised the question."

Perhaps the most delicious exchange between the two appeared a few minutes later. St. Clair had posed a question to Dean, but the Committee Chairman hadn't understood it completely and asked it be repeated.

St. Clair, momentarily off stride, asked the court to repeat it for him. Dean quickly interjected that he remembered the question and proceeded to repeat it perfectly to St. Clair and the Committee.

That display of Dean's memory flummoxed the noted attorney and he never recovered his aplomb. He concluded his interrogation shortly after. Any thought he entertained about a triumphant performance had soon evaporated.

John Dean wrote a sparkling account of his troubling tenure in the White House and his subsequent roller coaster ride through fame, Congressional hearings, trial and imprisonment. But, in *"Blind Ambition"* he doesn't even allude to this episode which had to be particularly savory, given the abundant opportunities for either victory or failure.

Of all the rather large group of participants in the White House who engineered the crimes and subsequent cover-ups, few have escaped the embrace of total obscurity: Haldeman and Ehrlichman didn't enjoy a long stay on the planet. Most of the others simply vanished without a trace. Only John Dean has endured and prospered. His face appears at regular intervals on TV. In addition, he has written at least six books, all well received on a national basis. I'm pleased to say I've read most of them.

CHAPTER XI

Once Special Prosecutor Cox was fired and the Saturday Night Massacre ensued, Nixon couldn't possibly survive in office. Once again, that date was October 20, 1973. Each week for the next nine months he would absorb another crippling blow to his credibility; still he would cling to the Oval Office with a grimness that exceeded belief. As a liar he had attained an astonishing level of conviction so that he could issue a continuing stream of untruths with enough sincerity to convince enough people that he was firmly allied with the truth.

His principal attorneys, whom he had personally selected, flew down to his winter home in Key Biscayne, Florida. (He maintained two large homes there in one of the priciest areas in Miami — one home for himself and the other for official visitors. Both units were entirely financed by the government.) Their mission was to persuade him to resign. He refused even to give them an audience.

On March 1, 1974, a grand jury would indict seven of Nixon's staff members, including four of his inner circle: Charles Colson, John Ehrlichman, Robin Haldeman and John Mitchell. Nixon would be added to the list, but as *an un-indicted co-conspirator* whose name would be withheld from the public.

For the next five months the president would hold the entire country hostage while he wiggled, and squirmed and lied, all in a futile effort to avoid the inevitable.

In the House of Representatives, where 22 bills had already been introduced seeking impeachment hearings, the Judiciary Committee was chosen to conduct those inquiries. Peter Rodino, Jr. was the chairman and had yet to distinguish himself. Still, as 1973 turned into the next year, the American people would begin to learn more and more about that chairman and view him in an ever more favorable light.

He had already selected John Doar to head the committee staff and in him had found a civil rights veteran of imposing credentials. Doar had spent considerable time in Philadelphia and Neshoba County, Mississippi under the Kennedy and Johnson Administrations. Under Rodino and Doar the Committee would operate in an atmosphere largely devoid of rancorous partisanship. It was comprised of 21 Democrats and 17 Republicans; the objective of the majority was to retain the good will of the minority.

One of the many facts the nation would slowly learn about Rodino was his self-effacing, gentle nature combined with a notable reluctance to seek publicity. As soon as this nation found itself engaged in WWII in December, 1941, he had enlisted in the Army and in due course was engaged in heavy combat with the First Armored Division. He became a member of a select group of soldiers in the Army who received a battle-front promotion to officer status. Before receiving his discharge he twice more was promoted and finished his career as a captain. Peter Rodino Jr. was no cut-and-run expert.

The Judiciary Committee began a serious inquiry into a possible impeachment case immediately after the Saturday Night Massacre on October 23, 1973. In order to hire a sufficiently large staff to conduct the investigation, the chairman obtained an initial grant of $1 million. Included within the staff was a young attorney, Hillary Rodham, a graduate from Yale Law School. Within a few years she would add the name "Clinton" to her own.

The newly hired staff had obtained the files of the Senate Watergate Committee, now disbanded, as well as other sources, including some from the White House. Once again enlisting material from "*The Final Days*," Bernstein and Woodward's second book on Watergate we learn: "There was a pattern of flagrant abuse –wire-tapping, concealment, half-truths, outright lies, consistent misuse of the executive power –but there was very little to tie specific criminal activities directly to the president."

Chairman Rodino would very succinctly outline to the full Committee the problem before it. "The manner in which we proceed is of historic performance, to the country, to the presidency, to the House, to the people, to our constitutional system, and unquestionably, to future generations. Our whole system, since the founding of the republic, rests on the principle that power itself has constitutional limits and embodies a trust. Those who govern are regularly accountable to the people, in elections, but always most highly accountable to the law and the Constitution itself. We ourselves are accountable."

As he gravely viewed his small audience, he continued: "Whatever the result, whatever we learn or conclude, let us now proceed with such care and decency and thoroughness and honor that the vast majority of the American people, and their children after them will say 'That was the right course. There was no other way'."

The committee staff first had to define the nature of impeachment charges; after all the U.S. Constitution uses only a bare few words in describing an impeachable offense. "The President, Vice-President, and all Civil Officers of the United States, shall be removed from Office on impeachment for, and Conviction of, Treason, Bribery, or other high crimes and misdemeanors."

The staff would in due time report back to the full committee precisely what White House conduct warranted impeachment proceedings. In preparing their conclusion they would review at least 400 years of British Parliamentary history.

Defining that elusive term "High crimes and misdemeanors" generally pointed to a violation of duty and trust. They then moved to discern what delegates to our Constitutional Congress in 1787 had in mind when considering impeachment crimes. They reviewed the advocacy of Alexander Hamilton, George Mason and James Madison. The latter had doubtless been more involved than any other delegate in highlighting impeachment discussions.

After sifting through mountains of material, the staff members narrowed their recommendations to three rather inclusive categories:

"1.) Exceeding the constitutional bounds of the powers of the office in derogation of the powers of another branch of government.

2. Behaving in a manner grossly incompatible with the proper function and purpose of the office.

3.) Employing the power of the office for an improper purpose or for personal gain."

Within a few days of receiving this report, John Doar sent a letter to the President's attorney, James St. Clair, requesting tapes of presidential conversations "prior to and following March 21, 1973." That was the date when John Dean had told the President about the demand for huge sums of hush money from Howard Hunt and members of the burglary team. Dean had placed special interest on March 21, in his testimony to the Senate Watergate Committee.

The president quickly replied to this demand in what could only be called a brilliant example of obfuscation. "I intend to cooperate with the Committee in its investigation consistent with my constitutional responsibilities as President." He was, of course, 'stone walling' and had absolutely no intention of providing the tapes.

These tapes would eventually destroy his presidency and for them Nixon was solely indebted to his chief-of-staff, H.R. Haldeman. Shortly after the Nixon gang had moved into the White House, Haldeman persuaded the president to install an elaborate taping system. His admiration for Nixon was little short of idolatrous, and so he could envision this taping system elevating the president to a figure of grandeur, perhaps the greatest chief executive of the 20th Century. There would of necessity be a delay until after Nixon's term of office was completed and *after careful and selective editing was done.*

Lamentably, the tapes did nothing of the sort. Rather they guided the president along the path leading to impeachment. It can be argued with conviction that without the tapes, he would have survived the ordeal, although noticeably bruised. After John Dean's testimony more people still believed in their president than they did in Dean's assertions. In short it was Dean's word against the president's.

After all in November of 1972, the Nixon team had just won a smashing electoral victory, losing only the State of Massachusetts. The continuous barrage of lies stemming from the White House – from the president himself as well as from his chief aides, was very effective. But then Special Prosecutor Archibald Cox made a determined effort to force Nixon's hand and surrender a small number of those miserable tapes. With that the Saturday Night Massacre was set into play and the national firestorm resulted.

The tide now turned against Nixon and his prevaricating clique, slowly at first but then with increased force. Nixon's decision to terminate the Office of the Special Prosecutor was hastily rescinded. Leon Jaworski, appointed to succeed the fired Cox, became relentless in his determination to listen to the tapes and demanded no fewer than 64 of them. The Judiciary Committee, not wanting to appear laggard, subpoenaed 42.

Now followed some contrived nonsense on the part of the White House gang. They attempted to mollify the Committee with edited, *selectively edited* mind you, transcripts. Chairman Rodino rudely rebuffed this transparent effort to hide the truth and demanded the tapes, and only the tapes. No substitutes.

Nixon's desperation sought refuge in the court system. His first efforts were met with failure so he pursued this enfeebled venture all the way to the Supreme Court. On July 24, 1974, that court ruled unanimously that he must relinquish all 64 tapes to the Special Prosecutor.

To illustrate how inexorably the tide had turned against him we need only proceed to the televised debate of the Judiciary Committee which started the very next day. There were 38 members on that panel, 21 Democrats and 17 Republicans (since the Democrats were the majority in the House). Speaking to the television audience was Caldwell Butler, a life-long Republican from Virginia. He begins by addressing his gratitude to the president. "And I am deeply grateful for the many kindnesses and courtesies he has shown me over the years. I am not unmindful of the loyalty I owe him."

For this extensive segment I am once again indebted to Bernstein and Woodward and their engrossing book, "*The Final Days.*" Representative Butler would continue, "There are frightening implications for the future of our country if we do not impeach the President of the United States. If we fail to impeach, we have condoned and left unpunished a course of conduct totally inconsistent with reasonable expectations of the American people.

"The people of the United States are entitled to assume that their President is telling the truth. The pattern of misrepresentation and half-truths that emerges from our investigation reveals a presidential policy cynically based on the premise that the truth itself is negotiable."

Each of the panel members was allotted 15 minutes for his or her presentation. All 17 Republicans were white males. Comprising the 21 Democrats were three blacks, one of whom was female; three Jews one of whom also was female. Finally, a Catholic priest.

The committee could easily have drawn up six pertinent articles for impeachment, but chose to confine the number to three. After calling the roll on Article I, the final tally was 27 for impeachment and only 11 against. Seven Republicans had broken rank and voted with the solid front presented by the Democrats.

On the second article, the result was the same with seven Republicans joining the 21 Democrats. Article III produced a 21-17 result. Richard Milhous Nixon had been recommended for impeachment to the House of Representatives on three counts.

Before proceeding further with the hearings, I find it pertinent to comment on the voting pattern of Representative Trent Lott of Mississippi. On all three articles he found it impossible to vote for impeachment. However, 24 years later as Senator Lott from Mississippi, he had no problem whatsoever in voting three times to convict President Bill Clinton of soiling Monica Lewinsky's blue dress with semen. Back in 1974, Lott knew the way the political game was played in Mississippi – racism wins elections. Lott then belonged to a slightly sanitized version of the Ku Klux Klan, a somewhat subdued variety of a White Citizens Council. The savage brutes around Philadelphia and Neshoba County had undergone a notable degree of civilizing. Still no question exists in my mind that had the persecutors produced a video showing Nixon entering the Watergate office in question, along with the burglars, ol' Trent would quickly have manufactured extenuating evidence to exonerate his man.

When we review the true nature of the Nixon presidency, which Lott and his small cadre guarded with such zealous dedication, it is particularly instructive to note what critics of that rancid regime had to say. One such critic, Arthur Schlesinger, Jr., was among the greatest of our 20th Century historians. "In his first term, President Nixon kept his Cabinet at arm's length; and in his second term he had put together what, with one or two exceptions, is the most anonymous Cabinet within memory, a Cabinet of clerks, of compliant and faceless men who stood for nothing, have no independent national position and guaranteed not to defy Presidential whim."

In Haldeman and Ehrlichman, the president had his two Dobermans, twin aides with unprecedented discretionary power. No other president in our history had ever permitted associates to accumulate authority on such a terrifying level. For instance, it was a rarity for even an important Cabinet member to have an audience with the President without one or both of them in attendance. But in allowing them to garner so much administrative strength, Nixon planted the seeds of his presidential destruction.

Once the Supreme Court decreed that Nixon had to relinquish control of the 64 tapes, there was no way for him to survive. His new Presidential Aide, Alexander Haig, who replaced Haldeman, was at times extremely concerned that Nixon would take his own life. Both he and his wife, Patricia, were drinking heavily. Nixon, always a loner, was becoming increasingly isolated and detached, but still clung to the possibility that the Senate would preserve his tenure in office. The Constitution dictates that two-thirds of the Senate must vote for conviction and it appeared he still retained the good will of 40 Republicans in that body.

But one by one the 40 Republicans were deserting their chief. The thought of a lengthy, agonizing trial in the Senate was too dreadful even to contemplate. Both his attorneys, James St. Clair and Fred Buzhardt were anxious to resign, but remained at their post for the good of the Republican Party.

Finally on August 7, the three most important Republicans in the Senate, Barry Goldwater, Hugh Scott and John Rhodes asked for and received an audience with Nixon. He shook hands with each of them and was remarkably friendly and even serene considering the circumstances. Goldwater had been designated as the spokesman. By now he was completely disgusted with the manner in which Nixon had continually lied to them, even employing crude language in describing him. Finally, when Nixon asked for a head count of who could be counted on in the Senate, Goldwater threw the knock-out punch. "I took kind of a nose count today, and I couldn't find more than four very firm votes, and those would be from older Southerners. Some are very worried about what's been going on, and are undecided, and I'm one of them."

When Goldwater mentioned older Southerners as still being firmly wedded to Nixon, he had James Eastland of Mississippi in mind. It's good to remember that soon after the three civil rights workers disappeared in Philadelphia, Mississippi, he scornfully suggested to President Johnson that the case was nothing but a hoax and further assured Johnson that no Klan Chapter exited in Neshoba County. Eastland was older and more skilled at playing the race card in Mississippi than Trent Lott.

Even Nixon's full-time professional ass-kissers were revolted by the stream of unwelcome revelations escaping from the newly released tapes. Patrick Buchanan, perhaps second only to Haldeman in the degree of adulation accorded to the president, had grown outraged. Buchanan has accumulated a burdensome amount of baggage through the years with his not infrequent outbursts of anti-

Semitism. As quickly as one of these utterances would create a momentary outpouring of indignation within the media, he would retreat and mumble a modest apology.

The tapes would gradually reveal to a startled world that Buchanan's beloved mentor, Richard Nixon, possessed a deep well of aversion for an ethic group he sometimes referred to as 'kikes.' It is true that Henry Kissinger, Nixon's chief foreign affairs advisor, was Jewish, but the regard each had for the other was close to contempt, approximating hatred. Since they needed each other to flourish, they sublimated those darker feelings in public, and tolerated each other.

Following Goldwater's unvarnished appraisal of the outlook in the Senate, Nixon reacted by alternately sulking, drinking heavily but groping his way toward resigning the presidency. His son-in-law, Edward Cox, was strategically positioned to see the President frequently and close-up. He reported to Nixon's staff how the President was not rational at times. He too, like Alexander Haig, Nixon's Chief of staff, was deeply troubled that his father-in-law might commit suicide.

As Bernstein and Woodward assert in *"The Final Days,"* the young man related to confidants how "the president was up walking the halls last night, talking to pictures of former presidents, giving speeches, and talking to the pictures on the wall."

Goldwater's brutally effective speech was the final goad Nixon needed to make his decision. He asked his speech writers to draft the last address he would make from the White House. At noon the next day, the signing machine used for his signature was closed.

A bare few minutes later, Ron Ziegler appeared in the press room. "Tonight at nine o'clock, Eastern Standard Time, the President of the United States will address the nation on radio and television from the Oval Office."

That night, in a sparse message, the President announced that he would resign, effective at noon tomorrow.

At noon on August 9, 1974, Nixon's presidency ended.

CHAPTER XII

It's a 'downright rotten, lowdown dirty shame', a highly descriptive phrase filched from a Duke Ellington jazz composition, that the Republicans continue electing first a rotten criminal like Nixon, then a low down dirty shame to introduce the nation to MCI Reagan. Not content with those assaults on presidential dignity and honor, they contrived to place an amiable doofus like George Herbert Walker Bush in the White House. For what it's worth, Richard Nixon had a low regard for Bush, but George Herbert Walker had just enough ability to fill posts like the U.S. Ambassador to the U.N., or Republican National Chairman, or Ambassador to China. Mao Tse Tung, the Chinese dictator, was so impressed with Bush's credentials that the Ambassador was never granted an audience with Mao, and never spoke to him. Cognitively Impaired Reagan was equally disdainful of Bush. As Vice-President to Reagan, the Bushes were never permitted access to the Reagan living quarters, upstairs in the White House.

Of course the most monumental affront to presidential history was nominating George Walker Bush for the presidential post in 2000. The clueless clown from Crawford, Texas was so ill-suited to take up position in the White House! Still, his Supreme Court victory in *Bush v. Gore* in December, 2000, demonstrated what the expenditure of more than $200 million spent in his election could accomplish.

Now in his eighth year as current occupant of the White House, he already has established his position in presidential rankings. That is, firmly established his position as the nations most woeful Chief Executive of the White House, and by an impressive margin. The heirs of Warren Harding can now feel relieved that their ancestor no longer holds that 'honor."

For a quick, accurate appraisal of the Nixon persona we should turn to President Harry Truman, ranked number seven, high up in the Presidential hierarchy. In an incisive riposte to Nixon dismissing the 20-year term in office of Franklin Delano Roosevelt and Truman as "20-years of treason," Truman said this of Nixon. "Richard Nixon is a no-good lying bastard. He can lie out of both sides of his mouth at the same time, and if he ever caught himself telling the truth, he'd lie just to keep his hand in." President Truman saw no sense in uttering diplomatically couched phrases when plain English is so much more effective.

Jimmy Carter, very likely the nation's unluckiest president, dismissed Nixon in this manner, "In the hundred years of history, he's the most dishonest president we've ever had. I think he's disgraced the Presidency."

Distasteful as it may be for some, we must return to the Nixon reign of ruin and consider his coalition of criminals. Those who either pleaded guilty to, or were convicted of, one or more felonies were:

- The five break-in experts whose efforts were so skillfully organized by G. Gordon Liddy and E. Howard Hunt. Burglars United would never have recommended any of those seven for meritorious practices.
- Then John Dean whose testimony before the Senate Watergate Committee 34 years ago, I still remember vividly and recall it with fondness. It wasn't so much a statement as a performance worthy of awe and admiration.
- Then the Big Four – the dedicated Dobermans, H.R. Haldeman and John Ehrlichman. Next, John Mitchell who permitted a program involving multiple felonies to be discussed in the Attorney General's office. Who can ever forget Charles Colson, he of the 'orchides forum trahite' motto? There were an additional eight miscreants of lower rank to bring the total to 20 who served time in prison. Ron Ziegler, who derided the idea of "A third rate burglary" being in any manner associated with the Nixon administration, escaped servitude but was never heard from again.

During the 20th Century seven Democrats were elected to the office of President. None of them required Supreme Court decisions, as in the case of Bummy Bush, or of a special partisan board, as in the case of Rutherford (or Rutherfraud) Hayes to gain admission to the White House. Woodrow Wilson served eight years; Franklin Delano Roosevelt and his Vice-President, Harry S. Truman, occupied the office for 20 years. John F. Kennedy and his V.P., Lyndon Johnson, were in office eight years. Jimmy Carter completed a single term; finally, Bill Clinton resided in the White House for eight tumultuous years. That totals 48 years.

In a very sharp distinction, the Democrats may point with pride that in those 48 years not a single administrative figure was ever indicted, much less tried for a felony committed while in office.

Yet, when Bush and Cheney invaded the Oval Office in January, 2001, having stolen the election in an outrageous manner, they proclaimed to the world their dedication to cleanse that office of every taint of scandal and sin. They must, they insisted, restore honor and dignity as only Republicans can.

Which Clinton associate was indicted or tried for a felony committed during the Clinton years in office? The answer is there was none. Not a single one!

After this extensive revue of the Nixon hearings conducted by the Democratic Congress and examining the protracted criminal activities of Nixon, we should in turn investigate the impeachment hearings and Senate trial of President Clinton.

The composition of the two Judiciary Committees is most revealing. In 1973-74, the 17 Republican members were all white males. The 21 Democrat members contained three blacks (with one woman), three Jews (with one woman), and a Catholic priest. In the 1998 hearings, the Republicans had the majority, 21 members, of whom 20 were white males, with one woman, Mary Bono, who succeeded her husband Sonny Bono killed in a skiing accident. Her presence on the Committee was purely the result of this tragedy. The combined total of the two Republican Committees was 37 white males plus one entirely accidental white female. To a neutral observer it would immediately become apparent that the Republicans were striving heroically to maintain their image as the "Party of the Big Tent."

As previously noted, Chairman Peter Rodino went to inordinate lengths to avoid contentious partisanship from arising, and in that effort was uniformly successful. At no point did his Republican opposites on the Committee claim that the Chairman was unfair or biased. The group operated behind closed doors and not a single leak filtered through those doors. In his opening message to the members in 1973, he implored them "to proceed with such care and decency and honor" that future generations will insist "that was the right course." Recall that Rodino had enlisted in the army as soon as Congress declared war on Japan and Germany and in short order was assigned to an armored division. He would be promoted repeatedly from a private to a captain, an uncommon procedure in the army. None of the 17 white males on the Republican side had seen military service. Very few Republican Congressmen ever did.

The Republicans on the Committee, mostly lacking in either character or conscience, were resolute in their desire to nail Bill Clinton to the impeachment cross and cared little what process they employed. Consider for a moment that 11 of the 21 members were Southern conservatives, which meant they were in complete accord with white supremacy. That is *white male* supremacy; remember, there is not a single black Republican in Congress and there hasn't been since J.C. Watts quit in disgust with his fellow Republicans some years ago. (The Democrats have 44 black members.) An additional six were from mid-western Republican enclaves. Even today, in a Democratic Senate, 17 of the 22 Senators from the 11 former Confederate States are Republican and of these 17, only two are women. Of the five Democrats in those 11 states, two also are women. In the Senate there are 16 women members, 11 Democrats and only five Republicans. Here again we see the dogma of the Republicans being the "Party of the Big Tent" firmly in place.

The Clinton impeachment ordeal was a judicial travesty that *never should have happened*, should never even have been considered. One part of the persecution team, and these were persecutors, not prosecutors, was the Republican Congressional contingent. The first hearings were held in the summer of 1995 by the Senate Banking Committee under the chairmanship of Alphonse D'Amato. This proved to be a most regrettable action on the part of the senator since in his next election he would be easily defeated by Chuck Shumer, the current Senator from New York. His defeat could be attributed to the casual relationship he maintained with the truth. Repeatedly he would tell an excited press, and through it the entire nation, that he was in possession of a "smoking gun" concerning the president, implying that impeachment articles would be forthcoming.

In this endeavor he received considerable assistance from Lauch Faircloth, the senator from North Carolina. The two senators fulminated at great length about the felonious activities of their target in the White House. Unhappily for Senator Faircloth, he too would be denied his senate seat by North Carolina voters that same election.

Reviewing the blizzard of near lethal blows coming at the Clintons from several sectors and how newspapers that would normally be even-handed in their treatment of the proceedings were actually slanted towards the prosecutors, it's amazing that the President and First Lady emerged as un-bloodied as they did.

Consider the attitude of Newt Gingrich, who in January, 1995, became Speaker of the House of Representatives, arguably the third most powerful position in American government. Privately he told his avid flock of Republicans, who now controlled Congress, that he would relentlessly pursue the President and begin a stream of investigations which he hoped would lead to impeachment charges. He insisted that the President "had presided over the most systematic, deliberate obstruction-of-justice cover-up to avoid the truth we have ever seen in American history."

Before the Judiciary Committee would hold its first official impeachment hearings, the 1998 Congressional election still had to be held. Gingrich was a veritable cyclone, whirling around the nation forecasting a huge electoral victory for his party. He was confident of 30 — 40 new seats in the House alone. At the same time he projected exuberance at the prospect of successful impeachment articles passing in the House, especially under his leadership as Speaker.

On election night, the Republican headquarters in Washington was bursting with expectant joy anticipating an impressive victory. But shortly, as the individual results began to filter in, the rapture began to diminish. Fewer and fewer of the anticipated triumphs were materializing. Before the evening finished, the party had suffered a net loss of five seats.

Robert Livingston, a senior House member from Louisiana, quickly went to work to dethrone Gingrich. The Speaker was widely disliked even among his fellow house members for his autocratic demeanor. In victory his leadership was tolerable but following this unimaginable defeat his services were no long required. Within days Gingrich realized he was finished, and within a few more days decided to resign from Congress. His decision occasioned few tears in that body.

Nemesis, the Greek god of retributive justice had intervened in the affairs of Newton Gingrich. Nemesis found himself in a favorable atmosphere and decided to pay a visit to several more senior Republicans in the House before departing to where Greek gods go. He selected Robert Livingston for his next call.

Before venturing into this truly bizarre scenario, it is necessary to introduce a character unique to American history, Larry Flynt. He had attained a measure of fame by publishing a salacious magazine called *"Hustler,"* generally considered the raunchiest of its genre. The magazine became the crown jewel of his publishing empire and rewarded him with an abundance of wealth. En route to this new found wealth, he also encountered a certified nut case, a White Citizens Council type in a nightclub who shot and permanently paralyzed him.

Years after this untoward incident, and upon reading the incessant chorus of sexual hypocrisy coming forth from the Republicans, Flynt paid for a full page ad in the Washington Post. In the ad he offered a modest $1 million for irrefutable evidence of "an adulterous sexual encounter," especially with Republican Congressmen.

Sidney Blumenthal, in *"The Clinton Wars"* highlights this episode in a manner which is a pure delight to read. In an interview shortly after the ad ran, Flynt observed, "If these guys are going after the president, they shouldn't have any skeletons in their closet. This is only the beginning."

Livingston was the Speaker Designate, following Gingrich's abrupt departure. He longed to preside over the impeachment trial of the much despised William Jefferson Clinton, which was due to commence the following day. The Republicans had been sipping liberally from the fountain of hypocrisy, but on this very day an extraordinary item appeared on the Internet. Livingston, it divulged, had been luxuriating in an extramarital affair!

Later that same day he was forced to appear before a Republican conference. Reading from a prepared statement he shamefacedly announced, "I have on occasion strayed from my marriage, and doing so nearly cost me my marriage and my family. I sought marriage and spiritual counseling and have received forgiveness from my wife and family, for which I am eternally grateful. This chapter was a small but painful part of the past in an otherwise wonderful marriage." In short order he too would resign from office and slink in anonymity.

Nemesis, once again stalking the Republican ranks for retribution, selected another victim. This was Bob Barr, doubtless one of two Republicans in the House most avidly pursing the impeachment route. He was clearly revealed to be a fraudulent piece of goods when his ex-wife disclosed he had forced her to undergo an abortion, and then lied about his action in the divorce case.

Following that, Professor Alan Dershowitz of Harvard Law School, whom we met while Bush was stealing the election from Vice-President Gore, exposed Barr for being seriously involved with a noxious racist group called the Council of Concerned Conservatives. Initially Barr attempted to lie his way out of the charge but damning photographs revealed his presence at their meeting.

Earlier Professor Dershowitz gave his evaluation of the charges against the president. "The false statements of which President Clinton is accused fall at the most marginal end of the least culpable genre of this continuous of offenses and would never even be considered for prosecution in the routine case involving an ordinary defendant." The professor, you might recall, had earned a full professorship at Harvard Law School at the tender age of 28, the youngest ever to do so in the school's history.

Accompanying Dershowitz was another very well known voice; this belonging to A. Leon Higginbotham, Jr. described in the "*The Clinton Wars*" as a former federal judge and one of the most distinguished black jurists and legal scholars in American history. He in turn cited Supreme Court Justice Oliver Wendell Holmes on degree and proportionality. Judge Holmes is one of the frequently quoted judges in American jurisprudence. Here is Judge Higginbotham weighing in for President Clinton: "Perjury has gradations. If the President broke the 55-mile-per-hour speed limit and said under oath he was going 49; that would not be an impeachable high crime. And neither is this … President Clinton's alleged perjury regarding consensual sexual relations clearly falls on the end of the spectrum with my example of perjury regarding a traffic violation. Assuming his statements were false and material, they did not cause anywhere near the gravity of injury required by the Constitution for impeachment."

Congressman Barr haughtily rebutted this scholarly statement with a considerable degree of asperity. "I'd be depressed but I realize there are two Americas out there. There's a real America that doesn't buy the professor's talk about gradations. Real Americans know that perjury amounts to impeachment."

The problem here is that since Barr was deeply immersed in the affairs of White Citizens Councils and Judge Higginbotham was black, their worlds almost never became entwined. A further problem existed in that Barr had perjured himself in his testimony during his divorce case. Perjury should be perjury whatever the judicial level.

Representative Barr would dip into the marriage pool three times and thus become eligible for the Triple Marriage Crown, a level of accomplishment he shares with Newt Gingrich. Republican presidential candidate, Rudy Giuliani also qualified but what truly distinguishes Rudy is he is the third husband of his current wife.

The Democrats old friend Nemesis, still hovering over sanctimonious impeachment seekers, next selected Henry Hyde for retribution. Smack in the middle of all this political turmoil taking place in Washington, *www.Salon.com*, the online magazine, dropped another depth charge on the Republicans. It highlighted Hyde's long ago affair with a married woman, Cherie Snodgras, which began when he was 40 years old and continued for five years. In the process, it destroyed the Snodgras marriage.

Hyde was completely dismissive of this rather sordid event in his life and referred to it as a "youthful indiscretion." Bummy Bush also reached 40 when he finally abandoned the wasteful life of youthful frivolity.

In printing this information, Salon's editor justified it in this manner: "If the public has a right to know, in excruciating detail, about Clinton's sexual life, then surely it has an equal right to know about the private life of the man who called the family 'the surest basis of civil order, the strongest foundation for free enterprise, the safest home of freedom' – and who on Monday indicated that he believes impeachment hearings are warranted."

Three Republicans remained that were yet to be chastised by Nemesis, although the Greek god would be ably abetted by Larry Flynt's efforts – Dan Burton, Representative from Indiana whose every act and utterance tends to cast disrepute upon the quality of the House membership. He was quickly exposed as having fathered an out of wedlock child years before.

Burton now became involved in a Republican vortex of supreme lunacy. Six months after Bill Clinton was sworn into office, one of the president's aides, Vince Foster, had committed suicide. The unfortunate, depressed man had driven to a nearby park, placed a gun in his mouth and pulled the trigger. The suicide weapon still remained in his hand. Immediately the president's fierce enemies, and they were legend, set about to contrive a murder scenario. Burton volunteered his services.

He called a press conference at which he predicted he would conclusively demonstrate that Foster had been murdered. At the conference he produced a watermelon and proceeded to fire several bullets into it from his hand held gun.

He felt he had put on a convincing performance. He had put on a performance all right, but the assembled press was perplexed about what they had just witnessed. They remembered that Burton had once called the president "a scum bag."

The "Reverend" Jerry Falwell would soon be hustling videos at $43.00 apiece which proved beyond question that Hillary Clinton had Foster murdered in her secret hideaway then had his body moved to the park. In the video, evidence was arranged so that it appeared a murder had taken place. Falwell liked a well defined cleavage or separation between church and state.

When casting disrepute upon the House membership, none did a better job than Helen Chenoweth from Idaho. She too soon confessed to an adulterous affair in her life. What distinguished her, however, was her repeated claims that she had seen large, black helicopters, belonging to the United Nations, circling overhead in her Idaho aerie. She was never able to find corroborating witnesses to these sights.

This brings us to Tom DeLay who escaped with his sexual virtue intact, but who is currently awaiting trial in Texas on a variety of charges. It's reasonable to state that without his feverish, almost demonic enthusiasm, no impeachment trial would ever have been held. It's also reasonable to state that the likelihood of his conviction and sentencing is quite high.

Bill Clinton's arrival in the White House fomented a monstrous level of anguish among fundamentalist organizations like the Christian Coalition inducing it to proclaim that his presidency was "a repudiation of our forefather's covenant with God."

The members of that organization doubtless would be aghast to learn that of our first four presidents, none of them even belonged to a church. George Washington, John Adams, Thomas Jefferson and James Madison were Deists who felt no need for religious services but did serve our country in an exemplary manner. Their view was bolstered by Benjamin Franklin and many signers of the Declaration of Independence. Mr. Franklin, who played a very important role in our Revolutionary War, once observed that after a shipwreck, it's more prudent to build a lighthouse than a chapel. Surely those august figures would qualify as forefathers.

It is also fair to point out that Honest Abe Lincoln never was a member of a church and he is easily the greatest of all Republican presidents. He would scarcely deign to enter the same church pew with the current occupant of the White House.

That argument aside, the fundamentalists passionately believed that our country was meant to be a Christian nation with life presenting an implacable struggle between Good and Evil. It required only a small step to conclude that their political opponents were aligned with the Devil.

After Vince Foster's suicide, several different sources produced videos linking the President and perhaps the First Lady with an entire series of unexplained deaths. As early as 1994 one such conspiracy group published a list of 34 people who had perished under what was considered highly suspicious circumstances – each somehow linked to the President. The Falwell version, already mentioned, "*Jerry Falwell Presents Bill Clinton's Circle of Power*" was merely one of a series of similar videos.

Falwell, it must be remembered, had openly preached segregation from his pulpit for years, and had a pronounced far right political orientation. Also, his Liberty University in Lynchburg, Virginia, was staggering under a mountainous load of debt. This tenacious crusade against Bill Clinton didn't lack for financial motives.

"*The Clinton Chronicles,*" another Falwell production, was issued and vigorously promoted on the 200 or more radio stations that carried "The Reverend's" programs. Although a bare few of these stations refused to air blatantly unchristian messages, most did without a second thought.

That a significant portion of the American public would purchase these videos and accept unthinkingly the content is shocking. But it's important to realize that most of these transactions took place in rural or small town areas in Southern States. In their fundamental churches they listened to preachers whose message was consistent: anti-abortion; fierce homophobia; anti-evolution; unrestrained hatred of same-sex marriage and a warning against eternal hell fires. There followed a blatant Republican message. All eleven ex-confederate states twice voted for Bush.

There never was a reminder that our Constitution insisted upon a distinct separation between church and state.

I find it extremely difficult to believe that the Clintons, in observing what befell their tormenters in the House, didn't come away from the imbroglio with not merely a feeling of satisfaction but a smile on their faces. The political axe neatly lopped off the heads of Newt Gingrich and Robert Livingston. Bob Barr would shortly be defeated by a youthful black lady in Georgia, and in a rematch would fall even harder. In the impeachment hearings, Henry Hyde would be made to appear even more foolish than nature intended. Helen Chenoweth is now deeply immersed in obscurity; Tom DeLay's destiny may be the worst of all, a prison cell. Only melon-head Dan Burton remains still pretending to be a fair-minded Congressman from Indiana.

In the Senate, retribution sped in swiftly as Alphonse D'Amato of New York was easily defeated for reelection by Chuck Shumer, now the senior Senator from New York. And who is the junior senator? Why, Hillary Clinton, of course.

Returning to the impeachment travesty – Following the embarrassing defeat at the polls in November of 1999, it appeared the Republicans would give up their quest for the President's scalp and settle for a censure vote or possibly even an apology from Mr. Clinton.

One of these outcomes was more than likely except for one Republican, Tom DeLay. His nearly maniacal need to drive the president from office overrode all other political considerations. He placed inordinate party pressure on every Republican on the Judiciary Committee whose desire for impeachment might be lacking. He played the retribution card, using every trick and wile at his command to coerce either the unwilling or the hesitant members into line. It worked.

Before proceeding further it is necessary to digress for a moment to review how the impeachment process even got under way. After the 1994 election when the Republicans regained control of Congress for the first time in 40 years, and with Newt Gingrich the newly installed Speaker of the House, they began their drive to scour the Clinton presence from the Oval Office. They intensified pressure on the Democratic Attorney General to appoint a special prosecutor to investigate the inflammatory nonsense about Whitewater. The Clintons had become involved in an ill-advised real estate venture outside Little Rock, Arkansas, on which they actually lost money. Tossing logic on its ear, Gingrich and his fired up minions demanded that justice be served with the entire episode being subjected to a thorough airing.

Janet Reno was the highly competent Attorney General and totally unlike the two imposters appointed by Bush to succeed her. Bill Clinton had continued the tradition of Democratic presidents in the 20th Century of appointing skilled administrators of justice in *The Justice Department*. Likewise the Pampered Parasite has perpetuated the tarnished tradition of Republican presidents by appointing indictment dodging Attorneys General like Harry Daughtery, who served under Warren Harding; Edwin Meese III (to whom we've been introduced) and now Blood Thirsty Alberto Gonzales.

Reno finally relented and selected Robert Fiske as the special prosecutor. Fiske was chosen because of his exemplary credentials. Once again borrowing from Sidney Blumenthal's *"The Clinton Wars"* — "During the Reagan Administration, Fiske had been chairman of the American Bar Association's standing committee on the federal judiciary, which reviewed nominations and issued ratings in a procedure that had virtually been an official part of the process since the Eisenhower Administration. Among the criteria to which Fiske had paid special attention were a candidate's record on women's and civil rights." Fiske was a life-long Republican.

He proceeded with dispatch and quickly proved that the Whitewater event was without merit. His initial findings exonerated Bill and Hillary from any significant participation in a Whitewater fraud or cover-up. Far from profiting in that real estate endeavor, they had lost a sizeable amount of money.

Fiske drew attention to the damning editorials about Vince Foster in the Wall Street Journal. That tragically depressed man tarred the Journal in his suicide note, "The Wall Street Journal editors lie without consequence."

Rather than manifest any sense of remorse for those unconscionable editorials, the paper continued its vendetta against the Clintons. It referred to Fiske's efforts in the most demeaning manner; shortly their editorials turned to rage and called his findings "The Fiske Cover-up."

Nor was the sainted New York Times either guiltless or guileless in this shameful attempt to tar-and-feather the President. Its chief Clinton hater demanded a more vigorous investigator. A man I consider a journalistic cockroach, William Safire, vented his rotten wrath against the highly respected Robert Fiske. "What's with this non-independent counsel who helps Democrats avoid oversight? Find a way to get rid of him."

I read the New York Times avidly each day and look forward to perusing it. Still, the paper insists on having one or more Safire-minded types on its payroll in an effort to "give balance" to its output. Its rivals like *The Weakly Standard* don't feel that need. In the buildup to the Iraq War, Judith Miller's articles, strongly urging invasion, were quoted extensively by the super-hawks in the administration to justify blasting into Baghdad. In one widely quoted instance, her Saturday article was used on the Sunday talk shows to great advantage by Dick Cheney and Condi Rice in an effort to promote that monstrous assault on a nation posing no threat to us.

It is with considerable jollity that I remind readers that Safire was the impassioned speech writer for Spiro Agnew. That's the Vice-President who was confronted with 57 felony counts by federal prosecutors appointed by Richard Nixon.

Can one ever forget that imperishable description, "Nattering nabobs of negativism," a phrase proudly authored by Safire so that Sinful Spiro could give voice to it before frenzied reactionary Republicans during the pre-Watergate Nixon era? Before attaining that high degree of notoriety, Safire was busy writing inspirational messages for an authentic wing-nut Republican who became governor in Florida. His name was Claude Kirk but critics promptly dubbed him Claude Quirk, and he became a one term governor. Kirk or Quirk reached a political level unattained by any other politician I'm aware of. He began his career as a Democrat, switched sides to Republican status, but finally decided he preferred to be a Democrat after all. Perhaps Safire provided guidance for these soul-wrenching decisions.

The New York Times erred massively in poisoning the information well it presented its readers. It carries a high degree of responsibility to the American people since it is so widely quoted in other newspapers and TV. To provide a billboard for a creature like Safire, who no doubt still adores Richard Nixon, was unpardonable. To publish the flagrant toxins of a Judith Miller was equally unforgivable. The Bush Administration welcomed her screeds with enchantment and used them to catapult this nation into attacking Iraq.

With the Republicans in total control of the investigation and media jackals like Safire and his like baying for the President's hide, Fiske would be fired by a three man court of right wing judges. In his place, Kenneth Starr was appointed. Practically speaking he became an auxiliary member of the Republicans on the Judiciary Committee.

Starr's counterpart in the Nixon case was Leon Jaworski, who made every effort to be impartial and treat both sides fairly. Totally unlike Starr he drew no conclusions from the evidence being presented as Starr would do consistently. He most assuredly did not draw up any articles of impeachment against Nixon. Starr, by complete contrast, proposed 10 articles against Bill Clinton. Jaworski believed that "making recommendations would transgress the boundaries of his office and usurp the power of the House."

In Starr's aberrant resolve to drive the President out of office he wouldn't be stayed by any of these judicial niceties. He shattered every precedent established by Chairman Peter Rodino and Leon Jaworski; he trampled under foot any effort to be objective.

Starr and the prosecutors he hired had contempt for Bill Clinton that approached loathing. Considering their intense religious convictions, the antipathy they felt for the President made them feel the man lacked the moral stature to hold the office. For instance, Starr had added Sam Dash to his staff as ethics counselor. Dash had been the chief counsel for the Democrats back in 1974. In "*The Clinton Wars*" he makes this observation. "I saw decisions made on moral grounds that had nothing to do with criminal grounds. They believed that someone was a bad person, a sinful person, who ought to be punished for it.

They distorted their judgment. Ken allowed his personal concepts of morality to interfere with the role of a prosecutor."

Once more mining the rich mother lode of *"The Clinton Wars,"* we find this critical analysis of Starr's methodology rendered by Robert W. Gordon, professor at Yale Law School. "He cranked up the machinery of the criminal process, spent millions of dollars (at least 45 million), fed a major national scandal, and hauled the President of the United States before a grand jury, in order to catch a civil party in a lie that was not central to Paula Jones' case but so peripheral to it as to be almost completely irrelevant, and which concerned underlying conduct that is not criminal at all. It's a sure bet that no other prosecutor in the history of the republic has spent millions on a criminal investigation of an offense like Clinton's, a lie in a civil deposition about a consensual affair that was totally collateral to any issue of importance in the case."

What do we know of the man who headed up the Office of Independent Counsel? Kenneth Winston Starr entered this world in a backwoods portion of Texas, the son of a part time minister of the Church of Christ, a branch of the Christian faith which dips deeply into the world of bible literalism or inerrancy. His family had an extreme puritanical approach to life – fun was viewed with a certain measure of aversion, so that normally accepted activities such as drinking, dancing, card playing and movie going were proscribed.

Young Kenneth, in due time, was sent off to Harding College, an educational arm of the Church of Christ located in Searcy, Arkansas. One of its distinguishing features was that it extended no invitations to blacks. Its president promoted the cause of the John Birch Society, a group of hallucinating right wing extremists who insisted that President Dwight Eisenhower and Secretary of State John Foster Dulles were card carrying Communists. The organization has long since suspended operations.

Arkansas at the time was scarcely a nationally renowned center for the Arts-and-Culture and Searcy was doing its part to uphold that standard. Still, one has to wonder what the young man's major was. Perhaps Medieval Religious Superstitions" or "Religious Tolerance in Italy and Spain during the 16th Century," might have appealed to him.

We might interject here that Ronald Reagan graduated from Eureka College in Illinois, a college with a near identical educational loftiness.

Stemming from this aesthetically withered background, it is little wonder that Starr's mind gradually welded together bigotry and hostility. Life presented no gray areas – everything was all black or all white. Bill and Hillary Clinton were black while he, Judge Starr, was the knight bedecked in dazzling white.

He gathered about him a small group of white men, and only white men. No blacks or women were admitted. They all had mind sets frozen into intolerance coupled with extreme scorn for those unlike themselves. To these True Believers the Clintons were common criminals who, because of presidential power, were able to cover up their manifest breaches of the law. Occupying the White House was the single most unforgivable offense; hence the presidential couple must be removed by whatever method.

Starr and his resolute band of crusaders no doubt had assimilated huge portions of the Bible, and could easily quote from it at length, but unaccountably their memories never established any linkage with any portion of "The Sermon on the Mount." It is nearly impossible to believe they ever entertained the thought that the chilling and concluding eight word directive coming from Christ might be aimed directly at them. "Do part from me you workers of inequity."

So, who were the "workers of iniquity?" Starr retired to become the Dean of the Law School at Pepperdine University in Malibu, California. (In ranking its law school, comparing it to Harvard or Yale, it might as well be Pepperoni U.) Bill Clinton's rating is as high as any politico in the land. "The former first lady has survived nine Republican candidates for the White House, plus six Democratic aspirants."

It is without question that no other president in our history was beset with so formidable a pack of jackals as was Bill Clinton. Yet the high degree of incompetence and the sorry level of their professionalism enabled him to escape their snares with no long term damage. One could easily conclude that he was indeed fortunate in having those individuals as his tormentors.

Consider the composition of the House Judiciary Committee that would conduct the impeachment hearings. On the Republican side were 20 white males plus Mary Bono, the widow of the national celebrity, Sonny Bono, who had died in a skiing accident. Mrs. Bono's position on the committee was purely an accident. The 20 white males were no accident; there were 11 Southerners whose political axis ranged from hard right to reactionary. Six more were from deeply conservative Midwest districts. The President had no reason to expect even a dram of charity or compassion from any of that lot.

The Republicans, having abandoned all pretense of being the Party of the Big Tent, had to look at the Democratic make-up. Of their 16 members four were black, three were women and six were Jews.

The Republicans on the committee at once abrogated their constitutional duty and essentially made Starr, not a fair-minded judicious Independent Counsel, but their unrelenting inquisitor. He became their only witness. As we have observed, he was neither fair-minded nor independent. The committee operated as a grand jury and under the Federal Code of Criminal Procedure it is illegal to disclose any evidence unearthed within the hearings. That restriction applies to both the prosecutor and his staff.

Starr and his group of True Believers however were ladling out evidence to their favorite members of the media as fast as it developed. Those favored members just happened to have a considerable detestation for the Clintons. When challenged by the President's attorneys, Starr would become quite indignant and deny that he or his minions were responsible for the leaks.

When Peter Rodino chaired the same committee for the Nixon hearing he very graciously allowed the Nixon attorneys *unlimited time* for questioning witnesses. But, under the 1998 hearings the super hypocrite, Henry Hyde, allowed David Kendall, Attorney for Bill Clinton, a trifling two hours.

Shortly after the hearings started, Hillary Clinton appeared on the Today Show and told the host, Matt Lauer, "that a vast right wing conspiracy has been conspiring against my husband since he announced for president." That same evening the President gave his State of the Union address. The Democrats responded in a most pleasing manner and gave him a whole-hearted, lengthy applause. Both episodes only enraged the ill-humored Republicans more.

All during this time the Grand Inquisitor was issuing a veritable blizzard of subpoenas for anyone even remotely linked to the case. Included in that group were Bill Clinton's attorneys and closest advisors. Soon they too were called to testify before the grand jury.

All of these decidedly un-judicial happenings motivated the president of the American Bar Association, Jerome Shestack, to issue a painful spanking to the prying persecutor: "Does prosecutorial zeal justify sting operations and unauthorized wire-tapping in order to leverage the hiding of a non-criminal sexual indiscretion into a criminal obstruction of justice? Is the special counsel a fourth arm of government lacking any meaningful accountability and realistically immune from removal? Are prosecutors entitled to ignore ethical prescriptions on the ground that their pursuit of truth or common practice justifies departure from professional standards?"

When David Kendall, the President's Attorney was finally granted an opportunity to interrogate Starr, the time limitation quickly came into play. Kendall's probing questions were highly effective and shook the studied composure of the Inquisitor. When his two hour period was exhausted, Kendall requested an additional hour but Hyde, with characteristic lack of graciousness, permitted only thirty more minutes. When that expired, another thirty minutes was asked for and denied.

This almost contemptuous treatment of the President's attorney, beseeching more time during one of the most celebrated trials of the century, was in bold contrast to Peter Rodino granting, not hours but days for Nixon's Attorney to complete his inquiries. But, of course, Hyde and his thirsting zealots had no interest in a proportionate division of time. Their decision had been arrived at long before the proceedings even started.

When the farcical hearing at last concluded, the verdict was predictable. Of the 21 Republicans, 20 voted for impeachment on three of the four articles; on the last article, every one of them demonstrated their ardor for his removal from office.

Before the final vote was taken, Sam Dash, whom Starr had personally chosen as the ethics advisor for the committee, resigned in disgust at the tactics employed by the Republicans, and Starr in- particular.

In a letter publicly released, Dash condemned the Special Investigator for "serving as an aggressive advocate for the proposition that the evidence in your referral demonstrates that the president committed impeachable offenses. In doing this, you have violated your obligations under the independent counsel statute and have unlawfully intruded on the power of impeachment which the Constitution gives solely to the House."

For Starr and his 21 Republicans, their minds resolutely frozen and resistant to any change, Dash's letter was a fruitless exercise. It is highly questionable that any of them gave it any credence. However, a new poll taken by the New York Times/CBS showed that Starr's rating in the nation had cascaded to a miserable 11%, while that of the President had levitated to 73%.

It would have been ill advised to think any of this would result in any cognitive or reflective activity on the part of the Republicans in the House. Their votes in the full body revealed their aloof disdain for the two Clintons. The first vote almost exactly mimicked the political division then existing – 228 for impeachment, 206 against. The second vote was a tad closer, 221 – 212.

The Republicans paid scant attention to the manner in which the American people were weighing this travesty. In *The Best of Times,* an utterly engrossing book by Haynes Johnson, he points out that "During the Watergate impeachment trauma in 1974, some 47.3 million viewers saw some or all of the Nixon impeachment hearings on network TV. In 1998, some 1.6 million viewers watched the Clinton impeachment hearings on cable TV, which *alone covers them in their entirety.*"

It's certainly worth noting that Haynes Johnson is a Pulitizer Prize-winning journalist, frequently seen on TV. But, what's even more exceptional is that his father, Malcolm Johnson, won another Pulitizer for his newspaper articles entitled *Crime on the Waterfront*, which eventually was adapted for that magnificent Hollywood production *"On the Waterfront."* I know of no other father-son winners of that coveted prize.

The U.S. Constitution provides a clear guideline for the next procedure. The full Senate must vote and two-thirds of its members must vote for conviction. Only once before had an American president been tried by the Senate. That occurred in May, 1868, when the President was Andrew Johnson, a Democrat. On two separate articles of impeachment the Senate twice failed by one vote to obtain the necessary two-thirds majority to convict Johnson. On both outcomes, seven Republican Senators voted not to convict.

January 19, 1999, would prove to be a pivotal day for Congressional Republicans and the President. In the Senate the case for impeachment was being tried by seven House Managers, all members of the Judiciary Committee and all his remorseless enemies.

That same evening he would deliver his annual State of the Union which would prove to be a riveting spectacle for the country. From the moment he entered the chamber he was greeted with boisterous applause and even cheers from the outnumbered Democrats; from the Republicans, only morose silence. He faced the badly divided audience with supreme confidence, totally at ease with himself and his surroundings. A casual visitor would never have imagined that only a short time before he had been impeached.

He instantly projected a pleasant magnanimous note of bipartisanship completely at variance with his dour opponents. At times he even became playful, virtually toying with the Republicans. Never in the entire speech spanning some 77 minutes did he utter that hateful term, *impeachment*. It turns into a bewitching performance and before the end, his entire audience was captivated.

The morning papers showered his efforts with effusive praise. Mary McGrory in the Washington Post poses the obvious question. "Was there any question in his mind about his survival in office? Apparently not. What the Senate is grinding through is the past. He is about the future."

During the period of that Senate trial the untruthful media torpedoes were busy spreading their lunacies. In *"The Clinton Wars,"* two such beyond-bizarre cases were delineated. In one the "Reverend" Jerry Falwell gushed, "Who will be the antichrist? Of course he'll be Jewish … if he is going to be the counterfeit of Christ, he has to be Jewish. The only thing we know is he must be male and

Jewish." A strong undertow exists that the Falwell antichrist must also be alive and employed by that awful Clinton.

In the other example, one of the right wing's premier nutcases offered this bit of enlightenment. Bill Clinton had sired a black son by a prostitute. Southern reactionaries had been hurling that racist charge against their progressive opponents for generations. Karl Rove would trot it out in 2000 when his boss, Bummy Bush, was campaigning against Senator John McCain. The South Carolina rednecks eagerly gobbled up that sterling example of ethical campaigning. As we have previous seen, the Bush family knows a good thing when they see it.

The seven House Managers didn't slog through the sludge to that depth but they had long abandoned any semblance of a righteous plane. They quickly discovered that their Republican counterparts in the Senate were more than reluctant to continue the unseemly tactics of the House Judiciary Committee and Kenneth Starr. A fair amount of sentiment existed on both sides of the Senatorial aisle to limit the chastisement of the President to mere censure or even a sincere, public apology.

But Tom DeLay, the self-appointed scourge of the Democrats would have none of this. The former bug exterminator from Texas had long been estranged from his mother and barely on speaking terms with several of his siblings. At length the Republican leadership in the Senate capitulated to this hectoring not only from DeLay, but Hyde and other outspoken House Managers.

The seven House Managers would make their individual presentations first. Not a word of any of their assaults on the President is worth preserving; it was only dreary repetitious material already spoken in the House hearings. Hyde and the others were incapable of forceful, memorable delivery since they had exhausted all their material long ago. Eventually the Clinton defense team would have its turn at bat.

Charles Ruff, confined to a wheel chair led off. His was a professorial approach, his words articulated in an impressive manner. "Be wary," he cautioned the senators, "be wary of the prosecutor who feels it necessary to deceive the court." He easily deconstructed the flimsy edifice piled together carelessly by the seven, sloppy persecutors.

Cheryl Mills, whose title was White House deputy legal counsel, would soon make her appearance. I can easily remember watching her on TV and marveling at the easy blend of professionalism and sincerity she projected. She was youthful, attractive and black, a radical contrast to the solid phalanx of stolid white males on the other team. I still recall how delighted I was to witness her composure, her eloquence and most especially her effectiveness. She made a most valuable contribution to the President's defense.

I believe her most forceful moment came when she very pointedly told the senators, "I stand here before you today, because President Bill Clinton believed I could stand here for him." The likelihood of an Afro-American being appointed to the Republic House Judiciary Committee was absolutely unthinkable. (Since there are no black Republicans to be found among the 535 members in today's Congress, feel assured it is still impossible) For these highly conservative white males to elevate a young black woman to the role of a House Manager was well beyond conceivable.

The last person to speak on behalf of the President was Dale Bumpers, only just retired as the senior Senator from Arkansas. He had known Bill Clinton for twenty-five years and the two had worked together for the 12 years of the Clinton governorship. In his natural folksy manner, he strung together a magisterial defense of his old friend.

He then accused the seven Managers of "wanting to win too badly. There's a total lack of proportionality, a total lack of balance in this thing. The charge and the punishment are totally out of sync." At this the entire senate body rose and vigorously lauded this bravura effort.

The Republicans, had they been astute politicians, would surely have realized they had failed in their impossible dream to drive the President from office. Common sense would have dictated a strategic retreat in a final effort to conceal their failure and with whatever dignity was available to them.

Of course, common sense is often a dearly purchased commodity. Voltaire, one of the French nation's greatest sons – a philosopher, playwright, poet and fabulous wit – casually observed, *"Le sens commun n'est pas si commun,"* common sense is not so common. The Republicans though were uncommonly slow to discern that simple fact.

Instead they blindly plodded on, expecting at some point soon to find salvation after all their ceaseless but heroic efforts. Following much internal wrangling among themselves and negotiating with their Republican brethren in the Senate, they settled on the stratagem of questioning live witnesses. Eventually they decided that three would have to suffice. Monica Lewinsky, of course, would be the most important. After all, it was her sexual relations with the President that had triggered the entire impeachment adventure.

Starr and his fervid inquisitors had scarcely covered themselves with glory when interrogating her early in the case. They had held her in custody for a period of 12 hours and during that entire period had subjected her to the most intense grilling. This was despite her repeated entreaties to have counsel present.

It's well beyond belief that at no time during this period while she time and again demanded to have an attorney by her side did any of them remember the Miranda Edict. Every police department in the nation had been forced, by settled law, to recognize that every person being questioned is entitled to two basic rights – they *must be informed* of their right to remain silent. Second, they absolutely *have the right to counsel*, either one they employ or one provided by a local court. This principle was determined by the Miranda v. Arizona Supreme Court decision in June, 1966. In Monica's case she was willing to provide her own attorney.

Under any normal set of conditions, failure to observe these and other conditions will rule out a prosecuting attorney from using any testimony developed during the ensuing questioning. At the time of Monica's predicament, that principle had been in force for over 30 years. Additionally, Monica wasn't even a suspect or accused of any crime. Still, the future Law Dean at Pepperoni U. had permitted his judicial goons to deny the most basic right to Miss Lewinsky. Following that episode, they then grilled her mother so vigorously over a period of two days that the poor lady collapsed and had to be led out of the hotel room by two people visibly supporting her.

Her interrogator was Bruce Udolph who, a number of years earlier, had cost the citizens of Atlanta $50,000 awarded by a court settlement involving a false imprisonment suit. Udolph subsequently fled town and ended up a member of the Starr troop of law breakers.

Starr was slowly becoming unfrocked, with his true nature revealed. Ultimately his approval rating plunged so low that even the House Managers decided that his services were dispensable. At that juncture, his popularity rating was at a near irreducible 11%. That was the exact level of Newt Gingrich's popularity among the American people when his Republican teammates threw him overboard.

Still, these Republicans were intolerably slow learners, a trait manifested once again when they elected to take-on Monica Lewinsky for a second time. Sidney Blumenthal in "*The Clinton Wars*" describes this encounter, held in her expensive hotel suite in Washington D.C.

In a particularly felicitous manner, he describes the scene. "Monica Lewinsky befuddled these conservative, provincial, middle-aged Republicans. She had confused Starr and most of the men in Starr's office, too. An articulate young woman of her worldly sophistication, way beyond their comprehension or ability to acknowledge. They were unprepared for the actual Monica Lewinsky."

It must be pointed out that nearly without exception, Hyde's team was comprised of men from smaller communities, often Southern, who were remarkably free of any taint of urbanity or familiarity with high cultural levels. They were uncomfortable with symphony orchestras or art museums. To be sure, they were attorneys but a thoughtful individual would not hire them for his defense counsel for anything more important than a minor traffic case.

Mr. Blumenthal continues the narrative. "For the House Managers, Lewinsky had been worse than a hostile witness. She had been in control throughout and had undermined their case in every way. She had refuted their premises of Clinton's criminality almost off-handedly."

After being chastised by this first of three hostile witnesses, and without giving heed to common sense, the House Managers selected Vernon Jordan as the next witness. This was doubtless an even greater mistake. Here was a man who was a senior partner at one of the most prestigious law firms in Washington, a man who usually charged clients $500.00 an hour for his services.

Moreover, he was a large, imperious black man from the South, no stranger to the deadly effects of segregation. He did little to hide his scorn for this conservative Southern Congressman who was a mere graduate of Bob Jones University.

The Congressman, Asa Hutchison, approached his task with a self-complacent, slightly condescending air. He was anxious to link Jordan closely with the President. In Peter Baker's "*The Breach*," a revealing account of this wrenching episode in American history, we learn that the Jordans and the Clintons were more than just friends. "They vacationed together, played golf together, spent the holidays together." The witness soon revealed that "Every year since his presidency, the Jordan family has been privileged to entertain the Clinton family on Christmas Eve."

The entanglement with Vernon Jordan had failed to produce a single nugget of helpful material for the House Managers. Now they were down to their last witness, Sidney Blumenthal, whose engrossing book "*The Clinton Wars*" has been repeatedly used to great advantage here. He was a senior adviser to the President and a confidant to both the Clintons. Before that exalted period of his life, he had spent 27 years as a distinguished journalist. His intense grilling by another of the House Managers bore as little fruit as had the first two.

All that remained was the vote in the Senate, which took place on February 12, the birthday of Abraham Lincoln. I refuse to believe that Honest Abe would have been anything but deeply disturbed to view the repugnant procedure under way in the Senate Building. By the time of his election to the Presidency, in 1860, he had become a greatly admired attorney in Illinois. He would have found himself in complete accord with the president of the American Bar Association, Jerome Shestack, whose stern rebuke to Starr we have already seen. "Are prosecutors entitled to ignore ethical prescriptions on the grounds that their pursuit of truth or common practice justifies departure from professional standards?" One doesn't acquire an exalted sobriquet like "Honest Abe" by abandoning professional standards.

The man who rose to such transcendental heights in the Republican Party, would have felt shamed to be linked to this sorry group, and would have objected forcefully when it called itself the Party of Lincoln.

The vote itself was the ultimate anticlimax. On Article One, 55 senators were in favor of acquitting the President; only 45 disagreed. On the remaining Article, the vote was evenly split, 50 – 50.

On the question of impeaching the current resident in the White House, sound political considerations dictate that he remain in office. (It is unconstitutional to simultaneously impeach both the president and vice-president.) Better to permit this festering sore to occupy the Oval Office until January, 2009, rather than have the Republicans rally around their badly wounded chief.

Meanwhile the election committees for both houses can gather funds and momentum to build much larger majorities in Congress. By adding 35 – 40 more Democrats in the House and six – eight in the Senate, much desirable legislation would be eased into law. It would also place the wavering and quavering Congressional Republicans in an increasingly awkward position and force many of them either to remain silent or even on occasion speak out against their stricken leader.

CHAPTER XIII

Distasteful as it is, we must pursue our goal of revealing the true nature of the Republicans. We have already identified them as the Party of Big Business, or the POBB; very emphatically they are also the Party of White Males, or POWM. Beginning with the 1868 election, after Abe Lincoln's death, they descended to the Party of Objectionable Politics, or POOP.

President Lincoln's assassination was the second greatest calamity to befall this nation in the 19th century, the worst of course being the Civil War. In eliminating the President, John Wilkes Booth guaranteed brutal, murderous treatment for the four million newly freed slaves in the Confederacy for at least a century, and prevented a desperately needed restructuring of southern attitudes such as occurred in Germany and Japan immediately after their surrender in 1945.

In neither country was there so much as a hint of resistance to the occupation, nor did any terrorist organization gain a foothold. I entered Germany on March 27, 1945, almost exactly six weeks before the war officially ended in Europe on May seventh. I remained at my Army Air Corps Base until the first week in December and, in that entire time, was never aware of even the tiniest act of defiance to American occupying troops. At no time did I or my fellow G.I.s worry about our safety when traveling about the country. Had there been a problem the Stars and Stripes, our daily Armed Forces newspaper, would have warned us.

In Japan the occupation force was presented with the same level of acceptance and the same lack of defiance. Yet, in the South, our fellow countrymen resisted with considerably militancy. Southerners weren't about to allow their negras to vote or achieve any level of parity with their former masters. Only the calming, conciliatory, hand of an Abraham Lincoln could have effected the desirable change and that hand was forcibly removed by a hateful slavery lover.

We have already taken a modest peek into the eight years of the Grant Administration, beginning in 1869 and saw how super-laden they were with the bribery, corruption and prison terms. But, at least he conducted his campaigns relatively free of objectionable politics. Neither party was completely divorced from its taint.

However, in the 1876 election involving the Republican Rutherford Hayes, the POOP strongly asserted itself and established a pattern that has continued for 130 years, right through the 2006 model. In 1876, Hayes was opposed by Samuel Tilden, a highly successful governor of New York, truly distinguished by his destroying the Boss Tweed gang in New York City, a brazen collection of crooks and party hacks, many of whom were sent to prison by the governor. From the earliest days of the campaign, Tilden and his team set out to conduct a run for the presidency with smear-free tactics.

The Republican response was to assail Tilden with unalloyed venom. Vile derogatory terms were used to denigrate the unsuspecting candidate. He was called a drunkard, a swindler, a liar and even a syphilitic. He was denounced as "a menace to the United States." When these methods failed to produce victory at the polls, Hayes' managers resorted to a purely larcenist course, one that came to be known as "the U. S. Fraud of the Century." The thieving band allied with Bush would pull off an equally successful heist in 2000.

At least Hayes was a reasonably competent occupant of the White House and didn't blunder into a war on another continent. Then too, while nobody ever referred to him as "Honest Rutherford," his veracity was never challenged. The current occupant of that same White House has his truthfulness disputed nearly every time he makes an utterance.

The next quadrennial contest in 1880 involved James Garfield against Winfield Scott Hancock. Garfield, the Republican, had been involved in the noxious Credit Mobilier episode during the Grant Administration, which we have already touched on. While he had never officially been charged with a crime, his reputation had suffered some slight decline. Trifling matters like official corruption almost never deter Republican king-makers when it comes to selecting a presidential candidate.

General Winfield Scott Hancock had no such blemish on his record. Moreover, he had truly distinguished himself at the battle of Gettysburg and was one of its authentic heroes. He displayed high levels of bravery at several critical points in the struggle and was badly wounded.

During the entire campaign Garfield enjoyed a lavish superiority in campaign funding. This was a standard that Republicans would enjoy in virtually every presidential race right through 2004.

Even with this huge advantage he barely managed to eke out a tiny 10,000 vote victory margin. He also became the third consecutive president coming from Ohio.

As President, Garfield quickly revealed himself to be fiercely anti-union and resisted any effort for blue collar workers to organize or to seek improved working conditions. He considered their efforts to establish an eight hour day as an unwarranted interference with the employee-employer working relationship.

During that election year a previously unknown group called the Greenback – Labor Party made a determined effort to upgrade working standards for laborers. They pressed for an eight hour day, better factory codes, and ending child labor. These provisions of course were frightfully abhorrent to Garfield and his fellow member of the POBB, the Big Business Party.

When he also fought against the right of women to vote, regarding women's suffrage as "destructive of marriage and family," he began formulating the POWM, Party of the White Male. Ever since 1880 the Republicans have been faithfully ministering onto this passionate belief. We saw during the Nixon impeachment affair how their House Judiciary Committee was so fairly divided – 17 men and zero women. Fifteen years later they labored intensely and improved the lot of Republican Congressional women. The division of that committee was 20 males and *One Female*. Now, tell me that isn't progress!!

Garfield would fall victim to an intended assassination on July second, in his first months in office, cling to life for two months, then expire on September 18th. His vice-President, Chester Arthur, was now elevated to the presidency.

To suggest there was anything distinguished about Arthur's career before becoming president would be hopelessly inaccurate. He had attached himself to the Republican Party early in life and worked hard to elect Abraham Lincoln and then Grant. For his assiduous efforts on behalf of the Grant campaign, he was rewarded with the important post of Collector of the Port of New York and filled that role from 1871 – 1878. As such, it was his task to collect tariff duties from all ships entering ports in New York State.

After Rutherford Hayes stole the presidency in 1876, in atonement, he managed to accomplish a few items of note. One important task was civil service reform whereby political hacks would be removed from roles of significance and replaced with men of merit. And, of course, that meant men, not women.

Pursuing this plan, Hayes appointed a commission to investigate the source of the distinct odor of corruption arising from the Collector's Office of the Port of New York. The first witness called was Chester Arthur and he endured a grilling for six hours. Upon concluding its findings, the commission strongly urged Hayes to vacuum out the incompetents in the Collector's Office. After reviewing the report the president politely asked Arthur to resign; when he reused to do so he was suspended.

Now the Republican Party found itself with Arthur as President of the United States. One party bigwig, when informed of this state of affairs, loudly bewailed, "Chet Arthur is President? Good God."

One marvelously precise summary of the man came from the Chicago Tribune, always a champion of the Republican Party. "Mr. Arthur's temperament is sluggish. He is indolent. It requires a great deal for him to get to his desk and begin the dispatch of business. Great questions of public policy bore him. No president was ever so much given to procrastination as he is."

In 1888 the American voters beheld an astonishing event – a first for many of them – when a Democratic President would be elected. That hadn't happened since 1856 when James Buchanan won the seat. Grover Cleveland came to office and not even an exuberant Democrat would call him either a Liberal or a Progressive. What modest efforts his administration made to lighten the burden of the poor, or the working class, were thwarted by the Republican majority in the senate.

Running for reelection in 1888, he was opposed by Benjamin Harrison, another product of Ohio, who was the grandson of a former president, William Henry Harrison. This latter Harrison was only in office for barely a month when he succumbed to a bad cold, the shortest tenure of any of our chief executives.

Benjamin Harrison would win the office with a plurality of electoral votes but be outpolled by over 90,000 votes. Thus, twice within eight years the Democrats had won more votes but lost the contest. Adding these two results to the outrage of 2000, when a remarkably flagrant swindle took place, we must note three times where the Republicans received fewer votes but walked off with the elections. Strangely enough the Democrats have never been able to manipulate the election returns to produce a victory with fewer votes.

About the only significant legislation passed by the Harrison office was the McKinley Tariff Act which raised duties on imports to their highest levels. It was now an even 100 years since George Washington became president by acclamation; he wasn't even required to run for office. But 100 years was more than enough time for business and industry to operate profitably without a baleful subsidy resulting from a protective tariff.

The obvious result, a very predictable result, was a diminution of competition from foreign entities with a resultant rise in consumer prices. The POBB was performing skillfully for its benefactors while Big Business would continue to shower its partner with lush campaign funding. The consequence was a greedy alliance between the rich and a readily purchasable Congress.

This coalition of a pliant congress and entrenched interests was still alive and thriving in its 109th edition which ended in January, 2007. That group, mostly Republican, had only two aims – protect its financial supporters and continue to reelect itself. Providentially enough voters had the good sense to replace many of these mind-numbing mediocrities with Democrats so that the 110th Congress is in Democratic hands.

Theodore Roosevelt, second only to Abe Lincoln as the best of the Republican presidents, very aptly characterized the tenure of the Republican Harrison. "Damn the President! He is a cold-blooded, narrow-minded, prejudiced, obstinate, timid old psalm-singing Indianapolis politician."

In the year 1896, voters elected the Republican William McKinley who quickly became the quintessential POBB president for the entire 19th century. Ronald Reagan captured that title with effortless ease for the 20th century. While the 21st century is still only in a toddler stage, our boy Bush appears to have a strangle-hold on that title. Big business looks upon his never-ending efforts on its behalf with appropriate adoration.

Opposing McKinley was William Jennings Bryan, one of the most gifted orators of all our presidential candidates. The contest rapidly became known as the "Battle of the Standards." The Republicans were resolutely entrenched as defenders of the gold standard, while the Democrats eagerly espoused the silver standard.

Henry George, widely celebrated in the country during those years as a land reformer and economist, and whose book, "*Progress and Poverty*," enjoyed monumental success, very succinctly defined the issue. "The struggle is on the currency issue. But, these are only symbols, and behind them are gathered the world-opposing forces of aristocratic privilege and democratic freedom."

Besides condemning McKinley and his fellow Republicans for espousing high tariffs and upholding the gold standard, Bryan demanded a federal income tax for the wealthy. He and his followers were equally incensed at the widespread use of court ordered injunctions to end strikes and even picketing at the entrance to factories.

McKinley was supplied with a wealth of advantages in the campaign. His manager, Mark Hanna, a precursor of below-the-belt hitters like Lee Atwater and Karl Rove had amassed an unheard of hoard of cash for his candidate, $7 million. Bryan had to be content with a mere $300,000. The vast differential in money was only one aspect of the struggle. Hanna skillfully assembled a Speakers Bureau of 1400 members who faithfully spread the Republican message throughout the land. Campaign literature by the tens of millions was showered on the people, all of it proclaiming the obvious merits of their candidate. The campaign slogan was "McKinley and the Full Dinner Pail."

To ensure victory in that November, Hanna and his helpers set into motion a strategy to vilify Bryan as unfit for office. He was called a socialist and then a communist, although the two factions commonly despise each other. Amongst other names of an uncharitable nature propelled his way were lunatic, traitor and murderer. The two nationally known New York City papers, the Times and the Tribune, could scarcely contain their wrath in castigating the man.

And what had he done to deserve this outpouring of hate and vituperation? Mostly he opposed high tariffs and the gold standard both of which were oppressive burdens for farmers and the working class who constituted an overwhelming percentage of the populace. In his appeals for a graduated income tax, applied only to the wealthy, he was seeking desperately needed funding for more schools, roads and bridges. The latter was of critical need for farmers and rural dwellers. For the want of a bridge across a nearby river, they might have to travel a long distance by horse and buggy to find a crossing.

Here is one of his most frequently quoted statements: "There are those who believe that, if you will only legislate to make the well-to-do prosperous, their prosperity will leak through to those below. The Democratic idea, however, has been that if you legislate to make the masses prosperous, their prosperity will find its way up through every class which rests upon them."

Bryan's economic philosophy exactly paralleled that of Honest Abe Lincoln during his entire eight years in the Illinois Legislature. It was the same as that reiterated during Lincoln's single term in Congress. He never deviated from it during his entire lifetime, and throughout that lifetime would continue to repudiate *laissez-faire* or trickle down economics.

But here were the Republicans, the Party of Lincoln, denouncing the core values of Abraham Lincoln as socialistic and communistic!! That's strange indeed.

In the 31 years since Honest Abe's tragic death, every economic principle he stood for had been betrayed when the Republicans under McKinley and Hanna had sold out what residue of principle remained to them. Big Business owned them. Now it represented only the cause of the privileged white male and had become the POWM (Party of White Males). But far worse than that, it had wandered off course and ventured into forbidden territory. It could be called, with total legitimacy, the Party of Offensive Politics, POOP.

With McKinley's election duly purchased, the Republicans could now concentrate on their newly discovered passion. They would be resoundingly successful in their efforts to promote American imperialism. They lusted to expand the continental boundaries of the nation and their painstaking exertions were rewarded when the battleship Maine sank in the Cuban Port of Havana, following a mysterious explosion. The true nature of the explosion is still a mystery today.

Spain's widespread empire was seriously deteriorating and the Maine incident provided an unexcelled opportunity to declare war and strip it of its lone colony in the New World. Immediately an intense propaganda campaign was launched, American troops landed in Cuba and a new military figure was born. He would be Theodore Roosevelt who, with his cavalry regiment of rough Riders stormed up San Juan Hill; later, Santiago was captured and Cuba was ours.

Because of Roosevelt's truly heroic performance, his chances of a political career of some note increased exponentially. Great fame would shortly come his way.

No sooner had we added Cuba to our possessions than Admiral Dewey and the formidable Asiatic Fleet of the U.S. Navy was dispatched to the Philippine Islands where it met and destroyed the small, inept Spanish Fleet in Manila Harbor. Spanish resistance collapsed and we were able to take control of the entire Philippine Archipelago. When Spain agreed to a peaceable settlement, it ceded two additional small islands, Wake and Guam.

For a committed history devotee, the ultimate disposition of those three island entities is both fascinating and bitterly ironic. Only 43 years later, the militarists ruling Japan decided they wanted to include those same island entities in their rapidly expanding empire. Even after bravery on a monumental order and much loss of life on the part of American defenders, the Japanese were able to dislodge our forces. But only three short years later our American Army, Navy, Marine Corps and Air Forces re-invaded and re-conquered every acre taken from us.

Three salient factors deserve to be included before we depart from this epoch.

In the year 1898, the Hawaiian Islands would be annexed, thus making us a colonial power of some consequence. McKinley played a leading role in this unwarranted display of imperialism and aggression and in doing so was conspicuously faithless to his position expressed in the Inaugural Address delivered to Congress. "It has been the policy of the United States since the foundation of the Government to cultivate relations of peace and amity with all the nations of the world, and this accord with my conception of our duty now. We want no wars of conquest; we must avoid the temptation of territorial aggression. War should never be entered upon until every agency of peace has failed; peace is preferable to war in almost every contingency."

His administration would aggressively expand the continental limits of the United States. It captured Cuba, took by limited force the Philippine Islands. Then it annexed the Hawaiian Islands, Guam and Wake. Our country was now a colonial power. During the following year, Garret A. Hobart, the Vice-President, died in office. At that point in the nation's history there was no constitutional guideline about appointing a replacement so the position remained unfilled until the next election in 2000. That office had a slender significance so the McKinley Administration and the entire electorate remained untroubled until the nominating process began for the 1900 election.

The 1900 campaign in many ways replicated the earlier effort between McKinley and Bryan. Perhaps the greatest hurdle facing Mark Hanna and McKinley was selecting the Vice-Presidential candidate. Theodore Roosevelt, newly elected Governor of New York was one of the foremost candidates, largely because of his heroic performance at San Juan Hill.

There were a trio of important political figures who viewed Roosevelt in the Vice-President's seat with considerable distaste. The first was T.R. himself. He loved his new role as Governor of New York and had no wish to trade it for what he considered an inferior role. Then too, McKinley much preferred that the governor stay in New York. The third voice to weigh in on the subject was Hanna, who was especially chary of the Roosevelt boom. "Don't any of you realize that there's only one life between that madman and the president?" he boomed.

But a very, very important voice in New York Republican politics belonged to Thomas Platt, the official GOP boss in the state. He wanted T.R. out of the governor's chair, out of New York politics, and out of his hair, so that he could once again dominate politics there. The Governor was faced with a perplexing problem. Multitudes of his supporters avidly wanted him to be the vice-presidential candidate, so with notable reluctance he permitted his name to be entered for nomination.

In his brief term in office the new governor had managed to pass several trail-breaking pieces of legislation through a largely hostile State Assembly. In one of them he was able to cap the number of hours women and children could work in a day; he curtailed some of the more flagrant abuses in sweat shops. His taxation of corporations was one of the very first such bills in the country.

McKinley won easily by over 860,000 in the November election, a margin reflecting the wave of good economic statistics surging over the nation following the frightful "Panic of 1893." That panic, coming hard upon the heels of the similar "Panic of 1873" was more destructive than a recession and was a product of boom-and-bust business conditions. In polite Republican society it was referred to as *laissez-faire* economics which, as we have earlier seen, meant "let business get away with as much as it can." In the rough, realistic world of farmers and blue collar workers it was called trickle-down politics.

T.R. was not all that entranced with his new position as Vice-President, complaining he "now expected to be a dignified nonentity for four years."

Fate would shortly extend an incalculable benefit to him. On September sixth, 1901, only a half year since his second inauguration, McKinley was attending the Pan American Exposition in Buffalo when Leon Czolgosz, an anarchist, pumped two bullets into his stomach. For a few days the President appeared to be recovering, instead he slipped into unconsciousness and, on September 14, was pronounced dead.

Mark Hanna saw his most dreaded fear come into being. "Now look," he wailed to an associate, "that damned cowboy is President of the United States."

The "cowboy" designation that was attached to him by his critics was the result of time spent as a cattle rancher in the Dakota Bad Lands, following a twin devastation of death to both his mother, followed by his wife, within eleven hours of each other on February 14, 1884. "The light has gone out of my life," he wrote in his diary. He would spend much time in Dakota in an effort to emerge intact from his close bout with insanity, after this nearly unimaginable loss.

Far from being "a damned cowboy," Teddy, as he became popularly known, had a ferocious intellect, second only to the sainted Abraham Lincoln among Republican Presidents. He possessed a near unquenchable thirst for knowledge and that was coupled with a boundless intellectual curiosity. I tearfully regret to state that a near criminal contrast exists between Teddy and the current occupant of the White House when cognitive values are examined. Dubya's thirst for knowledge is quenched with the merest sip; his intellectual curiosity can be sated with slight slivers of material.

T.R. graduated from Harvard in 1880 with the signal honor of being magna cum laude; the P.P., as we have already seen, graduated summa cum laude from Yale, a higher level, but his award was for most distinguished party animal on campus – excelling in drinking, snorting cocaine and bedding sorority girls. A modest distinction must be observed.

The exceptionally enlightened cowboy set out with a grim determination to drastically alter the economic and social order in the country. In his first message to Congress he pointed out that "Combinations" (huge conglomerations of business) "govern by the law of greed and they threaten the integrity of our institutions." These combinations had made a small segment of businessmen unhealthily wealthy, while at the same time Americans by the tens of millions found themselves lacking anything resembling wholesome living conditions: They were without adequate housing, food or clothing. *It was even difficult for them to maintain decent health.* (But, 106 years later in 2007, at least 47 million Americans still lack any but the most rudimentary health insurance.)

Tuberculosis was common in the tenements. An accurate estimate determined that fully 60% of adult male workers failed to earn sufficient wages to maintain a family. Perhaps as many as 50 million Americans, farmers as well as blue collar workers, were poor.

For the wealthy there were no taxes to be paid, there were absolutely no government regulating bodies to pester them or interfere with the way they did business. They had only to answer to their consciences and pitifully few of them had any. Goodness glands were a rare commodity among the rich. What's even worse, these privileged few were especially fond of Social Darwinism. This dictated that the strong deserve their social position and riches while the weaklings had to deal with exploitation.

Recall that during the long, sterile darkness of the Middle Ages, the nobility, the aristocracy, and the church paid absolutely no taxes even though they owned as much as three-quarters of the land in a country like France. Indeed, they rented out huge tracts of that land in small lots to the impoverished peasantry.

Edmond Morris in his captivating work, "*The Rise of Theodore Roosevelt,*" firmly establishes the grandeur of his subject. Readers will recall that this is the same Edmond Morris who authored "*Dutch – A Memoir of Ronald Reagan*" and who referred to his subject as "Shatteringly banal, a cultural yahoo and vacuous."

In "The Rise," referring to the non-taxation of the rich, he commented how T.R. "took the opportunity to complain that farmers, market gardeners, tradesmen and small holders were bearing a disproportionate burden of taxation in New York State, while franchise-holding syndicates kept every dollar of their profits."

With his arrival at the White House, T.R. brought with him an intense desire to act as the embodiment of a nascent progressive movement. His family had been in this country since 1644 and was financially comfortable, but certainly not wealthy. It had been drilled into him as a child to scorn idleness, instead pursuing cultural goals and returning to society the gift of public service. There was this tradition with some members of his social class that they manifest a distinct social consciousness and accordingly do well for the community, or for the state, or if possible, the nation. It would naturally follow then that young Theodore would choose politics as his primary goal in life.

From his youth he had emphasized to family and friends that he "intended to be one of the governing class." Once introduced to politics, he saw the true nature of the "unnatural alliance" between the Republicans in power and Big Business and how the former embraced the latter with tender affection even though the alliance did grave harm to millions of citizens.

Morris resumes his account of T.R's first message to Congress. "There is a widespread conviction in the minds of the American people that the great corporations known as trusts are in certain of their features and tendencies hurtful to the general welfare. This is based upon sincere conviction that combination and concentration should be, not prohibited, but supervised and within reasonable limits controlled."

In that assertion can be discerned the very first intimation by a President that 'laissez is not that faire.' Previously any suggestion, much less law, that activities of big business be regulated was immediately targeted as "radical," or, as McKinley stated, "Class upon class," strongly implying class struggle.

Even today when a Democratic in Congress advances the idea of universal health care in this country, it instantly is attacked by a Republican in Congress as dangerously "socialistic." The yahoo, reactionary Republican obviously overlooks the established fact that this nation has the most expensive health care system on the planet while delivered pitifully inadequate service. All of the industrialized nations in Europe have a single payer system which delivers superior results at a much reduced cost, and health care for everybody. Today in the United States there are 47million people completely lacking any care.

T.R.'s initial confrontation with any segment of big business came when he chose to joust with the most powerful trust in the nation, the Northern Securities Company. J. Pierpont Morgan, the most important of the type T.R. loved to call robber barons, had carefully assembled a prodigious concentration of railroads and steel mills. That same year, 1901, he had purchased Andrew Carnegie's vast steel production empire for $250,000,000, thereby making Carnegie one of the nation's wealthiest men. It is noteworthy that Carnegie, this prince of the robber barons, had fashioned his affluence by working his steel mill employees 12-hours a day, six days a week for miserable wages. When they went on strike for larger paychecks and more humane working conditions he retaliated with bloody, even murderous means to break the strike.

In bringing suit against Northern Securities, T.R. craftily utilized the Sherman Antitrust Act of 1890. The painful irony for Morgan was that the Act had been used almost exclusively to stifle labor union activity and had never been applied against the business trusts. The suit charged that the company was acting in restraint of trade by owning too many railroads.

The imperious Morgan, normally treating presidents as associates rather than superiors, contacted Teddy and recommended a compromise "where they can fix it up." Once he was told that the new management in the White House wasn't interested in fixing it up, Morgan was astounded. He had never been ordered around in this manner before. Eventually, in 1904, the Supreme Court ruled in favor of the government and the mammoth trust combination of Northern Securities had to be broken up.

President Roosevelt pressed for another important piece of legislation, creating a Department of Commerce and Labor which would include a Bureau of Corporations, designed to probe the activities of companies engaged in interstate commerce. Throughout the nation businessmen were incensed that a government agency would investigate their financial affairs. In February of 1903 this bill, the Elkins Act, became law. With this act in effect, T.R. proved to the very conservative Congress and his adversaries in big business that he would continue to force legislation through a reluctant body.

Soon he began to call this program of reform legislation his "Square Deal," a very liberal precursor to the "New Deal," introduced to a most willing Democratic Congress by his sixth cousin, Franklin Delano Roosevelt in 1933 at the very depths of the Great Depression.

An excellent case can be made that Theodore was more liberal than Franklin.

As his popularity soared with the electorate he could begin to exercise a growing control over the "Combinations" and trusts. But the foremost item on his agenda, as it is with almost every man to hold the office, was to win the next election, this time on his own. In 1901 that appeared to be an unlikely prospect. There were no primary elections, so presidential nominations were determined by state chairmen. He couldn't count on the stubborn Congress or the important money men in business to be on his side.

His most formidable barricade to reelection was Mark Hanna, justifiably considered the most powerful Republican in the entire country. He had single-handedly guided William McKinley to the governor's office in Ohio, then twice to the White House. He was to McKinley what Karl Rove was to Bush, only he was exceedingly wealthy and a United States Senator from Ohio.

Early in T.R.'s tenure, it seemed obvious that Hanna was positioning himself to be the Republican nominee in 1904. Such was his power and arrogance that he even told Teddy, "Don't even think of running in 1904." But then fate intervened a second time for the new president. A virulent case of typhoid fever would permanently remove Hanna from the scene in February of 1904. That left only big business, and without their maestro to guide them, the path was clear to the nomination.

While all this legislative strife occupied much of his time and energy, he also had to deal with a problem of huge concern in Central America. The United States, and the entire world, desperately needed a canal which would unite the Atlantic and Pacific Oceans, thereby slicing transportation costs between the two oceans immeasurably. But, which route should be selected and in what country?

Edmond Morris in "*Theodore Rex*" most efficaciously explains the perplexity facing Theodore Rex. "Panama might possibly have been chosen, but that fetid little Colombian province was already a monument to the folly of the French canal engineers. After 22 years of mismanagement, scandal, disease, and death, all that was left of Ferdinand de Lessep's grand 'Canal du Panama' was a gang of lethargic workers, some crumbling buildings and rusty machinery, and an immense muddy scar reverting to jungle."

Secretary of State John Hay entered into negotiations with Colombia but was immediately faced with extortionate demands. The Colombian officials saw in this situation a once-in-a lifetime opportunity to enrich themselves when dealing with the rich Yankees. Meanwhile, politicos in the Province of Panama equally perceived a once-in-a lifetimes chance to make themselves independently wealthy so they declared independence from the mother country. This is, of course, was exactly what the administration wanted.

When Colombia made bold efforts to suppress the revolt, thereby reserving the untold riches for its officialdom, the U.S.Government responded with what it considered appropriate measures. One of the president's favorite maxims was, "Speak softly but carry a big stick."

The big stick involved dispatching a formidable flotilla of U.S. Navy warships to an appropriate port where it could menace the Colombian forces. After a period of delicate diplomacy and with a judicious application of money to assuage hurt feelings, the threatening forces departed and Panama was declared a free country. Work on the new canal began in earnest.

Theodore was fortunate that in the 1904 race he had as his Democratic opponent an honorable, decent man in Alton Parker but one completely lacking any charisma or magnetism. To add to his hopelessness, Parker didn't even bother waging a campaign. The result was the largest margin of victory for any presidential candidate, to that point.

Shortly thereafter T.R. would once again make clear his inherent progressive philosophy. "The great development of industrialism means that there must be an increase in the supervision exercised by the government over business enterprises. Neither this people nor any other will permanently tolerate the use of the vast power conferred by vast wealth, ... without lodging somewhere in the government the still higher power of seeing that this power, in addition to being used in the interest of the individual or individuals possessing it, is also used for and not against the interests of the people as a whole."

In the next sentence he would reveal how threadbare is the case for the States' Rights advocates which came mostly from the South. "No satisfactory result can be expected from merely state action. *The action must come from the federal government.*"

His next big battle would come up in 1906 when the Hepburn Act would be presented to Congress. The contest was in the Senate since the House passed it intact. Here he was challenged by a host of very determined reactionary Republicans who insisted that the federal government had no right to regulate the way commerce was conducted. He finally was able to squeeze the bill through that body, and with its passage came a major turning point on the government's effort to impose effective regulation on big business. Now an agency of the federal government would have the right to subject company records to inspection, and what was even better, to force huge companies to conform to regulations.

Very costly to his popularity was the 'Panic of 1907' which robbed him of a considerable amount of popularity nationwide and with it the power to combat Congress and big business. The latter would hold T.R. personally responsible for the financial panic insisting that investors had been scared off by too much government regulation of the economic system. The gullible public would fall victim to those lies.

Ideas that he would subsequently advance to improve the lot of the working class could not be forced through his fellow Republicans in the Congress. He had gone about as far as he could go with this lot.

He had invested much of his manifest skills into passing an income tax for higher earning levels and saw his efforts fail. Likewise his pleas for more merciful working conditions and shorter hours went unheeded. Perhaps his greatest disappointment came with his inability to prevent the exploitation of children in the work force. Wealthy businessmen, particularly wealthy Southern businessmen, were devoted to adding little kids to their workforce, even placing them in dangerous factories and mines. Little kids were to these corporate owners what slaves had been to plantation owners in the Confederate States.

Before leaving Teddy with his reelection campaign, a pleasing item needs to be inserted. At one point in that effort he became concerned that he might lose his home state of New York. To head off that prospect he appealed to two business magnates for large donations. E. H. Harriman, a supremely wealthy railroad tycoon, contributed $50,000 and generated another $250,000 from friends. Henry Clay Frick, head of U.S. Steel, denuded his assets to the extent of $100,000.

Soon after the election, the president resumed his program to regulate business with still more assaults on the "malefactors of great wealth." The two men felt utterly betrayed. Frick would fulminate against the man they had helped reelect. "We bought the son-of-a-bitch and then he did not stay bought."

Here is where we observe a striking distinction between Roosevelt and Bush. We need to observe Dubya's steadfast fidelity. Once he's bought he's going to stay bought, and he's ever so content to remain bought.

I belong to a number of environmental and/or conservationist clubs and receive timely reports from them. From the largest, and typical of the general tenor of all of them is the July 3, 2003, "Memorandum," coming from the desk of Bruce Hamilton, Conservation Director. "As I write this, the Sierra Club faces the largest challenge in its 110-year history. Every week we are witnessing a new assault on the environment by the Bush Administration and its allies. One week after another a new anti-environmental federal judge is nominated for a lifetime appointment." He continued his plea, "the Club must muster its focus, its energy and resources to counter the Bush Administration's assault on basic American environmental values. We're dealing with an administration that shows no respect for our nation's environmental values and holds nothing sacred."

Another from Earth Justice reads: "Powerful special interests – led by big oil, gas, mining and timber companies – are using their ever-tightening grip on Washington to weaken environmental law and sharply curtail the enforcement of those laws. If they succeed, decades of environmental progress will be lost and our ability to protect America's natural heritage will be weakened for years to come. Now with their massive financial war chests, well-oiled PR machines, and platoons of lobbyists, researchers, and high-paid corporate lawyers, they are attempting to undermine 30 years of environmental progress."

Other organizations such as Nature Conservancy and the Audubon Club savage Bummy Bush in like manner. So, now that we've established that he is the worst environmental chief executive in our history let's examine the first and still the greatest in our history. That would of course be Theodore Roosevelt.

"T.R. arrived at the White House with a deep abiding love of nature, including its animals, its plants, its places and its moods," so wrote John Muir, one of the two men besides T.R. responsible for the nation's conservation program. As of 1901, approximately half of the timber in the country had been harvested and an incalculable amount of previous top soil had been wasted, much of it washed out to sea. Again we quote from him. "Any fool can destroy trees, but only Uncle Sam can save them from fools." Uncle Sam would appear in the person of Theodore Roosevelt. When he assumed office, 560 million federally owned acres in the lower forty-eight states remained open to entry, exploitation and settlement. Over the length of his seven-and-one-half year term in office he would close millions of those acres in the form of national parks, national forests or wildlife refuges. These include portions of some of our most treasured national areas: Yellowstone, Yosemite, the Grand Canyon, the Petrified Forest, and Sequoia National forest. He would create 150 national forests, five national parks, and 51 national bird reservations.

T.R.'s own writings veritably sing with the beauty he found in nature: "Nothing could be lovelier, and nothing more beautiful than the view at nightfall across the prairies to those huge hill masses, when the lengthening shadows had at last merged into one and the faint after-glow of the red sunset filled the west. After nightfall the face of the country seems to alter marvelously, and the clear moonlight only intensifies the change. The river gleams like running quicksilver, and the moonbeams play over the grassy stretches of the plateau. The Bad Lands seem to be stranger and wilder than ever, the silvery rays turning the country into a kind of grim fairy land."

Those lines would be penned in his disconsolate years spent ranching in the Dakota Bad Lands following the near simultaneous deaths of both his wife and mother, as we already have seen.

His writings on nature were expressions of rapture yet he was steadfast in his belief that as President he was the steward of this country's natural resources. As such he was honor bound to care for them as if they were his own. This he did and the manner in which he implemented his practices has preserved our national beauty and wealth for over a century. Preserved it until an election thief stole into the White House and began to unravel T.R.'s stewardship.

In his tender solicitude for the nation's natural resources, President Roosevelt rapidly became alarmed. Birds were being slaughtered in the wildlife, many of them for their feathers, or plumes, to be sold to the millinery trade. These would end up as gaudy decorations for ladies' hats. Some were killed merely to collect their eggs, others simply for sport. In his various speeches and writings he constantly savaged those guilty of "decimating the nation's wildlife." He established what today we call the National Wildlife Refuge System. The first was at Pelican Island in Florida at the urging of the Florida Audubon Society. During his term in office, fifty more would follow.

Another area of great concern was protecting the American buffalo, or bison. At the beginning there were believed to be sixty million of the great beasts in North America. By the end of the Civil War none could be found east of the Mississippi. In 1901, when he was sworn into office, the species was nearly extinct in this country.

Two modest herds remained, one each in Canada and Yellowstone Park, perhaps 1000 in all. In his autobiography he outlined "the important steps to preserve from destruction beautiful and wonderful wild creatures whose existence was threatened by greed and wantonness." He went on to lament the plight of the animal. "Gone forever are the mighty herds of the lordly buffalo, but these great herds that for the first three quarters of this century formed the distinguishing and characteristic feature of the western plains, have vanished forever."

In 1902 he pried from Congress "the very first appropriations for the preservation of buffalo and establishment in the Yellowstone National Park of the first and now the largest herd of buffalo belonging to the government." His autobiography would further detail subsequent Acts of Congress in creating the Wichita Game Preserve in 1905 and then "in 1907 acreage totaling 12,000 were enclosed with a woven wire fence for the reception of the herd of 15 buffalo donated by the New York Zoological Society." In 1908 an additional act established the National Bison Range in Montana.

The bison herds increased slowly but steadily. Today there are an estimated 200,000, some of them in the Theodore Roosevelt National Park. "Above all," he would later write, "we should realize that the effort towards this end is essentially a democratic movement. It is entirely in our power as a nation to preserve large tracts of wilderness, which are valueless for agricultural purposes and unfit for settlement, as playgrounds for rich and poor alike, and to preserve the game so that it shall continue to exist for the benefit of all lovers of nature. But this can only be achieved by wise laws and by a resolute enforcement of the laws."

At this point it is fitting to bear witness to the role George W. Bush played where conservation or environmentalism is concerned. It is easy to state that as a six year governor of Texas he never conserved an acre of Texas soil. At no point in that six years did he even contemplate conserving an acre of Texas soil.

Consider next the environment – with Bush we sadly view a history of staggering incompetence wedded to an abhorrent blindness to the dangers of those policies. We see that pattern established as soon as he became governor of Texas which arguably was the most polluted state in America. He emphatically turned his back on any effort to crack down on oil refineries and electric generating plants busily befouling the air. Instead he permitted them to escape regulation under an umbrella of "voluntary compliance." Out of 850 of the worst polluters, exactly three voluntarily complied.

The P.P. would later inquire sanctimoniously, "Is the air cleaner since I became governor? The answer is yes."

An objective survey would indicate a far different case. What was happening wasn't mere inadequacy on the part of the Bush regime. It was mendacity, selling out the entire state of Texas, next the country so that he and the Republican Party could receive election funds of unprecedented amounts. Rather than the polluters using large amounts of money to clean up their pollution sites, they were giving Bush and his electoral buddies a portion of it and pocketing the rest.

No sooner did he become governor, and then occupant of the White House than the guard dogs protecting the people's rights were thrown out of their positions and a new batch was installed to protect the rights of the polluters.

A pattern in one industry after another was established. For instance, in the mining industry, the number of safety engineers was drastically reduced. Those on the job were directed to issue fewer fines and those fines would be smaller. Finally, the mine owners would pay only a portion of the fines.

The current head of MSHA, the Mine Safety and Health Agency, told a Senate Committee that he saw no reason for employing tougher safety laws. Which is in place here – incompetence or deliberate blindness to safety standards? Mining is doubtless the most hazardous occupation in America today. Yet Bush will select a loathsome toad, hired at a generous salary and with no apparent qualifications for the position, to modify or even eliminate prudent safety regulations which protected the miners. In numerous instances his appointees had been industry lobbyists whose sole task had been to keep profits from the mines at their highest.

This nation should be embarked on a gradual effort to reduce the amount of coal we burn and pursue a path toward low or no carbon usage. Bush and his fellow pollution loving reactionaries in Congress are most unlikely to take a step towards implementing that policy. It must come from the Democrats in the current 110th Congress.

There are at least three reasons of consequence why this change must be put into effect as quickly as possible. Old, inefficient coal burning power stations are contaminating the nation's air at an intolerable rate. This toxic air is one of the leading causes of preventable death, often harmful to infants and toddlers. There is no question that adding particulates to the atmosphere promotes global warming.

In the August 13, 2007 issue of Newsweek Magazine can be found a most illuminating article on global warming. It lays out in a most edifying manner how the opponents of the concept of global warming have marketed their strategy. "Since the late 1980s, this well-coordinated, well-funded campaign by contrarian scientists, free market think tanks and industry has created a paralyzing fog of doubt around climate change. Continuing, the article states that the "greenhouse doubters argued first that the world is not warming; measurements indicating otherwise are flawed, they said. Then they claimed that any warming is natural, not caused by human activities. Now they contend that the looming warming will be miniscule and harmless."

Becoming more specific the article more closely identifies the contrarians. "Individual companies and industry Associations – representing petroleum, steel, autos and utilities, for instance – formed lobbying groups with names like the Global Climate Coalition and the Information Council on the Environment. ICE's game plan called for enlisting greenhouse doubters to "reposition global warming as theory rather than fact," and to sow doubt about climate research just as cigarette makers had about smoking research."

The nation's best known doubter is the current occupant of the White House, the self-described 'Decider.' "The jury is still out on global warming," he solemnly intones whenever the subject arises. I strongly suspect that, for that greenhouse doubter, the jury will remain out until at least January, 2009.

For one of the most prestigious scientific groups in the world, the jury no longer is out, but has reached a definitive verdict. "The International Panel on Climate Change, or IPCC – the body that periodically assess climate research – has just issued its second report, and the conclusion of *its 2500 scientists* looked devastating for greenhouse doubters." The IPCC concluded, "The balance of evidence suggests a discernable human influence on climate."

A huge majority of climate experts in the European Union have arrived at an identical conclusion. They likewise are not awaiting a verdict from a mythical jury. For many years their scientific finds have been indicating that accumulating greenhouse gases, the result of burning carbon fuels, are altering the planet's climate in a potentially deadly manner.

None of this is considered conclusive evidence to the doubters. After all, think of the numerous psalm-singers just in America who devoutly believe that our earth was created on a specific day in October, 4004 B.C. and at 9:30 a.m. I don't believe they specify if that was Eastern Standard Time or Tokyo, Japan time. They firmly believe that to be a total verity because the Archbishop of Armagh, in Ireland, back in the 17th Century, arrived at this determination after an exhaustive study of the Old Testament.

All the branches of science concerned with the earth's formation, including biology, geology, paleontology and numerous others, are almost universally agreed that the earth came together closer *to four and a half-billion years ago.* This unanimity began coalescing at least 150 years ago and involved scientists from all the industrial nations. By now, those scientists that were in harmony with this theory easily number in the hundreds of thousands. Contrast that with the number of discordant voices, from scientists, and the number is in the dozens.

A typical lone voice, crying out in solitude, belongs to Patrick Michaels, a climatologist at the University of Virginia. Newsweek resumes its narrative, "Michaels has written several popular articles on climate change, including an op-ed in the Washington Post in 1989 warning of "apocalyptic environmentalism," which he called "the most popular new religion to come along since Marxism." The coal industry's Western Fuels Association paid Michaels to produce a newsletter called World Climate Report, which has regularly trashed mainstream climate science." A few sentences later the article reveals that Michaels has received a trifling stipend from industry for his unstinting efforts. How much? Oh, just a mere $165,000.

When a woman accepts payment for a sexual favor granted to a man, the law condemns the act, and calls it prostitution. The woman in turn is regarded as a prostitute, or perhaps a more opprobrious term, a whore.

Another word should be said about the crippling Panic of 1907 which did more than a little harm to the President's reputation. It was the third of the post Civil War mini-depressions, all the result of boom-and-bust fiscal policies, High Tariffs and the gold standard that helped bring them on as did unacceptably low wages for the working class and low prices for farmers.

This third Panic had arrived only 14 years after the previous one. The fourth, slated to appear in 1921, would also take only 14 years to strike. It would deal the entire farm sector a nasty blow and gradually nudge it into a depressed condition years before the rest of the nation felt its fury.

The fifth and last financial epidemic came upon an unsuspecting nation in only nine more years in 1930 and, because of its terrifying magnitude, has been forever after called The Great Depression. Thanks to Franklin Delano Roosevelt, sworn into office in 1933, and the New Deal he introduced to a bewildered and starving nation, it would prove to be the last.

CHAPTER XIV

Upon being sworn into office after his landslide victory in 1904, T.R. shocked his family and then the entire country when he declared he would not be a candidate in 1908. Gradually he warmed to William Howard Taft as his successor. Taft had been appointed Governor-General of the newly acquired Philippine Islands in 1901 by President McKinley. In that function he had performed heroically and improved the lot of the islanders in a variety of ways. He installed civilian rule by kicking the generals out of office; he rid the judicial system of its overwhelming corruption. Among other improvements he installed a network of English language schools.

In 1904 he returned to Washington where he began to form a close relationship with the President. He became Secretary of State and in that capacity acted as an increasingly important adviser to his chief. The association matured into one of trusted friendship.

It was a result of this close harmony that Roosevelt began to position his friend as the next presidential nominee. Curiously enough, Taft longed to become Chief Justice of the Supreme Court and much preferred that position rather than the presidential role. Continuous prodding by both T.R. and Taft's wife forced him to surrender. He was easily nominated on the first ballot at the 1908 Republican Convention.

The Democrats permitted William Jennings Bryan to be their standard bearer again; his defeat this time was even more emphatic.

Before closing the door on the Roosevelt Presidency, we need to take a peek at his attitude toward race and civil rights. Only weeks into his Presidency, T.R. learned that Booker T. Washington, easily the most famous black leader in America, was in the Capitol and invited him to dine in the White House.

Edmund Morris in "*Theodore Rex*" enlightens his readers on the instantaneous reaction in the South. He quotes from the Memphis Scimitar. (Scimitar is a grotesque title for a newspaper; it is a curved sword used by Turks and Arabs.) "The most damnable outrage which has ever been perpetrated by any citizens of the United States was committed yesterday by the President, when he invited a nigger to dine with him at the White House." (Note the word – the polite term negra was not employed.) "No Southern woman with a proper self respect would now accept an invitation to the White House, nor would President Roosevelt be welcomed today in Southern homes. He has not inflamed the anger of the Southern people; he has excited their disgust." In Charleston, South Carolina, Senator Benjamin R. Tillman endorsed remedial genocide," Mr. Morris instructs. "The action of President Roosevelt in entertaining that nigger will necessitate our killing a thousand niggers in the South before they will learn their place again." One can immediately see the kindly teachings of Jesus at play here. Today in Columbia, SC, the state capital, there stands a life size statue of Benjamin Tillman, also known as "Pitchfork Ben."

James K. Vardaman, U.S. Senator then running for Governor of South Carolina, an educational and cultural beacon in America at that time, gave vent to his feelings. The president he insisted was "a little mean, coon-flavored misceganist;" the White House "was so saturated with the color of the nigger that the rats have taken refuge in the stable."

The two greatest Republican Presidents, Abraham Lincoln and Theodore Roosevelt were both viewed in the south as utterly repellant creatures. Even today, more than a century later, there exists in the South more than a little residue of that toxicity, in spite of the South being the heartland of the Republican Party.

Anthropologists all over the world are united in their belief that our species, *Homo sapiens*, originated in East Africa, tenths of thousands of years ago. Over-population forced them into gradual migration. The closest area suitable for habitation was the Mideast. They next trekked into Asia. Slowly, their expansion took them into Europe. North and South America were the last areas to be occupied and that migration came from Asia. There is no dispute among anthropologists that the original group in East Africa was black, a dark hue of black, since the area is known for its high temperatures. No dispute exists that our species, *Homo sapiens*, arose from that group of dark-hued humans in Africa.

In evaluating the Taft Presidency, a neutral observer could grant him rather high marks. He handled the role of Chief Executive in a most acceptable manner. While he did nothing brilliantly, he also committed few errors. Towards the middle of his term, however, the exceptionally high regard that T.R. had for him began to dissipate.

Degree by degree Taft drifted further to the right than Teddy approved of, especially when the new president launched a campaign to elect conservatives to congress replacing the progressives that the ex-president preferred. Teddy was still aggressively pushing reforms including strict laws governing child labor. Taft militated against these measures to the point where open warfare broke out between the two. Roosevelt realized that choosing Taft to succeed him into the presidency was a grave mistake and was determined to seek the 1912 Republican Party's nomination, rather than allow Taft to have it.

To do so, he hit the campaign trail with both relish and enthusiasm, and in the ten primaries he entered against Taft he easily won nine, even inflicting a humiliating defeat in Ohio, Taft's home state. In many of these contests he won big, swamping his rival. He did that despite Big Business and the entire Republican establishment solidly against him. At the GOP National Convention in June, in an obviously rigged election, he fell short in garnering the nomination.

With that he and all of his 334 delegates made a noisy exit from the convention site. T.R. observed, "I regard Taft as the receiver of a swindled nomination." Teddy bolted the party that had parted from the principles of Lincoln.

From this point forward in our history, the Republican Party would have no further identity with Honest Abe, although still proclaiming itself to be the Party of Lincoln.

Seven weeks later Roosevelt and the estranged delegates met to form the National Progressive Party, but they soon decided to call themselves the Bull Moose Party because their chief said he was "as strong as a Bull Moose." The platform it settled on was unequivocally the most liberal this rather conservative nation had ever seen and more liberal than its Democratic counterpart under Franklin Delano Roosevelt formulated 20 years later in 1932. It is worthy of a serious review.

The platform demanded that legislation be passed in the new Congress which was very radical for its day. Woman's suffrage was high on the list; outlawing child labor, used as it was by brutal employers, especially in Southern Textile mills, was a form of slavery so the new party wanted it outlawed; an eight hour day with a limit of six days per week. A Social Security System; enactment of a program of national health service; an end to damaging labor injunctions; graduated income tax plus inheritance taxes; and another law the country today desperately needs – a national referendum to overcome badly flawed Supreme Court decisions. In use today this would deny Scalia, Thomas, Alito and Roberts the ability to have their injurious, unjudicial opinions become settled doctrine.

It's "a downright rotten, lowdown dirty shame" that this nation nearly a century later has still been denied universal health insurance, a right taken for granted in every upgraded European country. As moviegoers have seen in Michael Moore's *"Sicko,"* even Communist Cuba has it. In progressive countries like France, England, Germany, Italy plus numerous other European nations, people live longer, healthier, and happier lives and pay far less than we in this country do today.

The Great Decider, the current occupant of the White House, is perhaps the most fanatical foe of this service. To bolster his opinion he has several hundred RRRs in Congress.

The Grand Alliance that has an iron grip on health care in our country has persevered assiduously to see that these culprits are bought and paid for. The American voters need to understand these Republican Congressmen will remain bought and paid as long as they are in office.

Brooks Adams, a member of a nationally known family of historians, made this trenchant observation during T.R's tenure. "The privileged classes seldom have the intelligence to protect themselves by adaptation when nature turns against them."

In the year 2008, nature is most assuredly turning against them and if my fellow Democrats stay united, huge new numbers of our politicians will be elected to office at every level.

The 1912 election would feature three candidates: Taft, striving for reelection was confronted with two exceptionally able candidates, one being his predecessor in office and his formerly great friend, Theodore Roosevelt. The other was the Democratic candidate, Woodrow Wilson, who first attracted notice as a professor at Princeton where he authored a number of popular books and articles. This drew the attention of the university trustees who soon chose him as the school's president. He immediately set in motion a vigorous campaign to transform the old New Jersey school into a paradigm of higher education. In so doing, he drastically reorganized many departments within the school. He soon was persuaded to run for governor of the state in 1910; he agreed provided he was granted the nomination without having to contest any other candidates. In the 1910 election he won easily over his Republican opponent. As governor he compiled an impressive liberal record, and early on was recognized as a candidate for higher office. Nailing down the nomination for the presidency was a prolonged struggle but it finally came his way.

There wasn't all that much difference between T.R. and Woodrow Wilson. Actually the Republican was a trifle more progressive. This would be the first race involving more than two candidates since 1860, when Abraham Lincoln faced three rivals. Early in the fray it soon became obvious that Taft had drifted out of contention. It was also clear that the two remaining candidates were staging a race totally devoid of the usual Republican tactics of character assassination.

Wilson, an unusually intelligent and articulate candidate was opposed by an extremely intelligent man who in addition brought an enlivened personality and a freshness of expression to the race.

The Republican voters however were hopelessly divided allowing Wilson to coast in with a huge victory. Taft finished a distant third winning only in Utah and Vermont.

Wilson in his first term would push through a tidy program of important legislative acts and continue the progressive movement of social welfare begun by Teddy Roosevelt. In so doing he would lay claim to be the most effective Democratic Chief of State since the fabled Andrew Jackson who left office in 1837.

One of those bills was the Keating-Owens Act of 1916, previously alluded to, which actually barred goods manufactured by companies employing children from inter-state commerce. In one of the cruelest, most wretched decisions ever made by a U.S. Supreme Court, the Act was declared unconstitutional by a quintet of super-reactionary Republican justices. Their task was to evaluate the merits of the case but not decide if it would harm the profit margin of the firms involved.

When five unelected white males, all totally devoid of a conscience, or any ethical values, are able to override huge Congressional Majorities, legislative relief must be found. The answer is a nationwide referendum which would make the ultimate determination.

World War I would erupt in August, 1914, and prove to be a worsening headache for the new President. The Germans, in an attempt to limit supplies coming to England, would initiate a very aggressive submarine campaign, warning that they would sink any allied vessels approaching the British Isles. As the war progressed they would increase their efforts to prevent *any ships* from reaching England, and this soon would include American cargo ships. Then on May 7, 1915, they sunk the British luxury liner, the Lusitania, with a loss of 1198 passengers, of whom 128 were Americans. The administration, together with the overwhelming majority of Americans, viewed this as a crime exceeding international law. The President remonstrated strongly to the Germans, but they declined to apologize for their act of barbarism.

A nascent peace effort was attempted by Wilson but neither the Germans nor the British expressed much interest so a conference between the two was never set up. The war dragged on through 1915, then 1916. But then the British passenger liner Laconia was sunk; next four American freighters were torpedoed.

Finally, through intercepted messages came the shock that the German Government had undertaken negotiations with Mexico for an extensive treaty. It included several momentous provisions, including one that should American declare war on Germany, then Germany would assist Mexico in recapturing Texas, New Mexico and Arizona.

Without question the great majority of Americans wanted to remain neutral, but most of those were more than willing to do whatever the president advocated.

Wilson in turn felt that he had tried everything to avoid war, but now it had been thrust upon him. On April 12, 1917, he asked a joint session of Congress to declare war on Germany, strongly suggesting it be done "to make the world safe for democracy." In just four days Congress voted for a declaration of war by an overwhelming majority.

It needs to be observed that Kaiser Wilhelm II, the near dictator of Germany, was considerably less bent on territorial conquest than Adolph Hitler would be. That *total dictator* of Germany would follow the abdicated Kaiser into office in only 15 years. Nevertheless Wilhelm II constituted a grave menace to international peace and needed to be vanquished. Only the United States, of all the nations in the world, was capable of that action.

The war would prove frightfully expensive to both the President and the nation. More than a year would be required before American soldiers, called doughboys, could be trained, shipped over to France, and only then see action. Once they were introduced into combat, they performed brilliantly, even up against veteran German troops. Time after time they would provide the steely determination needed to take strongly held enemy positions. As more of our troops entered the battles, the tide began to turn against the Huns, as they were generally called.

Ever so slowly German morale started to erode and by September, 1918 it began to crack. The exhausted German infantrymen were up against numerical superiority; there were simply too many fresh, well trained, well equipped Americans.

The German High Command would arrive shortly at the obvious conclusion and start thinking of an appropriate time and place for surrender. The Armistice took place on November 11, 1918 – the eleventh hour of the eleventh day of the eleventh month. WWI had cost the American 53,000 lives and $33 billion.

For President Wilson some of his most daunting encounters lay ahead. He would travel to France to meet with heads of state of his three European allies – England, France and Italy, in order to hammer out a Treaty of Versailles. He had two goals which he wished so desperately to achieve – to make this the war to end all wars, and to establish a League of Nations. Until he could have that league securely in place, he was sufficiently prescient to know there would be no end to wars.

Almost to a man the Democrats in the Senate supported the Treaty of Versailles, a key portion of which was the provision for the League of Nations. In order for the treaty to become law, two-thirds of the Senate would have to endorse it. A problem of considerable enormity arose however following the 1918 mid-term elections. The Republicans regained control of the Senate by a single seat advantage but this tiny edge gave them control of the Committee Chairmanships; Henry Cabot Lodge would be the Chairman of the Senate Foreign Relations Committee. He would prove to be a never-ending nightmare for Wilson. Almost single-handedly he would insure that this nation never joined the League of Nations.

The Republican opposition in the Senate was divided into three distinct factions. The first consisted of a small group who became known as the "mild reservationists" and who only wished to amend the treaty provisions in a mild way. The largest contingent was called the "strong reservationists" and were led by Lodge who wished to restrict it to such a degree that it would be a toothless travesty. Of the 48 Republicans in the Senate, 39 belonged to this clique. (The Senate at that period in our history had only 96 members and there was one Independent.)

The President pointed out in a dramatic fashion that if Lodge had his way, "the League would be hardly more than an influential debating society." The third group, fairly small, regarded themselves as the "Irreconcilables" who completely rejected the very idea of a League of Nations.

This group of shameful cretins would still be polluting the Senate in the late 1930s when President Franklin Delano Roosevelt was engaged in a dogged battle to build up the nation's military. The irreconcilables then would do everything in their power to frustrate his efforts. Way to go, Republicans!!!

Presented with this obstinate phalanx of Senators, President Wilson took his case to the American public and began traveling across the nation in September, 1919. He would deliver about 40 speeches in twenty days and in the process absolutely exhaust himself. On September 24, he would fall victim to a slight stroke, cancel the balance of the tour and return to the White House. Barely back in office he then suffered a crippling stroke on October 2. This effectively ended his political career. He would die in early 1924.

When Lodge asserted that he wanted the Treaty ratified but with strong amendments, he was engaging in a cynical and disgusting charade. He wanted no part of a League of Nations; his goal was to frustrate the president to the point of humiliation. An additional factor had to be included. Lodge was looking forward to the 1920 presidential election and he could see partisan advantage to be gained by demeaning the President.

A massive nation-wide campaign was soon underway to build up hostility to the League. Republican oriented newspapers joined in the assault. These well-coordinated efforts brought about the desired result. With the President incapacitated, the Democrats could not muster the two-thirds vote necessary for passage. Had the League of Nations included the United States, a rather compelling argument can be made that WWII could have been |averted.

Benito Mussolini presented the first threat to peace coming from a European country. He came to power by gathering a small group of malingerers and marching on Rome in October, 1922. Mussolini would form the first openly fascist government in Europe. He would call himself *Il Duce*, the leader. In 1935 Il Duce dispatched his hapless Italian army into Ethiopia, then called Abyssinia. After a remarkable long period of strife it managed to subdue this near defenseless country.

In Germany Adolph Hitler, who called himself *Der Fuehrer,* the leader, paid close attention to the aggressive militarism of Mussolini. He came to power January 30, 1933, Franklin Delano Roosevelt's birthday. His was the second openly fascistic dictatorship in Europe.

In Spain Francisco Franco, who called himself *El Caudillo*, the leader, led a small group of Arab soldiers from Spanish Morocco into Sevilla in 1936, and after a ruthless, bloody three year conflict, subdued the country. His would be the third openly fascistic country in Europe.

Had the United States been a member of the League of Nations and then joined forces with England and France who were members, that seemingly potent entente could easily have dissuaded Italy to back away from Abyssinia. England and France made a tremulous effort in that direction but lacked fortitude. The effort required only a little more muscle for the Italian people were not keen on foreign conquest.

President Wilson openly predicted that if this country failed in its efforts to join the League there would be another and greater World War within a generation. It took just 20 years to bring it about.

In almost exactly the same time frame in which the League of Nations was derailed by the Republicans, they engineered a legislative measure of near-crazed criminality. I refer of course to the Eighteenth Amendment, otherwise known as the Volstead Act, otherwise known as Prohibition. This Act sought to deny alcohol – beer, booze or wine – to those who would partake of it.

The ancestors of those voters who would twice mark their ballots for Bush, and who are today's voters in the red states, were responsible for its enactment. It was the vengeance that rural and small town American took on urban, big city America. Then too, it was the symbol of Puritanism sprung to life. That of the native-born psalm singers militantly opposed to any social changes taking place in America. Big cities in their view were citadels of Satan where dwelled all manner of folk to be viewed with distrust – immigrants, Catholics, Jews. They conveyed a message filled with rancor, even hatred.

The reality it delivered was one of startling stupidity. Where the scene before Prohibition struck showed a reasonable number of neighborhood saloons, interspersed with an acceptable amount of night clubs and a realistic application of law and order was soon replaced with a far different scenario. Prohibition served to ensnare large numbers of law enforcement officers: city police, county sheriffs, politicians, even judges were rapidly corrupted with bribes. Drinking increased at a dramatic pace; women who would never have considered entering a legal bistro now eagerly sought out illicit dives. In the major cities of the more enlightened parts of the country, the local bootleggers were often thrust aside by threats and violence; soon they were supplanted by criminal syndicates organized on a regional basis.

Gradually a ruthless, even murderous element took over the manufacture, distribution and sale of alcohol. This movement, courtesy of migration from Italy and Sicily, was known among its members as the Cosa Nostra, Italian for Our Thing. Americans had been introduced to the Mafia. The movement soon proliferated into diverse sectors of the economy and would require many decades to uproot it. Yet to this day the Mafia still has not been completely eradicated.

Application of the law in regard to the sale of illicit spirits varied tremendously—in smaller communities it could be enforced with some vigor. In the larger cities where bribery was employed extensively, enforcement might be lax or non-existent. The Volstead Act went a long way toward turning this land into a law-breaking nation.

With the war's end at hand, President Wilson found his political popularity slowly foundering. Nothing seemed to please the electorate. Inflation played a key role as did a high degree of unemployment facing the veterans returning from the war. Strikes were prevalent, most of them unsuccessful, and somehow this soured relations between organized labor and the Democrats. On election in November, 1918, voters responded by returning control of Congress to the Republicans.

As the 1920 presidential election approached, the Republicans were presented with a dearth of talent, a familiar pattern for them. Accordingly, they selected what they themselves admitted was the best of a group of second-raters. Actually, the party leadership picked the man they regarded as the most malleable – Warren Gamaliel Harding.

In him they selected a candidate who was dedicated to pursuing the pleasure principle, seeking always to gratify his senses. Single square blocks in Boston could easily have unearthed at least several candidates far more prepossessing than this choice for the nation's highest office.

He had numerous bad habits. For instance, he liked to chew tobacco. Now, who does that remind you of? Well, Bummy Bush of course, who practiced this wondrously repugnant habit, while in college. Harding also had a special fondness for booze; the fact that its consumption was now illegal had no relevance for him. He also had a fondness for the wife of a family friend, Carrie Phillips, with whom he maintained a long standing bedroom relationship. In addition to Carrie, he sampled the delights of a young woman, Nan Britton. That association eventually produced an offspring.

Harding was more or less presented with the position of United States Senator, since that office didn't necessitate election by the public, only selection by the legislature. That body in Ohio was largely bought and paid for. Once in office his attendance could charitably be called lamentable. He was present for fewer than one-third of the votes of the Senate. While he was compiling his non-voting performance he did find time however to join with Senator Lodge in the Republican's disciplined effort to destroy the chances of the League of Nations being ratified.

His opponent in the presidential race was James M. Cox, the liberal governor of Ohio. As governor, Cox put into place meaningful reforms and tried hard to institute others that would improve living conditions for the working classes. Whatever his merits, as a candidate he couldn't prevail against the over-powering strength of the political organization the Republicans presented. They had four-times as much money and a highly skilled machine which proved to be superbly efficient at marketing their candidate.

Harding's vice-presidential running mate was a preposterous nincompoop from Massachusetts, Calvin Coolidge, and together they formed the worst president – vice-president tandem in American history. That honor was perhaps equaled or even bettered in 1968 when the two crooks, Nixon, the unindicted co-conspirator and Spiro Agnew of 57 felony counts fame, headed the Republican ticket.

To be sure, I'm betting on George Walker Bush and Richard B. Cheney taking the honors. On a near daily basis they are presenting such unchallengeable credentials to the American people which will surely prove to be superior to those of Harding/Coolidge or Nixon/Agnew.

Franklin Delano Roosevelt was the Democratic nominee for Vice-President. One plank of the Democratic platform showed unbelievable prescience when it looked to the League of Nations "as the surest, if not the only, practicable means of maintaining the permanent peace of the world."

Harding's campaign pitch reflected felicitous foolishness such as 'not heroism, but healing; not nostrums but normalcy." These reflected the same degree of validity as did candidate Bush in 2000, proclaiming that "he was a uniter, not a divider;" or the other impassioned whopper, "I am a compassionate conservative." The Republicans were scornful of President Wilson's plea for the League and would inflict an ignominious defeat on the Democrats, piling up 16 million votes to only nine for the opponents. In terms of percentage it was 60.4% to 34.2%.

In his inaugural address, Harding would inveigh against the League of Nations. "A world super government is contrary to everything we cherish and can have no sanction by our Republic. This is not selfishness, it is sanctity. It is not aloofness, it is security. It is not suspicion of others; it is patriotic adherence to the things which make us what we are."

A truthful speechwriter would have concluded this neat little paean by observing, "it is not sanity, this is stupidity."

WWI, just like our own Civil War, should never have happened. A silly archduke of the Austro-Hungarian Empire headquartered in Vienna, Austria, was assassinated on June 28, 1914. Because he was gunned down in Sarajevo, Serbia, the Empire insisted on outrageously punitive measures against the Serbs, measures which the country wouldn't accept. The huge empire was spoiling for a showdown with the small independent nation of Serbia. The empire would soon realize its goal.

Germany would quickly align itself with it and in turn be opposed by Russia, ruled by the Romanov dynasty, which would come to the aid of its fellow Slavs in Serbia. France and England, both democracies, would soon find itself linked with Russia, one of the most repressive nations on the planet.

Following four and-a-half years of savage warfare the Empire, together with its ruling dynasty, the Hapsburgs, would completely collapse and it would crumble into a host of small, independent republics. The other two dynasties, the Romanovs in Russia and the Hohenzollerns in Germany would cease to exist.

Had there been a League of Nations in place in 1914, arbitration might easily have produced a peaceful solution. Interesting parallels can be drawn between the haughty Southerners, before our Civil War lusting for separation from the North so that they could perpetuate its slavocracy. They knew that a forceful separation, such as bombarding Fort Sumter in Charleston, South Carolina, would produce a Civil War. Still, they were so supremely confident that their cultured, genteel lads would put to rout the louts from the North. So too was the hapless Hapsburg royalty, so anxious to subdue the inferior Serbs but blind to their own internal weaknesses and near total inability to conduct an effective war. The Hapsburg Empire and the plantation owners in the South eagerly sought the conflict that would prove to be catastrophic for both of them.

The Hapsburg dynasty closed up shop and went out of business. The South today, 143 years after the Civil War, still clings foolishly to many of its pre-Civil War ideals that never were in consonance with reality but which now keeps them mired in backwardness.

Harding's cabinet appointees were an accurate reflection of his own merit. After all, he had no plan, no goal for his presidency. To the office of Attorney General he appointed his campaign manager, Harry Daugherty, a man completely lacking any legal education or experience. As the nation would soon discover, he also lacked any familiarity with honesty or integrity. An appointee to the Veteran's Bureau, Charles Forbes, took the opportunity to liberate large amounts from the Bureau's cookie jar. He then left Washington rather hurriedly. Soon after, two of Forbes' associates took their own lives.

As soon as the Ohio Gang hit town they acquired "a little green house" on K Street which became the headquarters of a never ending party. The newly installed president would make his appearance there several times a week for lengthy, high stakes poker games. The liquor bar, illegal of course with the Republican sponsored Prohibition in force, was fully stocked and seemingly never closed. Call girls paraded through continuously as did figures from the underworld.

Harding's Secretary of the Interior, Albert Fall, would contribute his bit to maintaining the Harding standard of conduct, by arranging to lease oil reserves owned by the federal government in exchange for enormous bribes. Fall and Forbes would soon both be guests of the federal government's incarceration department. Harry Daugherty would be indicted, not once, but twice, and would get a hung jury both times. An impeachment effort made against him narrowly failed.

During this period, Harding was inducted into the Ku Klux Klan in a secret ceremony at the White House. His bad habits and profligate appointees would finally exact their toll; he would suffer a fatal heart attack on August 2, 1923, only 29 months into his presidency.

CHAPTER XV

With the passing of Warren Harding, a man completely undeserving of such high office, a man equally undeserving of even the Vice-Presidency, Calvin Coolidge, assumed the role of the Chief Executive of our fair land. His tenure in office was admirably summarized by the sardonic critic of the 1920s, H.L. Mencken, who said of him, "Coolidge's chief feat was to sleep more than any other of his predecessors. The itch to run things did not bother him. He was to let them run themselves." When Coolidge departed this planet some 10 years later, the nationally known playwright and wit, Dorothy Thompson, innocently inquired, "How can you tell?"

His critics were savage in describing him. They took turns eviscerating him and his presidency. "A neat little one cylinder intellect," said Frank Kent of the Baltimore Sun. "What he says is mostly non-committal, neutral, evasive. The weak and watery utterances of a passive and pallid little man." It has been quite amazing he could be so consistently and so unqualifiedly dull, and for so long a period. And yet he was highly regarded in the business community, for he was their duly ordained high priest of trickle down economics. These tenets were now enshrined in national business policy thanks to presidents like McKinley and Harding.

Coolidge would utter commandments that caused the titans of industry to salivate with approval. "The man who builds a factory builds a temple; the man who works there worships there." Another of his notorious maxims was, "the chief business of the American people is business."

The Republican Party of the 1920s regarded high protective tariffs as the rock upon which the party was constructed. Indeed, tariffs had considerable validity in the party's nascent years before and after the Civil War. We have previously touched on this subject and saw how Abraham Lincoln viewed them with fondness. At that period American industry was still in its youth and needed protection from huge, established industries like those in England and France.

By the turn of the 20th Century, high tariffs were harmful, even pernicious, to all segments of the economy except manufacturers and distributors of their products. By keeping out foreign products, domestic industries kept competition reduced substantially, but this resulted in higher prices. What it also resulted in was nice, fat profits.

During WWI American farmers enjoyed a booming economy. Since the fighting in Europe prevented the usual planting and harvesting, the demand for American farm products increased dramatically. Exports to Europe rose to record heights. Many of our farmers went into debt rather heavily to buy new and better machinery or to increase their acreage. Soon after war's end, European farm production increased and then returned to normal. By 1920 our farm exports sagged markedly, and with it farm prices.

Meanwhile productivity in our agrarian sector was soaring and soon the nation experienced a glut of farm products. Prices dropped precipitously. Instead of curtailing the acreage planted, the despairing farmers tilled still more land. With that prices fell to record lows. Before long the farmers were unable to pay off their bank loans, the value of the land plummeted and rural banks began to fold in record numbers. Quickly the farm turmoil spread to the small businesses in nearby towns. Entire areas began to experience the effects of rural depression.

I can still recall, growing up in a small town in Wisconsin, near Green Bay, the shocking conditions facing the farmers. My parents knew several of these families, so we would occasionally visit them. The entire agrarian sector was already in a profound depression long before the Great Depression struck the rest of the nation. Many of the individual farmers were doggedly fending off bank foreclosure but this was a battle too many of them lost. The prices they often received for wheat and corn barely covered production costs; in effect the long, tough hours spent in planting, harrowing and harvesting the crops produced nothing.

Few of them had electricity, perhaps one or two out of a hundred. Their kitchens and living rooms reeked with barnyard smells; in summer flies were everywhere. The furniture and carpets almost always were shabby, or even threadbare. A sense of isolation was everywhere as was the unimaginable boredom. Even as a small boy I couldn't imagine why people would choose to live this lifestyle.

Coolidge, without doubt, was completely impervious to the plight of the near hopeless farmers. He reinforced this attitude by vetoing the McNary-Haughton Farm Bill, not just once, but twice. By the terms of this measure, Congress would establish a government corporation to purchase certain crops when they were surplus, store them until the price rose or else dump the surplus. He expressed his indignation most emphatically in his first veto message. "Nothing is more certain than such price fixing would upset the normal exchange relationship existing in the open market and that it would finally have to be extended to cover a multitude of other goods and services. Government price fixing, once started, has alike no justice and no end."

Farmers evidently were not included in his famous edict that the business of America is business. What in the world were high tariffs if they weren't a blatant form of price fixing for Big Business? Coolidge enjoyed a luxuriant relationship with that element as he permitted the federal regulatory commissions, set in place by Teddy Roosevelt, to be either captured or neutralized by the very industries they were designed to keep in check. During the entire period of his presidency, industry was growing because of record profits which enabled them to expand almost exponentially through mergers. Often these commissions became almost irrelevant because Coolidge was convinced that business flourished with no regulation.

Take the case of the Federal Trade Commission. It had received formidable powers "to investigate, publicize and prohibit unfair methods of competition." This act, passed during the Wilson Administration in 1914, strictly defined unfair competition as involving "substantial lessening of competition to create monopoly." The maiming of the FTC under Coolidge quickly revealed how a reactionary Republican president, intent upon inflicting grave harm on the general public, can reverse legislation passed by a Democratic Congress. In 1925 he appointed an industry shill, William E. Humphrey, to head the FTC. Humphrey quickly manipulated his agency around so that each industry could formulate its own rules and by doing so laugh at any attempt to regulate it.

The American people came to learn how Ken Lay, former CEO of Enron could select the very people it wanted to govern Enron's industry. George Bush was only too happy to assist his big buddy, Kenny Boy Lay.

Kenny Boy had worked the shell game to perfection, or so he thought. Far from it, Enron entered bankruptcy, a huge percentage of its employees lost their jobs and nearly all the money they had placed in their 401K pension funds evaporated. Stock holders viewed with horror as the share value of Enron stock nose dived from $90.00 a share to just pennies. Kenny Boy had been touting the stock, ever exhorting his employees to continue making purchases. He, of course, was quietly selling his shares.

After protracted court sessions, a plentiful number of his company's high ranking officers found themselves peering between bars in a federal house of corrections. Ken Lay would be convicted on multiple felony counts, but would shortly thereafter succumb to a heart attack.

Peering into Coolidge's early career, one is immediately struck by the enormous disparity of his approach to social legislation when he was in the Massachusetts State House and when not too long after he became president. In those years "he instinctively voted for measures that would protect working people against the rapacity of exploiters." We learn this from a highly instructive biography of Calvin Coolidge fittingly entitled "Calvin Coolidge," by Robert H. Ferrell, published by University of Kansas Press. "He saw unfairness in laws, or a lack of laws that stood for fairness. He favored women's suffrage, which would bring local interests into politics. On the state level, he supported a six day work week, a limit on hours of work for women and children, pensions to families of firemen and school teachers, half fare on street cars for school children. Something happened to Coolidge's brush with progressivism."

To suggest that he succumbed to the shameless blandishments beckoning him toward *laissez-faire* economics and politics appears to be on target. As president, he became completely blind to the rapacity of exploiters and started to babble errant and insidious doctrine about the workshop being a temple where workers should worship.

In another of Coolidge's often quoted affirmations, he was arrogantly dismissive of Congress in its ability to produce helpful legislation. He referred to the "utter hopelessness of having considerable enterprise conducted by the Congress." That was undeniably true under *his Republican Congress*. But beginning in early 1933, *the Democratic Congress* under the inspired leadership of Franklin Delano Roosevelt and his enlightened legislative aides would reel off a string of 'considerable enterprises' that rescued this county from the nearly bottomless quagmire it was in.

Coolidge and the Republican election machine would seduce the electorate into viewing his years in office as Coolidge Prosperity. He would be given a renewal of his lease on the White House for four more years when he won big in 1924. The Democratic presidential candidate is too insignificant to mention, but not the name of the Vice-Presidential running mate. That young man's name was Franklin Delano Roosevelt.

The stock market began its ascent into the wild blue yonder during the last 18 months of Coolidge's tenure. It became known as the Coolidge Market. The New York Stock Exchange pontificated about its being "a market place where prices reflect the basic law of supply and demand." That pious credo actually reflected an egregious departure from truth and fact.

Had the vaunted Exchange not been so faithless to veracity it would more correctly have observed it was where "Wall Streeters traded on inside information, produced their own speculative booms and crises, blocked fruitful competition, made obscene amounts of money and used it to corrupt politicians and the press." Those marvelously incisive words can be seen in *"The Great Crash,"* John Kenneth Galbraith's monumental depiction of the Wall Street meltdown, culminating in October, 1929. The book underwent innumerable printings following its initial appearance in 1954.

Continuing, he observed that, "The sense of responsibility in the financial community for the community as a whole is not small. It is nil." There was both a "mass exodus from reality" and a "tendency toward self-immolation."

In a particularly priceless example of the atmosphere then prevalent, he pointed out, "but it was plain that an increasing number of persons were coming to the conclusion that they were predestined by luck, an unbeatable system, divine favor, access to inside information or exceptional financial acumen for becoming rich without work."

Sometimes the insider wolves were able to shear the outsider sheep. "A number of traders pooled their resources to boom a particular stock. They appointed a pool manager, promised not to double-cross each other, and the pool manager then took a position in the stock which might also include shares contributed by the participants. If all went well, the public would come in to buy, and prices would rise on their own. The pool manager would then sell out, pay himself a percentage of the profits and divide the rest with the investors."

In his final State of the Union delivered on December 4, 1928, Coolidge would contribute to the aura of lunacy pervading the investment community. "No Congress of the United States ever assembled, on surveying the State of the Union, has met with a more pleasing prospect than which appears at the present time. In the domestic field there is tranquility and contentment and the highest record of years of prosperity. In the foreign field there is peace, the goodwill which comes from mutual understanding." The President would conclude this example of boundless optimism by noting: "The main source of these unexampled blessings lies in the integrity and character of the American people."

Had any integrity or character existed in the Coolidge Administration, the looming stock market meltdown might easily have been averted. In addition to the snoozing, do-nothing President there was the important Secretary of the Treasury, Andrew Mellon, a holdover from Harding's gang. The Secretary of Commerce was Herbert Hoover, another Harding refugee, and the next president. All three were devoted disciples of silence and inactivity on economic and stock market matters.

By the time Coolidge had uttered his imperishable words on the condition of America, as of December 4, 1928, a new president, Herbert Hoover had already won a very convincing victory in the November election. In defeating Alfred Smith, the Governor of New York, he piled up a plurality of 6,430,000 votes. Coolidge's successor was the third of the mind-numbing mediocrities that would fill the role of the president for 12 years.

In his acceptance speech at the Republican National Convention the previous summer, Hoover proclaimed to the jubilant delegates, "We in America today are nearer to the final triumph over poverty than ever before in the history of our land. The poor house is vanishing from among us. We shall soon with the help of God be in sight of the day when poverty will be banished from this nation."

In this 1928 race, Smith had to confront two enormous handicaps, the first being religion. The New York governor was Irish Catholic, a fact of life that would aid Hoover immeasurably. As the campaign opened Hoover maintained an air of tolerance on the question of religion. "By blood and conviction I stand for religious tolerance both in act and spirit. I abhor bigotry." Hoover demanded that his associates were to wage only a positive campaign and to omit mention of religion or prohibition.

The country however was still in the fierce grip of racial and religious inflexibility and the Ku Klux Klan was absolutely supreme in the South. Whatever the candidate's true position was, his campaign workers drove home Smith's Catholicism at every opportunity, and nothing would stop them.

These Hoover campaigners were again igniting the Republican Party image that burned so brightly during the McKinley — Bryan race in 1896; then it was the Party of Offensive Politics or POOP. POOP would prevail in 1928.

A whispering and rumor campaign was started, sometimes involving the Pope, who according to the rumor had already made arrangements to depart for Washington as soon as Smith won. Oh! And a grand tunnel from the Vatican, extending all the way across the Atlantic was already under construction. Protestant ministers launched a veritable crusade to keep Smith out of the White House.

Hoover's busy assistants were belaboring Smith from every angle. One of them appeared before a very large audience of Protestant ministers and importuned them to take to their pulpits to spread the word that this was a contest between "the loose elements of morals" on the one side while on the other, the Republican side, was "the very highest and best morals."

In their earnest desire to keep the loose-moraled Smith out of the White House, the Republicans discovered more ammunition in demon rum. Smith was vehemently opposed to Prohibition, highly unpopular in civilized parts of the country. In marked contrast, Hoover maintained a solid defense of the law, saying it was "a great and economic experiment noble in motive and far reaching in purpose." Organized bootleggers were completely in accord with its being far reaching in purpose. Somehow Hoover never could find the words to stop or even slow the avalanche of religious bigotry being issued by his party.

Reading about this nauseating episode, refreshens my memory about the 1960 contest between the Catholic John Fitzgerald Kennedy and Richard Nixon. Much of the religious distemper used to advantage against Kennedy sounded remarkably similar to the material employed in 1928.

The unbelievably powerful role played by the Ku Klux Klan in the South requires an adequate airing. Its ranks included small-town businessmen, police officers and, of course, sheriff's deputies. We have already seen how the Klan had a strangle hold on Philadelphia, Mississippi 35 years beyond this election. At least one of its U.S. Senators had more than a little identity with it. In that wretched town the sheriff, his deputy and the Klavern's chaplain were all deeply mired in its murderous activities.

Speaking of its 1928 character, the Klan enjoyed widespread acclaim amongst the Southern Baptist and Southern Methodist clergy. The reason for this acceptance was what the organization opposed with such violence, societal elements routinely found within liberal ranks. The Klan was anti-black, anti-Jew, anti-Catholic, anti-evolution, anti-immigrant, anti-feminist, anti-intellectual and disturbingly homophobic. What it stood for was the literal interpretation of the Bible, white male dominance and a willingness to invoke almost unimaginable cruelty to its enemies. Xenophobia was everywhere present.

Herbert Hoover was one of the unluckiest presidents in our history. Whereas Coolidge floated through the five and-a-half years of his tenure, merely riding aloft on the bubble of "Coolidge Prosperity," Hoover had been in office barely seven months when the first ripple of the Great Depression struck. That was when the stock market crashed with a thud heard 'round the world.' Never before or since has there been such a detonation felt on Wall Street as took place in October, 1929. Had the economy been sound, supported by strong elements across the nation, the imploding market might not have had such a horrendous impact. But as we have seen the farm belt was already undergoing its own depression and too much of the laboring force was struggling to stay afloat. Starting in November the national economy began a precipitous slide and by March of 1930 was in headlong retreat, hurtling the entire country into the Great Depression.

During WWI Hoover compiled a near legendary reputation for his heroic efforts in providing relief for the starving hordes in Belgium in areas ravaged by the invading German troops. He quickly established a system to deliver food, medicine and other vital necessities. His efforts were so successful that he received universal acclaim. Once the effects of the Depression had descended on his own land, he proved to be utterly incapable of administering desperately needed relief to his countrymen.

A reasonably close examination of Hoover's cabinet reveals his tragically circumscribed outlook on American society with particular emphasis on business cycles and trickle-down economics. Of its nine members all were WASP males and nearly all of them millionaires. There was not a single Catholic, Jew, Southerner or woman.

Harding, Coolidge and now Hoover all gave utterance to appalling lies about the condition of the economy and the stock market. No control over Big Business was in place since the regulatory commissions established by the two liberal presidents, Theodore Roosevelt and Woodrow Wilson had been almost completely emasculated by this cunning trio of presidents. *Laissez-faire*, or more properly, trickle-down economics was in the driver's seat. Here existed a tiny percentage of the country reveling in riotous luxury while at the same time inordinate numbers were either at or below the subsistence level. Calamity was right around the corner.

The new president simply could not rid himself of ancient precepts about the sacred nature of capital and property. When it came time for the federal government to provide food for hungry bellies and arrive at a determination that human rights were superior to property rights he remained immobile. "Money for hungry people would turn them into *mendacious parasites*," he would stoutly maintain. Which is better, a starved-to-death True Believer or a live mendacious parasite?

I am continually reminded of Abraham Lincoln's astute and merciful approach to human life during the Civil War. When his generals wanted to execute sentries who had fallen asleep on guard duty he would invariably commute the sentence. "It's far better to have a live soldier above ground than a dead one below the ground," he would casually observe.

Everywhere across the nation existed glaring examples of outrageous discontinuity. In the cities people in large quantities were starving while at the same time crops were rotting in the fields. An almost inconceivable degree of deflation had taken root and forced the price of produce down to the point where it was no longer profitable to harvest.

Hoover and his nine wealthy males were positive the American spirit would find the way to muddle through this economic mess just as it had during the harsh Panics of 1873, 1893, 1907 and 1921. He would then bestow to the eagerly waiting nation this dictum, "Where people divest themselves of local government responsibilities they at once lay the foundation for the destruction of their liberties. The spread of government destroys individual opportunity and initiative and thus destroys character. *Bureaucratic federal aid would damage the sense of an American community.*"

By 1931 in large cities across American, hospital records noted that the cause of death of a patient was starvation. It was happening with increased frequency.

152

The Governor of New York, Franklin Delano Roosevelt, had a far different approach to individual opportunity and initiative. He demanded of his legislature that it provide unemployment relief, *not as a measure of charity*, but because it was *their social duty.*

The man I regard as the *greatest unelected presidential candidate* in our history, Hubert Horatio Humphrey, gave expression in a most felicitous manner to the social duty of a government. "The moral test of government is how the government treats those in the dawn of life, the children; those who are in the twilight of life, the elderly; and those who are in the shadows life – the sick, the needy, the handicapped." He was defeated in 1968 by a man for whom I have bottomless scorn, Richard Milhous Nixon.

Quickly the vault of my memory bank provides me with the names of four men who would have been in absolute accord with those sentiments. The first three are our three greatest presidents – Franklin Delano Roosevelt, Abraham Lincoln and Theodore Roosevelt – one Democrat and two Republicans. And the fourth? Why that of course would be Jesus Christ, earth's first and greatest liberal. The politicians are listed first as a convenience and not to delegate order of importance.

With equal swiftness that same memory vault provides the names of four more men who would be in total denial of those precepts. Again the name of Richard Milhous Nixon comes up in bold relief, followed by Ronald Wilson Reagan. Completing the quartet are George Herbert Walker Bush, pere, and son George Walker Bush. The last one may be in the most emphatic state of denial.

As the months of 1930 passed into history more businesses careened into bankruptcy, unemployment increased on a weekly basis and the rate of bank failures steadily grew. Still President Hoover maintained his air of unconcern. A growing divide could easily be noted between his perception of economic conditions and the stark reality of everyday life. In May of 1930 he would explain to a Chamber of Commerce gathering, "I am convinced that we have now passed the worst and with continuing unity of effort, we shall rapidly recover." In the following month a delegation came to seek his help for the growing number of unemployed and he would blithely dismiss them. "Gentlemen, you have come sixty days too late. The Depression is over."

That timeless observation by Hoover is richly deserving of commemoration and should be cast in bronze so that it can be seen for all eternity, or at least as long as the bronze casting lasts. I also believe Republicans should demand that a similar casting be made for Dick Cheney's perspicacious forecast made in mid-2003, shortly after the fall of Baghdad that "the insurgency is in its last gasp."

That was before an estimated 4000 *more American lives* were needlessly thrown away, and an estimated 35,000 *more* serious wounds were suffered by our valiant troops. The insurgency at the time consisted of nothing more than a mild uprising.

In declaring the Depression to be ended, Hoover erred ever so slightly. By year's end business failures totaled 26,355. In only the last months of 1930, bank closing would reach 600, bringing the year's total to 1352.

Already in that year he had taken part in a legislative barbarity – the Smoot Hawley Tariff Act, considered by many observers of Congress to be one of the most monstrous acts ever passed by the United States Congress. It was to tariffs what Bush v. Gore was to election law. When he signed the bill, Hoover knew it would cause instant tariff reprisals world-wide. He was absolutely correct. But, much worse, it heightened the sense of nationalism in several European countries. In one country, Germany, the shocking rise of nationalism would portend unthinkable developments in a mere handful of years.

In the spring of 1930 an obscure group called the National Socialist German Worker's Party, was nearly moribund. Whenever the party was recognized it was just the butt of crude jokes. In the fall elections it would gain eight times as many seats as it previously held in the Reichstag, the German Congress. For the party the terrible times in Germany were a precious gift. The United States and Germany suffered the most because of the world-wide downturn in business.

The party quickly became known as the Nazis; its head was Adolph Hitler. In the words of William Shirer, the author of *The Rise and Fall of the Third Reich*, "the Nazis were, "a conglomeration of pimps, murderers, homosexuals, alcoholics and black mailers who flocked to the party as if to a natural haven." A The New York Times book review called this epic chronicle "one of the most important works of history in our time."

In summarizing his own work, Mr. Shirer would say, "It constituted the blueprint of the Third Reich, and what is more, of the barbaric New Order which Hitler inflicted on conquered Europe in the triumphant years between 1939 and 1945." As outlined by the author, Hitler had "a burning passion for German nationalism, a hatred for democracy, Marxism and the Jews. … and a certainty that Providence had chosen the Germans to be the master race." Mr. Shirer had spent many years in Germany as a reporter and remained there until December 11, 1941, the day Hitler declared war on this country, just four days after Pearl Harbor.

From my personal point of view, Adolph Hitler and the Nazis cost three years of my life during the period I served in the Army Air Corps, much of it under harsh privation and much of it under extreme discomfort. I entered

Germany on March 27. 1945, almost exactly six weeks before the war ended. During that summer I was able to fly into Berlin twice. I toured around a significant part of the Germany which was under the control of our Army. The remainder of the country was divided between the British, Canadian, French and Russian occupying forces. The magnitude of the ruin, the total devastation is very difficult to describe. The German people would need at least 10 years of extraordinarily difficult effort to rebuild their country until it began to approach its prewar condition.

Previous to that I spent the last six months of 1944 in Normandy and Northern France, every day living in an unheated tent. For at least the last three months of the year the nighttime temperatures would plummet into the low 20s. For a period of at least four months I experienced the luxury of exactly one shower, outdoors, in near freezing weather and lasting for no more than two minutes. Our uniforms suffered from similar neglect, remaining unlaundered for the same period.

Under these stark living conditions we had to acquire a pervasive stench from both our bodies and our clothing, but strangely enough none of us seemed to notice it. We didn't dare complain about the quality of life because the suffering GIs in the Infantry and Tank Corps were under enemy fire on a near daily basis and were being killed or wounded in significant numbers. Our brave pilots, whom we got to know from daily meetings in the weather truck, were equally at risk and altogether too many of them failed to return from combat missions.

Could WWII have been avoided had the United States Senate ratified the League of Nations Treaty? A formidable case can be made that with the backing of the U.S. Government, the leaders in France and England might have had sturdier backbones and stood up to Mussolini and Hitler. As has been documented, important figures in the Republican Party went to heroic lengths to prevent that from taking place. As we have also seen, and in the same time frame, Prohibition was inflicted on an unsuspecting nation by the Republican Party.

The war produced pitifully few results for which the world could be grateful. When the Third Reich was born on January 30, 1933, Hitler announced it would endure for a thousand years. Referring to that Reich, Mr. Shirer pointed out, "It actually lasted twelve years and four months, but in that flicker of time as history goes, it caused an eruption on earth more violent and shattering than any previously experienced, raising the German people to heights of power they had not known in more than a millennium, making them at one time the masters of Europe from the Atlantic to the Volga, from the North Cape to the Mediterranean, and then plunging them to the depths of destruction and desolation at the end of a world war which their nation had cold-bloodedly provoked and during which it instituted a reign of terror over the conquered peoples, which in its calculated butchery of human life and the human spirit, outdid all the savage oppressions of the previous ages."

My admiration for Mr. Shirer and his work knows no bounds but that has to be the longest sentence I have ever read.

CHAPTER XVI

What were the causes of the Big Depression? From the extreme right wing, that is the Republican political spectrum, comes the view of Milton Friedman. For many years until his recent death at age 95, he held steadfast to his theory that the great economic upheaval was the result of the Federal Reserve Board having clamped down on the money supply available to business. Let's sift through the evidence.

By the summer of 1929 at the latest, sales were tumbling in four major categories. Automobiles were no longer rolling out of dealer show rooms as fast as they had been. The manufacturers in Detroit could produce far more vehicles than their dealers could sell. Builders were constructing houses faster than they could sell them. Steel production had been curtailed due to falling demand. One widely viewed index was railroad car loadings — the amount of box cars loaded each month. These too were down.

Under these conditions would automakers, home builders or steel manufacturers hurry down to the bank, borrow money and increase production? That seems highly unlikely.

In a remarkably accurate and pithy summary of the causes of the Depression, John Kenneth Galbraith of *"The Great Crash"* fame highlights the five weaknesses in the economy that constituted the major factors. First was the bad distribution of income. This had already been treated at some length. He was also decidedly emphatic about the Milton Friedman dictum. "There was no shortage of production capability in any industry so it would be pointless to invest it there."

He next alludes to the bad corporate structure. "American industry had permitted itself to be invaded by large numbers of promoters, grafters, swindlers, imposters and frauds." He explains how, through the use of unlimited leveraging, holding companies could build huge business edifices and thereby control unhealthy segments of the railroads and public utilities. A holding company would obtain the bare minimum amount of stock in a smaller company needed to operate it. Using that as leverage it purchased yet another company through the mechanism of selling corporate bonds. Leverage can exert a near magical effect when the economy is expanding. But, when the economy begins to contract, as it started to do in 1929, leveraging also has a magical effect, only in reverse. The holding company is unable to meet its debt payments and begins to sell off some of its acquisitions. It would be hard to imagine a corporate system better designed to continue and accentuate a deflationary spiral."

In 1929 the banking system wasn't merely weak, *it was rotten*. Starting in the early 20s, the Roaring Twenties, as the reigning Republicans liked to call them, an average of over 500 banks would self-destruct on an annual basis. In 1929, easily the most bountiful year of the century, the rate accelerated to 659. We have already seen where the failure rate reached 1352 in the year 1930. "Speaking of banks," Mr. Galbraith pointed out, "the weak destroyed not only the other weak, but weakened the strong."

On a personal note, during this period of the Hoover doctrine which gradually wrecked the economy, my father, an immigrant at age three, learned to profit from the stock market. Unfortunately the two banks where he maintained a modest account failed to survive the upheaval. Very little of my dad's bank balance did either. From one bank he salvaged 10%, from the other only 5%.

Mr. Galbraith takes us to "the dubious state of the foreign balance." Seeking to clog up the arteries of world trade, the Republican Congress in 1922 passed the Fordney McCumber Tariff Act which set import duties sufficiently high to create havoc in world trade. American businessmen lobbied hard to obtain schedules that would largely prevent manufactured goods and raw material from abroad to enter this country. There is little question but what this irresponsible bill played a discernable role in the economic debacle awaiting us. Bad as that was, the Smoot-Hawley Tariff Act of 1930 was far worse. Congress and Hoover might just as well have declared war on our trading partners by passing and then allowing the Tariff Act to become law. Before signing that senseless product of avarice, over 1000 economists signed a petition pleading with the president to veto the bill. Nonetheless he went ahead and signed it. Immediately, European nations retaliated in kind. Global business in trade diminished drastically from around $36 billion in 1929 to a wretched $12 billion in 1932. Reviewing this act, it seems almost impossible to believe that a Republican Congress, acting in concert with a Republican head of state would deliberately perpetrate such an economic monstrosity on the American people.

Mr. Galbraith's fifth cause of the Depression was "The poor state of economic intelligence." The Hoover administration never missed an opportunity to worsen the eroding fiscal climate. On a consistent basis, it listened to bad advice. It was unrealistically concerned with the ill effects of inflation at a time when farm prices were at rock bottom. Its attention should have been drawn to *the horrors of deflation.*

While Coolidge, Hoover and Mellon could see no evil or detect any danger on the distant horizon, observers with more acute judgment perceived ominous signs on the near horizon. We once again enlist the words of Mr. Galbraith. "Writing in the March 1929 issue of the *Atlantic Monthly*, Paul C. Cabot stated that dishonesty, inattention, inability and greed were among the common shortcomings of the new industry. These were impressive disadvantages, and as an organizer and officer of a promising investment trust, the State Street Investment Corporation, Mr. Cabot presumably spoke with some authority."

There were only a few other voices of dissention. An important figure, Paul M. Warburg of the International Acceptance Bank, volunteered his appraisal of the market. Unless the unrestrained speculation is brought to a halt, he predicted that "disastrous collapse" would result and cause "a general depression involving the entire country."

A third echo of discord needs to be noted. Roger Babson, a man normally accorded a considerable degree of deference in financial circles, cast a dire warning early in September, 1929. "Sooner or later a crash is coming and it may be terrific." His speech would end with this verbal missile, "Factories will shut down; men will be thrown out of work. The vicious circle will get in full swing and the result will be a serious business depression."

Only a year before Babson had spoken to an audience prior to the Hoover — Smith election and made this portentous forecast. "If Smith should be elected with a Democratic Congress we are almost certain to have a resulting business depression in 1929." On the other hand he cheerily notes, "The election of Hoover and a Republican Congress should result in continued prosperity for 1929."

Far from taking heed of the remarks of these three naysayers, they instead were issued stern rebukes and their prescient forecasts were dismissed with hauteur.

The antics of illustrious clowns in caps and gowns prancing around on Ivy League campuses sorely need noting. Joseph Stagg Lawrence of Princeton University gave frequent, immoderate expression when addressing anyone who had the temerity to question his judgment about the market. Even the august Federal Reserve Board could not escape his wrath. During the fateful month of September 1929, when the market had already reached its tipping point and was beginning to head downhill, he accused it of "doing its utmost to cast the proverbial monkey wrench into the machinery of prosperity."

Several points about the Board need to be stressed hurriedly. That group had previously done exactly nothing to moderate the insanity taking place at the New York Stock Exchange. Had the Board been able to locate a monkey wrench, it would not have had the faintest idea what to do with it. Mr. Galbraith described it perfectly when he called it, "A body of startling incompetence." Had President Hoover possessed the tiniest resolve, he would have fired the entire outfit.

Lawrence of Princeton, not wishing to be adjudged timid, spoke out in a most forthright manner. "The consensus of judgment of the millions whose valuations function on that admirable market, the Stock Exchange, is that stocks are not at present over-valued." Not to be outdone in radiant confidence, Professor Irving Fisher of Yale boasted: "Stock prices have reached what looked like a permanently high plateau."

(I once owned a stock during a like period of a permanent high plateau. I possessed 20,000 shares of a hot item which reached $16.00 a share. I feel it necessary to divulge this minor incident in my life in order to demonstrate my superior skills in the realm of market investing. This was during the Clinton Administration. Not too long after Bummy Bush became the occupant of the White House, its value declined a trifle. I parted company with the issue when its value had receded to 20-cents a share.)

The roseate declarations of Lawrence of Princeton and Fisher of Yale richly deserve a place in history. So too, does the Cunard Steamship Line when it flaunted its latest creation, the *Titanic*. The proud owners declared it to be not only the largest and most luxurious liner afloat, but unsinkable as well. No other ship builder had ever made such a boast. The Cunard spokesman directed attention to the 16 water tight compartments which prevented the ship from taking on water.

On the Titanic's maiden voyage from Southampton, England to New York, five of its water tight compartments sprung leaks after striking an iceberg. In slightly more than two hours, on April 13, 1912, the unsinkable liner began its deathward plunge, carrying with it 1513 victims.

We should dwell for just a moment on the diverse attitudes of New York City's two greatest newspapers, the New York Times and the Wall Street Journal. Mr. Galbraith deftly summarizes the position of the former. "By far the greatest force for sobriety was the New York Times. Under the guidance of the veteran Alexander Dana Noyes, its financial page was all but immune to the blandishments of the New Era. A regular reader could not doubt that a day of reckoning was expected. The time was coming when the optimists would reap a rich harvest of discredit. But it has long since been forgotten that for many months those who resisted reassurance were similarly, if less permanently, discredited."

The sharpest of contrasts could be discerned on the financial page of the Wall Street Journal in September 1929. The Stock Exchange was already manifesting unhealthy tremors. Still, the Journal notes, "price movements in the main body of stocks yesterday continued to display the characteristics of a major advance temporarily halted for *technical readjustment.*"

To fully comprehend the potential of an innocuous phrase like technical readjustment, we need only look at the downward progression of an investment trust, the progenitor of today's mutual fund. United Founders, one of the larger trusts in 1929 with assets of $301,385,504, saw its share price climb to $75.00. After several years of undergoing technical readjustment, its share price contracted to 75 cents, a tidy loss of 99% for its investors.

On March 4, 1929 Herbert Hoover was sworn into office. The economy, a product of the Coolidge Prosperity, was displaying increased signs of fatigue and beginning to appear despeptic. The farm sector already was in a state of acute distress. Homebuilding and auto sales were languishing while steel mills were cutting hours of production.

By September 3, less than six months since the new president's inaugural speech, the stock market, supposedly on a permanent high plateau, began to explore lower latitudes. This despite loans from stock brokers to market players buying stock on margin. Just for the month of September those loans rose to the giddy level of $670 million. While the floor under the market was becoming shakier, the passion for speculation remained undiminished.

The market continued to flutter ever downward as September turned into October. Time Magazine, however, continued to place internationally known financiers on its front cover. Ivar Krueger would adorn a cover in October; a week later Samuel Insull would appear. In roughly a year-and-a-half Krueger would fire a bullet into his head as his fraudulent ways were catching up to him. Not too long later Insull would turn international fugitive. Such are the shifting circumstances of international fame.

By Saturday, October 19, conditions now more than a little precarious, worsened. On opening again on Monday, the market began to plunge. Huge numbers of players, who were financing their stock purchases with broker's loans, saw their paper fortunes dissolve. They not only were wiped out, they were ruined, many of them for the remainder of their lives. Often this was accompanied by loss of job, foreclosure on their home and soon, loss of pride.

In 1930 the ranks of the unemployed grew by 5,000 000. The year 1931 saw that figure swell to 10,000,000. By the time 1932 came to its dismal end, certainly the worst year in our nation's history, the unemployment total would balloon to 15,000,000. Bank failures were keeping pace. When Hoover was finally swept out of office on March 4, 1933, the entire banking system in this formerly prosperous country was in a state of complete collapse. In 38 of the then 48 states, all banks were closed, by orders of their governors. In the remaining 10 states almost no banks were open for business.

I can't resist relating an incident told me by my father when I was perhaps nine years old. Fortunately for our family he remained employed but had a wretched job in North Dakota, two days travel from our home in Wisconsin.

In this small town in North Dakota, a retail hardware store owner walked across the street to his friendly neighborhood bank and deposited $650.00 in cash in order to pay his suppliers and remain in business. To the small businessman, that sum of money represented an enormous fortune. The following morning the store owner discovered the bank had its shades drawn and was obviously not open for business. With that he walked to the bank, pounded on the front door, and because he was well known to everybody in the bank, was admitted.

The banker, with obvious embarrassment told his friend the bank could no longer stay in business and was a victim of the Hoover Administration. The depositor politely asked that his money be returned to him. The banker replied that because of banking regulations he would be unable to comply with that request.

Whereupon the store owner returned to his shop, selected a revolver out of stock, loaded it and again pounded on the front door. After he gained admittance he pointed the revolver at the banker's head, and with considerably more insistence, demanded that his deposit be returned to him. The banker allowed as how, under these changed conditions, he could now accede to that request.

On Monday, October 21, after another loss in the morning, prices rose slightly in the afternoon. Tuesday even produced a slight overall gain. Wednesday was a far different story. After the Exchange had been open for five hours, a tidy $5,000,000,000 was lost taking out another large host of investors who couldn't meet their margin calls. In 1929, $5 billion was a gargantuan sum of money.

Since many of these investors had scrambled around frantically the previous week seeking money to meet the demands of their brokers, they could no long unearth any more resources. The Exchange was in a state of panic. For many desperate sellers, there were *no buyers at any price*. This had never happened before on the Exchange.

The big banks in New York City, now realized their condition was approaching insolvency. Needing to cope with this suddenly malignant crisis, six of the city's largest banks pledged $40,000,000 apiece to buy up many of these orphans for which there had been no buyers.

By noon, now that word had spread that "organized support'" had been delivered, an entirely different emotion was unleashed. Thomas Lamont, a senior partner with J .P. Morgan and Company, made a dramatic appearance on the floor of the Exchange. "There has been a little distress selling," he casually announced, but he attributed that to a "technical condition." Next, Richard

Whitney, a vice-president of the Exchange began to make unusually large purchases of stock.

With that the panic, the uncontrolled fear, fled the scene and buyers, eager to snap up some of these newly found bargains, reentered the market. Stock prices surged.

While all this tumult was taking place reassuring voices could be heard throughout the financial world. The key word they embraced was some variant of 'fundamental' accompanied by 'progress' or 'sound'. Hoover added his bit of soothing balm by declaring, "The fundamental business of the country, that is production and distribution of commodities, is on a sound and prosperous basis." Obviously he knew not whereof he spoke.

What the scoundrels back on the Exchange floor had perpetuated was an artificial stimulus to the market. They merely wanted to force prices up momentarily, sell their own securities at a favorable price, and quickly depart. The unfortunate suckers who were lured back into the market were once again victimized.

Some years later Richard Whitney, who by that time had risen to the head of the New York Stock Exchange, was found to have expropriated client's funds left in his care. It took until 1938 for justice to catch up with him, but in that year he could be found in a federal prison, dressed in the humble garb of an inmate.

On Friday, the market continued its forward movement still buoyed by the momentum from the previous day's spurious activity. The next day it relinquished those gains but in two days it hadn't lost any ground. Many investors now believed that the big banks would not permit any more panic selling as had happened on Thursday morning.

Monday, October 28, the market immediately opened on a dismal note and continued in that manner. There would be no intervention from white knights forming a cavalry of organized support from the big banks. The last hour the Exchange was open proved to be the most unpleasant; more shares changed hands in that 60 minutes than would on an entire frantic day.

Tuesday, October 29, 1929, a day that still resonates in history, was not only the most unpalatable in the entire annals of the New York Stock Exchange but almost certainly of any exchange anywhere in the world. Repeatedly throughout the day no buyer could be found for a stock *at any price*. On that single day the New York Times Industrial Average, the forerunner of today's Dow Jones Industrial Average, lost as much as it had gained in an entire year.

All this took place in spite of the incessant incantations from respected voices in the Hoover Administration, from among the learned clowns in caps and gowns, and from exalted figures in the financial community. The stock market and the economy were fundamentally sound – how those soothing phrases would be echoed and re-echoed past October 29th, even well into 1930.

The almost unimaginable sum of $32 billion of stock market profits had evaporated beginning early in September when the market reached its highest point.

January 1, 1930 finally saw the end of the "Roaring 20s", actually a low, dishonest decade. During the year 26,355 businesses closed their door permanently. Every industrial group showed a sharp decline in profits and sales. As an individual factory saw its volume of business shrink, it would first curtail inventory, fire workers, then reduce wages and finally shorten its work day. By the end of the year, 4,340,000 men were unemployed. Farm income would drop to $4.1 billion, its lowest in many years.

Hoover's acceptance level among the electorate would undergo a slow, steady erosion for the entire year. Looking stolidly at this grim picture Hoover, Mellon and the other rich, white, male cabinet declined to do <u>anything</u>.

Instead, they relied on exhortation while waiting for the immutable laws of economics to take over. Even though there had been four, full-blown Panics since the Civil War and even those eruptions had caused great havoc for many people, always the economy eventually returned to normal.

Accordingly, they viewed this upheaval with equanimity; even the horrendous melt down on Wall Street failed to register. Governmental interference in the market place was not only considered bad economics but represented 'socialistic schemes' which Hoover viewed with total abhorrence.

The November 1930 election brought about a newly energized Congress. Hoover's impressive Republican advantage vanished; he had a one seat majority in the Senate and only two in the House. But, before Congress convened five Republican House members died so he lost his advantage in that body.

The Democrats very shrewdly refused to organize the House as they were entitled to do, preferring to allow their Republican foes to suffer all the political fall-off.

One aspect of Hoover's personal life deserves scrutiny. The image that he presented in his daily routine in the White House was difficult to admire. His newly found airs of royalty lent themselves to ridicule. As he was about to enter the dining area for his evening meal, he insisted that a bugler musically announce his arrival. He always dressed formally for the repast even though he and his wife often dined alone. He simply was unable to treat the White House staff, all Afro-Americans, with any degree of humanity.

They may as well have been robots for the manner in which he regarded them.

Meanwhile, Congress set about to ameliorate the baleful effects of the worsening Depression. It soon passed some badly needed legislation. Under the direction of Senator George Norris of Nebraska, a Republican, Congress selected a site on the Tennessee River in Alabama called Muscle Shoals, where it was determined it would be advantageous to produce cheap electric power for both residential and industrial use. Two most important byproducts would also result. One, it would harness some of the ruinous annual floods on the river at that location. Secondly inexpensive nitrate fertilizer could be extracted to aid neighboring farmers.

After Congress passed the bill, Hoover unleashed his veto pen and killed the measure. This type of legislation nearly sent the President into convulsions. The private electrical companies, extracting large profits from selling electricity, were equally aghast. Hoover at once declaimed, "It is my view that the federal Government should not go into the business of either generating or distributing electrical power." Continuing in this vein, he added, "The spread of government destroys individual opportunity and initiative and thus destroys character."

In just two short years the White House would be graced with the presence of the man destined to become the nation's greatest president. With his practical and searching mind, Franklin Delano Roosevelt quickly realized the near limitless potential of Muscle Shoals. In short order the Tennessee Valley Authority, the TVA, would be law, passed by a huge Democratic majority in Congress and signed by an enlightened and gifted chief executive. From that legislation would evolve the Rural Electrification Agency, which would bring electric energy to a still largely rural America.

At that point in our history, no more than one or two farms out of a 100 had electricity. A mere 10% of rural America possessed it. In the brief 20 years of FDR and Harry Truman presidencies, that 10% would explode to 90%.

But of just as much import was another by-product of what Muscle Shoals and the entire Tennessee River would deliver to the nation. Hoover's enshackled mentality would have been completely incapable of envisioning this by-product. It was Uranium-235, fissionable uranium and plutonium, which not long before was considered a science-fiction dream.

In August, 1945, Americans and the Japanese nation would instantly be made aware of what that by-product, U-235, could accomplish.

An armed device called Little Boy would explode over Hiroshima, Japan on Monday, August 6, and with that the world would be introduced to nuclear power.

Little Boy would be the result of an exhausting effort on the part of hundreds of scientists at Columbia University in New York, the University of Chicago and the University of California at Berkeley.

An important ingredient in the production of U-235 was the manufacturing facility created at Oak Ridge, Tennessee. One of the key reasons for its selection was its ready accessibility to seemingly inexhaustible amounts of cheap electricity produced by the hydroelectric plants on the Tennessee River. Every watt of that electricity was generated by those federally owned plants. Every particle of work done on the Manhattan Project, including overall supervision and production was funded by the Federal Government.

A willing Congress passed the Wagner – Garner Act providing $1 billion to alleviate the growing hunger and malnutrition in the country. Once again Hoover would veto the legislation providing Congress with another neat sermon about preserving the moral fiber of the nation.

Quite evidently he either had forgotten, or perhaps had never read one of Abraham Lincoln's most famous dictums. It certainly bears repeating. "The legitimate object of government is to do for a community of people whatever they need to have done, but cannot do at all, or cannot do so well for themselves in their individual capacities."

There existed a forbidding chasm between the man who should have been Hoover's ideal President and this vain creature who needed a bugle blaring his entrance into the dining room.

To a growing number of voters he appeared as a Great Scrooge, exhorting Congress and the public to preserve the moral fiber of the nation. Cartoonists delighted in portraying him as a merciless skinflint, now that hunger and homelessness were becoming more common. Many of these unfortunate men erected flimsy shelters made out of cardboard or scrap lumber. Small clusters of these shanties would accumulate and be called Hoovervilles. Our small town in Wisconsin had one on each side of the city limits.

Farmers converted non-functioning automobiles into worthwhile transportation by removing the heavy engine and hitching a horse to the contraption. These were known as Hoover cars. Newspapers covering homeless people sleeping on park benches became Hooverblankets.

1931 was an utterly disastrous year for the economy and the entire nation. Joblessness grew with every month- bank failures kept pace and every aspect of the financial system would continue to sink. Finally, as the last page of the calendar for the year was removed, 1932 arrived and it with the November election process began.

Both parties would meet in Chicago, only a week apart. The Republican Convention was dull, even dispirited. Will Rogers, the famous entertainer and wit, suggested the Republicans open up the churches in town "to liven the place up a bit." Hoover was renominated with no opposition and no enthusiasm.

The Democrats arrived in town the following week and provided a spirited contrast to the previous group. Franklin Delano Roosevelt was the favorite, but because the nominee had to have a two-thirds majority of the delegates, he needed four ballots to pull off the victory. One of the key planks on their platform was the removal of the hated Smoot-Hawley tariff.

The Democratic nominee bore a physical handicap of frightening proportions – both legs had been completely paralyzed for 11 years, ever since had had contracted poliomyelitis in the summer of 1921.

In his acceptance speech he very confidently proclaimed to the delegates, "I pledge you, I pledge myself, to a new deal for the American people." That expression, "new deal," would describe his platform and his Congressional program and still to this day identifies FDR with what he accomplished in the first year of his administration. Then he would exhort the delegates, "This is more than a political campaign; it is a call to arms. Give me your help, not to win votes alone, but to win in this crusade to restore America to its own people."

He very emphatically told his audience that the federal government had "a continuing responsibility for the broader public welfare." This was clearly an evocation of Abe Lincoln's deathless maxim about government's legitimate object in providing assistance to the people in time of need.

Both the Democratic Party and their standard bearer demanded repeal of the 18th Amendment, that dastardly Prohibition. Aid to the stricken agricultural sector was called for as was unemployment and old age assistance; a shorter hour work week was sought. Federal regulation of securities such as stocks and bonds was demanded.

Each of these considerations was regarded by Hoover and his RRRs as an absolute abomination. In a nominating speech for Hoover, he was warmly praised "as the man who taught the nation to resist the temptation of government paternalism." Tariffs were still viewed as a blessing to be preserved.

On the campaign trail FDR was most insistent in his demand for a new order. "A government that could not care for its old and sick, that could not provide work for the strong, that fed its youth into the hopper of industry, and that let the black shadow of insecurity rest on every home was not a government that could or should endure." He continued in a more strident vein, "Any business unable to make a fair return except by child labor, long hours, dog's wages, lying and cheating was not a business that the country wanted."

A listener to that pleasing pronouncement could not fail to construe the precise meaning of those words; no misinterpretation was possible. Abraham Lincoln would have beamed with pleasure; Theodore Roosevelt would have been delighted.

But for the six or seven other Republican Presidents ending with Hoover, those words would have caused inner turmoil; they represented a repudiation of everything the Republican Party stood for.

Considering his disability, FDR conducted an astonishing campaign, speaking 60 times in every portion of the country. Hoover limited his addresses to 10. Where the Democratic nominee was met with amazingly large, friendly audiences, Hoover most always encountered ominously quiet, smaller groups. Frequently boos rang out. It was not unknown for a rotten egg or an overly ripe tomato to be hurled his way.

Yet he would tear into his rival, shamelessly assailing him for advocating a program, "that was the same philosophy of government which has poisoned all Europe, the fumes of the witch's cauldron which boiled in Russia." It was painfully obvious he considered FDR not only immoral but a malevolent Communist to boot. By electing that man and removing the high tariffs which the Republicans worshipped, Hoover would prophesize, "the grass will grow in the streets of a hundred cities, a thousand towns; the weeds will overrun the fields of millions of farms."

On several occasions since then I have heard Republicans predict the grass and weeds routine, but in spite of their ominous warnings, neither the grass or the weeds ever developed. In 1993 when newly elected President Bill Clinton advocated his tax increase for the upper one-and-a-half percent of taxpayers, Representative Dick Armey reechoed Hoover's words. Armey was another vacuous Texan who, together with every Republican in Congress voted against the bill. Passage of the legislation resulted in the greatest expansion of the economy ever seen in our history, an expansion that lasted for the full eight years of the Clinton Administration. Subsequently Armey's wife would be paid $300,000 by Ken Lay's Enron Corporation at a time when mountainous debt was piling up and bankruptcy for the infamous company was imminent. At the time Armey was the number two man in the House hierarchy. What was Mrs. Armey paid for? Well, it appears largely for being Mrs. Armey.

Up until election day, Hoover would assert that only an experienced old hand like himself should be at the tiller to guide the ship of state and that it would be supreme folly to turn control of the government over to a relative neophyte like Roosevelt. Of course, by election day the experienced old hand had permitted the entire banking system in the nation to plummet in collapse. In 1932 there were still only 48 states, all in the lower 48 as the humorous statement defined it. Already 38 governors had completely shut down the banking system in their respective states. Pitifully few banks remained open anywhere in our country.

How was Hoover coping with the problem? In the identical manner with which he dealt with all the other matters of grave concern, he did nothing! Of course in one vital area the Republicans were exceedingly active. They began spreading rumors that the Roosevelt family name was actually Rosenfelt, a Jewish name. FDR's physical condition wasn't caused by polio – no his malady was syphilis. It escaped these spreaders of vicious rumors that in the entire history of syphilis it had never caused paralysis.

One last item must be related. Shortly before the election, Hoover was in Charleston, West Virginia, dedicating a memorial. The usual 21 gun salute was fired. After the smoke drifted away from the scene, and as Hoover was standing there gazing at the memorial, one elderly man was heard to exclaim in disappointment, "by gum, they missed him."

CHAPTER XVII

On an unusually bright, sunny day for that early in the year, Franklin Delano Roosevelt was sworn into office on March 4, 1933. In his inaugural address he proclaimed, "This is preeminently the time to speak the truth, the whole truth, frankly and boldly. This great nation will endure as it has endured, will revive and prosper. So, first of all, let me assert my belief that the only thing we have to fear, is fear itself – nameless, unreasoning, unjustified terror which paralyzes needed efforts to convert retreat into advance." His voice then took on a grim, hard edge as he proceeded. "Plenty is at our doorstep, but a generous use of it languishes in the very sight of the supply. Primarily this is because rulers of the exchange of mankind's good, having failed through their stubbornness and their own incompetence, have admitted their failure, and have abdicated…the money changers have fled from their high seats in the temple of our civilization."

In the week following this astonishing address, over 450,000 Americans wrote to him. The mail room would soon need 75 full-time workers to process this deluge. Hoover's mailroom required but one person. In their new president the people quickly realized they now had a leader, one who was brimming with optimism. On Sunday, the very next day, he issued two presidential edicts. One called Congress into session on the coming Thursday, and the other declared a bank holiday wherein every bank in the nation would close. Almost all of them had already closed.

During the four day interim some of the men working on the banking bill were from Hoover's cabinet. Both his Secretary of the Treasury, Ogden Mills, and the Under Secretary, Arthur Ballantine, played principal roles in formulating this vital bill. When presented to the House of Representatives it passed by voice vote unanimously. That same day the Senate adopted it completely unchanged; by evening the new President signed it. Its official title was the Emergency Banking Relief Act which enabled the government to issue more currency and to assist insolvent banks.

Why hadn't Hoover done that weeks or months earlier? Why, that would have been governmental intrusion on the sacred province of private enterprise.

The previous morning on March 8, FDR conducted his first press conference. He gathered around him an estimated 125 reporters in the Oval Office. He quietly informed them he would like to do this twice a week and they should feel free to ask any questions of him. In doing so he established a compelling difference between himself and his Republican predecessor who had insisted that questions be submitted in writing, in advance. Hoover had been aloof and nearly disdainful of the reporters.

Instead FDR was treating them like friends, calling many of them by their first names. He had grown familiar with them from his four years as Governor of New York. For the next 45 minutes he would joke with them, even engage in good natured teasing.

Immediately a firm bond of affection was established with the reporters, a virtual love affair, that would last for the entirety of his 12 years in office. During that entire period not one photo ever revealed to the public his terrible physical handicap. On one occasion a press photographer, new to this assignment, snapped a picture of FDR which revealed his paralysis. Quickly his camera was seized by others of the press, the film removed and promptly destroyed. The culprit learned his lesson. FDR's handicap would remain un-photographed.

The new President would soon deliver the first of several dozen of what came to be known as Fireside Chats. It would be broadcast at 10:00 p.m. Eastern Standard Time, on Sunday, March 12th. That time had been carefully selected to draw the largest listening audience and have the maximum impact across the nation's four time zones. FDR had been the first politician of note to use the relatively new medium of radio to speak to his constituency, initiating the practice as Governor of New York. It proved to be an unbelievably effective means to rally support from the public for his proposed legislation in the face of a reluctant legislature. It worked brilliantly, chiefly because of the sterling quality of his voice, which reflected the tone of a Harvard educated patrician. But instead of that being a detriment it had a positive effect. His manner of expression conveyed a captivating intimacy, a nearly caressive appeal.

George W. Bush attended Harvard for two years but nobody, not even Laura or Barbara, has ever detected the faintest wisp of a patrician tone or an expression of captivating intimacy. His delivery is more reflective of Midland and Crawford, Texas. When he is remembered at Harvard it is more for the cowboy boots and the chewing tobacco. Somehow the image of Franklin Delano Roosevelt with a mouthful of chewing tobacco is too difficult to conjure up.

There were upwards of 60,000,000 listeners tuned into the radio that night to hear their new president; that represented nearly half the nation. He began to speak to that audience in a pleasing, reassuring manner. "I want to talk for a few minutes with the people of the United States about banking. I want to tell you what has been done in the last few days, why it was done and what the next steps are going to be." He urged listeners to deposit their cash in the bank, where it now would be safe, rather than hiding it under the mattress. "Let us unite in banishing fear," he pleaded. "We have provided the machinery to restore our financial system; it is up to you to support and make it work. It is your problem no less than it is mine. Together we cannot fail." No other president in our history had ever done anything remotely similar.

The next day, following his 15 minute conversation with the American people, banks in the 12 Federal Reserve Bank cities reopened their doors. One day later all banks in cities with clearing houses opened. The effect upon the nation was beyond expectation. Within 10 days since FDR took office, the spirit of the country had undergone a bewildering change of attitude. Deep despondency had been replaced with hope and expectation. By the end of March, 12,500 of the nation's 17,800 banks were doing business as usual. Nevertheless, a few thousand were completely liquidated.

March 22nd would bring another popular victory to the President. Congress overwhelmingly passed the Beer and Wine Act, which partially nullified the hated Volstead Act of 1919 and which now allowed the sale of beer and wine. By year's end, Prohibition would be history, with the passing of the twenty-first Amendment, permitting the sale of all types of alcohol. By first allowing beer and wine to be sold, badly needed tax revenues were raised, thus mollifying some of the die-hard drys.

FDR would have little difficulty in obtaining passage of legislative bills his administration sent to Congress. When in November he was elected by a 7,000,000 vote margin his coattails brought into the Senate 59 Democrats with only 36 Republicans. In the House the division was even more pronounced – 313 of his party and a mere 117 Republicans.

Moving along at breakneck speed Congress next passed one of his pet projects, the Civilian Conservation Corps, soon called the Cs. This nation rarely received as great a return on its minute investment as it reaped from that monumental project. Just as fast as barracks could be assembled, 250,000 unmarried, unemployed young men were put to work in the nation's forests, lands which had been so neglected, and so abused for so long. The volunteers were paid $30.00 a month, of which $25.00 had to be sent home to their families. That $25.00 was a positive bonanza for starving families living in squalor.

Within our forests huge swaths of trees had been clear-cut, leaving nothing standing. This was common practice of greedy, thoughtless lumbermen interested only in large profits but leaving behind barren ground, ripe for massive soil erosion and ruinous flooding.

The new recruits, many of them big city kids, set about planting trees, called saplings, by the thousands, then the millions, finally the tens of millions in total.

To control forest fires in the uncut areas, they built fire-breaks and lookout towers. Desperately needed bridges were constructed. They ventured into beautification programs by erecting campgrounds and nature trails.

Over its complete tenure, the Cs employed an estimated three million unemployed young men; it went out of business early in 1942 after our nation found itself at war with both Germany and Japan.

Beginning with the Japanese attack on Pearl Harbor on December 7, 1941, the Civilian Conservation Corps served as an outstanding recruitment program for the armed forces. It would prove to be an agency of overwhelming popularity and a tribute to the prolific imagination of FDR. Herbert Hoover, as might be expected, viewed it in unreserved disdain.

Congress, together with the entire Roosevelt Administration, worked feverishly during the first three months in session. On May 12, two legislative acts of startling importance were passed. The first, the Agricultural Adjustment Act, the AAA, would provide the outline for federal farm policy for the balance of the century. In the words of Raymond Moley, one of FDR's closest advisors in the early days, the Act "was the revolutionary assumption of public responsibility for the economic well-being of the thirty million farmers and dependents of the nation."

Farms were being repossessed by banks and mortgage companies at a fearful rate and this Act would slow down or even halt the process.

Its twin legislative Act was the Federal Emergency Relief Act (FERA) which provided for a half-a-billion dollars to be distributed around the states, so that they, rather than the federal government could tackle work programs for the unemployed. Bear in mind that in 1933 there were at least 15 million men out of work.

FDR did not lack for critics. Typical of them was Simeon D. Fess, a Senator from Ohio. He could hardly find "parliamentary language to describe the statement that the States and cities cannot take care of conditions in which they find themselves but must come to the federal government for aid." Simple Simeon obviously overlooked the fact that with little exception the States and cities were themselves bankrupt and hardly in a position to help anybody.

Confronting the Depression head-on, FDR chose next to introduce to Congress the Tennessee Valley Authority, the TVA. It passed in record time and with it followed a prodigious program of dam building, along with hydroelectric generating stations, and attendant flood control projects. Its jurisdiction was not limited to the Tennessee River and its feeder streams, but to the entire drainage basis of that river.

That encompassed parts of seven states; Alabama, Georgia, Kentucky, Mississippi, North Carolina, Tennessee and Virginia. It must be emphasized that those seven states were among the most destitute in the nation. They had the lowest per capita income, a poverty rate of staggering proportion, and health conditions that were a national calamity. Malnutrition was prevalent throughout the region. Accompanying that condition were dietary scourges such as pellagra and rickets. Malaria and meningitis, both often fatal were widespread and were the result of the swarms of mosquitoes in the warm weather months.

Education ranged from lamentable to non-existent. By 1933 many of the rural elementary schools had folded from lack of pay for the teachers. Entire towns were bankrupt. The wide, rapidly coursing Tennessee River frequently overflowed its banks causing widespread death and destruction. The TVA would shortly control that problem forever. In this seven state region not even one percent of farms had electricity. Again, the lowest in the nation.

Utility company executives were enraged at this radical approach to electricity production. They tongue-lashed FDR and his administration for invoking this dastardly state socialism, and venturing from the path of honorable *laissez-faire* economics.

The TVA did much more than produce cheap electricity; a 650 mile navigation channel was dug to facilitate increased river traffic. Doing so made the Tennessee River completely navigable. The cheap electricity that readily became available was a monumental incentive for new industrial development.

As each dam was finished, and there were more than 50 of them, a lake of imposing dimensions formed behind it from the impounded water. Some of those lakes grew to spectacular size. An impressive mosquito eradication program was soon in place and with it the malaria and meningitis threat disappeared.

None of this would have been completed, much less even contemplated by local utility company executives.

Earlier we touched ever so briefly on the Manhattan Project whose near term goal was to produce Uranium-235, which the scientists concluded was the fissionable component of the bomb. It had to be separated from its natural and more abundant companion, Uranium-238 and could be done only by extraordinary difficult physical methods. This diffusion method needed a huge, complex facility which in turn demanded an inordinate amount of cheap electricity. Soon that triumph of design and construction came into being; it was called Oak Ridge conveniently close to the Tennessee River.

Could private industry have furnished this super abundant, cheap electricity? Shit, they couldn't even provide a few cheap kilowatts for the nearby farmers.

What's truly frightening about the Manhattan Project is how totally unlikely it would even have been envisioned, much less funded, much less brought to fruition without the prolific imagination of Franklin Delano Roosevelt. When the concept of an atom bomb was first presented to him, no appreciable form of atomic energy existed anywhere on the planet! Starting from that position, the idea of assembling a nuclear device was way, way out there in the wild blue yonder.

The first sketchy outline of the atom bomb was undertaken when Albert Einstein addressed a letter to the President suggesting the possibility of such a device being completed. Mr. Einstein was probably the most famous nuclear scientist in the United States and had been forced to flee the Nazis who had already begun their infamous and murderous campaign against the Jews.

The letter was delivered in person to the President by two highly qualified scientific figures. FDR readily grasped the fantastic potential of this weapon and appointed an advisory committee on Uranium. By June of 1941 the project gathered additional momentum when the Office of Scientific Research and Development was established.

Our entry into the war in December of that year stimulated still more forward movement and unleashed a torrent of funds for the orderly achievement of the plan. The pilot plant at Oak Ridge was built and energetically expanded. Mountainous problems confronted the scientists and the engineers at every turn. The President never faltered in his determination to see the project through to fruition.

It's sad to say he never lived to see the results of his fertile imagination and driving energy. He died of a massive cerebral hemorrhage on April 12, 1945. His vice-president, Harry Truman, would authorize delivery of the ultimate military weapon over Hiroshima on August 6th.

Could any of the Republican presidents or presidential aspirants of that era had sufficient imagination or determination, which FDR possessed in abundance, to start and complete a plan of that bewildering complexity? Let's pass them in review. How about Harding? Enlightened know-nothings likely were more competent. What about Coolidge? Much smarter than Harding, but still several levels below FDR. OK, let's consider Herbert Hoover. Hoover was a well-qualified mining engineer but to suggest he would have allocated more than a moment of his time exceeds probability. Besides, he was a Quaker, a total pacifist.

Let's try Alfred Landon, the Republican nominee in 1936. Landon was a progressive Governor of Kansas and had belonged to Theodore Roosevelt's Bull Moose Party in 1912, but he quickly reverted to more conventional Republican politics. Not too long after the campaign ended he became deeply embroiled in the America First movement.

The organization's principal goal, indeed its sole reason for existence, was to frustrate FDR in his valiant effort to rebuild the country's sadly deficient armed forces. This organization was tragically slow to realize how unprepared the country was for a conflict with any foreign power. In only a few years two extremely well prepared nations, Germany and Japan, *would declare war on us*. Only then would the America First organization cease its opposition to rearmament and slink from public awareness.

TVA was the opening act of a nationwide public power program that expanded into the Rural Electrification Administration, the REA. This program did more than any government action to change the nation's rural life. By 1950, nine farms out of 10 not only had electricity, but had it in abundance and at cheap rates.

Next up on the legislative agenda was the Federal Securities Act. For the first time in the nation's history, stock and bond sales were to be regulated; full disclosure of important information about the securities were required. No longer was the credo, "let the buyer beware" be the sole criterion in place. From now on it was also, "let the seller beware." In the following year the Act would become considerably strengthened under the Securities Exchange Act, the SEC, which is still in place today. Under this new, harsher law, the seller of bogus stocks could easily exchange his position in society for a prison cell.

Two very important bills were passed on June 16, the day Congress adjourned, after being in session exactly 100 days. That preliminary session of the new Congress is celebrated even today as "The First Hundred Days" and it enacted a torrent of vital legislation the likes of which this nation had never seen. The Glass-Steagall Act was passed first; it created the FDIC, the Federal Deposit Insurance Corporation which guaranteed the safety of bank deposits placed in banks offering that protection.

Since that legislation was passed a few banks might have closed their doors in bankruptcy, but not a single depositor would lose so much as a dollar. I should point out it initially covered only the first $5,000. Today it guarantees the first $100,000 and it has never cost the taxpayers a penny; the insurance part of the Act is payed by the banks.

In the opinion of the Roosevelt Administration, the prime piece of legislation of the first 100 days was the Act which established the NRA, the National Recovery Administration. The NRA would put in place codes that fixed the maximum hours that could be worked by day, or by week, plus the minimum wages that must be paid, industry by industry.

One of its key provisions was the elimination of child labor, the use of which was so beloved of Big Business. My abhorrence of child labor is exceeded only by my loathing of slavery. The 11 states of the Confederacy were forced to abolish that insufferable institution only at the point of a bayonet. The Big Depression was a fact of business life nearly as compelling as the point of a bayonet, so business and industry most grudgingly assented to the direction of the NRA and agreed to forsake child labor.

An additional ingredient in the NRA was a provision to fund the Public Works Administration, the PWA, with a $3.3 billion allotment to pump up the economy across every region in America. Beside the PWA, there were several other manifestations, such as the WPA, Works Progress Administration, and the CWA, Civilian Works Administration. While reactionary critics like Hoover mercilessly derided FDR's effort to feed starving men and their families, these various agencies provided the money and the expertise to complete upwards of 30,000 projects nationwide.

Hundreds of post offices were built as were desperately needed bridges in rural areas. Airports popped up across the land, thanks to the largesse of the federal government. So did sewer plants and other additions of consequence, including jails, railroad stations, city halls, even playgrounds for children. Innumerable hospitals in small communities were erected. The little town in Wisconsin where I grew up owed its hospital to one of these agencies.

Most of the communities where these projects were completed were destitute by 1933. Many of them couldn't even afford to pay its teachers; some even closed their schools. St. Petersburg, Florida, where I spent more than four decades, lacked the means to pay its employees in cash and so resorted to script. Local merchants accepted this paper, but only after discounting it to a considerable degree. From a strict fiscal standpoint, the script was worthless paper money.

It is highly likely that no less than 25% of the overall population came to benefit from these activities. For each person receiving a pay check, several more received aid.

The vultures on the far right, the trickle-down economy types, viewed these projects with scarcely concealed malice. The fact that millions of Americans were either suffering from malnutrition or nearing starvation meant not a thing to them. The belief was firmly embedded in their thought processes that the needy, whether they were newly begotten poor, or had long been poor, were themselves responsible for their precarious situation; in some arcane manner poor people became transgressors against the social order. As such they had no right to seek alms from the public purse.

Some of the more vehement protesters were nearly incoherent with rage at the thought of the moral fiber of the nation disintegrating in this wave of creeping socialism.

Herbert Hoover was typical of that designation. With his goodness gland desiccated beyond revival, a heart frozen into glacial insensitivity, and a social conscience long since fled, he constituted the very determined opposition to *everything* the New Deal was striving to put into practice.

How did the Rotten Reactionary Republicans arrive at the conviction *they* were entitled to complete dominance in a far rightwing regime? It certainly wasn't from the founding fathers or the priceless document they produced. Consider Gouvenor Morris, a delegate from New York to the Constitutional Convention in 1787. He was one of the most conservative members of that body but yet warned that if left unchecked, the rich would exploit the poor; hence restrictions must be written into the Constitution. Otherwise he predicted, the rich and powerful would almost surely saddle this land with an undemocratic tyrannical regime.

Since George Washington assumed office in 1789 until Herbert Hoover surrendered that office in 1933, 144 years had passed; realistically speaking that was the condition of the government, a conclusion that FDR had arrived at when he took over the stricken government.

After Congress had adjourned following its epochal first Hundred Days, the mood of the country was improved to an almost unimaginable degree. Federally funded projects were underway or about to begin in every corner of the land. The banking system was functioning at a higher level than ever seen before, particularly now that deposits were guaranteed by the federal government. Even in good years during the Twenties, on average about 500 banks would fail. That nightmare would never take place again. Thanks to FDR and the New Deal the people throughout the nation had reasonably full bellies again. Still all the calamitous residue of the Depression would be impossible to eradicate until well into 1939.

The First Hundred Days amounted to governmental interference on an unprecedented scale. The country required strong medicine, a purgative, to purge it of the poison of trickle-down economics. According to the RRRs, this was rampant socialism which would destroy the very fabric of our society.

Nonetheless, he had pulled off this seeming miracle of rescuing the nation from the effects of the catastrophe that had befallen it. Because of the skills he had gained while governing New York, plus his unrivaled talents, plus his unshakeable faith that he could move the country to safe ground, the economy was on more certain footing. This in itself was a victory beyond compare. Certainly no other politician in America could have pulled this off. But considering that he had been the victim of a bitterly cruel affliction, the total paralysis of his legs, the triumph was all the more priceless. What many of his closest advisers came to believe was that the paralysis had defined his character.

Spending years overcoming this frightful burden added immeasurably to his abundance of toughness, inspired his infectious optimism and stiffened his refusal to accept defeat. It infused him with limitless quantities of hope which he in turn could transmit to his associates and then to the entire country.

His trial by fire, as his wife Eleanor characterized his bout with polio, transformed his personality. "Anyone who has gone through great suffering," she commented, "is bound to have a greater empathy and understanding of the problems of mankind." After this hideous trial was completed, he lost much of his arrogance and smugness. He would instead become far more focused, more complex and much more interesting. As a direct result of his rendezvous with disaster he evolved into what his biographers believe was the most enlightened politician of the 20th century and easily our greatest president, surpassing the beloved Abraham Lincoln.,

FDR in 1928 was most assuredly a beneficiary of benign fortune. In that year, against all his wishes and contrary to his instincts, he became the Democratic candidate for Governor of New York. He and his close advisor and confidant, Louis Howe, were utterly convinced that it would be a year of Republican conquest and so were reluctant to run a race bound to be a loser. The outgoing governor, Al Smith, was now the Democratic nominee for the Presidency, and was unrelenting in his insistence that Franklin enter the race. FDR continued to demur but eventually was forced to accept the challenge.

Even though Hoover would sweep into the White House by a landslide and carry New York State by 100,000 votes, FDR would eke out a slender victory by only 25,000 votes. He had pulled this off despite his grievous handicap. No other polio victim had ever won high office before. He overcame this formidable barrier by using the automobile for traveling around the state and politicking hard, day after day. Each step he took was painful and amounted to a test of endurance.

As a new governor two very discernable differences could be observed that distinguished him from his fellow governors or from any president to that time. One was his considerable reliance on women, not merely for clerical help, but for serious consultation and even elevating to high office in his administration. He immediately appointed Frances Perkins as a state labor commissioner.

Early on in his new office, he urged the establishment of an unemployment insurance program for workers, pointing out how unfair it was for them to be faced with financial insecurity. Two other women who would play important roles in both Albany and Washington were Grace Tully and Marguerite LeHand. Additionally then he had the extraordinary wise counsel of his wife, Eleanor, whose opinion carried an enormous amount of weight.

Totally unprecedented would be the astonishing number of Jews he turned to for assistance: Adolph Berle, Felix Frankfurter, Max Lowenthal, Bernard Baruch, Henry Morgenthau and Sam Rosenman. They were differentiated by being nationally known college professors, some were influential businessmen, others merely possessed distinguishing qualities. *All served without pay.* These factors placed them in painful juxtaposition to the contemptible party hacks appointed by the current occupant of the White House who dredges up men from nowhere, selected solely on the basis of their personal loyalty to him and who earn a trifling $125,000 a year or more. One's thoughts quickly stray to men appointed to run FEMA who lacked a single qualifying trait. One thinks also of individual lobbyists appointed to police that same industry and who badly need policing themselves.

It is utterly unthinkable to consider Harding, Coolidge or Hoover ever having even one Jew in an important position. Hoover, remember, relied exclusively on wealthy white males for his Cabinet. Once FDR was in the White House he would appoint still more Jews. It must be noted that his Republican critics, always gentlemanly patriots, would refer to his New Deal as the Jew Deal and as we have noticed insist that his family name was Rosenfelt and of course that his paralysis was really caused by syphilis.

Franklin was the first, and the only governor, to demand aid from the state legislature for the growing number of destitute unemployed. He told his largely conservative legislature that "the duty of the State toward the citizen is the duty of the servant to its master. The people have created it; the people by common consent permit its continual existence. One of these duties of the State is that of caring for those of its citizens who find themselves the victims of such adverse circumstances as make them unable to obtain even the necessities for mere existence without the aid of others. To these unfortunate citizens aid must be extended by government – *not as a matter of charity but as a matter of social duty.*"

The New York Legislature passed TERA, the Temporary Emergency Relief Administration, a precursor to near identical agencies he would introduce to the nation as president. Quickly he would discover Harry Hopkins, who would run the agency. Hopkins would evolve into FDR's most important presidential advisor and head up huge relief agencies while continuing to be the President's personal emissary to Prime Minister Winston Churchill of England and Josef Stalin, dictator of Russia.

Hopkins would hastily establish a plan to put to work over 10,000 youths in a program of soil conservation, tree planting and erosion control. Soon, this became one of the new governor's personal favorites and led him to introduce an identical bill in Congress, the Civilian Conservation Corps. It was one of the very first adopted by Congress and proved to be wildly successful.

In June of 1930 he would address the Governor's Conference in Salt Lake City where he would enthusiastically recommend to his fellow governors that they advance some form of unemployment insurance as was just passed in New York. Tragically almost nothing of its like was done. By 1933 most of the states were approaching bankruptcy and would be unable to assist their work force. Only the federal government could now do so.

It strains the imagination to the breaking point to believe he could have put in place the New Deal so quickly, so efficiently, without his apprenticeship in New York. Sam Rosenman, one of his most trusted aides in both Albany and Washington, made this observation. "In those messages and speeches from 1929 through 1932, you will find proposals for appropriate state actions in the same fields in which he later urged action by Congress: minimum wages and maximum hours, old-age insurance, unemployment relief through public works, regulation of public utilities and strict regulation of the banks."

It's pleasant to indulge in a phantasy of a meeting between Abraham Lincoln and FDR. Both were immensely likeable men. Lincoln doubtless possessed a superior brain but would have recognized in his companion a near twin. Both were polished raconteurs.

As presidents they were unmatched at negotiation and compromise; each would recognize in the other an accomplished administrator.

Would they have liked each other? I really believe so. Both were beaming optimists who radiated confidence. Both would have made each other laugh at their splendid anecdotes.

CHAPTER XVIII

Legislation passed in the famous First Hundred Days would leave its imperishable mark on the economy and on the nation. Many bright young men would stream into Washington looking to attach themselves to the New Deal. Many were from the most elite universities in the land. Others were on the faculty of less prestigious state colleges. Law professors were fairly common. Possessed as they were of a high degree of energy and enthusiasm for the task at hand, their dedication and sincerity was compelling. There were no industry lobbyists or campaign hacks amidst their ranks.

Reviewing the achievements of the First Hundred Days we first consider the NRA, The National Recovery Administration, whose most important goal was to revitalize the nation's economy, much of which was nearly comatose. It provided immediate employment for over two million workers, who according to Hoover's philosophy immediately became 'mendacious parasites'. The overwhelming bulk of these were of course parents striving desperately to feed and clothe a new generation of m.p.'s

Many of that new generation would, within not too many years, become members of our Armed Forces. Meanwhile Hoover, naturally enough, was laboring heroically through his peace-loving group, to deprive the Armed Forces of the funds to become combat worthy. It all made a great deal of sense to Herbert Hoover.

The NRA tried valiantly to end the downward spiral of deflation which was killing the farm belt and crippling business activity nationwide. To a considerable degree it succeeded. The NRA also attempted to improve business ethics as much as possible. In this effort it largely failed. Too much of American industry was mired in an unethical ethos. This New Deal agency effectively wiped out child labor, a loving source of fat profits for so many businessmen, most emphatically in the South.

After the First Hundred Days there was no question that FDR and the New Deal had not only saved this country from anarchy but positioned it on the road to recovery, however tenuous that path might be. The flood of legislation that had been enacted was nothing less than an economic, political and social revolution, absolutely unlike anything ever seen in this land previously. Unlike the French Revolution at the close of the 18th Century and the Russian Revolution early in the 20th Century, this upheaval in the United States was legislated into law with a total lack of bloodshed.

Nowhere had a guillotine been put to use as had been thousands of times in Paris and elsewhere in France. No shots had been fired by the all-powerful

Democrats, not a one. Contrast that with the wholesale executions by the Bolsheviks in Russia.

Mr. Roosevelt went to enormous lengths to cooperate with American business and to treat fiscal and industrial owners as allies. He abhorred any conflict with them. For example the NRA attempted to put into practice codes designed to produce more competition but in the process utilize collective bargaining and affect a shorter working week.

Some industries forced their employees to work a 60 or even a 70 hour week. Along with the shorter week the codes demanded more equitable minimum wages instead of the nickels and dimes per hour. These codes were still quite favorable to business, much more so than many of his Cabinet or advisory staff approved.

Far from agreeing with these modest proposals, much of big business protested vehemently, and saw in them attempts to introduce socialism, or even worse, communism. Whereas entire swaths of Americans looked upon their new president in a highly favorable light, even as a benign visionary, altogether too much of the business community regarded him as evil personified.

The history of strife between labor and industry in this country was often one of violence and spilled blood. The murder of labor organizers was commonplace, most particularly in the South. Governors would call out their National Guard units to suppress any hint of a strike, or even a picket line. The local police departments or sheriff's offices didn't hesitate at times to fire into a group of unarmed and peaceful pickets. The District Attorney in Johnstown, Pennsylvania, was quoted as saying, "Give me two hundred good, tough, armed men and I'll clean them sons-of-bitches on the picket line." The two hundred good, tough, armed men of course would be mostly criminals or worthless thugs, not family men trying to make a decent living.

The industry publication, *Fiber and Fabric*, religiously read among owners of textile sweatshops offered this editorial. "A few hundred funerals will have a quieting effect." Adolph Hitler was employing similar tactics on labor leaders in Nazi Germany, either that or tossing them into concentration camps. Both of these quotes reflected one of Calvin Coolidge's famous precepts. "The man who builds a factory, builds a temple; the man who works there, worships there."

FDR was most assuredly one of our most perceptive chief executives, so he soon came to realize that in the business community he did not have an equitable partner. Many members of his Administration were quick to point out to him that this supposedly reliable associate was not interested in the welfare of the nation; no, solely on their own profit margins. Business demanded that it be shielded from any invasions by progressive legislation or what it viewed as "social experimentation."

FDR would briefly allude to this subject in his next press conference. Business finally agreed to proscribe child labor, which after all, was only slightly less execrable than slavery and it voluntarily surrendered some ground in one or two other areas. Still he observed, "An organization that only advocates two or three out of the Ten Commandments may be a perfectly good organization, but it would have certain short comings in having failed to advocate the seven or eight other Commandments.

Many of his critics, chief among them Herbert Hoover, were savage in their denunciation of both him and his administration for causing a loss of freedom and liberty. This was strange language indeed pouring from the lips of such a pronounced failure as he represented. With the possible exception of Nixon no president evacuated the White House amid such a tidal wave of antipathy.

In another of his fireside chats, FDR would dispose of that issue with clarity and precision. "Theoretical die-hards will tell you of the loss of an individual liberty. Have you lost any of your rights or liberty or constitutional freedom of action and choice?" He would suggest that his millions of listeners review the Bill of Rights and then ask, "whether you personally have suffered the impairment of a single jot of these great assurances."

As 1934 approached, economic conditions, while still remarkably improved since March, remained forbidding and not too much had been accomplished toward ending the Depression. Only slight inroads had been made in the unemployment picture as upwards of 12 million workers were still without jobs. Farm prices remained resistant to increases. As a result the entire agrarian sector continued to look bleak. The New York Stock Exchange was scarcely bubbling over with delight.

The Big Depression had struck the nation with too much savagery for it to recover in such a short time. Big Business, having caused the Depression was supremely indifferent to the plight of the miserable millions of sufferers and made little or no effort to alleviate any suffering.

With 1934 now underway, and the economy remaining undernourished, the critics of the New Deal maintained their barrage of infamy against many of the programs being conducted in local communities. They loved to view them as boondoggles, despite the thrust of these efforts was to put food on the table and shoes on the feet of barefoot children. The idolaters of trickle-down economics dismissed this compassionate concept completely. While unquestionably there were numerous examples of workers idling away the hours performing chores of minimal value, federal agencies like the Public Works Administration were involved in hundreds of truly noteworthy undertakings.

One undertaking funded by the PWA, early in the FDR Administration, was priceless beyond compare. This involved smuggling enough money through the agency to construct two large, contemporary aircraft carriers, the Enterprise and the Yorktown. FDR had been the Assistant Secretary of the Navy during the Wilson administration where he came to realize how vital it was to have a strong, modern navy.

These two carriers played super heroic roles in defeating the naval forces of Japan at one of the most pivotal battles fought in WWII. This was the Battle of Midway, June 3-4-5, 1942, just under six months after Pearl Harbor. In it these two carriers sank all four of the Japanese carriers opposing us.

To place the event in its most charitable context, we were extraordinarily fortunate to win that battle. The Japanese had 10 large, formidable battleships; we had one, which was not as large or formidable as its opposite members. They had four carriers; we had three, one of which, the Yorktown, had suffered extensive structural damage three weeks earlier during the battle of the Coral Sea. The repairs required two months in dry dock. In our desperate circumstances, our repair crews did what they could in five days.

The strategy of the Japanese Commander, Admiral Isoroku Yamamoto, was to overcome the defenders at Midway Atoll and occupy the two small islands which made up the Atoll. By doing so he was convinced he would force the American Navy into battle when it attempted to recapture Midway. He was absolutely confident that he could then annihilate what was left of our fleet. At that point we would have virtually no naval forces left to continue the war; whereupon our government might easily decide to call off further conflict. Realistically his strategy was quite sound, at least on paper.

Two large problems existed which the admiral hadn't considered. Our naval intelligence had penetrated the Japanese naval code sufficiently to understand what the enemy was plotting. Next, the admiral didn't believe we had the means available to prevent his enormous strike and occupational forces from capturing Midway. He was certain our navy had lost two of its prized carriers at the Battle of the Coral Sea three weeks earlier. True, we had seen our carrier Lexington sunk, but the other, the Yorktown, remained afloat and as he would shortly discover, was still a powerful fighting machine.

That left us with three carriers waiting to spring the trap at Midway; the Yorktown, which the admiral believed sunk at Midway; the Enterprise; and finally the Hornet, which the admiral was convinced wasn't even in the area.

This carrier force had to possess superior battle tactics and a large measure of good fortune to stand any chance in the coming battle. In Admirals Chester Nimitz, the overall commander in the Pacific, and Raymond Spruance, in charge of the carrier group, we had on our side two gifted and daring leaders; in our navy pilots we had dozens of trained fliers who were more than willing to forfeit their lives. Tragically, many of them did in this battle.

The carriers Yorktown and Enterprise, their construction costs underwritten by PWA funds, and PWA a vision of Franklin Delano Roosevelt, turned all four of Yamamoto's carriers into flaming wrecks, three of them within a five minute span. The admiral, after this unseemly response on the part of the American Navy, was at first determined to continue with his plan to capture Midway. Upon further reflection it became apparent to him that his still formidable invasion fleet, now naked of any air protection, might also be at grave risk of joining his carriers on the ocean floor. Accordingly he rather ignominiously headed back to Japan.

This was only the first of what would prove to be a nearly unbroken string of defeats for the Japanese. Under the inspired guidance of President Roosevelt, the U.S Navy in the Pacific would be mightily enriched by a total of 38 carriers of different sizes and capabilities. Our combined air, army and naval forces would, in not too many months, smash whatever defensive forces the Japanese would present.

I find it instructive that in the 1932 election, 15,761,000 voters marked their ballot for Hoover. Al Smith in his futile race against Hoover four years earlier only garnered 15, 016,000 votes and that as a highly successful Governor of New York. Yet an entirely discredited candidate who seemingly could do nothing right, but did many things wrong, would net 750,000 more votes in his loss. Ethnicity, religion and rabid, unthinking partisanship would account for it.

It is highly probable that at least one-quarter of the nation's population in 1934 was either fully or partially reliant on the New Deal and its programs for survival. Naturally they not only were grateful but pleasantly disposed toward the President and his fellow Democrats. As election day approached, not much progress had been made in defeating the Depression. A like amount of progress had taken place in Europe. Still, the leaders of the Democratic Party viewed the election with more than a little apprehension, but they need not have worried. In this first test of the New Deal, voters added to the already generous majorities in Congress, the governors, and the state legislatures. In the House, their margin extended to 322 to only 103 for the Republicans. In the Senate the final count was 69 to 25 with two independents.

In the spring and summer of 1935 Congress would grapple with legislation having gigantic implications for tens of millions of Americans. On July fifth it presented FDR with the National Labor Relations Act, usually known as The Wagner Act named after the New York Senator who had shepherded it through Congress. The Act would establish a permanent board which would be given authority to hold elections about labor relations with businesses; it would also ensure that the business in question would not commit "unfair labor practices" such as firing workers involved in forming a labor union. The businesses were further enjoined from fostering phony employer-dominated company unions. The federal government now guaranteed that labor could hold collective bargaining campaigns and that a business had to recognize a union within its walls.

From this point forward no factory owner could call out the police, the sheriff's office or the National Guard to shoot at strikers or pickets in front of a plant. They could no longer obtain a court order, granted by a right-wing Republican judge to enjoin any gathering of workers seeking to improve working conditions or increase wages. At the very minimum this was a radical law and yet it whizzed through both houses of Congress.

In January 1935, FDR asked Congress to pass a law that was of vital importance to him and the nation – the first social security legislation. Throughout the country there existed a pent-up demand for old age pensions. The vote on the legislation was 371 – 33. The moment the bill passed the House every Republican, with one exception, voted to recommit the bill which was a strong indication they wanted no part of a Social Security Bill. Not a single Democrat joined them in that deeply disturbing action.

In June the Senate passed the bill but not before a typically worthless Republican whined, "Passing this measure will take all the romance out of life. We might as well take a child from the nursery, give him a nurse, and protect him from every experience that life affords." But, of course, stemming from a wealthy, white class that was exactly what his family had done for him. President Roosevelt, with great satisfaction, signed it on August 15.

For all the benefits it would bring to the working men and women, the bill was replete with gross inequalities and unfairness. Workers who were most in need of social security were denied it. These were domestic servants and farm workers. Realistically the federal government evaded all responsibility for its workers. In every country in Europe which had an old age pension program, the national government was entirely responsible for the funding.

In America the system was funded equally by employers and workers. Additionally, there was no provision for either sickness or job unemployment.

FDR justified it by announcing, "We put those payroll contributions there so as to give the contributors a legal, moral and political right to collect their pensions and their unemployment benefits. With those taxes in there, *no damn politician can ever scrap my social security program.*"

In this we see another area where his impressive prescience was on display. No damn politician attempted to tinker with it for over half-a-century, until the most reactionary president elected in the 20th century, MCI Reagan, attempted to do violence to it early in his tenure. Now Bummy Bush in 2005 made 60 visible efforts to rupture the formula, thereby staking out his claim to reactionary fame.

Mr. Roosevelt next made a most audacious move when he urged Congress to enact gift and inheritance taxes. He then made a much bolder request – a graduated income tax "on very great individual net income." In his message to Congress he wrote, "Our revenue laws have done little to prevent an unjust concentration of wealth and economic power. Inherited economic power is as inconsistent with the ideals of this generation as inherited political power was inconsistent with the ideals of the generation which established our government."

This tax, as presented to Congress, would dip rather deeply into the pockets of those with undue purchasing power, those who were FDR's most vociferous antagonists. Their cries of outrage were heard throughout the land. William Randolph Hearst, owner/publisher of a powerful chain of newspapers identified this new tax with blatant Communism. He demanded that his editors always describe the proposed tax as an effort to "Soak the Successful." Henceforth they were no longer to use the term "New Deal;" it now became the "Raw Deal." Also FDR was now to be called Stalin Delano Roosevelt.

En route to final passage the legislation was watered down extensively. Its final form did little to redistribute wealth; it raised an estimated $250,000,000, nowhere near what the administration wanted.

This second wave of corrective and progressive legislation came to be known as the Second Hundred Days. The economy which early in 1935 had surged forward slackened off to a disheartening degree toward the end of the year. But back it came in early 1936. FDR and his advisors came to view the political horizon with optimism. Starting in January the unemployment figure began a favorable decline, averaging 150,000 per month.

Accompanying this employment growth was a more robust farm economy where rural electrification had made serious inroads on the prevailing sense of despair and hopelessness. Farm wives were for the first time able to enjoy the luxury of an electric refrigerator or an electric stove. That minimized the constant drudgery of their previous life. Inexpensive automobiles were starting to replace the Hoovercars which had been so prevalent for so many years.

Business staged its own revival. Where it had rung up a net deficit of $2 billion in 1933 it now displayed a $5 billion profit in 1936. Over four million mortgages had been refinanced by the Home Owners' Loan Corporation, another example of unwarranted government intrusion in the private sector. Banks were staying afloat uniformly throughout the country and no depositors were losing any money.

The NRA, for all the merciless jibes it had endured, was successfully raising wages and measurably improving working conditions in factories. While it hadn't restored prosperity, it had reintroduced a sense of contentment in the country.

One family that was especially grateful was that of Jack Reagan in Dixon, Illinois. Jack headed up the local relief agency. It has since been well documented that each weekly paycheck received by Jack went a long way to ward off malnutrition and suffering for his family.

Nevertheless his son, Ronald, would spend eight years in the White House endlessly inveighing against the pernicious effects of the federal government interposing itself in local affairs. Previous to that period he had spent eight years as Governor of California trumpeting the same message; Government is the problem, not the solution.

I have long felt that Ronald Wilson Reagan was possessed of a bottomless well of ingratitude for all the federal government had done for his family, the people in Dixon, for the State of Illinois and finally for all the other states. His mindless message was — let no good deed go unpunished.

Because of FDR and his New Deal, newly formed labor organizations were growing at a pleasing rate. Chief among these was the CIO – the Congress of Industrial Organizations. It was energetically founding industry-wide unions, where none had ever taken hold, within such major units of industry as automobiles, steel, and tires. The Union members who had achieved much improved wages, shorter hours, and safer working conditions were only too happy to support the president. This meant a meaningful financial contribution for election costs; providing manpower to encourage voter participation.

FDR, without question the most innovative and resourceful politician-president ever, even unto this day, recognized the untapped value of ethnic and religious minorities. Before his first term was completed he had appointed 51 Catholics to the post of federal judges. Compare that to the miserly total of eight appointed by all three of his Republican predecessors. We have already seen how frequently he staffed his administration with the Jews. In the face of implacable and sometimes vicious opposition from Southern Democrats, he also included a sprinkling of young, educated Blacks to minor posts within his administration.

No other president had ever approached this level of non-WASP appointments. His cousin Theodore was the first president to appoint any non-WASPs and he did it on a minor scale. Woodrow Wilson increased the volume a bit. But President Roosevelt headed up a grand alliance of the previously neglected.

The 1936 GOP national convention was held early in June and selected with little fuss the two-time Governor of Kansas, Alfred Landon, known by his constituents as Alf. An immediate judgment of him would say he was infinitely superior to Harding, Coolidge or Hoover. Earlier in his life in 1912, Landon had joined Theodore Roosevelt's Progressive Party, and migrated back to safer Republican territory in 1916. In 1933 he was entirely willing to endorse the tenets of the New Deal because it was truly addressing the problems created by the Big Depression.

The party felt safe in selecting him because in both 1932 and 1934 he was one of only two Republican candidates for governor who escaped the wrath of the voters. His selection amounted to an overthrow of the old, reactionary types since he represented a compromise between the New Deal and the traditional Republicans. Its platform called for all the federal relief programs to be turned over to the states. This was nothing more than a rhetorical flourish since the states were hovering near bankruptcy and hardly willing to take on more debt.

The race would pit a relatively talented amateur in the ways of governance against a maestro of the political art.

In the speech given by the President on his acceptance of the nomination, he made a number of truly memorable statements. "Better the occasional fault of a Government that lives in a spirit of charity than the consistent omissions of a Government frozen in the ice of its own indifference." That sentence so beautifully demarcated the Liberal Democrat from a Herbert Hoover, a Ronald Reagan or a George Bush.

This would be followed by: "There is a mysterious cycle in human events. To some generations much is given. Of other generations much is expected. This generation of Americans has a rendezvous with destiny." I was only 13 at the time but his pronouncement made a decided impression on me. I felt the challenge he extended to be ever so exciting and alluring; to this day I remain astonished at how amazingly clairvoyant our President was.

As the campaign progressed the Landon forces unrealistically expected to profit from the Social Security issue. In some strange manner they convinced themselves that hostility to the program would increase as wage earners had to pay into their retirement program. Frequent radio commercials would point out menacingly that workmen would be given a number, and what was worse, made to wear an identification tag, as if that were a subversive Communist plot to ensnare them.

In mid election Mr. Roosevelt and his Congressional candidates were somewhat dismayed by the results of a poll conducted by Literary Digest, a well respected nationwide magazine. This was a survey taken only of people owning automobiles and telephones. Its conclusion was that Landon would carry 32 states with 370 electoral votes whereas the President's efforts would yield only 16 states with 161 votes.

On the night of October 31, before an overflow crowd at Madison Square Garden in New York City, FDR's favorite venue, he would counterattack with one of his most masterful speeches. The Garden was in active ferment with many horns and cowbells adding to the din. "Never before in all our history have these forces been so united against one candidate as they stand today. They are unanimous in their hate for me – and I welcome their hatred. I should like to have it said of my first administration, that in it the forces of selfishness and lust for power have met their match." He paused for effect and then his voice took on new power. "I should like to have it said of my second administration that in it these forces met their master." The wild cheering and noise making continued for a full hour after he departed.

The multitudes working for Landon and the executives associated with the Literary Digest discovered on election night that while a great many voters couldn't afford either a telephone or an automobile, they knew how to locate a voting booth. On election night President Franklin Delano Roosevelt piled up the greatest plurality ever recorded in a presidential election to that date – a victory margin of over 11 million votes. Landon carried rock-ribbed Vermont and Maine with a total of eight electoral votes while FDR came away with 523.

The Literary Digest quickly faded out of the business, selling what remained of its assets to Time Magazine. I have a slight confession to make. For a brief period when I was about 12 years old, in 1935, I peddled the Literary Digest for five cents a copy. Out of the five cents I could keep two cents. In those days an industrious lad didn't turn up his nose at two cents. But, like my parents, I was convinced President Roosevelt could do no wrong.

A final word needs to be said of Alfred Mossman Landon. He was a courageous advocate of civil liberties and had successfully battled the Ku Klux Klan in Kansas during the 1920s. He certainly would have represented an enormous improvement over the previous three Republican presidents, all advocates of trickle down economics. However, following the 1936 election, and as his status in the America First movement hardened to where he became a stout isolationist, Landon evolved into a less benign figure. With that Alf, his nickname, progressed to Alfalfa, which appeared to be one of the principal ingredients between his ears. The isolationists in The America First bunch advocated a program which would have done to the nation's defense what trickle down economics had done to the national economy. It merits repeating that the isolationists were almost exclusively Republican.

The rapidly developing threat of fascism in Germany was a major source of FDR's concern by the mid-1930s. He brought to the office of president a highly sophisticated knowledge of foreign affairs very likely greater than any chief executive even to this day. From his early childhood he had been reared in a cosmopolitan world, traveling frequently to Europe. With it came a considerable knowledge of both the French and German languages. He, along with his distant cousin, Theodore, had acquired an intuitive mastery of internationalism gained by both experience as well as personal observation. Both had been assistant Secretaries of Navy; both had served as governors of New York.

Attempting to compare Franklin Delano Roosevelt with the current occupant of the White House in this area is an exercise in total implausibility.

Adolph Hitler preceded the president into office by exactly thirty-three days. At nearly the same time as our new president was being inaugurated, the German people were conducting another election. Hitler, an extremely forceful and passionate speaker, made the most of the government owned radio network. Hitler convinced the nearly senile, 88 year old president of Germany, Paul Hindenburg, to issue a decree proscribing all civil rights. Hitler and his Nazi thugs now bludgeoned their way to total power.

It would be helpful to recall how William Shirer, in his magnificent book, *"The Rise and Fall of the Third Reich,"* described the Nazis. "A conglomeration of pimps, murderers, homosexuals, alcoholics and blackmailers who flocked to the party."

Hitler and his Nazi hordes now began a savage campaign of arrests, beatings and torture. Those tactics were accompanied by the introduction of numerous concentration camps sprinkled around Germany. With their majority in the Reichstag, all legislative authority was concentrated in their iconic leader, Der Fuehrer. They immediately became the only legal party in Germany, outlawing their rival groups. The German people, with a considerable assist from the Nazis, had bartered away their freedom for jobs and security. There would be no elections and no more freedom in Germany for 12 long years, until Hitler shot himself and the Nazi movement was crushed.

FDR had an impressive ability to peer far into the future and make forecasts with uncanny accuracy. It took him preciously little time after he assumed office to realize that the Democratic nations in Europe and the New World would have extreme difficulty living in harmony with Hitler and Nazi Germany. He also realized how citizens of this country looked upon WWI as a bloody, expensive and foolhardy venture into European politics. They most emphatically disavowed any further interest in that continent.

The president's efforts to drag and push this country into a meaningful rearmament program before we might be assailed by the fascist regimes in Europe were met not only with resistance but strident alarm. Our army was rated as low as 26th smallest in the world. It not only lacked size but effectiveness as well. Army rifles and machine guns were obsolete. In tanks and aircraft we fell short of many of Europe's armed forces.

A proposal was made in 1926 that Congress fund a modest-sized squadron of modern aircraft. President Coolidge, awakening from one of his long, daily naps, countered with a suggestion that we limit the purchase to one aircraft and allow the pilots in the squadron to take turns flying it. This was at a time when our Army Air Corps was still flying planes left over from the previous war and by now hopelessly outdated.

In 1935, Hitler felt strong enough to repudiate all the controlling strictures of the Treaty of Versailles. Specifically, he revealed the formation of the new German Army, the Wehrmacht, and even more ominously the air force, or Luftwaffe. The British and French did not lift a finger to stop him, even though these measures were in defiance of the terms of the treaty.

Hitler, becoming ever more emboldened, marched a battalion sized force of his Wehrmacht across the Rhine River on March 7, 1936 into an area called the Rhineland. This was absolutely forbidden territory for German forces and a complete abnegation of the Versailles Treaty. It was also one of the most salient acts of the 20th Century.

The French government wanted to take immediate measures to counteract this maneuver and force the small contingent of Germans to retreat across the Rhine. The French Army, easily the largest in Europe, was many times the size of the Wehrmacht. However resolute the government might have been, the French General Staff was equally irresolute. Its Chief of Staff, General Maurice Gamelin, with lips quivering and knees buckling "advised that a war operation, however limited, entailed unpredictable risks and could not be undertaken without decreeing a general mobilization." Each word of that statement was an outrageous exaggeration and manifestly untrue.

The German General Staff, when it heard that the French Army was rushing a much larger element to the area, wanted to withdraw their troops back to German soil. After the war the head of the OKW, the Oberkammando Wehrmacht, testified at the Nuremberg Trials, "Considering the situation we were in, the French covering forces would have blown us to pieces." That general, Alfred Jodl, was sentenced to death after his trial and was subsequently hanged.

If a finger could be pointed at one man who, besides Hitler, was the direct cause of WWII, it would be without any question, *General Maurice Gamelin.* Never in the history of mankind has one man been directly responsible for so many deaths and so much suffering. I would judge that an absolute minimum of 30 million people died cruel, savage deaths in the European theater as a result of this man's inconceivable lack of fortitude in not confronting Hitler's Wehrmacht.

During this period of French history this ancient and proud nation suffered from Anti-Bolshevism, despair and Pro-Fascism. I strongly suspect that the general suffered from parts of all three weaknesses.

What is truly heart-rending is the knowledge that, had the Wehrmacht retreated across the Rhine, Hitler's career would have quickly ended. During the previous war his rank was corporal; furthermore he wasn't even a German national since he had been born in Austria. Many high ranking German generals viewed him with contempt, nothing more than a reckless interloper leading the Wehrmacht into disaster. Hitler later admitted he would have been finished. "A retreat on our part," he conceded, "would have spelled collapse. We would have had to withdraw with our tail between our legs, for the military resources at our disposal would have been wholly inadequate for even a moderate resistance."

CHAPTER XIX

By the successful reoccupation of the Rhineland, and with no meaningful response from England or France, Hitler had completed the first step en route to fulfilling his dream of German conquest of the whole of Europe. He had learned much from Benito Mussolini's takeover of Italy in 1922 and who then became Europe's first fascist dictator. Hitler would be the second. Then in October 1935, Mussolini invaded Abyssinia, today's Ethiopia; using planes and tanks the Italians finally subdued their primitive opposition.

The next fascist conquest took place starting in July, 1936 when the exiled Spanish general, Francisco Franco, invaded Spain with Muslim troops from Spanish Morocco. It would take El Caudillo three full years to subdue the duly elected, democratic government of Spain and would remain in power until his death 29 years later in 1975.

During the conflict Hitler would hone the effectiveness of his expanding Luftwaffe, bombing Spanish cities and for the first time in history delivering terroristic tactics from the air. Mussolini would send troops by the tens of thousands to assist his fascist buddy.

France and England refused any aid to their fellow democratic country. FDR could not provide any assistance because of Neutrality Laws on the books.

During Hitler's 10-year campaign to seize power in Germany, he had developed both formidable and frightening skills. He was now in a position to employ each of these in gobbling up Austria. Assassination, intimidation, treachery and lies – all would now be employed. Another tactic that would serve him well in future conquests was the use of local infiltrators, usually home-grown traitors, desperately seeking power in a new regime.

The Anschluss, the rape of Austria, would take place according to Hitler's plan, and on March 14, 1938 he would enter Vienna to the plaudits of huge numbers of nearly hysterical Viennese.

Chief amongst these would be Arthur Seyss-Inquart, a local attorney, who would shortly become the Austrian puppet-ruler, dangling on a string from the puppet's headquarters in Berlin. On October 16, 1946 after a trial in Nuremberg, Germany, a much stouter string, actually a rope, would be affixed to Arthur Seyss-Inquart, and he would dangle until claimed by death.

What the world now observed throughout Austria, but particularly in Vienna, was a descent into police activities far worse than sadism, more closely identified with a sickening depravity. The city was home to more Jews than any other city in the world. With the arrival of the Nazis, the terrorized Jews were forced by the tens of thousands to scrub the sidewalks on their hands and knees and next to cleanse the gutters. They were jailed in formidable numbers. Everything they owned would be stolen from them. Construction of a large, grotesque concentration camp outside the city was quickly underway. Called Mauthausen, it would rapidly achieve world-wide recognition as a place of unspeakable suffering and death.

For this and other information on the Nazis, I owe a large measure of gratitude to a work possessing an astounding depth of knowledge on the subject, *"The Holocaust – The Fate of European Jewry,"* by Leni Yahil. "As early as March 1933, Heinrich Himmler established the first camp near Dachau, a town near Munich. Beginning in 1936, one new camp was established after another: Sachsenhausen in September 1936, Buchenwald in August, 1937 then Mauthausen in 1938."

The author describes in a most plaintive manner the conditions found in the camps. "Poor nutrition, appalling sanitary conditions, iron discipline, the humiliation of prisoners, and the imposition of unspeakably brutal corporal and other punishment for even the slightest transgression – all made the concentration camp "education system" into a hell with few parallels in the history of humankind."

In a most revolting manner the German 'security system' put in place by Himmler had a savage effectiveness. (Before he joined the Nazis he had raised chickens for a living, thereby meriting my description of him – the Nazi chicken-plucker.)

Leni Yahil continues her assessment of the camps. "Even before the establishment of the special extermination camps, a vast number of people died or were killed in detention. The camp inmates succumbed to exhaustion or illness as a result of malnutrition, debilitating labor and harsh punishment measures…As a result, the concentration camps cast a pall of terror over the entire population, and were an effective deterrent to disobedience of the government's orders, to resistance of any kind, and even to criticism."

Consider what Vienna had presented to the world before this flood of fascism occurred. In 1936 it was one of the most gracious, charming cities in the world. Its fame had been apparent for many hundreds of years.

For several extended periods in its history, Vienna had been the musical capitol of all of Europe. There Mozart had conducted the first performance of *The Magic Flute*; he had been born near the city. Three of Beethoven's greatest symphonies were heard for the first time in Vienna. A number of the world's most celebrated composers made their home there. In the 18th Century Mozart, Haydn, Beethoven and Shubert were represented; in the next century, adding to the city's musical fame, were Brahms, Bruckner and Gustav Mahler.

Hitler now would seek to replace this image with his own imprint, and the suddenly beleaguered city would fall victim to his psychopathic rages.

He had grown to maturity in the city, but every one of his years spent there were lived on the ragged edge of destitution. For police protection, Vienna now would be introduced to a Nazi security system, a type previously unknown to the civilized world. Its name was the Gestapo, shortened from Geheime Staatspolizie.

For the next nine years, until the end of the Nazi regime, the Gestapo would range across much of Europe, inflicting execution, torture and incarceration on a shocking scale. Himmler, the former chicken-plucker, was personally selected by Hitler to operate this security apparatus. It is quite unlikely that any police agency in all history ever shed so much blood, and inflicted so much suffering as did the Gestapo.

President Roosevelt, already acutely attuned to the dangers stemming from fascist elements in Europe, paid heed to the comment of Claude Bowers, our Ambassador to Spain. "With every surrender such as Abyssinia and Spain, the fascist powers, with vanity inflamed, will turn without delay to some other country, such as Czechoslovakia, and that the prospect of a European war grows darker."

Few men of political prominence in this county could be found in early 1938 who agreed with FDR and his Ambassador on this early diagnosis of the hazards over the horizon.

In January, 1938, the president introduced the first of what would be innumerable military appropriations bills to Congress. This was a slender request of $300 million to continue rebuilding the navy. The bill contained provisions for another two aircraft carriers which created a new concept for these vessels. The Essex Class carriers were 27,100 tons and would begin arriving in the South Pacific in the fall of 1943. When they made their appearance our carrier force consisted of the Saratoga, which in addition to being old and slow, was also undersized. (It had been commissioned in 1927). Japanese planes and submarines had sunk four: the Lexington, Yorktown, Wasp and Hornet. The fifth, the Enterprise, was laid up in dry dock for extensive damage repair.

The despairing admirals conducting the war in the Pacific, Chester Nimitz and William Halsey, had to be pleased that FDR had won the election in 1932 against Herbert Hoover, a Quaker who hated war. After the President demolished Alf Landon, an avowed isolationist, in 1936 they had to be utterly ecstatic. The record compiled by the Republican politicians on military funding, beginning in 1938, was worse than lamentable, beyond abysmal, even reaching unfathomable.

In light of subsequent events, consider the cantankerous assessment of FDR's presidency, issued by Hoover in 1952. "Along with currency manipulation, the New Deal introduced to Americans the spectacle of fascist dictation to business, labor and agriculture." Hoover neglected to mention the many millions of his fearsome "mendacious parasites" who, having been fed by the New Deal, matured in healthy condition. They then joined the Armed Forces, which had been splendidly nurtured by the Democrats in Congress and in short order defeated the two Evil Empires, Germany and Japan.

In response to Hoover's uncharitable review of FDR's twelve year term, I consider it only fair to reflect on a number of the conditions that Hoover introduced to America. There were, of course, Hoovervilles, Hoover cars, Hoover blankets and additional items prefaced by 'Hoover.' And, who could forget the Great Crash, the stock market collapse in October, 1929? What did Hoover and his reactionary clique do or say to prevent it? Surely he must have remembered that almost immediately following the Great Crash, Americans were buffeted with the full fury of the Great Depression. Did he or his Republican Congress lift a finger as little as a millimeter to ward it off? And then of course there was the total collapse of the entire banking system in the country. Perhaps he might have enlightened us on what measures he proposed to Congress to avert it, or at least alleviate it.

It required an inordinate level of forgetfulness for Hoover to overlook the vast naval armadas required *in both oceans* to conquer fascist forces in Germany and Japan. Hundreds of thousands of military aircraft of the finest design materialized in the nick of time because of FDR and the accursed Democratic Congresses. Large armies, splendidly equipped, sprouted up largely because of two military draft bills, both of which Republican isolationists bitterly fought.

How odd of Herbert Hoover to overlook these considerations! What isn't at all odd was the fact I couldn't recall the year in which Herbert Clark Hoover passed away. I had to check the history books. What also isn't odd that, in the case of Franklin Delano Roosevelt, I could instantly recall the year, the month, the day and even the exact time of day he expired. Going further, I knew the exact location – the city, the house and even the people present when he was suddenly stricken with a fatal cerebral hemorrhage.

CHAPTER XX

By now democracy had ceased to exist in four European countries: Italy, Germany, Spain and Austria, in each instance replaced by fascism. The likelihood of a fifth democracy disappearing increased markedly at a meeting in Munich, Germany on September 29, 1938 when the heads of state from four countries met. From England, there was Neville Chamberlain; Adolph Hitler from Germany; Edouard Daladier arrived from France and Benito Mussolini represented Italy. They met to discuss the fate of the Sudetenland, a prosperous region in the Republic of Czechoslovakia. Even though this area had never been a part of Germany, and even though a majority of its citizens were Czechs and not Germans, Hitler demanded it because it was home to a significant percentage of Germans. Hitler, truly a World Class Liar, insisted, "This is the last territorial demand I have to make in Europe." Stripping this area from the Czech Republic would fatally compromise its defense in the future.

Hitler was supremely confident that Chamberlain and Daladier would succumb to his threats since in private he referred to them as "mere worms." He couldn't have been more precise in his assessment of those two since they both readily caved in to his demands. Chamberlain would scurry back to London and present his case to Parliament where he would boast that he had "achieved peace with honor." Going a step further, he would crow that he had bought "peace in our time."

The man, who would shortly succeed Chamberlain as Prime Minister, Winston Churchill, in a most memorable rejoinder, would warn Parliament, "Do not suppose this is the end. This is only the beginning of the reckoning. This is only the first sip, the first foretaste of a bitter crop which will be proffered to us year by year, unless by a supreme recovery of moral health and martial rigor, we rise again to take our stand for freedom as in the olden time."

Throughout this oration, one still celebrated today for its uncanny look into future events, the next Prime Minister was mercilessly heckled and even booed by Chamberlain's reality-challenged Tory boobs. Tories present to Parliament the same message that Republicans do to Congress.

William Shirer in "*The Rise and Fall of the Third Reich*" was equally critical. "The British Prime Minister was gullible beyond comprehension in accepting Hitler's work."

Although the British people accorded Chamberlain a large initial measure of acclaim, they soon came to realize that he had sold out a thriving democracy and in a short span of time looked upon the idea of *peace in our time* with the same degree of acceptance as thoughtful Americans regard the P.P's duplicitous banner *Mission Accomplished* shown aboard the Aircraft Carrier Abraham Lincoln, on May 1, 2003.

Bush, in an act of unacceptable hypocrisy, would land on the carrier and swagger around on the flight deck in a fancy flight suit. Republicans are now careful *never* to show that unforgettable sequence, although they thought at the time they had a lovely campaign nugget.

A note of extraordinary sadness needs to be inserted here. A powerful group of high ranking generals were frightened that the Austrian Corporal was leading their country into disaster. To thwart any further aggressive moves on Hitler's part, they were prepared to arrest him and place him on trial for treason. This act was conditioned on his failure in the Sudetenland venture. This episode in German history is superbly documented by testimony from a variety of German sources at the post war Nuremberg Trials in addition to the Diaries of several members of the general's cabal. Their instincts were on target and future events proved them correct. Regrettably, by his craven conduct at Munich, Neville Chamberlain would foil their plans.

Herr Hitler wasted little time in the furtherance of his goal to conquer all of Europe. On March 15, 1939, he ordered his Wehrmacht into the remains of the Czech democracy and in so doing successfully absorbed another country without a shot being fired.

President Roosevelt was by now firmly convinced that European fascism, with especial regard to Nazi Germany, constituted a mortal threat to America, and to the entire free world. His impressive insight into future events persuaded him to abandon further efforts to strengthen the New Deal; instead to concentrate his efforts to rebuild every aspect of our military.

In this effort he was assisted by Southern Congressmen, all solidly Democrat. They too wanted a strong defensive posture. Congressmen from Western states were equally cooperative provided he could continue to persuade them he had no intention of embroiling the nation in European wars. It was only within Republican ranks that FDR encountered militant opposition.

From the first days of his Administration they had presented a belligerent front, always eager to combat any legislation the New Dealers proposed. Could it be the scant Republican minorities in Congress, beginning in 1933 were motivated solely by blind partisan opposition? That doesn't appear to be an unlikely answer. What other reason can be found for Senator Henry Cabot Lodge's obstinate desire to frustrate President Wilson from obtaining Senate approval for the League of Nations? Harding and his Republican hordes made resistance to the League one of the prime facets of their 1920 campaign. It was either that or an imbecilic reluctance to confront reality and in so doing hide behind the isolationist movement. Whatever their motive, it was placing the nation in a potentially hazardous position.

In a fireside chat soon thereafter, Mr. Roosevelt addressed the problem. "The nation could no longer cling to the illusion that we are remote and isolated and therefore secure against the dangers from which no land is free." His Republican foes would completely ignore the incontestable logic in his statement to Americans; instead they would nurture their deep, bitter hate for him while continuing their indefensible opposition right up to Sunday, December 7, 1941 – Pearl Harbor Day.

On a personal note, in the summer of 1939, I was 16 years old and everything appeared quite clear to me. War was not only inevitable but before long I would be wearing a uniform. Beyond that, every action taken by our president in rebuilding our country's neglected defenses appeared not just sensible but absolutely necessary. I actually joined the Minnesota National Guard the following year when I was but 17 and hence not of legal age.

My guard unit was a field artillery regiment, still using hopelessly obsolete and underpowered French 75 millimeter pieces remaining from World War I. In the artillery we would never utter the word <u>cannon</u>, always pieces. I attended two summer training camps, lasting a month each. We also participated in one-a-week sessions at night during the rest of the year. If my outfit ever fired a single round from one of our artillery pieces, I never heard it.

The regiment eventually saw combat in North Africa in 1942-43, after undergoing extensive training with our regular army and conducted itself in a competent manner. It was, of course, eventually fitted out with modern, effective equipment and also fitted out with new officers, since most of the old group wasn't up to speed. Since I had enlisted underage, my parents insisted that I withdraw. I did.

Hitler quickly followed up his absorption of Austria and Czechoslovakia by striking at Poland on September 1, 1939. He had been duly warned by England and France, after his recent take-over of the remaining part of the Czech Republic, that any further aggressions in Europe would be met with armed resistance. To bolster that new stance, both England and France had signed a pact with Poland, guaranteeing its territorial integrity and promising to go to war to defend the country. Hitler placed no faith in this treaty and continued with his plan to conquer the entire continent.

To his utter astonishment on that day, he was now challenged with an ultimatum— either pull back to the original border or war will be declared. Der Fuehrer ignored the threat and continued to unleash his Wehrmacht and Luftwaffe on the weak Polish defenses.

The Luftwaffe now introduced Poland and a horrified world to death and destruction from the skies on a scale never seen previously. To be sure, the Spanish city, Guernica, had been largely demolished by this same Luftwaffe during the Spanish Civil War, but now devastation of an entire country was underway. Warsaw, the Capital of Poland and a lovely cultural center, was immediately subjected to a terrifying assault from the sky.

On Sunday, September 3, Germany found itself at war with England and France. World War II was officially underway. Hitler, the master of prevarication, had deceived the German public beginning with his introduction into politics in 1923, to his consolidation of power in 1933. Now he would subject his gullible audience to an additional untruth. "You know," he would convincingly proclaim, "the endless attempts I made for peaceful clarification and understanding of the problem of Austria, and later of the problem of the Sudetenland, Bohemia and Moravia. It was all in vain."

But it wasn't all in vain. This too was a monstrous lie. The ease with which untruths would fall from his lips, plus his continued aggressions had produced the exact results he dreamed of. At no cost in blood or expenditure of bullets, his Nazi government had assimilated two peaceful democracies and was now rapidly annihilating a third country.

The declaration of war on Germany was as far as the English and French would move. Had those governments unleashed their armies, acting in concert, as they had during WWI, the chance for success was quite good. The Wehrmacht, when presented with a campaign on two widely separated fronts, might easily have floundered. This situation would also have presented an additional opportunity to the deeply troubled German generals to stop Hitler. Unfortunately for the craven Allied leaders, the mere worms as seen by Hitler, the declaration of war signaled a period of inactivity.

The out-manned and out-gunned Polish Army quickly succumbed to the combined onslaught by both the Wehrmacht and Luftwaffe. The conflict was over shortly.

Joseph Stalin, the Soviet dictator, had made repeated overtures to form a military alliance with England and France, part of which would have secured Polish sovereignty. Instead he was rebuffed each time, at least once in a belittling manner. In Neville Chamberlain the British had a Prime Minister who was totally blind to the continued treachery of the psychopath heading up the German nation. Additionally he was deeply fearful of Russian Communism which presented no threat to England. The threat from Hitler, by contrast, was now only dire, but in well under a year would prove near fatal.

Because of the ease with which the Wehrmacht had conquered the Polish Army, Hitler's vanity grew apace, and he began to think of himself as an authentic military genius. No small number of his generals also began to subscribe to Hitler's assessment of himself. These generals would soon percolate to the top of his army hierarchy.

The military genius quickly drew the bulk of his combat troops from Poland and started to position them for his next assault in Europe, which he planned for in early spring. On April 9, 1940, he invaded Norway for a variety of sound political and strategic reasons. Germany had suffered irreparable harm from the British naval blockade during WWI, so by seizing that country before the quietly dozing British could act, he would remove the future threat of another blockade.

On the same day he also sent his troops into the neighboring Denmark; this netted him five countries that had fallen under his Nazi terror regime. Wasting little time, Hitler quickly struck Holland, Belgium, Luxembourg and France on May 9. Holland was completely subjugated in only five days. Belgium and Luxembourg required only a little more time. Meanwhile the combination of the Wehrmacht and the Luftwaffe were defeating the combined British and French troops with relative ease.

On May 19, General Maurice Gamelin was relieved of duty with, I strongly suspect, lips still quivering and knees still quavering.

The French government had invested prodigious sums of money in a defensive position called the Maginot Line which they were certain would make them invulnerable to a future German attack. Whether or not it would have done so will never be known, since the Germans simply outflanked the Line and made no effort to assault it. The Maginot Line had ended at the Belgian border and it was at that juncture where the Wehrmacht made its move.

It took the Germans only 15 days to split the combined British – French forces and drive to the French coast. Half the allied forces were to the north of where the Wehrmacht held 15 miles of French water front, the other to the south of the German Army. Hitler could now chew up both elements easily and at his leisure.

At this crucial period in history monumental good fortune intervened when the German military genius halted his attack for five days to allow his slower moving foot troops catch up with the swift tank divisions. The exact reasoning has never been determined but it appears Hitler seemed confounded by the Wehrmacht's success and decided not to push his good fortune.

The combined British-French troops were desperately fighting for their lives, penned into a narrow enclave around the small French coastal town of Dunkirk. Starting May 30 a wondrous evacuation plan got underway; it utilized both the Royal Navy and upwards of 900 small and medium sized individually owned motor craft. In five seemingly hopeless days the Brits were able to evacuate 338,226 troops, the great majority English. By the time the Germans resumed their assault on the area, almost all of the troops were safely back in England.

The French government requested an armistice on June 17 and the peace treaty was signed on June 22. Not since France, under Napoleon Bonaparte in the early 19th Century, had one country and one man dominated so much European real estate.

Just as the French Army finally rid itself of its General Gamelin, so did Parliament, in a move long overdue, deposit their Prime Minister in the dust bin of history. Conrad Black, in his mesmerizing biography, *Franklin Delano Roosevelt* continues the narrative. "Winston Leonard Spencer Churchill, aged sixty-five and a veteran of thirty-nine years in Parliament and eight different cabinet positions … was invested with practically unlimited authority at the head of a national unity government. No one had assumed the great office of prime minister in more dire circumstances, but he did so serenely, his 'whole life a preparation for it'."

Three days later on May 13, 1940, Churchill would address Parliament and, by radio, the world eagerly awaiting his message. From him would come one of he most hallowed statements of the war. "I have nothing to offer but blood, toil, tears and sweat…Our policy is to wage war by sea, land and air with all our might…against a monstrous tyranny, never surpassed in the dark, lamentable catalogue of human crime. Our aim: Victory — the victory at all costs, victory in spite of all terror, victory however long and hard the road may be." Mr. Black goes on, "for everyone but the Nazis and their sympathizers, this was a refreshing change, and for few people more than the President of the United States… Franklin D. Roosevelt would have someone who knew the nature of civilization's enemies and the requirements of mortal combat, and with whom he could plan and achieve the repulse of the barbarians."

No question that safely delivering over 300,000 trained British troops back to England was a stroke of great good fortune, but left behind in Dunkirk were 40,000 more who immediately became German prisoners. Also left behind was every stick of army equipment. As the new P.M. sagaciously pointed out, "wars are not won by evacuations."

On June 4th Churchill gave one of his most widely celebrated addresses which caressed the hearts of millions of despondent Americans. "We shall go on to the end. We shall fight in France, we shall fight in the seas and the oceans, we shall fight with growing strength and growing confidence in the air, we shall defend our island, whatever the cost may be. We shall fight on the beaches, we shall fight on the landing grounds, we shall fight in the fields and in the streets, we shall fight in the hills; we shall never surrender."

Our President knew exactly what needed to be done. Ignoring objections from many in his government, he demanded that they come to England's aid. Lying around in army depots were 500,000 old Enfield rifles, left over from WWI. At least 1000 French 75 pieces could be found; countless millions of rounds for rifles and perhaps a million or more shells for the artillery. Cagy FDR knew it would be illegal for the U.S. Government to do so because of neutrality laws on the books. But he could work around that barrier by selling all this material to private corporations who could then legally sell it to the British.

He would implement this forceful action with an additional message of hope, help and good cheer when he rode in his presidential train to Charlottesville where he would deliver the annual commencement address at the University of Virginia. There he made scathing reference to those Americans "who still hold to the now _somewhat obvious delusion_ that we can permit the United States to become a lonely island in a world dominated by the philosophy of force."

While the relatively slender group of students and faculty in attendance were deeply impressed by being in the same auditorium with the popular President of the United States, his listening audience must have numbered in the tens of millions. With the power of radio at his command, FDR would reach a worldwide audience of deeply troubled human beings. To these listeners his appeal would bring comfort and expectation.

Too much emphasis cannot be placed on the deep divide between FDR and his two Republican rivals for the Presidential seat. Both Hoover and Landon, had they been in the White House, would have lashed out in vehemence against any pernicious involvement in _foreign entanglements_. Both were possessed of a bewildering blindness to the threat of what the President called "the contemptuous, unpitying masters of other continents…and a world dominated by force."

The British people were now faced with the most mortal threat to their existence since the successful Norman Invasion in 1066. Their rather diminutive island nation was only 22 miles distant from France, now under complete control of the Nazis. Separating the two lands was the Pas de Calais, or as the English preferred, the English Channel. Once again a most benign intervention was taking place.

Hitler was supremely confident that the British would agree to his terms so that there would be no need for an invasion. Meanwhile he was reveling in his magnificent accomplishments; nine countries conquered, doubtless the greatest European ruler in all history. After the peace treaty with France was signed he would spend a hurried day sightseeing in Paris, and spending a little of it visiting Napoleon's tomb. Upon his return to Berlin the crowds greeting him exceeded all expectations in their level of adoration.

His level of confidence was inflated still further by General Maxime Weygand, who supervised the surrender of the French forcers and who predicted, "In three weeks England will have her neck wrung like a chicken."

More than a year later, once the threat of invasion had vanished, Winston Churchill would have great sport with that declaration. Speaking to the Canadian Parliament he mocked the defeatist general. "Some chicken," he roared. Then following a long pause for dramatic effect – "some neck."

After frittering away weeks during which the Brits were feverishly preparing for invasion, reality slowly returned to the military genius. His rotund head of the Luftwaffe, Hermann Göring, bursting with certitude, kept insisting to Hitler that he could bring England to its knees, using only the fearsome Luftwaffe. Many Germans playfully referred to him as Der Dicke, the fat one or just plain fatty.

Two very old and famous cities in Europe had just recently endured the potency of the German air power, Warsaw in Poland and Rotterdam, in the Netherlands. Each suffered a mighty pounding from the skies as Hitler used this new weapon to terrorize and intimidate.

As July waned, Hitler slowly assented to an all-out attack on Britain, using only the Luftwaffe. A code name was arrived at – Adlerangriff – Eagle Attack, which was to begin soon after August 5th. Finally the actual day was set August 13th, Adlertag or Eagle Day.

Göring and Hitler were by now completely persuaded that the Luftwaffe would need only to fly over England, deposit loads of bombs on the luckless British cities, and the Brits would soon plead for peace. When Adlertag proved too cloudy, a one day delay went into effect.

Over the bombers came the next day, escorted by thick numbers of fighter planes. The Battle of Britain was underway. Along with the standard bombers was the Junkers 87 which had terrorized ground troops in Poland and France. This bomber was totally unlike anything England, France or Poland used. In the U.S. only the carrier based SBD (Dauntless) was comparable. The Army Air Corps didn't use dive bombers. Only a relatively small number of the SBDs had sunk all four Japanese carriers at Midway.

As the sailors aboard those carriers quickly discovered, the dive bombers were deadly accurate. So was the JU-87; it was also fitted with a siren which screamed a fearful message on its downward path. Once the bombers pulled out of their dives and headed skyward again, their velocity was what was called stall-speed, a rather slow, extremely unhealthy rate for a few moments.

In Poland and France these bomber pilots had never encountered a fighter plane like the one they were about to meet. This was the British Spitfire Supermarine, a sleek instrument of death that carried eight machine guns and was flown by highly trained pilots. The Spitfire, about the fastest fighter plane in the world at the time would follow the JU87 down and when it pulled up, would present a lovely, slow moving target.

On this opening day of the Battle of Britain, Göring would include 40 of these dive bombers in his air armada. The Spits quickly sent 10 of them downward in their final, fatal dive. Many of the others released their bomb without a dive and headed homeward.

The Battle of Britain would continue through the year. Hitler had been absolutely certain his ground forces could invade the country and overcome its defenses as it had in Poland and the six newly conquered lands in West Europe. But until the RAF was neutralized this would be impossible. Despite Göring's vain boasts the British pilots continued to shoot down Luftwaffe planes at an unacceptable rate — more than 1600 would be knocked out of the sky. Of the modest numbers in his RAF, Churchill had the rarest praise. "Never in the history of human conflict was so much owed by so many to so few."

The German military genius ached with desire to attack the nation he considered his ultimate enemy, Russia, and although he dreaded to leave behind an unconquered foe, in the form of England, he had unbounded optimism in his Wehrmacht to defeat the Communist country. After all look at the ease with which it had subdued Poland and six other nations in Western Europe. Accordingly he began to withdraw his air force shortly after year's end.

Londoners had suffered 40,000 fatalities and horribly large numbers of wounded. Tragically, major British cities had felt the wrath of the German bombers. On March 19th, London was subjected to its most dreadful raid. It wasn't until May 10, 1941, when the city suffered its last onslaught that the Battle of Britain finally ended.

On June 22, 1941, exactly a year after the signing of the peace treaty with France, Russia would feel the might of Hitler's forces.

CHAPTER XXI

At the time Hitler continued his military adventure with the take-over of Czechoslovakia, the United States army consisted of 176,000 troops, a total which positioned it in a hazardous military situation. It also meant that 25 other nations had an army larger than ours. At this point President Roosevelt began requesting the first of what would be numerous defense appropriations bills. Up until Pearl Harbor Day, each of these would be accompanied by outpourings of indignation and outright rejection from the Republicans in Congress, and it must be stressed, *only the Republicans.*

Senator Gerald Nye of North Dakota could always be relied upon to be negative; he was most forthright in his denunciation of this first military bill, referring to it as "undue military preparedness."

We turn once again to Conrad Black's engrossing work, *"Franklin Delano Roosevelt."* " Roosevelt had recognized from the earliest moments of the Third Reich that Western democracy probably could not coexist with it. He came to believe, by early 1939 at the latest, that the United States would be called upon to rid the world of Nazism and that it would then emerge not only as a post isolationist country but as the preeminent nation on earth. Supreme political artist as he was, he cannot have failed, by the beginning of 1939, to have glimpsed this destiny that would carry his county to heights no nation had ever occupied and himself to a position in American history, rivaled, if at all, only by Washington and Lincoln.

"Like an agile predator he knew when to emerge, reveal his design, and execute it. And once determined to lead opinion and implement a policy, he was unflappable, devious, utterly determined, and unusually inspiring. Now, in early 1939, his course, though indiscernible to others, was clear to him. It could be summarized in six points. First, he had to complete the conquest of the Depression by arming America. Second, He could arrange a virtual draft to a third term as the candidate of peace through strength. Third, he could complete the acquisition of an overwhelming level of military might. Fourth, and assuming a new world war was already in progress, he would engineer righteous hostilities with Germany and the lesser dictatorships, ensuring that the dictators would be seen as aggressors. The fifth stage would be winning the war and leading the world to a post imperial Pax Americana, in which, Sixth, Woodrow Wilson's goals of safety for democracy and international legality would be established in some sort of American led international organization. Nothing less or other than these goals can explain Roosevelt's conduct from Munich on. No other American leader had ever conceived such an immensely ambitious plan for making over the world. The few leaders of other countries who were ambitious, Napoleon, Lenin, Hitler — were not as, or not at all, benign. And no one, benign or otherwise, would be more durably successful in implementing a grand design for reorganizing international relations."

Arguably FDR's most astute appointment was George Catlett Marshall as his official Army Chief of Staff. Officially the appointment came on September 1, 1939, the same day WWII started. Unofficially he was already acting in that capacity much earlier in the year. The general inspired Congress with such a high degree of confidence in him that he could persuade it to pass defense measures where the President might fail.

The 1938 midterm elections had materially increased the Republicans in Congress — they added six seats in the Senate but 80 in the House, advancing from 89 to 169. With them came more partisan rancor, some of it venomous.

Always yapping at the President's heels was Herbert Hoover who relieved himself of this sentiment. "Certain types of propaganda are today fertilizing our soil for entry into war."

His lamentations came immediately after FDR asked Congress to fund 6,000 planes. This number was far fewer than he wished, but already General Marshall thought the President was placing too much importance on aircraft and not enough on tanks. Curiously enough, one of the main reasons why Roosevelt selected Marshall over a multitude of higher ranking officers was because the general was willing to challenge the Commander in Chief. Here was one instance, and the general prevailed.

It's good to recall that when Coolidge was asked by the Air Corps in 1926 to obtain an expenditure in Congress for a mere squadron of new planes, he suggested they purchase only one plane and allow the various pilots to take turns flying it.

As Hitler enlarged his newly conquered domain in Europe, FDR appeared before a joint session of Congress on May 16 and asked for another, and more realistic, defense bill of just under one billion dollars. He pointed to the need to make our nation "an arsenal of democracy." In tandem with that request he declared that "this nation should plan at this time a program that would provide us with 50,000 military and naval planes." And then suggested the seemingly impossible goal of 50,000 planes *annually*.

The lobotomous Republicans reacted with ridicule and blind fury at what they considered a ludicrous proposal. Yet the President would be able to demonstrate to the world how farcical were his opponents when by the end of 1943 the nation's defense industry would be producing planes at the rate of

100,000 a year. These opponents were consolidating their position as "the let's get it wrong, all along, throng."

At the end of May, the equally visionary General Marshall presented a timetable for the buildup of the army to fighting strength. He insisted on 500,000 men by July , 1941. A full million by January, 1942, and 1½ million by July, 1942. He stressed the obvious that waiting for voluntary enlistments would never fill the needs of the nation's military.

To implement this bold plan Roosevelt and Marshall realized that a civilian draft would be absolutely necessary. But never in the nation's history had this ever been put into effect in peacetime. With much of the Republican opposition motivated by their hatred of FDR, plus their willingness to overlook the mortal threat of fascism, it became obvious that General Marshall should spearhead the intense effort to pass the Selective Service and Training Act. Pursuing that plan, General Marshall made separate appearances before the Senate and House Military Affairs Committees.

Congress had such complete faith in his testimony that they would endorse legislation he had proposed while being far more reluctant to pass the same legislation if presented by the President. Roosevelt was more than a little convinced that some of the more outspoken isolationists in Republican Congressional Circles were being bribed by Nazi Advocates.

On September 14, 1940 the Selective Service and Training Act was passed by Congress. In the House the vote was 232 for passage and 134 against. Since that House was represented by 169 Republicans, it's fair to say that just about 75% were opposed to the draft bill, truly one of the most vital acts of defense legislation passed during the Roosevelt Administration. In his testimony before the Congressional Committees Marshall had pleaded with them to pass the draft bill. He pointed out in the most plaintive manner that the United States *had no army* worthy of the name. Not only was it tragically small in numbers, but even those few number lacked modern weapons, still using a rifle that first was introduced in 1903.

High ranking officers persisted in clinging to the concept of horse cavalry even though the Wehrmacht had conclusively demonstrated the lethal striking power of its panzers, the tank corps. Upon assuming the role of Army Chief of Staff General Marshall had reviewed the combat capability of 24 major-generals; he promptly retired 23 of them.

Contributing to the feverish current of revolting isolationism was the Wall Street Journal which added this silliness, "Stop foreign Meddling; American wants peace." So obviously did the considerable cabal of Republicans representing the Party of Lincoln. Upon being sworn into office President Lincoln soon demanded of Congress a draft bill so that the United States could properly defend itself against intrusion from the armies of the newly formed Confederate States. He also, just like President Roosevelt, requested from Congress gigantic appropriations to build up the army and navy. To a mortal threat Honest Abe reacted in an aggressive manner, the same as FDR was now doing. The Lincoln of the Party of Lincoln would not have gazed approvingly at the sorry cabal in the 1940 Congress.

Adding to the poisonous brew of rumors spread by the isolationists was the latest hot item — both Eleanor and Franklin were Jewish and were firmly wedded to the Alliance of Jews working to embroil this country in a war with Germany.

The moment the draft legislation was completed, FDR had to concern himself with the 1940 presidential election — he would be venturing into new and forbidden territory, his third term in office. His opponent was Wendell Willkie, a candidate with qualities not seen by the Republicans since the departure of Teddy Roosevelt in March of 1909. He was not only articulate, but intelligent and moderate as well. After his defeat Willkie would prove to be an important asset to the war effort.

All during these hectic times for our country, the British were reeling from the savage onslaught of the Luftwaffe. Prime Minister Churchill had already persuaded our President to contribute 50 overage destroyers to the British to help combat the threat of Nazi submarines which were sinking English freighters at a forbidding rate.

He then beseeched FDR to come to Britain's aid once again. The British government was rapidly approaching bankruptcy and soon would be unable to pay for its military and economic assistance. The President was most anxious to respond favorably to his ally's compelling cry for help but first he had to contrive an adequate rationalization for this act — one he could sell to Congress and the American public.

To implement his plan he undertook a short cruise in the Caribbean aboard the cruiser Tuscaloosa. It was during this delightful interlude that he slowly and painstakingly arrived at the concept of Lend-Lease, an idea that had been ripening in his mind.

Conrad Black once more treats us to a critical analysis to FDR's thought process. "It was one of the most brilliant ideas of his career, and it changed history. Essentially, the president's concept was that the United States would lend Britain whatever it needed, at no cost, and Britain would repay in kind, by giving back what it had borrowed, or in other agreed equivalent consideration, when it could. This avoided the dispute about gifts, sales, cash loans, and all that wrangling that had gone on over war debts." Mr. Black would then quote Robert Sherwood, the famous American playwright, "FDR, a creative artist in politics, had put in his time on this cruise evolving the pattern of a masterpiece."

The Administration introduced the legislation, Bill 1776, on January 15, 1941. Two of its principal and strongest witnesses were Republicans who FDR had brought into his government the previous year in an ardent desire to seek a bi-partisan approach to governing. First to appear before the House Foreign Relations Committee was Henry L. Stimson who had been Herbert Hoover's Secretary of State. Following him was FDR's Navy Secretary, Frank Knox, Alf Landon's running mate.

Prior to the vote in the House, FDR made his plea for passage. "If Britain goes down, an unholy alliance of the dictators would continue to pursue world conquest and all of us in the Americas would be living at the point of a gun. We must become the great arsenal of democracy."

The President with all his eloquence together with the impressive list of witnesses in favor of Lend-Lease might just as well have saved their words. On this legislative Act the House Republicans in opposition numbered 135, one more than voted against the draft bill. Each was impervious to the logical and patriotic importuning presented to them. Their minds were shackled in a hermetical seal with no possibility of even a wisp of a discordant idea gaining entry.

Nor were only the Congressional Republicans opposed. Many of the Party's big guns lined up against this necessary legislation —Hoover, Landon, Thomas Dewey, who had been an important figure in the 1940 vote for presidential candidate and who would be the candidate in both 1944 and 1948. Others in Congress such as Robert Taft and Arthur Vandenberg added their voices.

When the House was voting on the bill, I turned 18 years of age and was already positive that war was inevitable. I had no particular insight into world politics, but my opinion was shared by a large percentage of the population, including the President and most likely his entire Cabinet. The Republicans in Congress were generally three or four times my age and most had college educations. They were not a group to be consulted for advice. Nor should you choose an attorney from amongst their ranks to defend you in anything important.

One has to wonder which side these 135 Republicans were pulling for. There is no question that a small percentage of Americans were in favor of a German victory, but they were intense Germans, some born in Germany. Consider that 236 Democrats were in favor of the legislation which was totally non-partisan.

Consider also that both America and Great Britain were in a savage battle to preserve civilization against the fearful onslaught of the Nazi war machine.

With the vote in the House now completed, bill number 1776 moved to the Senate. Following established protocol the Senate Foreign Relations Committee conducted hearings and then reported the bill to the Senate floor with a vote of 15 in favor and 8 against, virtually a straight party vote. The churlish Republican isolationists tried mightily to prevent passage of the measure but were defeated at every point by the enlightened Democrats.

Winston Churchill, in addressing his Parliament, spoke of Lend-Lease as "the most unsordid act in the history of any nation," one of the most widely quoted utterances he ever made. He expressed his and the British peoples, "deep and respectful appreciation of this monument of generous and far reaching statesmanship. The most powerful democracy has declared that they will devote their overwhelming industrial and financial strength to insuring the defeat of Nazism." Continuing he said, "The government and people of the United States proclaimed by precept and example the duty of free men and free nations to share the responsibility and burden of enforcing them. In the name of all freedom-loving peoples, we offer to the United States our gratitude for her inspiring act of faith."

Only two days following Churchill's history making oration, FDR appeared before the annual White House Reporter's Dinner. "This decision," he told the correspondents, "is the end of any attempts at appeasement in our land; the end of urging us to get along with the dictators, the end of compromise with tyranny and the forces of oppression. The great task of this day, the deep duty that rests upon each and every one of us is to move products from the assembly lines of our factories to the battle lines of democracy — now."

Sometime in the mid 1950s I began to notice the appearance of small paperback books exploring every facet of WWII. They cost 25 cents per volume. Soon I was traveling extensively in pursuit of my business, and would purchase several of these works every week. Within a few years I had read every history book to be found and calculated I had devoured easily 600 of these works. They covered every conceivable phase of the war, from basic training to combat training to the Army's involvement first in North Africa, then Sicily on to Italy and finally D-Day in Normandy. Then there were our mighty operations in the Pacific beginning with our occupation of Guadalcanal.

Had the Selective Service Act not passed in 1940, much of that could not have been undertaken. The renewal of that Act in 1941 passed the House by the margin of a single vote, and even that required some chicanery. Had the Lend-Lease bill not been passed the following year a different outcome might have resulted. It wasn't until our nation was attacked on December 7, 1941, at Pearl Harbor that the Republicans finally ceased their impassioned and insane opposition to the war effort. Hitler declared war on us four days later. It was only then that Winston Churchill and the British finally felt secure and knew that Hitler would never conquer their storied isles.

By this critical juncture in the nation's history, FDR realized that the days of Congress passing any more New Deal legislation were finally over. This was a certainty. Equally certain he knew that Congress, which by now had turned considerably conservative, could not undo any progressive bills already passed.

Examining the long term consequence of Roosevelt's programs we see them as a grand and radical change under which he majestically and methodically put together a legal, unbloodied overthrow of the POBB's economic and social edifice. John Maynard Keynes, he of the Keynesian Theory of economics, wrote to FDR: "You have made yourself the trustee for those in every country who seek to mend the evils of our condition by reasoned experiment within the frame work of the existing social system."

The United States under the enlightened guidance of our President had become a brightly shining beacon for untold multitudes of people hungering for a government with social justice.

The New Dealers emphasized the total repudiation of the values of the 1920 decade. FDR's rejection of it was emphatic, referring to the 20s as "a decade of debauch." Others in his inner circle declared it "a decade of empty progress, devoid of contribution to a genuinely better future." The Roosevelt group embraced experimentation, always ready to attempt new approaches. Almost to a man they decried the Coolidge/Hoover theory that the frequent Panics and the final, terrifying Depression were part of a natural rhythm that had to be endured. They had sufficient insight into economic theories so that they could readily observe that the largest share of the enduring was borne by the bottom end of the economic ladder.

Hence they focused on stability and a more equitable distribution of the economic pie. From that came the continuous experimentation — the Cs (Civilian Conservation Corps), the Rural Electrification program which transformed farm life, the NRA, the Securities Exchange Commission, FDIC, which effectively ended bank failures.

The President was safely en route to being adjudged the most admired and beloved figure in the entire world. History soon would crown him as the greatest figure of the 20th Century. Amongst the nation's presidents in that century, only his distant cousin Theodore could remotely challenge him.

CHAPTER XXII

The Republicans, beginning with Ulysses Grant in 1869 had perpetrated an unending series of sordid acts, veering ever rightward, putting vast distances between themselves and Honest Abe Lincoln. Their Administrations were the direct cause of hundreds of prison cells being filled. Their Attorney's General were easily the worst in our nation's history — sleazy crooks who richly deserved imprisonment but like Harry Daugherty under Harding and Edwin Meese III under Reagan successfully eluded it.

Some of their behaviors strongly suggest they were sociological cretins, utterly incapable of shame or interspection. How else can one characterize the performance of Henry Cabot Lodge and the Senate Republicans in 1919 when he and they labored so mightily to derail the majestic cause of the League of Nations. Their activities were truly memorable for the frightening level of stupidity.

At the conclusion of WWI, Woodrow Wilson, an exceptionally intelligent Democrat President, wanted above all else to craft a worldwide organization to promote peace. The conflict had been called the War to End All Wars. In pursuit of that goal he would appoint a committee. That committee created the Draft Covenant of the League of Nations. Here was the outline of a world-wide structure whose purpose was to prevent further military aggression and instead promote world peace. Wilson then presented the Draft Covenant to the Senate. Immediately Lodge, who as chairman of the Foreign Relations Committee had enormous power, put that power to work. He and his blind, uncomprehending Republican cabal, authored a resolution that opposed not only the Covenant but the League itself.

Wilson next made extensive revisions in the proposal to counter objections from the 39 Republicans. He presented the legislation to the Senate with this message. "The stage is set, the destiny disclosed. We can only go forward, with lifted eyes and freshened spirit, to follow the vision. The light streams upon the path ahead, and nowhere else."

It must be pointed out that the Democrats in the Senate were nearly unanimous in their support of the League. When the President presented this amended version to the Senate the result was predictable. Lodge countered with a list of 14 reservations, massively tinctured with deceit and hypocrisy. The cabal operating under Lodge's direction called themselves "strong reservationists," which meant that their reservations about the League of Nations were so strong that this country's membership in it would have no significance. The group should have been called "strongly irresponsible."

In attempting to sell the concept of a world peace organization to the public, Wilson made 40 speeches in 20 days, traveling 10,000 miles. In doing so he overtaxed his health and suffered first a mild stroke, but then a crippling version which would effectively end his political career.

We have previously seen how Wilson predicted, with astounding prescience, that if this country failed to join the League of Nations, a second and far more ruinous world war would come about in a generation. Actually it required less than 20 years.

The Republicans, by considerable contrast, enjoyed the same level of perspicuity as did their fellow, revolting House members in 1940-41 who voted first against the draft bill and then Lend-Lease.

The culmination of this forgettable period was when an extremely able, highly intelligent Democratic President would be followed into office by a lazy, unfocused, cognitively challenged Republic klutz by the name of Warren Harding. The klutz would drag in with him as his Vice-President, Calvin Coolidge, who was famous for sleeping 12 hours daily.

This scenario would be repeated two more times. In 1981, a very able, very intelligent Jimmy Carter would have as a successor a lazy, unfocused, cognitively challenged Ronald Reagan, accompanied by George Herbert Walker Bush. This president, who I am pleased to call MCI Regan, declared his favorite President to be Calvin Coolidge, doubtless because both took extreme delight in sleeping for inordinate periods.

The third example was surely the most egregious, when a polymath named William Jefferson Clinton would view with extreme distaste an election thief slink into the White House by a side door, courtesy of the U. S. Supreme Court. George Walker Bush was most emphatically lazy, unfocused and cognitively challenged. There are a growing number of Americans who serious question whether Bush's I.Q. equaled his internal body temperature.

Is it possible that the case of *Bush v. Gore* is touched on at Pepperoni U. where Kenneth Starr is Law Dean? This is the K. Starr who first attended college at Harding in Searcy, Arkansas. One might legitimately inquire if K. Starr dwells to any extent on *Miranda v. Arizona*, one of the most famous decisions in the history of the Court. As we have seen Miranda guarantees two absolute rights to anybody detained by law enforcement officers: One, the right to remain silent; two, the absolute right to counsel (except of course in Texas).

However, when Monica Lewinsky was kept sequestered for12 hours under intense, continual grilling by Starr's legal goons, these two important rights were conveniently overlooked, and she in fact was denied either right. Miss Lewinsky wasn't even a suspect for any crime. His troop of goons weren't law enforcement officers either. K. Starr, the Law Dean at Pepperoni U. never bothered to address the matter.

CHATPER XXIII

In reviewing how FDR engineered complete victory over Germany and Japan, one has to stand in absolute awe at the magisterial manner in which he became the architect of the "Arsenal of Democracy." Starting as early as 1935, and with his visionary mind in high gear, he spirited funds through Congress for the aircraft carriers Yorktown and Enterprise. The Yorktown, before it was sunk at the Battle of Midway in June, 1942, had repaid its cost multiple times. Only three weeks earlier, at the Battle of the Coral Sea, it helped cause sufficient damage to the large Japanese carriers, Shokaku and Zuikaku, so they could not participate at Midway. Had they been present it is extremely doubtful we would have won that convincing victory.

The President earlier had played an enormously vital role keeping England in the war. Even as keen an observer as George Catlett Marshall, Army Chief of Staff, was positively convinced that England was doomed in the Battle of Britain. Still worse, there was scarcely any important officer in either the Army or Navy who disagreed with that assessment. As already noted, Mr. Roosevelt insisted that 50 Navy destroyers be delivered to the Brits; they were of no value to our Navy and had been taken out of service. At the President's insistence, immense amounts of rifles, artillery and ammunition were hurriedly transferred to England over the often violent objections of key military advisors.

On June 22, 1941 Hitler invaded Russia with three million men, consisting of at least 150 divisions. (It is doubtful on that day that we had even 15 combat worthy divisions). He would also utilize 3300 tanks, 2700 planes and 600,000 motor vehicles.

FDR's Cabinet was about evenly divided on the question of providing military assistance to the Russians since Marshall and the entire combined Army and Navy staff were persuaded that Russia was doomed. In their collective opinion, the Russian Army's life expectancy wasn't more than 90 days. Their extreme reluctance flowed from their conviction that any armament sent East would fall into German hands.

Once again he overruled his military and domestic advisors. First he sent his most trusted aide, Harry Hopkins, to interview Winston Churchill and in Moscow, Joseph Stalin. Churchill, militant anti-Communist that he was, strongly urged immediate assistance to the now beleaguered Soviets. Stalin was very convincing in his argument that his armies would contain the onslaught, but would require immediate and massive, aid.

Because of the inspired direction of the President, and his continual prodding of Congress, that somewhat reluctant body had approved expenditures of around

$30 billion for rebuilding our armed forces. That, despite the sullen, rearguard defiance of the isolationist, obstructionist Republicans.

Without FDR's relentless effort to provide the Soviets with immediate aid, very little assistance would have resulted. His firm demand that they be included in Lend-Lease was motivated by his conviction that Soviet survival had weighty consequence for our own national security. In that appraisal he was once again right on target. The Russian Army and the Russian winter would rip apart a significant chunk of the Wehrmacht and the Luftwaffe.

During the first summer Hitler's hordes forced the Russians into a continuous retreat and in the process took upwards of four million prisoners. Of that, roughly 95% would not survive captivity. Finally, in late September the annual autumnal rains would fall and with the still primitive state of roads in the Soviet Union, the German juggernaut began to slip and slide and slow down. In October cold weather set in. Now the roads were slippery in their iciness, and presented hazards at every mile. In November the numbing chill of Russian winters nearly paralyzed Hitler's war machine. Engines, lacking anti-freeze, froze over; the internal combustion engines were destroyed. The German infantrymen were still wearing summer clothing since Hitler and his entire general staff were convinced the Russian Army would disintegrate within 90 days.

At about the 180 day level the Russians struck back and recaptured several hundred miles of lost territory. This was the first reverse ever suffered by the troops of the German military genius. His army would never again be as good as it was on June 22.

Meanwhile the President and his military staff were anxiously viewing the increasingly turbulent scene in the far Pacific. Doris Kearns Goodwin, in her enchanting biography of Eleanor and Franklin Roosevelt, *"No Ordinary time,"* outlines the predicament the President was encountering.

The top naval commander in the Pacific Theater, Admiral Harold Stark, had warned his President on November 27. "Japan may attack the Burma Road, Thailand, Malaya, the Netherlands East Indies, the Philippines, the Russian Maritime Provinces ... The most essential thing now from the United States viewpoint, is to gain time." FDR insisted that this county continue to maintain peace with Japan. "We must strain every nerve to satisfy and keep on good relations with this group of Japanese negotiators," he told Secretary of State Cordell Hull. "Don't let it deteriorate and break up if you can possibly help it."

At about 7:30 a.m. Honolulu time, the Japanese launched a surprise attack on Sunday, December 7th. Even though peace envoys from both Japan and the U.S. were still engaged in diplomatic talks, the Japanese had launched this perfidious and deadly air assault on our naval vessels. "I never wanted to have to fight this war on two fronts," Franklin told Eleanor, "We haven't got the Navy to fight in both the Atlantic and Pacific…So we will have to build up the Navy and the Air Force and that will mean that we will have to take a good many defeats before we can have a victory."

Ever since Pearl Harbor Day, the pitiful Roosevelt haters have spread all manner of execrable lies. Mrs. Goodwin presents us with their detestable argument. "Roosevelt was aware of the Japanese plans to attack Pearl Harbor but deliberately concealed his knowledge from the commanders in Hawaii in order to bring the U.S. into hostilities though the back door. Unable to swing Congress and the public toward a declaration of war against Germany, critics contend, the president provoked Japan into firing the first shot and then watched with delight as the attack created a united America."

The attack on Pearl Harbor happened because our forces were negligently unprepared. "Neither Army or Navy Commandants in Oahu regarded such an attack as at all likely," Secretary Knox explained to Roosevelt. (Remember, that Secretary Knox was the running mate for Alf Landon in 1936.) "Both General Walter Short and Admiral Husband Kimmel felt certain that such an attack would take place nearer Japan's base of operations, that is, in the Far East." The author continues the narrative. "Lack of readiness characterized every aspect of the base — from the unmanned aircraft batteries to the radar station whose sentries went off duty at 7:00 a.m. that morning."

It should be made clear that not a single high ranking officer ever uttered a statement, or authored a document that impugned the President's actions leading up to Pearl Harbor Day. But which of his critics were certain that his true name was Rosenfelt, or that his paralysis was caused not by polio but by syphilis?

At last the reprehensible isolationists were finally silenced. The old fool Herbert Hoover bayed a different note. "American soil has been treacherously attacked by Japan. Our decision is clear. We must fight with everything we have." Of course had he been reelected he would have insured we had nothing to fight with.

Continents away, Adolph Hitler blamed our President for provoking the war. "This man alone was responsible for the Second World War," he proclaimed to the Reichstag, and because of his foul deeds, Germany "considers herself to be at war with the United States, as from today."

That outburst was as faithless to the truth as were the charges by FDR's critics, all Republicans naturally, that he had deliberately provoked the Japanese attack.

Only after the Joint Chiefs of Staff had absorbed the twin devastations of Pearl Harbor on December 7 and Hitler's declaration of war four days later, did they and the President arrive at an understanding that Nazi German constituted this nation's gravest threat. The Japanese would have to be contained as best as possible.

Hitler, the German military genius, had engaged his nation simultaneously at war with Russia, this country and England with its British Empire. On the day of his war declaration, the Wehrmacht was engaged in a savage struggle for survival not too far from Moscow. While it would endure this challenge, it would have to absorb the loss of nearly a half-million of its highly trained men killed, wounded, captured or missing in action. What was nearly as bad was that this mighty juggernaught had sacrificed a worrisome amount of its original equipment. Wholesale quantities of tanks, motorized artillery and other mechanized equipment had been destroyed or abandoned.

The diminuendo days of that once unstoppable force were just over the horizon. In well under a year it would be subjected to an even more destructive episode at a major industrial center on the Volga River called Stalingrad.

Joseph Stalin considered that city nearly hallowed ground since he had renamed it in 1925, shortly after becoming the absolute dictator of the Soviet Union. Adolph Hitler was fanatically determined to conquer it mostly because of its name. For these reasons its importance ascended far beyond its military or strategic valve.

Before this cataclysmic contest would end, well in excess of a million lives would be expended – not merely combatants from both sides, but countless civilians, most of them workers producing vital supplies for the Russian Army. The entire Sixth German Army, or what remained of it, would surrender to the Soviets, an army which at the beginning of the battle numbered 350,000 men. With it was lost every rifle, machine gun, artillery piece, truck and tank which it possessed.

As the fight for Stalingrad approached its conclusion the American army would, on November 8, 1942, initiate its first offensive against Hitler. It would take place in North Africa. Half of the thrust would be on the Atlantic Coast, the other half along several Mediterranean ports.

The idea of this invasion in North Africa would be passionately debated among FDR's military advisors. Generals Marshall and Eisenhower fiercely opposed it, opting instead for an assault somewhere in occupied France. Eisenhower was so adamant that he predicted the resulting fiasco "would go down as the blackest day in history".

FDR, as we have already seen, was frequently at odds with his Joint Chiefs and, in this situation, with the two generals most involved. Before proceeding further, I must confess my sincerest admiration for George Catlett Marshall, without whom the war would never have been brought to such a speedy, successful conclusion. However, the President was equally convinced that the North African invasion was badly needed. In his vaunted ability to peer into the future, he needs to be compared to Abe Lincoln, who had the same luminous insight into military affairs.

For it was Honest Abe who insisted on retaining Generals Ulysses Grant and William Tecumseh Sherman in spite of heavy opposition from his war department. It was he, who also fostered the careers of Generals Phil Sheridan and George H. Thomas. Once he had those four commanders in place, union victory became inevitable.

For insight into merely one problem facing the planners of any seaborne invasion, one only has to witness what took place on the morning of November 8, as cargo ships prepared to unload. "In this first encounter with the enemy, the army was determined that American boys have the best equipment their country could give them: the new streamlined Sherman tanks, new multiple gun mounts, amphibious tractors, submachine guns. The proliferation of materials had made the loading process in the states a nightmare. Unschooled in logistics, inexperienced loaders invariably stored the small-arms ammunition and other cargo needed first in the deepest holds of the ships. Heavy equipment that should have gone into bottom storage arrived later and was put on top instead.

Of the dozens of books available on this period in our history, none presents this argument in such a succinct and enlightened manner as does Doris Kearns Goodwin in her completely absorbing "No Ordinary Times – Franklin and Eleanor Roosevelt: The Home Front in World War II. This is just one of several best selling books she has penned. In this work she delineates "a brilliant narrative account of how the United States, an isolationist country divided along class lines, still suffering the ravages of a decade-long depression and woefully unprepared for war, was unified by a common threat and by the extraordinary leadership of Franklin Roosevelt to become only five years later, the prominent economic and military power in the world." This quote is from the book jacket.

After first engaging French troops, which often offered only dispirited resistance, the Americans next would next clash with the seasoned German veterans led by field Marshall Irwin Rommel. Our troops always fought with valor but were inexperienced in battle and were sometimes poorly led. Our tanks were not as good, other equipment less than adequate and as a result our side suffered some disconcerting setbacks. All of these conditions would improve with time. Fortunately time was on our side. Within six months, our invasion force, working in concert with the British driving west from Egypt, would force the surrender of over 200,000 German and Italian troops. All of North Africa would be in allied hands, as of May 13, 1942.

What needs to be considered is that Rommel's forces suffered from want of sufficient numbers of tanks, trucks and most importantly, gasoline. His only supply line, from Italy, was undependable. British submarines and bombers sunk altogether too many of the German cargo ships. The Wehrmacht in France didn't suffer from these afflictions. All of these considerations pointed to the obvious fact that our army wasn't ready, in 1942 or even 1943, to go up against the Germans in France.

Franklin Roosevelt could visualize these manifest problems – surprisingly Marshall and Eisenhower couldn't. Both lacked the President's uncanny ability to envision the entire picture, beginning with geographical knowledge and recognizing the frightening inadequacies of our army.

Slightly less than two months after the surrender in Tunisia, the Allies staged their second invasion in the Mediterranean region, this time in Sicily on July 10, 1943. In only 31 days the entire island would be cleansed of German and Italian troops. This campaign was conducted on a much higher level of efficiency. Loading and unloading vital supplies were handled in a more expeditious manner. The commanding general for the Americans was George Smith Patton, a certified genius in conducting bold, inspired offensive thrusts. Patton would garner world-wide celebrity in his daring forays against Nazi troops in France, the following summer. Of the six biographies of Patton I have studied – questionably the most authentic is that of Carlos D'Este entitled "Patton – A Genius for War".

By D-Day in France the following June, both the allies in the west operating out of England, and the Russian in the East, would have delivered a continuing series of crippling blows to Hitler's legions. It had taken all of 1942, and months of 1943, for the Army Air Corps to build up its bomber and fighter groups to the level where they could punish the Germans on the continent. Our eighth Air Force concentrated on demolishing as much of the enemies' military production as possible. As D-Day neared the focus turned to isolating the Normandy battlefield area so that the German forces were considerably hampered in their movement. This meant knocking out bridges and vital railroad centers.

In order to deceive Hitler and his general staff about the eventual invasion site, the Royal Air Force worked in close harmony with our Air Corps and plastered two widely separated areas in France – the Pas de Calais region directly across the channel from England and also Normandy. The allies strived desperately to convince the German military genius that the assault would be near the French coastal city of Calais. This region contained several small seaports, vital for landing troops and handling supplies. In this effort they were pleasingly successful.

Both allied air forces went to enormous and costly lengths to blast German gasoline refineries, thereby making it more difficult for both Nazi ground forces and the Luxtwaffe to function efficiently. Here again their efforts were fruitful.

This unimaginable progress could have been forecast by listening to the President's State of the Union delivered on January 6, 1942, less than a month after Pearl Harbor. In it he boldly laid out his production goals for the year. He predicted the nation's factories, now busily converting to military output, would turn out 60,000 fighter and bomber planes; 45,000 tanks; 20,000 anti-aircraft guns.

He summarized the feeling of his administration by adding, "the militarists of Berlin and Tokyo started the war. But the massed angered forces of common humanity will finish it". Finished as well were the formerly surly, spiteful Republicans who now found it expedient to join ranks with our optimistic military leaders and a very determined populace. The President's ardent desire to make this nation the arsenal of democracy would be fulfilled.

To fully comprehend just how stalwart the arsenal would become we should turn to the "West Point Atlas of American Wars" which presents an overflowing of statistics compiled by the Department of Military Art and Engineering, the United States Military Academy. Its chief editor was Colonel Vincent Esposito, Professor and head of the department. "The major factor in the increased mobility and efficiency of the Russian Armies was Allied Lease Lend. During the war, the U.S. alone provided Russia with 385,883 trucks , 51,503 jeeps, 7,056 tanks, 5,071 tractors, 1,981 locomotives, 11,158 freight cars, and 14, 834 airplanes.

Colonel Esposito firmly establishes his opinion of the transaction. "Generally speaking, Lend-Lease to Russia was carried out in the same atmosphere of mixed-idealism, enthusiasm and naiveté." It pays to recall that FDR's Joint Chiefs of Staff were nearly unanimous in their opposition to sending anything to the Russians since they were possessed of a complete conviction that the Russian Army would collapse in as little as 90 days. Even after Stalin's troops held firm against the Nazi's and then began sending them into retreat, these same military advisers could not rid themselves of a visceral hatred of the Communist regime in Russia.

There is no question that the Soviet Army was infinitely improved by the providential shower of Lend-Lease equipment coming from America, just as there is no question that the Russian military employed it with praise worthy results. By the time the Americans landed in Normandy on June 6, 1944, the Nazis had been forced to relinquish almost all of Russian territory they had conquered during the idyllic days of easy triumphs in 1941-42.

At this point the Nazi high command was busily filling the dangerously depleted ranks of its infantry with Ost soldiers, men from the East, mostly captured Poles and Russians. To be sure these replacements could shoulder a rifle, but their devotion to the Nazi cause was never very fervent.

The Wehrmacht opposing the Americans on D-Day was substantially weakened from its high level of destructiveness before the Russian campaign. It was critically hampered by an inability to maneuver quickly due to months of air attacks on bridges and railroad centers. The inventory of locomotives and rolling stock available was shrinking, often times caused by sabotage from French Resistance fighters.

D-Day, the beginning of the invasion of France, was originally set for June 5, 1944, but miserably inclement weather forced a postponement for a day. Looking for guidance from the "West Point Atlas of American Wars" we learn that, "In selecting the landing areas, SHAEF(Supreme Headquarters Allied Expedition Force) planners considered many factors, the most important being the requirement for air cover, adequate beach and port capacity, German strength and dispositions, and availability of landing craft and transport aircraft. The choice was narrowed to the LeHavre – Calais and the Caen – Cherboury areas; the second was eventually selected, primarily because of its better beaches and weaker defenses.

"On 6 June, the strengths of the Allied force (all numbered services) was 2,876,000 men. The organization of the ground component numbered 45 divisions. The task of equipping and supplying this tremendous force had been staggering, but by virtually converting the United Kingdom into one huge military base, it had been accomplished".

This had been accomplished because of the nearly unfathomable torrent of supplies shipped over from American factories. By D-Day there was a plentitude of equipment for every branch of service, a fact that played a supreme role in the success of the invasion.

To this day I am continually astounded by the super abundance of equipment and supplies that arrived where it was needed. Much of that was freighted by Liberty ships. No Liberty ships existed before 1941. No shipyards existed to build Liberty ships before 1941. Moreover the concept of a Liberty ship had as yet not been born. What's still worse – our shipping industry had been indolent for more than a decade and this country ranked far down the list of nations with fleets of first rate ocean freighters.

Just as FDR had set a seemingly impossible goal for building military aircraft as he did when he requested funds for 60,000 annually, so he did for constructing desperately needed new ships. German submarines were sinking them at a savage rate. To do this he turned the project over to Henry J. Kaiser who could best be described as an entrepreneurial genius who had quickly constructed two mammoth dams, Boulder and Grand Coulee. At the time Kaiser didn't know much more about building ships than did my mother, but with his exceedingly fertile mind the President was confident he was the man for the job.

The techniques put to use by Kaiser turned out craft lacking in impressive form and pleasing design but each could carry nearly 3,000 jeeps or 3,000,000 meals for our troops. Besides that about 2700 of them flowed out of his shipyards.

The landings in France on June 6, 1944, officially known as D-Day, were the most magnificent invasion in the history of military conflict. Absolutely nothing compared to it in size or concept. Just after midnight two complete divisions of airborne infantry, the 82nd and the 101st, came cascading from the sky. There were 13,000 of these heavily armed, extremely well trained paratroopers. Numerous factors, including German anti-aircraft fire caused them to be wildly dispersed, sometimes many miles from their drop zone. The result was not always undesirable. Reports coming into German unit headquarters inflated the real numbers beyond belief. Adding to the confusion, thousands of dummy parachutists, small-sized fakes fluttering down with miniature chutes, were setting off fireworks upon landing which simulated small arms fire. The totally bewildered Germans estimated that 96,000 Americans had plummeted onto French soil – this caused them to send their forces over a huge area searching for imaginary Americans.

The German defense had been stormed along a lengthy span of Normandy coast-line, 59 miles to be exact. In the two American beachheads, Utah and Omaha, elements of five different infantry divisions began to land at daybreak. At Utah, the most southern point of the invasion area, the landing force met almost no hostile fire. To some degree this was the result of 269 Marauder medium bombers, sweeping in at low level and plastering the area with thousands of bombs, killing or wounding many of the defenders. Just a short distance to the North, the Omaha sector, the assault troops were cut down mercilessly by German machinegun and artillery fire, often times before they could even move out of their landing craft.

The commanding general of our ground forces was Omar Bradley who began receiving radio reports from the beach area that pointed to looming disaster.

By nine on that first morning he was giving serious thought to abandoning Omaha and reinforcing the British and Canadian forces to the north. By this time navy ships, principally smaller vessels like destroyers, could work their way into shallow waters and fire their five inch guns with considerable accuracy. This artillery fire was sufficient in enough positions to enable the beleaguered infantry to fight their way off the beaches and onto higher ground, away from the lethal German rifles and artillery.

In an isolated position, Pointe du Hoc, a precipice 100 feet above the shore line, 225 superbly trained American Rangers began the climb to the summit. By day's end only 90 were still battle worthy. This scene has been reenacted in several famous movies about D-Day, but the magnificent Rangers scaled those heights to complete their mission successfully.

Due to the repeated heavy shelling from Navy ships, the German communication system was battered and sometimes even destroyed. Good fortune on occasion intervened. A German division assigned to a critical area was instructed by higher command that the invasion was hurled back and the situation was completely under control. Scenarios of this nature are known as "the fog of war" and are common place in battle.

Adolph Hitler, the self-proclaimed military genius, habitually remained awake until well after midnight, and only then went to bed. He normally arose around noon. When informed on June 6 of the landings he remained unconcerned, serene in the knowledge that this was only a devious plot by the cunning allies and the real invasion would come well to the north. German generals acted under his strict control and could not undertake any significant movement of troops without his explicit approval. He gave none until later in the afternoon.

Geoffrey Perret has authored a work, "There's A War to be Won," of very pleasing expression. In it he reveals a staggering attention to detail. "By nightfall on D-Day there were 30,000 men ashore at Utah; 26,000 at Omaha; and another 17,000 paratroopers and gliderists in the Cotentin. There were 83,000 British and Canadians in their sectors. Allied casualties had been projected to run as high as 25,000. Overall losses came in around 10,000.

"Even though it fell short of the highest hopes, Overlord covered the bottom line – it put the troops ashore."

The American 82nd Airborne division had secured the small town of Ste-Mere Eglise on D-Day, the first inhabited dwelling place in France, part of Hitler's Festung Europa, Fortress Europe.

The Nazis had more than sufficient troops, tanks, and assembled fire power to drive the Allies back into the sea, but they were beset with a multitude of problems, not the least of which was their military genius heading up the defense. Added to that were the continuous air attacks which constituted an onerous burden. Each effort in the daylight hours to assemble a group of tanks and motorized vehicle drew savage destructive reprisals.

Slowly, but inexorably the allied ground forces pushed the Wehrmacht back as troops, equipment and supplies piled into the expanding bridgehead. On D-plus 30, July 6, the first American fighter group began landing near the village of Ste. – Mere-Eglise; our little weather forecasting detachment accompanied it. The airfield was nothing more than Normandy pasture land on which a heavy steel mesh was laid to give the wheels on the fighter planes a firmer landing surface. The front line was not much more than 20 miles distant; we knew the Germans lacked the means to break through our front lines. The once omnipotent Luftwaffe rarely appeared and when it did only one or two fighter planes would show up and they were none too eager to inflict any damage.

At the apex of this extraordinary war effort was the Commander-in-Chief, Franklin Delano Roosevelt, who led the still large majority of Democrats in Congress. Without their help in passing the colossal military appropriations bill beginning in 1938, no D-Day would have been possible. Then reflect on how the clueless, churlish Republicans overwhelming opposed the draft bill in 1940. Volunteers couldn't possibly have sufficed to create 45 infantry divisions, the numerous armored (tank) divisions, the army air corps requirements and of course the highly expanded navy.

We must reflect as well on what our colossal torrent of military supplies under Lend-Lease did for the Russians in the crucial years of 1942-43. Then see what the Russians did to the Nazis in those years and were continuing to do right up to June 6, 1944.

Even facing a severely mauled Wehrmacht on that day we needed the charitable hand of Dame Fortune in order to succeed. It quickly becomes too stomach-churning to contemplate the scenario of a victorious Germany and a defeated Russia in 1942. Yet that could easily have happened without Lend-Lease to the Russians which began very shortly after Pearl Harbor Day.

What of the 134 Republicans in the House who voted against Lend-Lease in 1941? Did even one of them subsequently become contrite and plead to be forgiven for this unseemly treachery? Ha! They immediately banded together to find where next they could do combat with the hated Roosevelt.

In a delicious application of military chicanery, we must bear witness to a campaign which the devilishly clever Allies in London perpetrated on the unsuspecting Nazis. The German Secret Service, working under the auspices of the Gestapo, labored assiduously to infiltrate spies into England. As soon as each one entered the country, he was immediately apprehended by the English counterparts. The spy had been directed to report to his next in command. That spy however had already been arrested, so before the new agent could begin work he was already in custody. He could agree to cooperate with his captors and become a double agent, just as his next in command had done, or he would be executed. In the former role he would transmit bogus information about the state of allied preparedness back to German. Surprisingly few chose the other alternative.

In this grandiose hoax, the handlers in England first created the fourth American Army, a huge imaginary military force of trained infantry slated to land in Calais, the area closest to England. Numerous small ports existed in nearby towns; delivering army supplies and equipment could be easily facilitated. A part of this army would also be diverted to invade Norway.

In order to make this ploy even more deceptive, numerous elaborate stratagems were put into practice. Squads of radio operators sent information about this army back and forth. Lightweight rubber tank models, by the thousands, were set in place so that German reconnaissance planes could easily spot them. These were amazingly realistic in appearance, especially when viewed from hundreds of feet above. It was all very deceptive and the Germans bought into the ruse. Hitler and his important generals were utterly convinced.

Bear in mind that this torrent of material was streaming into Berlin from its own spies, trained by German Intelligence; the Nazi High Command had every reason to believe it was authentic. Not a single piece of evidence pointed to the fact that these spies were captives and co-opted by the British and Americans. It was largely on the strengths of these reports that Hitler placed so much emphasis on defending the Calais area rather than Normandy.

To be sure Normandy was not left undefended, but the majority of German troops in France were in the wrong location. Earlier in the campaign, troops were being withdrawn from Norway and used to bolster the defenses in France. Once he was convinced that this fourth army might actually invade Norway, Hitler began to reverse the flow. The swollen multitude of troops in that country remained there until they surrendered to the Allies after the war ended and never participated in any battle.

Had this monumental deception not been swallowed by the Germans the allied invasion force would have had a much smaller likelihood of success.

I readily confess that for the past 50 years and more, I have been a devoted and unrepentant junkie on all facets of World War II history. After all it covers the most melodramatic period in all of mankind's history.

Once the Americans, together with their British and Canadian allies had secured a continuous front in Normandy, they began the grueling task of ridding all of France from German occupation and in turn destroying the Wehrmacht. In doing so our infantry divisions, while inching forward during June and well into July, were sustaining brutal casualties. By the time the Americans had captured St. Lo, the first city of note and no more than 20 miles distant, they had suffered 40,000 killed or wounded, and this only 41 days after D-Day on July 17th. American cemeteries in Normandy, while tastefully designed, were filling too rapidly with crosses.

On July 20th, an attempt was made on Hitler's life by high-ranking German officers. Only a fluky intervention of fate at nearly the last second saved him from destruction by a powerful bomb placed only feet away.

Once St. Lo had been captured, the Americans had burst into open country and could exploit this advantage. They soon evolved a radical new concept in military thinking – saturation bombing from an air armada of around 2000 planes, both large four engine and smaller two engine bombers. Moreover they would confine that unprecedented striking power to a relatively tidy area – three miles by one-and-a-half miles. It was code-named Operation Cobra.

This plan was the distillation of thought by both General Omar Bradley, head of all American ground forces in France, and Elwood "Pete" Quesada, a much younger air corp general. The two shared breakfast each morning.

When put into operation on the morning of July 25th, it's effect on the Germans was demoralizing. An entire panzer or tank division that had been blocking our advance was simply demolished. Into this breach raced three of our armored divisions. An entire infantry division soon followed. For the first time in history, every man in this division rode in a fast moving truck; none walked.

In the rank of world class armies, this one had by now risen to the very top. The Wehrmacht unleashed by Hitler against Poland on September 1, 1939, was easily the greatest of all time, particularly when it operated in close concert with its air component, the Luftwaffe. What assailed the British and French armies in May of 1940 was a much improved version of German might. Still more destructive was the Wehrmacht of June 1941.

However, following two years of embroilment with toughening Soviet armies and enduring two savage Russian winters, Hitler's hordes had suffered a continuing emasculation.

By the end of December 1942, the Russians under Stalin now held the honors as the best army in the world. That army of course had been opulently fortified through Lend-Lease, beginning immediately after Pearl Harbor Day. The 134 Republicans in the House who voted to kill Lend-Lease would have preferred not to discuss the matter.

By the beginning of August, 1944, our invasion force in France was without a peer in military annals. Concurrently, the Naval task force rampaging through the Pacific was equally nonpareil, as the Japanese defenders on the various islands we wished to take were soon to discover.

Three days after Cobra was launched, George Smith Patton assumed command of the newly organized Third Army. Georgie Patton, as he was called by his men, was an authentic military genius, the only one the American armies produced in World War II. His guiding philosophy in warfare was a French expression he frequently put to use – l'audace, tojours l'audace – audacity, always audacity.

One of his numerous biographers, Carlo D'Este in his work of inestimable insight on his subject, "Patton – A Genius for War" sums up General Patton correctly. "The Patton who trained himself for greatness with a determination matched by no other general in the 20th Century. In North Africa, Sicily, France and Germany, he earned the reputation of being the allied general the Germans most feared and respected."

Immediately upon taking command of his army, "he put the Third Army on that one road south, pushing 200,000 men and 40,000 vehicles through what amounted to a straw." This passage is from "There's a War To Be Won – The United States Army in World War II" by Geoffrey Perret. The author continues, "Every manual on road movement was ground into the dust. He and his staff did what the whole world knew couldn't be done. It was flat impossible to put a whole army out on a narrow two-lane road and move it at high speed. Everything was going to come to a screeching halt. He even intermingled units, yet out the other end of the straw came divisions intact and ready to fight. If anybody else could have done that, no one ever got that man's name."

Patton instilled audacity into all unit commanders under his leadership. In their daring forays he drove them to approach recklessness. Once his offensive got underway, his German adversaries were sent reeling backward in utmost confusion as American tank units suddenly appeared behind enemy lines raising complete havoc.

When his division commanders voiced concern about the enemy attacking from the flanks, he would berate them, telling them not to take counsel of their fears. He constantly admonished them to let the Germans worry about their flanks.

As D'Este explains, "Patton's cavalier dismissal of his flanks was not as casual as it appeared." First of all he had "Ultra" working for him. Back in London the wizards in the Allied Intelligence Service had broken the secret radio code of the Wehrmacht; the result was the allied generals were constantly apprised of German plans. Any orders from Hitler's staff would quickly wind up in the hands of generals like Patton. In the Pacific our Naval Intelligence had performed in a like manner with the Japanese secret code.

Next, Patton could rely on an extensive network of armed, trained resistance fighters from the F.F.I, the Free French of the Interior who were in touch by radio with our army units. They continuously alerted these units to any German forces starting to assemble on the exposed flanks.

In addition General Patton had at least 2000 deadly fighter planes working in close concert with his infantry troops. The pilots had direct radio communication with the infantry and tank units and could quickly break up any attempt on the part of the German generals to organize a flank attack.

One of Patton's most effective weapons was his personal use of aerial reconnaissance. He would fly over the rapidly moving battlefield in a small, two-seat Piper Cub; the pilot was the only other occupant. He continually risked his life doing so because German anti-aircraft fire might bring down his plane. No other American general ever did this.

Galvanized by the dynamism of this one man, the Third Army was employing lightening-like thrusts into a German army approaching defeatism. The Germans were being assaulted by hundreds of thousands of superbly armed, well-trained young men whose morale was bubbling over. Contrast that with the Wehrmacht which had now been battling for almost five years-first in Poland in 1939, France in 1940; then in Russia in 1941, North Africa in 1942-3; now in France again in 1944. Their infantry ranks were dangerously compromised by captive Polish and Russian soldiers eagerly awaiting an opportunity to surrender to the Americans. In many instances these Ost soldiers, before running over to the American lines waving a white flag of surrender might first try to kill several of the German troops.

The lethal striking power of the Third Army came from two dimensions. On the ground the overwhelming might of the tank divisions, buttressed by motorized artillery, which were led by superb unit commanders. From the skies the Germans could count on frequent visits from our planes; fires would then break out in a convoy of enemy tanks which included gasoline and ammunition trucks, both readily flammable. Often the fires would spread from one vehicle to another.

Patton put to use tactics that became terrifying assaults for the Germans. His tank commanders were trained to probe for small undefended or lightly defended areas in the enemy defensive front and instantly hurl large numbers of fast moving tanks into the breach. The aggressive tankers would then roam at leisure behind enemy lines and with their machine guns and artillery weapons shoot up everything in sight. Wehrmacht veterans of the campaigns on foreign soil had witnessed similar attacks against enemy troops. Now they were being subjected to them only delivered with far better, faster tanks.

These violent attacks created a debilitating effect on the enemy so that thoughts of surrender became more frequent. It must be realized that when Patton took command on July 28th, the German defense lines were stretched to a near breaking point. Each German in France that was killed, wounded or captured was one less soldier available to fight. Hitler was unable to spare any further reinforcements, since his armies in the East fighting the Russians were everywhere in retreat.

Once Patton's forces punched through the rather thin defensive line, as happened after Cobra, there were no reserves to stop them. Georgie seized upon this advantage and began a wide loop around the entire Seventh German Army in France. In an amazingly short period of time he was on the brink of entrapping that army.

Carlo D'Este focuses on the scene. "The Allied triumph that ended the Normandy campaign ensured that Germany would ultimately lose the war. The magnitude of the German defeat was starkly visible around the villages of Tron, Saint Lambert and Chambois, which were littered with unburied dead, thousands of dead horses and cattle, and smashed and burning vehicles. Patton's divisions across southern Normandy met with little opposition. Le Mans, Orleans, Chartres and Dreux all fell to the Third Army."

Once enemy positions began to collapse, the other Allied Armies, the Canadian and the British began to thrust forward. The three Allied forces could easily, very easily completely encircle the German Army trapped in the general area of Falaise.

Patton's superior officer, Omar Bradley, was exultant. He referred to this as "an opportunity that comes not more than once in a century. We're about to destroy an entire army. We'll go all the way to the German border."

Only one man prevented the U.S. Third Army from going all the way to the German border, and of course ending the war no later than November 1st. That man was Omar Bradley. The British and Canadians were charged with the responsibility of closing their sector of what became known as the Falaise Gap. They proceeded to do so, not at a leisurely rate but at a glacial pace. The Third

Army could have easily done what their Allies were unable to do. But Bradley stubbornly refused to grant Patton authorization to move the slight distance necessary to enclose the trap. The tortoise speed of the Canadians required a full week to finally join up with Americans.

Meanwhile enemy troops were able to flee north toward Germany in the vacant area. They moved on foot and abandoned every bit of motorized equipment. Estimates vary on the number of Nazis who escaped – some historians place the total around 50,000 seasoned troops. The Americans would have to engage in a bloody slugfest with these same troops in December in the Battle of the Bulge – a battle that should never have happened, since the war should have ended.

Pages could be devoted to quote the many historians who have subjected Bradley to a remorseless indictment for his failure of leadership at this momentous occasion. Martin Blumenson, one of the most respected of these historians and author of three separate biographies of different phases of Patton's career, is merciless in his appraisal of Bradley's conduct during this entire scenario. Bradley, he insists, "halted Third Army at the Seine River and at Dreux, Chartres and Orleans and thereby killed the pursuit at the very moment he ought to have been encouraging it. He made instant decisions, then second guessed himself. He initiated potentially brilliant maneuvers, then aborted them because he lacked confidence in his ability to see them through to completion."

One of the most tragic mistakes in our invasion of France was selecting Bradley to command our forces. Patton had been Bradley's commanding officer when we invaded North Africa in 1942 and then again in our conquest of Sicily the next year. But on two separate instances Patton had slapped an American soldier in a field hospital in Sicily, both times because these combat veterans were suffering from post-traumatic stress, or combat fatigue. These episodes nearly destroyed Patton's career. Following the second incident, Eisenhower relieved Patton of his command and in a role reversal made Bradley the senior officer.

Blumenson continues his appraisal of the situation. "Had Patton commanded the Army Group (the group to which the Third Army was attached) as indeed he would have had he not self-destructed his career in Sicily – the events of August 1944 would have been very different."

D'Este has this to say. "Had Patton been in command of the Americans in France, there would have been a much earlier end of the war; there would not have been indeciveness."

Another highly respected biographer, Ladislas Farrago, in his revealing work, "Patton-Ordeal and Triumph", renders his verdict on the subject. "It is, therefore, regrettable that after the initial and incidental oneness of Eisenhower's and Patton's outlooks, the Supreme Commander gradually departed from these views and plans. Instead of pursuing them boldly and rigorously in cooperation with Patton, he abandoned them in favor of more cautious estimates and actions.

"But Ike's proximity to Bradley soon began to dilute his own concepts and weaken his determination. Within a week he was to succumb to Bradley's influence and stand idly by as the bold campaign Patton was improvising along Eisenhower's own lines was halted and diverted, resulting in the enemy's escape from the trap to delay victory in the Battle of France".

With that decidedly uncharitable verdict arrived at, let's zoom in on the man in question. Ike, his preferred nickname, remained at his fashionable headquarters in London, seldom visited with Bradley and almost never with Patton. Instead of being present and participating in the decision making process, he permitted Bradley to rein in the best general we had in France.

As August was coming to an end Georgie Patton would suffer still another rude rebuff, this time at the hands of Eisenhower. At this pivotal juncture in the campaign, Ike finally decided to assert a leadership role.

Eisenhower's new strategy called for the American First Army, much, much larger than Patton's Third Army, to assume the brunt of the offensive. Courtney Hodges, commander, would coordinate his efforts with British and Canadian troops under the British commander, Field Marshall Sir Bernard Law Montgomery.

Patton's Third Army would be relegated to a minor role, principally because that army had advanced the greatest distance and was much farther removed from the Atlantic ports. Eisenhower put this plan in effect by allowing the other two generals to have most, or nearly all the available gas, and in doing so forcing Patton to the sidelines.

Since the Allied Armies had in August advanced so far, so fast, their supply lines had fallen hopelessly behind. No shortage of gas or other supplies existed – the shortage was in the transportation system, of being unable to deliver these supplies hundreds of miles from the Atlantic ports.

Patton had been pleading for a more equitable share of gas or other supplies. He told his staff, "if Ike gives me the supplies, I'll go through the Siegfried Line like shit through a goose". Georgie delighted in using very colorful, profane language. The Siegfried Line was on the German border, but Hitler had no troops to man it. Since June of 1944, for every German in France that had been killed, wounded, or captured, there had been at least two on the Russian front.

A military campaign can be likened to a horse race. In Patton, Eisenhower had in his stables, unquestionably America's greatest thoroughbred, whereas in Hodges and Sir Bernard he had a pair of undistinguished steeds. Neither ever exhibited any sterling qualities.

Yet Ike rewarded them by placing them in the race and in effect kept Patton in the barn. As a general, Courtney Hodges was a plodding type to whom l'audace was an ill-considered concept. Sir Bernard proceeded forward with cautious hesitancy.

Predictably Eisenhower's chosen generals proved to be slow-motion tacticians who failed to put a dent in the German lines. The campaign next moved into an uncertain area and then migrated into calamity. On December 16, 1944, Eisenhower discovered to his immense discomfort, that the Germans had launched an unbelievably fearsome attack against his troops. The Battle of the Bulge was underway.

The epic battle came perilously close to disaster for our troops. Our two top commanders, Eisenhower and Bradley preferred to ignore repeated warnings that the Germans were preparing a major offensive in the sector of the Ardennes Forest. By complete contrast, Patton's G-2, his Intelligence Chief, Colonel Oscar Koch had for several weeks been highly suspicious of the unusual degree of activity taking place among the Germans in the Ardennes Forest area near the Belgian border. He could see there was much too much railroad movement in a region that should have been quiet. He reported this to Patton, adding, it was obvious that a buildup of combat troops was underway. Even more ominous was the sudden complete radio silence from the Nazis.

This information was scarcely unknown to Eisenhower and his Intelligence Section. Colonel Benjamin Dickson, the G-2 for the First Army, had been telling his boss, Courtney Hodges, essentially the same information that Koch was telling Patton. General Patton however, was avidly listening to Koch and planning for any eventuality. Hodges thought Dickson was working too hard and very likely had a feverish imagination. He sent Dickson to Paris for a well-needed rest, one day before the battle began.

Within the Wehrmacht an unbelievable transformation had taken place. Gone was the shattered morale and deadly pessimism of the previous September. It had been replaced by the resurgence of a fighting spirit. By December the once proud German Army had regained a considerable amount of élan and once again was a fighting force of stature.

Adolph Hitler, working alone, had conceived this bold stratagem which he called 'The Watch on Rhine'- Das Wacht Am Rhein. Perfectly and boldly executed he expected to cut the Allied forces in two and then destroy each half at will, just as he had done to the combined French-British forces in May of 1940. To do so he needed Dame Fortune to intervene more than a few times.

He received kindly intercessions almost immediately. It was absolutely vital that the secrecy of his attack go undetected. As we have already seen it was detected by two different colonels trained in the business of ferreting out information of enemy activities, but the top three allied generals paid these officers no heed. On the very morning of the Ardennes Offensive, Sir Bernard issued this proclamation. "The enemy *cannot* stage major offensive operations." Eisenhower and Bradley were in complete accord with Montgomery's belief.

The next most important ingredient for the 'Watch on the Rhine' to be successful was for the weather to be favorable. For Hitler that meant complete overcast skies with low hanging clouds and for an extended period of time. That condition would prevent American planes from attacking his troops. Based on my many months of forecasting weather for that part of Europe, that was not unusual weather for Belgium in December. The weather on December 16th was exactly as Der Fuehrer would have liked and that condition remained for seven days. Then the weather began to turn favorable for our side.

Hitler couldn't have selected a more fortuitous sector to launch his offensive than in the Ardennes area. The troops along the 85 mile front where the attack came were very likely our worst units in France. The 106th Division had zero combat experience with nearly no combat training. Alongside it was the 99th Division which was only slightly more combat worthy. If that wasn't bad enough the two divisions were spread much too thin across the 85 miles.

Without doubt the absolutely worst break that Hitler could have received was the set of circumstances that thrust Patton into a position of command over the battle. Bradley was relegated to the role of an observer. Courtney Hodges was in over his head and unable to assume any authority. Sir Bernard was still hesitant in his caution and didn't bestir himself until January 3, and even then didn't overtax himself or his troops.

Eisenhower, not knowing what else to do, placed Georgie in charge and indeed Patton took immediate charge. Martin Blumenson, one of the war's most accurate historians said of Patton, "This was the supreme moment of his career." Omar Bradley was unstinting in his summation of Patton's role in this battle. "His generalship during this difficult maneuver was magnificent. One of the most brilliant performances by any commander on either side in World War II. It was absolutely his cup of tea – rapid, open warfare combined with noble purpose and difficult goals. He relished every minute of it, knowing full well that this mission, if nothing else, would guarantee him a place of high honor in the annals of the U.S. Army." Other than that remark, Bradley was usually stinting in his praise of Patton. As for Eisenhower, in his words of praise for Patton, he was even more frugal.

During this entire conflict I was stationed about 70 miles from Bastogne, Belgium which witnessed the bloodiest part of the battle. Since that time I have studied the battle in enormous detail by absorbing countless books on this period of the war.

In the battle's initial phase, the American forces were continually pushed back, trying desperately to contain the surging Nazis by forming a united front. Their gradual withdraw forced them to gather around Bastogne, a mere hamlet of some 4,000 souls. It's prominence in the eyes of both the American and German commander was in its strategic, geographical location. Seven ordinary roads all led through the town. These roads were crucial to the Germans in order to move their forces.

Hence, the enemy forces had to take control of it in order to reach their destination, the Meuse River. The Americans, by denying the town to the Wehrmacht, could contain the invasion.

Carlo D'Este in his glorious work "Patton-Genius for War" now reveals his subject at easily the most majestic moment of his career. "After more than thirty-four years, it was as if destiny had groomed him for this single, defining instant in which the fate of the war rested upon the right decisions being made and carried out by the men in that dingy room. While others debated or waffled, Patton had understood the problem facing the Allies and had created a plan to counteract the Germans and occupy Bastogne- which although not yet surrounded, was clearly soon to be besieged."

Patton now came to the rescue of Eisenhower and Bradley-he proceeded to halt the forward progress of his Third Army, turned it in a completely different direction and then raced to the rescue of Bastogne. This was done on relatively narrow, slippery roads and in freezing weather. Once more Blumenson weighs in on Patton. "Altogether it was an operation only a master could think of executing."

Quickly it comes to my mind the top four commanders in France who couldn't even visualize the execution of such an immensely challenging plan, much less successfully implement it – they were of course Eisenhower, Bradley, Hodges and Sir Bernard.

Two other points need to be addressed. For 18 acutely critical days for the Americans, starting on December 16, Montgomery refused to lift a finger to come to their aid. Secondly, throughout this entire episode in the Bulge, Patton remained serenely confident that all his subordinate generals and every one of their subordinates would act in a skilled manner and justify the immense risk he had just taken.

By the time Patton took charge of the battle, three American divisions were in Bastogne, and nearly surrounded. The weather finally cooperated sufficiently on December 23, so that our Air Corps could conduct limited strikes and also drop badly needed supplies to the men on the ground.

It wasn't until the day after Christmas that one of Patton's best tank divisions broke through German forces and reinforced our lads in the besieged town. They had christened themselves "The Battered Bastards of Bastogne". While this dramatic event virtually assured the town's defenders that now they would survive and not be captured, it hardly meant that their troubles were over. Illness was creating as much distress as the raging battle. That winter was the coldest of the century so with all the combat troops forced to live outdoors, flu and other respiratory diseases became a real menace. So did trench foot. This nasty condition was ever present and turned feet black, which if not treated quickly could result in gangrene, often followed by amputation.

While the hazardous period of mid and late December was over, the bloody conflict still continued. The Americans would attack in one area; the Germans would probe for a weakness in another.

It was becoming increasingly obvious from captured Nazi troops they were suffering from hunger and lack of supplies. Ever alert to weakness, Patton aimed for a bold counter attack that would surround the entire enemy force at Bastogne. But now that defeat was no longer a threat, and Patton had bailed him out of troubles, Eisenhower began to reassert his superior rank and deny Georgie permission to use any bold strokes.

As we have repeatedly seen, Ike and Bradley continually kept him on a short leash in Normandy and denied him unlimited movement at a time when audacity would have ended the war in Europe. Eisenhower and Bradley wanted no part of l'audace.

Since Patton was now restricted in his maneuvers by higher command and the Germans retreated ever so reluctantly, the war of attrition ground on. And so did the casualties. By the time the epic battle concluded in January, 31 days after it started, the American ground forces would suffer 80,897 casualties. Of these 10,276 were killed; 47,493 wounded; 23,218 missing in action.

None of those 80,897 casualties should ever have occurred. One of my classmates from high school was a fatality.

It wasn't until March 17, that Ike managed to issue his <u>first</u> congratulations to Patton. At one of the rare moments when he personally visited with Patton his compliments were effusive but not extensive. Georgie pointed out that this was the first time in two and a half years and that included the times they met in North Africa and Sicily.

Shortly thereafter when Ike was writing to George Marshall, his boss in Washington, he went to great lengths to extol the merits of Bradley and Hodges. He placed emphasis on the fact that "others had received credit for things that Bradley and Hodges were primarily responsible for."

That praise would come as an inordinate surprise to Patton's numerous biographers. Generally they were far more likely to belittle Hodges than praise him. Bradley merited a higher regard from them.

Hitler had gambled all his remaining resources on a roll of the dice at the Ardennes Forest. When it failed, his once invincible Wehrmacht could no longer sustain the blows coming from the Russians and the Allies.

By the time I entered Germany late in March, 1945, the bitter struggle had nearly ended. Nazi's were surrendering in ever growing numbers except for isolated smaller units. The principal Wehrmacht generals would meet with their American conquerors in Rheims, France to arrange surrender terms. The cease fire would come two days later. The war in Europe would officially end on May 8.

In America two consequences of note would directly flow from war's end. Omar Bradley would be widely lauded back home and shortly thereafter become the Chief of Staff, the highest ranking officer in the Army of the United States.

As the conqueror of Adolph Hitler, Dwight David Eisenhower would ride his celebrity into the White House in 1953. His was the first Republican presidency following the 20 years of FDR and Harry Truman.

In December of 1945, George Smith Patton would die as the result of a strange auto accident. Riding with three other generals, his vehicle would be struck by a truck. Only Patton was injured, but his spinal column would be crushed and the damage would prove terminal. Patton died on December 21.

He was interred in an uncompleted military cemetery outside Luxembourg City, Luxembourg, in a grave site dug by German prisoners of war. His headstone, a simple small cross, is identical to that of each of the 5,076 fallen American heroes. His wife Beatrice had hurriedly flown to his hospital. Once he was convinced he would not live much longer, he told her he most definitely did *not want* Eisenhower admitted to his funeral. He gave this judgment of his comrade in arms, "I hope he makes a better president than he was a general."

Mrs. Patton was given a choice of three cemeteries where her husband could be buried with the bodies of other Third Army men. She immediately selected the one near Luxembourg City for its close proximity to Bastogne, where he conducted his most famous battle. She refused to consider having his body returned to America for his final resting place.

At West Point today there are large heroic statues of Patton and Eisenhower, not far apart. Symbolically, their backs confront each other.

Patton had several serious flaws as a human being, most emphatically when considered from the prospective of a Liberal. He, like nearly all the top U.S. generals, was alienated from black people and considered them inferior specimens. Certainly Eisenhower, Bradley, and MacArthur shared that failing. He was also an outspoken anti-Semite. But he reserved his fiercest enmity for the Russians, even though Russian armies had killed, wounded or captured far more Nazi troops than had the Americans.

After his Third Army, advancing east, and the Soviet army moving west, met at the Elbe River in Germany on April 25, he was forced to celebrate with Russians at the site. His assessment of them was brutal. "Soviet officers, with few exceptions, give the appearance of recently civilized Mongolian bandits."

In numerous histories of this phase of the war can be seen candid photos of top Russians officers. None, not a single one, manifest any appearance other than a Caucasian visage.

Well after WWII had ended and while he was still stationed in Germany, his hatred of the Russians surfaced; he professed a desire to arm the captured Nazi troops and with them form a new army to attack the Russians. In a conversation with Eisenhower's new deputy, Joseph T. McNarney, Patton revealed his feelings. "We are going to have to fight them sooner or later; within the next generation. Why not do it now while our Army is intact and the damn Russians can have their hind end kicked back into Russia in three months? We can do it easily with the help of the German troops we have; if we just arm them and take them with us; they hate the bastards."

Once he uttered those words his future in the U.S. Army would be short lived. Eisenhower had no alternative but to relieve Patton of his command and reduce him to an inferior position.

The virulence of Patton's hatred and his total lack of political reality occasioned no sympathy amongst the GIs or the civilians in American. Eisenhower by contrast had warmed considerably to the person of Marshall Georgi Zhukov, his counterpart in the Russian Army. Zhukov was like Patton, a brilliant military tactician, and merited considerable praise.

Also the Truman administration, (now that FDR was dead), together with the New English and French governments, wanted to make deadly certain that Germany would never start another war, having started both World Wars.

Closing the chapter on Georgie Patton: if you want to win a war quickly with a minimum of bloodshed, opt for Patton. On other political matters, or foreign policy, never chose Patton.

The very last consequence of the tragic failure to end the war in Europe long before the Battle of the Bulge needs disclosure. There was a needless loss of life among European civilians of very easily two million. It is widely believed by many historians that because of Hitler's insane hatred of the Jews, and his passion for exterminating them that an additional 1,000,000 of that doomed ethnic group perished between August, 1944 and May, 1945. Somewhere around 500,000 in Hungary alone were rounded up and slaughtered.

Added to that huge throng were hundreds of thousands of German civilians clustered in large cities who failed to survive allied air raids. Additional hundreds of thousands more non-combatants died in countries throughout German occupied Europe from starvation and general neglect.

When every military advantage favors your army it is infinitely superior wisdom to pursue audacious tactics rather than those of caution. L'audace, l'audace, tojours l'audace.

Before abandoning the European war, two remaining scenes need to be presented. On April 28, 1945, Italian anti-fascists had captured Benito Mussolini; whose regime had been thrown overboard the previous year. His captors executed him and flung his bloody body onto a square in Milan. Soon thereafter two elderly Italian ladies took turns squatting over his face and emptying the contents of their respective bladders on that face. One can only hope that each bladder was completely full.

One can also hope that his longtime fascist friend in Germany, the Nazi military genius, had learned of the circumstances of Il Duce's death. Two days later Adolph Hitler, with complete resignation, inserted a German Luger pistol into his mouth and pulled the trigger.

CHAPTER XXIV

Only nine days after D-Day in Normandy, the Navy undertook its own D-Day halfway around the world in the Mariana Islands in the Central Pacific. The mammoth invasion fleet was named Task Force 58; it consisted of 535 combat ships, together with an additional assemblage of troop ships which held 127,000 trained combat forces.

Their primary target was the island of Saipan; the other two islands in the group were Guam and Tinian. As we remember, Guam had originally been annexed by this country during the presidency of William McKinley. Subsequently, it was conquered by the Japanese invaders in 1942. Now, barely two years later, it was about to be liberated by the triumphant Americans. Tinian would achieve a remarkable degree of immortality since it hosted the two B-29 bombers which dropped the nuclear bombs on Hiroshima and Nagasaki in August of 1945.

The task force proudly arrived on the scene, June 15, with 15 large carriers and 900 combat air craft; in addition it contained eight smaller carriers with 200 planes.

Only about 18 months earlier our entire carrier fleet in the Pacific consisted of the Saratoga which was small and slow, in addition to which it was old. Lexington had been sunk at the Battle of the Coral Sea in May, 1942; Yorktown only three weeks later at Midway. Wasp and Hornet had gone to the bottom later in the year. Enterprise was back in the states following heavy damage by the Japanese bombers.

Saipan was 3500 miles from Pearl Harbor, in the Hawaiian Islands, but still 1200 miles from Japan.

For a confirmed addict of World War II history, "The Carrier War" by Clark G. Reynolds and the editors of Time-Life Books reveals a treasure-trove of delectable information about carriers and the Navy's participation in that war. The U.S. superior industrial and technological base enabled it to produce far more ships – and better ones – than the Japanese. No fewer than 33 fast carriers of two entirely new designs were on the way: nine 11,000 ton Independence Class light carriers and two dozen 27,100 ton carriers of the Essex Class."

The Essex-Class carriers surpassed all their predeccors. They were more maneuverable; they had thicker armor and greater numbers of anti aircraft weapons. Following the naval tradition of carrying on the name of ships that had succumbed to battle, two of the new Essex-Class flat tops were christened Yorktown and Lexington, others would later be named after Hornet and Wasp.

The Battle of the Marianas was, by an incalculable margin, the greatest engagement of naval forces in the history of warfare. The combined forces on both sides were at least four times as extensive as in the Battle for Midway, more than two years previously. The American Navy would achieve such a masterful victory that the Japanese could never again assemble a striking force of naval and airpower as they had on June 15, 1944.

Oil, or lack of it, would play a definitive role in this momentous defeat. Whereas early in the war, the Japanese pilots, most particularly their naval fliers, were far better trained than ours, now the roles were reversed. The enemy lacked sufficient gasoline to waste it on pilot training. As a tragic consequence for their side, 395 Japanese planes were shot out of the sky.

From this point forward our Navy would be in total command in the entire Pacific combat zone; this ensured Japan's ultimate defeat. Conquering the main island of Saipan cost the lives of 3,426 ground troops with another 13,099 wounded. Tinian next would be invaded; the death total here was a much reduced 389. The taking of Guam resulted in 1435 combined deaths and missing in action. MIA almost always was the result of an artillery shell landing directly on one or more soldiers. These death totals were comparatively modest when likened to the hideous harvest of fatalities that awaited our troops in the taking of Iwo Jima and Okinawa.

Iwo was a volcanic island which however possessed great strategic value because of its location plus the fact that the Japanese had already conveniently constructed two airfields on it. It was 625 miles north of Saipan and nearly the same distance from the Japanese capitol of Tokyo.

When our gigantic B-29 super fortress bombers were returning from a mission to enemy cities, these airfields would provide landings for damaged planes or planes that had developed flight problems. The island had still another advantage – it could house the short range P-51 fighter planes desperately needed to provide protective escort for the B-29s.

When the Marianas were at length pacified, our Air Force began to build up to a suitable size. Already by August 10, our bombers began missions to Iwo to eliminate all enemy planes and to soften it up preparatory to invasion. Initially these were B-24s, a much smaller bomber than the majestic B-29s.

The B-29 was the world's largest four engine bomber and could fly farther while carrying a larger bomb load than any plane that existed. Truly its design and startling innovation represented a gigantic leap into the future of airplane design. Neither the Luftwaffe nor the Japanese would produce anything remotely comparable to it. The same could be said of our Allies, the British and the Russians.

Normally developing a plane of such striking concept would require five or more years. Unfortunately years were not available so testing and production was being undertaken concurrently. Indeed design changes were still being made when the plane was already flying in combat. The ultimate product was unexcelled. It would make the B-17, also produced by Boeing, appear anemic by contrast. Fully loaded the super fort, as it came to be known, would weigh 142,000 pounds; the B-17, one of our work horses in Europe was a puny 54,000 pounds.

The parent company, Boeing, could not possibly produce the thousands of these craft which the Air Force demanded; so much of the work was parceled out to at least a dozen large corporations and yet again to many hundreds of lesser companies. Before long Boeing was forced by the overwhelming magnitude of the project to turn over management of the entire operation to the Army Air Force (what in the world would Ronald Reagan have to say about this blatant governmental intrusion into private industry?)

On November 1, 1944 the first of these majestic giants was circling over Tokyo taking thousands of aerial photographs.

This country was fortunate beyond measure to have visionary planners overseeing this project, and so, as early as June 16, 1941 – nearly six months before we were at war, contracts were signed to produce a slender number of these giants by January, 1943. Once again Dame Fortune smiled and by September that order was amplified enormously to 250. Our armed forces were vastly benefited by not having any Republican isolationists in the procurement process.

The moment the Japanese attacked Pearl Harbor on December 6, the original order was doubled to 500 planes. So from June to January production goals were raised from 14 to 500.

By this time the B-29 was being called the three billion dollar gamble as developmental problems were arising all too often. Many doubters were also questioning the two billion dollar gamble called the Manhattan Project. Providentially both gambles paid off in a most handsome manner, thus shortening the war with Japan by perhaps years. The savings in lives would not be measured in the tens of thousands, but more likely in the hundreds of thousands since we would be spared the invasion of the Japanese homelands.

Well in advance of U.S. forces landing in Saipan, Japanese planners in Tokyo came to the realization that the various island chains closer to Japanese must be defended to the death or defeat would prove inevitable. The three rather diminutive islands that comprised their homeland would never be able to withstand the formidable amount of U.S. power that would appear.

With grim resolve they completed their defenses in Saipan, Tinian and Guam and then set about to fortify Iwo Jima. The defense system set in place was cunningly executed and was manned by 21,000 veteran Japanese troops fanatically devoted to their emperor. The final subjugation of the Marianas took until August 10th, nearly two months since the invasion of the first island on June 15th.

American admirals and generals began planning for Iwo's invasion while our forces were still attacking Saipan. First though, the formidable Japanese Air Force on that island had to be neutralized and that proved to be a burdensome task. Our air force sent over bombers by the score to render the airfields useless on the island; we coordinated that with bombardment from our large naval vessels.

From these two sources, Iwo received an inordinate amount of steel, but as quickly as we delivered it, Japanese repair crews would restore the runways to operating status.

Beginning in October, B-29s began arriving in Saipan intent on bombing Japan. Frantically the Japanese on Iwo struggled to eliminate that threat by attacking those planes parked on the restored runways. Successive attacks proved to be serious and either crippled or ruined altogether too many of these wondrous birds of prey.

Starting on February 17, 1945, Iwo was subjected to a near nonstop pounding from hundreds of our bombers and fighter planes. Simultaneously hundreds more appeared over Tokyo and plastered industrial plants. Two days later a gigantic naval armada approached the besieged island. Included in the fleet were eight brand new, very powerful battleships which administered a lethal shelling from close in. D-Day for Iwo Jima was at hand.

All of these tactics contributed to an unrealistic confidence that the island would be easily secured and with a minimum amount of casualties. Instead our troops found themselves fighting a huge enemy force largely untouched by the bombing, and artfully concealed in protective pillboxes. These deathtraps could only be detected from a short distance away.

Progress would be measurely just by the yard and then only after a horrifying amount of death and bloodshed.

Before Japanese resistance finally ceased on March 26, the Army and Marines suffered 5934 deaths; included in that total were 46 listed as missing in action. Since there was no place to hide on the island, M.I.A. meant the men involved were quite literally blown apart to the point where no recognizable portion of their body could be found. An additional 17,272 were wounded, many of course maimed for life.

Nor did the Navy escape unscathed. When smaller vessels edged too close to the shoreline they were sometimes hit by Japanese artillery fire. A total of

433 men were killed. They also suffered an intolerable loss of 448 M.I.A.s. Once again since there is no place to hide aboard a naval vessel, the obvious conclusion is that they were blown overboard after a large shell exploded on deck. Many, perhaps most of these men, were in fragments. The Navy also listed 6,815 wounded.

Immediately after the details of the Iwo Jima conquest found their way back to the States, the Hearst Newspaper chain attacked the entire episode in a remarkably malicious manner. The campaign, the papers insisted, was not only wasteful of human life, but unnecessary as well. Recall that the owner, William Randolph Hearst, demanded that the editors of his various newspapers refer to the New Deal as the Raw Deal and also call the President, Stalin Delano Roosevelt.

The Chicago Tribune gleefully joined the assault. Its owner, Robert McCormick, had given himself the title of Colonel, earlier in life. As soon as FDR was sworn into office "the Colonel" never missed an opportunity to assail the President or ridicule every part of the New Deal. On two separate occasions his paper revealed that our Intelligence group had broken the Japanese Naval Code. These were treasonous acts. "The Colonel" was one of the ringleaders of the terrifyingly stupid America First program that fought FDR's valiant effort to rebuild our Armed Forces.

On December 7th when Japan attacked us at Pearl Harbor and December 11th when the Germans declared war on us, how would we have retaliated had we listened to "the Colonel"? We would have had no draft bill; instead we would have had a much smaller Army. We would have had no new aircraft carriers in the Pacific. We also would have been without tanks and aircraft for use against Hitler.

"The Colonel", in short, was an abhorrent phony and a worthless hypocrite. An honorable man would have maintained a discrete silence about Iwo Jima.

Long before the conquest of Iwo Jima was completed, the Joint Chiefs of Staff in Washington unanimously decided on the large island of Okinawa as the next target. Its nearly available airfields would position our B-29 bombers within 360 miles of the most southerly of the Japanese islands, Kyusho. D-Day was set for April 1, 1945.

But even before Iwo was totally subjated, the B-29s began their bombing runs to Japan and its capital, Tokyo. In one raid alone, on the night of March 9, 1945, nearly 85,000 residents in that city were incinerated. In this and subsequent raids, Japanese homes by the hundreds of thousands were consumed from mammoth fires, spreading through the flimsy, wooden structures.

Japanese military officials knew that if the Americans added Okinawa to their lengthening list of captured islands, their nation would surely be defeated. In desperation they began to recruit suicide bomber pilots by the hundreds. These young men would be given only rudimentary flight training, and then sent out on a one-way mission to crash their plane, with a single large bomb, into an American naval vessel. This tactic had first been employed in Iwo Jima with considerable success. This new stratagem was called Kamikaze, or Divine Wind.

To illustrate how effective this new diabolical maneuver was, we need only observe what took place when one of these Kamikaze planes slammed into one of our newly minted carriers, the Franklin. At the moment it was struck, the carrier was aligning its hundred or so planes for take-off. Instantly these craft, each with several hundred gallons of fuel, plus hundreds of large caliber bullets for its machine guns, turned into fearsome weapons dealing out death or terrible injury, to everybody on the deck.

The captain and his staff, or what survived, began evacuating the remaining crew from the stricken ship, except for a small emergency unit trained in fire fighting measures. Tow lines were hastily attached and she was towed away from other nearby ships.

A total of 724 men were either killed or their bodies were never found. Nevertheless the crew of battered lady slowly extinguished the flames and regained power. She then made the 12,000 mile trek to San Francisco. The ship was eventually scraped, far too damaged to be of any use. The Franklin was widely recognized as the most heavily damaged ship still able to remain afloat in the entire war.

Well before any invasion of Okinawa could be undertaken, a relentless process of "softening up" the enemy forces defending the island would be required. The nearly unimaginable deluge of military might that had poured into this theater of operations insured the success of the campaign.

Japanese air power in the region had been skillfully decimated by our naval pilots during the conquest of Iwo Jima. Still remaining were believed to be two or three thousand based on the main target of Okinawa and its surrounding islands. We had gained a considerable advantage in that we could now use Iwo as a staging area for the Super Forts. In addition the Super Forts would be based on the several airfields located there.

Next came the awesome fire power of the battleships and heavy cruisers which maneuvered to within firing range of the island. Complementing these agents of destruction were 1213 naval craft of all types which gradually assembled for the invasion.

D-Day, was April 1, 1945, Easter Sunday. The hundreds of small landing craft were now put to use to ferry the 127,000 invasion troops from the huge transport ships to the shore. Larger craft were employed to convoy tanks, artillery and other necessary implements of modern warfare.

We must not forget that huge numbers of these men, the pilots, the crews on the warships, the invading ground forces, were sons of the mendacious parasites who were fed, clothed and housed by that slayer of laissez-faire economics, Franklin Roosevelt and his New Deal. Herbert Hoover would have far better preferred that the families of those combat personnel suffer from malnutrition and homelessness rather than be nurtured by the federal government.

It also bears reiterating that Hoover's supporters in congress, who considered laissez-faire economics to be sacred doctrine, fought FDR in the most dogged manner every time he introduced another military appropriations bill, beginning in 1938. Nearly without exception, each one of them was a Republican and usually an isolation to boot.

The 77,000 Japanese defenders were more than willing to fight to the death and that they did. They put to lethal use natural caves and cleverly designed machine gun nests that were hard to detect.

The Kamikaze planes contributed greatly to the ghastly total of American fatalities. An estimated 1900 suicide attempts were made on the Navy. The great bulk of them were blown from the sky from superbly designed gunnery systems aboard our Navy ships, but not before 32 of those ships had been sunk, with another 368 damaged. The death total from these attacks was around 4900 killed or missing in action.

Fighting on land didn't end until nearly every one of the 77,000 defenders was either killed or who self destructed. Only a mere handful surrendered. Final resistance ceased on July 2. The combat fatalities on land were 7613.

Huge fleets of the Army's B-29s could now subject all of the large Japanese cities to remorseless attacks. Perhaps of even greater importance, the Japanese civilian government, which had a firmer attachment to reality than did the military, now realized that the war was irretrievably lost, and was anxious to work out a permanent settlement.

The ranking military, however, much preferred honorable death to a dishonorable surrender. For this element, the Americans under their new President, Harry S. Truman, were in the process of completing two agents of death and destruction never witnessed by man on this planet. Actually never before even contemplated except by tiny groups of physicists working under intense secrecy.

One such group was in Nazi Germany where their scientists started on an atomic bomb project several years before the Manhattan Project was even a concept. Thankfully, Adolph Hitler, the military genius concluded that the bomb wouldn't be necessary since his Luftwaffe and Wehrmacht could easily conquer Europe. Besides it was frightfully expensive and too many obstacles remained to be overcome. The winters of 1941 and 1942, when his Wehrmacht struggled against the Russian Army, should have revealed the error of his thinking.

America, by contrast, had in Franklin Roosevelt, a President who was acutely perceptive when presented with revolutionary concepts and who could take forthright steps to fulfill the promise of those concepts.

Before beginning the discussion of how this country came to develop an atomic bomb, it is first necessary to review the earliest, baby steps taken so that we could even contemplate working on nuclear energy.

A decidedly vital segment of the important physicists that completed the two atomic bombs, which brought World War II to a successful conclusion were Jews. Each of them had been forced to flee for their lives from Hitler's maniacal drive to exterminate all of Europe's Jewry.

Except for Lise Meitner, all were men. The role she played was absolutely crucial. While living in Berlin she had worked with fellow scientists at the Kaiser Wilhelm Institute. After she decamped to Sweden to save her life, two of her former colleagues in Germany related to her how they had successfully penetrated the nucleus of an atom.

She immediately told her nephew, Otto Frisch, who had escaped to Denmark, about this potentially frightful development. He in turn quickly relayed this awesome news to a fellow Jewish physicist Niels Bohr, who was leaving Denmark for the United States.

As quickly as possible Mr. Bohr recounted this amazing achievement pulled off in Berlin, to a large group of American physicists meeting in our nation's capital. Bohr was not a run of the mill scientist; he had already been awarded a Nobel Prize for work done in Denmark. He was also an authentic genius when it came to theoretical physics.

This information set the group of scientists in feverish pursuit of experimentation in nuclear energy. Laboratories were hurriedly set up or enlarged at three of America's top schools – Columbia University in New York City; the University of Chicago; the University of California at Berkeley.

Early in the race to assemble a workable bomb before the Nazis in Germany did, the select group of scientists working in these three schools soon came to the realization that their ultra secret project, called the Manhattan Engineer

District, could only be completed by a contractor with a proven record of great accomplishments. That had to be the United States Corp of Engineers.

The outstanding officer in that military unit was Colonel Leslie R. Groves. He had just supervised construction of one of the largest buildings in the world – the Pentagon in Washington. Moreover he completed the project well ahead of time and well below cost estimates. When first offered the coveted position, the Colonel declined to accept. His long held dream as a West Point graduate was to lead men in battle. His superior officer told him he was the only man for the job, promoted him to Brigadier General, and then ordered him to report for his new assignment.

Choosing Colonel Groves to take charge of this impossibly complex project was one of the smartest decisions made in the war. Several historians of this segment of World War II have categorically asserted that without his driving force, enormous confidence and intuitive brain power the task that soon became the Manhattan Project would never have produced the bomb.

All of the scientists working in these University labs failed to realize that in order of prominence, having a continuous supply of uranium available was the number one consideration. Brig. General Groves however, immediately grasped the importance of this scarce element.

To alleviate everybody's concern, a huge supply soon turned up, right on the doorstep of New York City. In another of Hitler's gifts to the Project, a Belgian Jew who had departed to America had providentially shipped 1250 tons of the material to America several years earlier. He had been one of the owners of a very large uranium mine in what was then the Belgian Congo.

Immediately Gen. Groves arranged to buy the entire shipment from Edgar Sengier, the Belgian refugee.

Groves and his staff began an immediate search for areas where they could construct the facilities for manufacturing an atom bomb. The scientists were conducting a frenzied search for an ability to reach critical mass, the term they used for igniting a spontaneous reaction whereby the neutrons would begin to career off each other endlessly and with increased volatility until they stimulated the greatest manmade explosion in all of human history.

The first area chosen was Oak Ridge, Tennessee, a short distance from Knoxville. They purchased 50,000 acres in a site that offered the maximum degree of isolation. This would help maintain the desired degree of secrecy and help mask the true nature of the enterprise. In this remote location they could also minimize the destruction should there be a violent explosion. Eventually over 20,000 workers would be hired in Oak Ridge.

One other reason for its selection – Oak Ridge was close to the Tennessee River, and all that super abundant supply of electricity. The facility would require inordinate amounts of that energy. Of course the reason for the abundance of cheap power were the huge dams built by the Rural Electrification Agency (The REA) using money supplied by the federal government. This was an agency that created endless heartburn for Herbert Hoover and his laissez-faire loving cronies who considered this agency just another insidious application of governmental socialism. But to Groves and the men who managed Oak Ridge, those dams and the profusion of available electricity certainly came in handy.

The next site chosen was at Hanford, Washington. Hanford was a tiny village situated in a remote area of the state, a condition always desirable in producing an atom bomb. It also had the other necessary attribute; it was located on the banks of the mighty Columbia River, reasonably close to two tremendous dams, Grand Coulee and Bonneville. In each location, the scientists, engineers and technicians had a specific role to play in the production of the bomb. Hanford's task was to produce the extremely rare plutonium, a derivative of U-235, also quite rare. At Oak Ridge their workers had to reduce the more plentiful U-238 to U-235.

The third remaining location was at Los Alamos, New Mexico. Here would be constructed the laboratories for the large contingent of nuclear physicists who would arrive shortly. This area was even more remote than the previous two, a plateau atop a desert mountain. Unlike Oak Ridge and Hanford, it didn't require unusually large amounts of electricity.

But here were sequestered, under forbiddingly strict secrecy, the numerous European Jewish Physicists, all refugees from Adolph Hitler, and Heinrich Himmler, the Nazi chicken plucker and head of the Gestapo.

From Germany came Hans Bethe and Otto Frisch, Lise Meitner's nephew. From Denmark would arrive Niels Bohr, already alluded to. Hungary would produce a bumper crop of truly brilliant scientists: John von Neumann, whose specialty was mathematics, a genius whose talent outshone most other mathematicians in the 20th century; Leo Sziland; Edward Teller and Eugene Wigner. Italy would deliver Enrico Fermi – not a Jew, but married to one. He too was a genius. Present day Poland would send us I. I. Rabi, not as a refugee however. He too was the recipient of a Nobel Prize for his work in observing atomic spectra.

Robert J. Oppenheimer, also Jewish, but locally grown, was personally selected by Gen. Groves to supervise these highly unusual, even idiosyncratic, scientific specimens.

Although only 39 years old, Oppie, as he was usually named was called upon to direct this large group of scientists who began the effort to engineer a project that had much of the allure of peril and mystery. It is important to understand that atomic power had the potential explosiveness of 20,000 pounds of TNT.

Into this isolated setting, twenty miles from the nearest town, the scientists were allowed to bring their families, but only after a protracted battle with Groves, who felt the families would compromise secrecy.

Everybody employed at Los Alamos lived a Spartan, nearly primitive life. There was little in the way of entertainment or diversion. Some of these men had world-wide reputations, but what kept them secured to their tasks was the knowledge that they were in a deadly race with the Nazis to develop the bomb. They also were brutally aware that the fiendish Nazis had a five year head start in the race.

It is beyond question that this assortment of scientific talent, and even genius, gathered together at Los Alamos, represented the most exceptional aggregation of aptitude ever seen on earth.

Right from the beginning the Manhattan Project represented a decided gamble– the odds of it succeeding were long. New materials had to be invented or drastically reconfigured; unheard of production methods had to be found. All of this engineering had to fit together in a harmonious, workable manner.

Before all the pieces were put together, 600,000 workers were on the payroll and $2 billion was expended. The project of necessity was a deep, deep secret which was kept from all of Congress except for a mere handful of important committee chairmen.

The long months of stupendous effort to create the world's first atomic bomb finally paid off. The detonation of an actual bomb was set for July 16, 1945 at an U. S. Army facility called the Alamogordo Bombing Range about 50 miles from the New Mexico town of Alamogordo. It was also 200 miles from Los Alamos.

A few of the physicists who actually worked on developing the bomb were more than a little fearful that the bomb possessed monstrous capabilities and might destroy Alamogordo. Some were concerned that the entire state of New Mexico might be at grave risk.

The location where the device would be exploded was completely flat with only a 100 foot steel tower holding it in position. After the explosion nothing remained of the tower; it had completely vaporized. All personnel were at least 10,000 yards away, flat on their stomachs and turned away. Nobody was injured.

Completely assured now that the Los Alamos devices worked, the first atomic bomb designed for a war-like application was under way to Tinian in the

Marianas, a sister island of Iwo Jima. It possessed two 8500 foot runways and a B-29 carrying a 9000 pound bomb needed every foot of that runway.

President Truman had broadcast a message to the Japanese government offering it an opportunity to surrender or else suffer "utter devastation of the Japanese home land." The message was sent worldwide and contained no threat of any unusual explosive bomb.

Truman and his advisors anxiously awaited an answer from their Japanese counterparts. The message they received after several days was both evasive and noncommittal. Within that government existed a whirlwind of conflicting attitudes. The civilian portion wanted to pursue the path to surrender; the army generals were defiant and seemed to prefer to fight to the death. At this point the generals prevailed.

While the bomb was enroute to its destination, the first target had already been selected – Hiroshima with a wealth of reasons why it should be leveled. The city contained numerous large factories engaged in war productions. A more superior argument for its selection was that it housed the headquarters of an entire enemy army headquarters.

Harry Truman now gave the signal to drop the bomb, but not before carefully soliciting the opinions of all his principal advisors, both civilian and military.

On August 6th, the Enola Gay, a B-29 named after the pilots' mother, took off from Tinian with Colonel Paul Tibbets at the controls. On board was "Little Boy," the first atomic bomb to be used against an enemy. The military unit that had been established to rehearse the bomb drop, was the 509th Composite Group, and the Colonel was its' commanding officer. The Group had been practicing it's tactics for well over a year, both back in the States and on Tinian.

The Enola Gay, as well as other bombers in the Group, had carefully rehearsed the extreme tactics to be used the instant the bomb was released over the precise target – a hard right hand turn away from Hiroshima and back to Tinian. The crew expected a violent reaction and it soon arrived. The first sound wave of fiercely compressed air struck the plane and pitched its crew members around like toy soldiers. Almost immediately came a second wave, and then the plane was safely away from danger. No damage was realized to either the plane or its crew members.

Back in America it was still August 5th. The President was on a naval vessel headed back to America from a historic meeting in Potsdam, Germany with Winston Churchill and Josef Stalin. He issued a prepared statement: "It is an atomic bomb. It is harnessing the basic power of the universe. The force from which the sun draws its power has been loosed upon those who brought war to the Far East." Mr. Truman then added, "If their leaders do not now accept our terms they may expect a rain of ruin from the air the like of which has never been seen on this earth."

Even before "Little Boy" landed on Hiroshima, many of the nation's top military leaders thought it unnecessary to employ this device. They were convinced that conventional bombing would lead the Japanese to surrender. Three of the most important Army Air Corps generals passionately believed that to be true. General Eisenhower also thought so. Even Harry Truman was very reluctant to have the bomb dropped. Only when General Marshall confronted him with the grisly estimates of American casualties in an invasion, did he agree that only the bomb would end the war.

The estimates presented by General Marshall were based on the radio intercepts obtained by Naval Intelligence which revealed that the Japanese had 5,000 suicide planes cleverly hidden, sometimes underground, ready to greet our invasion forces. The general forecast casualties of easily 275,000 of our troops would be killed or wounded.

The Hiroshima bomb jolted the leaders in Tokyo to a considerable degree, but not enough to come to terms with the Americans. While the civilian portion of the government were even more anxious to agree to surrender terms, the obtuse generals remained resolute in their determination to continue fighting.

Accordingly, the President ordered the second bomb dropped. For this mission the pilot selected Frederick Bock, whose plane was called Bock's Car. The bomb was named "Fat Man," and was to be released on August 9th.

Unlike the earlier mission by Tibbets where no problem developed, this flight was dogged by one misfortune after another. The first two cities chosen as targets had to be bypassed for various reasons. As the plane approached Nagasaki, two large predicaments appeared – the skies over the city were completely overcast and the crew's orders were to release the bomb only when the target was visible. Additionally, they were low on gas. Finally, a large enough hole developed in the clouds and "Fat Man" dropped on Nagasaki.

The Nagasaki bomb was far more technically advanced than its predecessor dropped at Hiroshima. Uranium – 235, used in the first bomb was discarded entirely in favor of plutonium. This was a nuclear bomb as opposed to the atomic bomb. Each, however, had produced an incandescence far brighter than the sun.

At Hiroshima nearly all of the hospitals had either been completely destroyed or rendered nearly useless. The city's physicians had been decimated to a pitiable state – either dead, dying or injured to some degree. The condition of the nurses was identical. As if that wasn't horrific enough, almost nothing remained of medical equipment and supplies.

Verifiable estimates of the dead were put at 140,000. The heat, which easily soared into thousands of degrees Fahrenheit near the drop zone, when cooled with exponentially expanded air pressures and winds, completely destroyed two-thirds of the cities' buildings.

On the morning following the Nagasaki explosion, Russia invaded the huge area of Manchuria which had been captured by the Japanese from China beginning in the middle 1930s. The Japanese Army, which had been withdrawing men from that area to defend Iwo Jima, Saipan and Okinawa, now had little in the way of military power left to defend its holding on the Asia mainland.

Even after the second catastrophic bomb drop, a few leading generals continued their defiant posture. Now it was obvious that the only person in Japan capable of breaking the deadlock within the Cabinet was the revered Emperor, Hirohito. The very next day he addressed the full cabinet. "The time has come when we must bear the unbearable. I swallow my tears and give my sanction to the proposal to accept the Allied proclamation on the basis outlined by the foreign minister." With that he left the room.

Announcements of the emperor's decision were sent by cable to Japanese embassies in Europe where the message would be relayed to foreign governments in Washington, London and Moscow. No ambivalence was present in the dispatch. "The Japanese government is ready to accept the terms enumerated in the joint declaration issued at Potsdam on July 26, 1945, with an understanding that the said declaration not compromise any demand which prejudices the prerogatives of His Majesty as a sovereign ruler."

The diplomatic niceties were firmly in place now that the American government agreed that the Emperor would be retained in the New Japanese administration. He would have virtually no authority in the future.

On August 14, 1945, President Truman told an ecstatic nation that Japan had surrendered. Except for the occupation of the country and peace treaty formalities, the war was over.

There remained however, considerable trepidation that fanatical elements within the Japanese Army might attempt further hostilities. Extreme care was taken to prevent this. It wasn't until August 28th that the first American troops began landing at a Japanese air force base close to Tokyo. Hirohito had ordered the entire nation to capitulate without any hostilities and his directive was observed. The occupation continued without a single untoward incident.

On September 2nd, the formal peace was signed aboard the battleship Missouri, especially chosen since it represented President Truman's home state. Immediately after all the dignitaries had put their name on the document, a glorious formation of 1900 American and British planes flew over the warships in a magnificent tribute to the occasion. The Missouri was merely one of several hundred American naval vessels comprising this enormous flotilla gathered in Tokyo Bay.

World War II had reached its fitting climax. Nearly six years earlier, on September 1, 1939, it had begun when Adolph Hitler unleashed his feverish Nazi hordes on Poland. Guns around the world had finally grown silent.

CHAPTER XXV

It is only fitting and proper to return to the day Franklin Delano Roosevelt passed from the country's midst. We need to devote sufficient space in this chronicle commensurate with the impact he had on this nation and the entire world. It is entirely reasonable to conclude that in the brief span of time between the news of his death, on April 12, 1945, and his interment at his ancestral home in Hyde Park, New York, more tears of bitter anguish and actual heartbreak were shed than for all our deceased presidents combined.

When his casket was placed aboard the train at Warm Springs, Georgia, where he had died the previous day, it was placed on an elevated level so that it could be seen from both sides of the track. The casket was in the last car of the train which was fully lighted.

Between Warm Springs and Washington, mourners numbering in the hundreds of thousands stood patiently waiting at crossroads, many waiting for hours, merely to have a brief glance at that last car. Larger clusters of sobbing admirers of the President gathered at the railroad stations throughout the route, anxious to pay their final respect to the man they so loved; the man who had so improved their lives.

After the train reached Washington, the funeral motorcade rolled from the train station to the White House, past enormous throngs of mourners lining the streets.

At each intersection looking down both side streets, could be seen still more multitudes of weeping citizens who openly loved their President.

Since the news of the President's death was first broadcast, torrents of tears beyond measure were being shed. Now compare that incalculable volume with the mere cups full trickling out when news of any of FDR's three predecessors was announced. The tears cast following the deaths of Warren Harding, Calvin Coolidge and Herbert Hoover could easily be measured and perhaps even counted.

The Roosevelt's, Franklin and Eleanor, were disdainful of any display of ostentation. FDR's vacation home at Warm Springs, where he died, was small and plain to the point of being Spartan. The funeral service in the East Room of the White House reflected that philosophy of life.

That same evening the train once again bearing the President's coffin began the distant trek to the family estate at Hyde Park, a considerable distance from the White House.

Once again truly impressive crowds bore silent but melancholy witness as the train wended its way along the banks of the mighty Hudson River. All during the night, wherever there was room for gathering, hosts of mourners, imposing in their numbers, came together. It is widely believed that at least two million mourners saw the train and the casket hurry by.

The burial ceremony at the Roosevelt estate at Hyde Park, while moving, was brief. The President was laid to rest on a plot overlooking the Hudson River. At the foot of his grave on a small, simple plaque can be read:

Franklin Delano Roosevelt

1862-1945

He was only 63 years old, when after 12 years in the White House and subject to unrelenting turmoil and tension, he fell victim to a massive cerebral hemorrhage.

The long years spent delivering this nation from the Republican Depression, while almost immediately thereafter turning the country into an arsenal of democracy, unquestionably shortened his life. Then playing a very paramount role in conducting the wars simultaneously in Europe and the Pacific contributed to his body's deterioration.

But very likely his most worrisome burden was the long, incessant warfare he was forced to fight with the malignant, obstructionist Republicans in Congress. They fiercely contested every legislative initiative he proposed. After they increased their numbers in Congress following the 1938 elections, the isolationists, all Republicans, acted like jackals in trying to thwart his every effort to rebuild the country's anemic defenses.

Without any question the obituary with the most forceful impact I ever read was that of the New York Times on April 13, 1945. Of course I didn't read it in the Times since I was in Germany on that day. Subsequently, I have seen it reproduced in several of FDR's biographies.

From "No Ordinary Time" by Doris Kearns Goodwin, we find this delectable morsel. The author first says, "Even the normally staid New York Times was extravagant in its editorial praise." Then follows the obit. "Men will thank GOD on their knees a hundred years from now, that Franklin D. Roosevelt was in the White House....It was his hand, more than that of any other single man, that built the great coalition of the United States....It was his leadership which inspired free men in every part of the world to fight with greater hope and courage. Gone, now, is this talent and skill....Gone is the fresh and spontaneous interest which this man took, as naturally as he breathed air, in the troubles and the hardships and the disappointments and the hopes of little men and humble people."

This extravagance of emotion is echoed and reechoed by many of his biographers. FDR doubtless had more writers penning his history than all other Republican presidents combined since those of Lincoln.

From Conrad Black in his work "Franklin Delano Roosevelt – Champion of Freedom", this pleasing message, "It is the contention of this book that Franklin D. Roosevelt was the most important person of the twentieth century, because of his achievements as one of America's greatest presidents and its most accomplished leader since Lincoln."

Lest the reader think this is another Liberal idealizing his subject, permit me to quote three stalwart Republicans giving voice to their appreciation of Mr. Black's effort. From George F. Will: "Conrad Black skillfully assembles powerful arguments to support strong and sometimes surprising judgments. This spirited defense of Roosevelt as a savior of America's enterprise system… is a delight to read."

From William F. Buckley, Jr., a veritable cornerstone of America's conservative movement. "An enormous accomplishment, a learned volume on FDR by a vital critical mind, which will absorb critics and the reading public."

Henry A. Kissinger offers this assessment. "No biography of Roosevelt is more thoughtful and readable. None is as comprehensive."

On April 17, five days after FDR's death, Winston Churchill rose in Parliament to deliver this heartfelt and impassioned eulogy to his longtime friend and ally. "He devised the extraordinary measure of assistance called Lend-Lease, which will stand forth as the most unselfish and unsordid act of any country in all history."

Again from Mr. Black, "Churchill declared that Roosevelt was the greatest of all American leaders, because if he had failed, Western civilization would have been enslaved, whereas the consequences of the failure of Washington or Lincoln would have been confined to America."

"There is nothing remotely resembling a precedent in British history for so elegiacal a tribute to any deceased foreign leader. The British and Winston Churchill in particular, perceived before anyone how preeminent a titan of the twentieth century Roosevelt was."

The Roosevelt reign of righteousness lasted 12 years, one month and eight days. That magisterial reign most assuredly included Eleanor, usually referred to by Franklin as "my missus." The two of them working as a team labored tirelessly to improve the lives of tens of millions of underprivileged people throughout the nation.

Almost single-handedly FDR created the modern America which in turn revolutionized other progressive countries. In evolving this insurrection he peeled off the once supreme power from the hands of what his cousin Theodore called "robber barons of industry" and permanently denied them the ability to regain it. In so doing he summoned up the implacable hatred his name would have for the Rotten Reactionary Republicans even to this day. Some how they felt they possessed the right to have dominion over other men – force them to work long hours for 'dogs wages' and in the process be ill-housed, ill-clothed and ill-fed, in the words of FDR.

By the time of his death, a huge percentage of blue collar workers had more than doubled their wages, working conditions had vastly improved, and they were free to form unions. Now, for the first time, laboring men were paying income taxes as well as contributing to their social security pension – and happy to be doing both.

Child labor had been finally banished, never to return. Instead, children were in school, learning.

Gone was the specter of another crushing panic such as had been endured in 1873, 1893, 1907 and 1921. Gone was the concern about another cataclysmic Great Depression. Gone for all time was the wrenching concern that their bank would close its doors and steal their deposit.

Still, it must be realized, that joining the swelling multitudes of American men and women down on their knees thanking GOD for having placed this president in the White House, were other crowds a plenty. They were also thanking a just GOD for having seen fit to remove this socialistic monster from the political scene forever. Now with the help of that same just GOD, these Republicans hoped they might be able, once again to restore trickle-down economics – oops, laissez-faire economics.

As these patriotic Republicans in Congress had witnessed the flood-tide of $300 billions spent for national defense, some of it on Lease-Lend given to helping communistic Russia, they were convinced that the profligate Roosevelt was bankrupting the country.

They had done their part. These white males who comprised the 75% majority of the Republican membership in the House of Representatives, had tried mightily to hold down costs by voting against the Selective Service Bill in 1940, and the Lend-Lease Bill in 1941. Passage of these measures had tortured their parsimonious souls.

These same Republicans took great pleasure in deriding the President as "The Great White Father" who endlessly squandered billions of dollars on his New Deal legislation. They were scornful of this legislation which they considered odious socialism.

Little did they realize that to millions of recruits in the Armed Forces, Franklin Roosevelt was indeed The Great White Father, the only President they had ever known. Worse than that, these young troops looked upon him with awe as a kindly, all-knowing leader directing them to victory over the evil forces of Germany and Japan.

To those of us in Germany, we knew that by April 12th the war was won in that theater. The Luftwaffe had simply disappeared. The once invincible Wehrmacht was reduced to isolated, disorganized groups of German soldiers increasingly eager to surrender. We regarded our Army and its Air Corps as the greatest fighting force ever assembled – and it was. For that we thanked Franklin Delano Roosevelt, the Great White Father.

CHAPTER XXVI

As the October page of the 1943 calendar appeared, President Roosevelt presented a bill to Congress, called the Serviceman's Readjustment Act, which was post war veteran's legislation. In doing so he was acutely aware of what an unfeeling, ungrateful Republican Congress had granted the World War One veterans in 1919, those returning from France. He had held a position of some prominence as undersecretary of the Navy, under President Woodrow Wilson and had witnessed the miserly benefits the Republicans, then in control of Congress, had doled out to the doughboys. They were issued a check for $60.00, plus a ticket for a train trip home. Five years later they were given another modest stipend, a bonus of $625.00, but with an important proviso – it was a government bond not due for payment for 20 years, not until 1944.

In the summer of 1932 a large group of homeless, jobless veterans conducted a march to Washington. This bonus Army, numbering at least 40,000, came together to make a plea to Congress for an early payment of that bonus.

In this summer of 1932, in the very heart of the Great Depression, and doubtless the worst year this country has ever endured, the veterans had been especially hard hit. More than 100,000 of them had suffered grievous wounds in battle, many of which had gone untreated or insufficiently tended to. The Hoover administration was not one to throw money around recklessly, nor had the Coolidge or Harding governments done so. The Bush collection of incompetents still reflects that attitude towards the Iraq war vets, a war which it alone provoked.

In larger cities in 1932, veterans could be seen selling apples at 5 cents each, a slightly elevated form of begging.

Herbert Hoover obstinately refused to meet with any spokesmen from the Bonus Army. In his feverish, reactionary brain he regarded these woeful, poverty-stricken vets as nothing but Communists intent on overthrowing the government. Instead, he appealed to the head General of the Army for assistance in removing these unwashed hordes from the nation's capitol. Douglas MacArthur, who in turn could easily discern a communist hiding behind many trees in Washington, went on record as saying he "detected a whiff of insurrection in the air."

Accordingly the fearless general mobilized the Army's might, which included tanks, infantry and tear-gas guns and charged into this pitiful assembly of unarmed, hungry men, some with family. The Bonus Army scattered, more hungry, and embittered than ever.

Following this resolute display of forcefulness in the face of dire threat, President Hoover now proclaimed that he was thankful that stability had been regained by the timely action of the Army. Playing a prominent role in the action were two Army majors – Dwight Eisenhower and George Patton.

The bill FDR introduced to Congress in October 1943 would be called the G.I. Bill. (All U.S. Army troops in this war were called G.I.s, short for Government Issue.) In it the President could demand from a now more conservative body far more benefits for the troops than could be obtained for the entire populace.

He soon discovered that in the American Legion he had a very helpful accomplice. The Legion was a huge veteran's organization that carried an equal measure of clout, and had been founded immediately after WWI.

Like Roosevelt the Legion distrusted the thought of a cash bonus. What together they would demand for the returning troops was the opportunity to acquire a useful education. This meant either attending college or a vocational training school. Remember that when they either enlisted or were drafted, half the troops lacked a high school diploma.

Both the President and the American Legion could now work in concert to provide vast benefits to a majority of the returning veterans, benefits on a heroic scale far, far in excess of what had been done in 1919.

Early in January, 1944 FDR appeared in person before Congress where he made a detailed and forceful appeal for passage of the bill that would bring such enormous help to his "soldier boys." With great emphasis he stressed that "lack of money should not prevent any vet of this war from equipping himself for the most useful employment for which his aptitudes and willingness qualify him. I believe this nation is morally obligated to provide this training and education."

Quite obviously in the 12 years that Harding, Coolidge and Hoover stumbled through their tenure in the White House, never once did any of them feel any moral obligation to provide anything in the way of training and education. Neither of course did the Republican Congress which held power for those 12 years. It's equally obvious that Bush and Cheney have never had much in the way of an impulse to assist the Iraqi War vets, particularly the ones desperately crying out for medical or psychiatric treatment.

With his probing mind in high gear, President Roosevelt realized that if millions of ex – G.I.'s took advantage of these unusually generous benefits, this would delay their pursuit of a job in a market not yet ready to absorb job seekers. He could foresee victory in the not too distant future – all the large factories through the nation would then cease production of tanks, planes, trucks and all the other warlike items that already were flowing so bountifully to the front lines. It would then take months before these plants could readapt to civilian needs.

Meanwhile the vets could be in college or gaining advanced job skills in repairing car engines, or radios, or refrigerators. Untold thousands could even forego the job market and start their own business, which in turn would require new employees.

For those undetermined about their future, and needing time to recover from the trauma of combat, FDR strongly urged a program which was called the 52-20 Club – a payment of $20.00 a week for up to 52 weeks considering the future. Although this proposition initially evoked anguished screams from the right-wingers who were certain that many vets would loaf around for the full year, for those who signed up for unemployment compensation, the average stay was around 18 weeks.

Although the radical legislation encountered some very rough spots in its passage through both house of Congress, the President signed the final bill on June 22, 1944. In neither chamber was a single negative vote cast.

June 22nd was the third anniversary of Hitler's invasion of Russia. On June 6th the Americans had firmly established themselves in Normandy and could no longer be driven off. Meanwhile the Russians were mauling the once invincible Wehrmacht everywhere on the Easter Front. The Third Reich, which the German military genius was confident would endure for a 1000 years, would crumble into ruins in less than 10 months.

A great many historians of the era firmly believe that the G.I. Bill was the greatest of all gifts President Roosevelt bequeathed to the nation. The 78th Congress which passed the bill was a pale shadow of earlier counterparts in the Roosevelt administration. More Republicans were in this body than ever before since he came into office. Meanwhile the Southern Democrats were becoming ever more truculent in their attitude toward New Deal measures and Republicans, by their very nature, hated to help needy people.

The G.I. Bill came ever so close to failure because of it's inclusion of benefits for all veterans, black and white, and that meant the 50,000 southern blacks.

Plantation owners, who up to passage of the bill, could hire blacks for a dollar a day, and that was a day lasting more than eight hours, became nearly apoplectic at the thought of "their blacks" receiving $20 a week for not working.

The Congress had to be literally shamed into passing the bill because of the near universal feeling amongst the American public that nothing was too good for the gallant troops. Under the inspirational leadership of the President and the constant goading of the American Legion to pass the legislation intact, and without any crippling amendments, the reluctant Congress did so.

A number of presidents of elite colleges were positively aghast at this proposed invasion of their esteemed sanctuaries by hordes of unwelcome, under qualified veterans. Many of these proposed students would spring from the laboring class, a group previously unrepresented in their school.

These college presidents were quite reminiscent of the learned clowns in caps and gowns whom we previously encountered during the Roaring Twenties. Then they presumed to guide the economy, and they did. Only they guided it down its path to utter destruction.

Two of this type most frequently cited were Harvard's James Conant and from the University of Chicago, Robert Hutchins. Both were certain their hallowed precincts would become hobo jungles because of the entry of combat veterans.

This 78th Congress, where reality didn't always reign, was convinced that probably only 500,000 or at most 1,000,000 former military would apply for the educational benefits offered by the bill. They were well aware that more than half of the 15 million men and women in uniform failed to finish high school.

Heretofore a college education had been limited to the children of white upper class professionals. Admitting men who should be lining up for the dead-end factory or mining jobs, which their fathers were limited to, was totally unreasonable and could easily upset the regular order of things. Colleges of the elevated order of Harvard or Chicago were no place to institute a massive public works program.

What occurred from the moment the veterans hit the college classrooms was vastly different. These were older students who had been all over the world and who were compelled by a fervent desire to learn; in short order they radically altered the system and the attitude in the elite colleges.

Conant quite obviously arrived at a similar conclusion and his perception of these unusual pupils. "The mature student body which filled our colleges in '46 and '47 was a delight to all who were then teaching undergraduates. Before the advent of the G.I. Bill the educational system was perpetuating, more than we realized, a hereditary class of highly educated people."

The G.I. Bill extended great generosity towards the veterans. The bill provided for full tuition costs, plus textbooks and any incidental fees. A married vet was also given $90.00 a month living expense; single vets drew $65.00. These stipends were raised in 1948.

I was one of the 7.8 million G.I.'s who took full advantage of this marvelous legislation. I never met up with even one enrollee who felt guilty about accepting this largesse from the government. Without fail we were convinced we had earned it and more to the point we deserved it. Not a one of us felt we were clients of a welfare system.

FDR summed up the problem facing America at the conclusion of the war with this most pleasant expression "America's own rightful place in the world depends in large part upon how fully these and similar rights have been carried into practice for our citizens. For unless there is security here at home, there cannot be lasting peace in the world."

Extracting another nugget from Conrad Black in his glorious work, "Franklin Delano Roosevelt – Champion of Freedom" we find: "The New Deal and winning the war were complimentary objectives, and world peace depended on America's prosperity and moral credibility as a just society. Isolationism, laissez-faire economics and racial segregation would all be endangered species in postwar America." The G.I. Bill, he would say, "was the most indisputably successful measure of the entire Roosevelt presidency, and was entirely his original conception and his achievement."

In another work, and a huge bestseller, David M. Kennedy's "Freedom from Fear – The American People in Depression and War 1929-1945", we find this jewel, which completely reinforces Mr. Black's attitude. "The G.I. Bill thus stood out as the most emblematic of all World War II – era political accomplishments. It aimed not at restructuring the economy but at empowering individuals. It roared on after 1945 as a kind of after burner to the engines of social change and upward mobility that the war had ignited, propelling an entire generation along an ascending curve of achievement and affluence that their parents could not have dreamed of."

By the time the G.I. Bill ceased paying out benefits on July 25, 1956; about 2.2 million veterans had attended college on some level. The peak year was in 1947 when 1,150,000 were hitting the books; that amounted to 49.2% of all college students.

Then upwards of three million more would receive training below the college level. Of that two million were taking on the job training. Among the favorites were auto mechanics, refrigerator repair, machine tool operation and of course radio repair. Merely because of the educational portion of the bill the educational level of the American people would be significantly elevated, and for all time. This new standard motivated parents to strive for a college degree for their children.

In order to process all these new applicants, the existing campuses would be forced to expand. Within a remarkably short period of time, Harvard would double its enrollment, and improve its scholastic rating in the bargain. New schools sprouted up all over the land. I attended one of them – Mexico City College – in Mexico City, of course.

All of these benefits funded under the educational provisions of the G.I. Bill cost the taxpayers $14.5 billion and the average cost per applicant was $1,858.00. For that expenditure, the country received in turn a bounty priceless beyond compare.

Various economists have calculated that each college graduate earned in his lifetime $250,000 more than non-college type. Factor in the huge number of participating vets who, instead of going the college route, opted for on the job training. Large numbers of these elected to start their own businesses; many of these would hire additional employees.

In a very enlightening study of the bill and its impact on America, Edward Humes in his "Over Here – How the G.I. Bill transformed the American Dream" outlines in a most pleasing manner what the U.S. Treasury received for its expenditure of the $14.5 billion.

"Considering college benefits alone, The Joint Economic Committee of Congress made a detailed cost-benefit analysis in 1988. Updating the findings with 2006 dollars, this study revealed that the cost to the government of sending every G.I. to college who wanted to go after WWII amounted to 51 billion dollars. The return on that investment was found to be 260 billion dollars in increased economic output from those educated G.I's – their average incomes were that much higher than their peers. Another 93 billion in extra taxes paid on that income rolled in. That's a gross profit of 353 billion dollars. Seven dollars earned for each dollar invested is a pretty good return."

At this point, I'm simply unable to resist the impulse to comment on MCI Reagan's approach to governmental assistance. Reactionary Republicans have established an adoring cult in honor of the man.

Reagan virtually made a career out of proclaiming that the nine most dangerous words in the English language are, "I'm from the government and I'm here to help."

Suppose for a moment we venture back in time to Dixon, Illinois – the year is 1933. Jack Reagan, longtime resident, is about to encounter agents from the Public Works Administration, one of President Roosevelt's nationwide, New Deal Agencies. Jack, who is future President Ronald Reagan's father, has been having more than a little difficulty paying the rent on the family's humble abode. To make matters worse, the cupboard is a long way from full.

The question is – how does Jack react to this meeting? Does he react with haughty indignation, proclaiming for all to hear – "depart from me, ye workers of iniquity"? Or does he promptly drop to one knee and kiss the hand of the leader of the group? The PWA was in Dixon to establish projects that badly needed doing and hiring local men, long out of work, who badly needed employment. They also needed a few dollars to keep from starving.

Readers will recall that ex-President Herbert Hoover branded any man who received public aid, such as offered by the PWA, a "mendacious parasite". Jack Reagan was immensely pleased to join the ranks of the m.p's, as were many millions of men across the land. It is entirely possible that other members of the Reagan family notably rejoiced at the new status of the father. Sometimes, just sometimes, a man from the government who is there to help can prove to be a blessing.

One more ingredient in the life of Jack Reagan needs to be added. Jack was appointed head of the local chapter of the PWA, and as such was the chief mendacious parasite in Dixon. His job was to supervise the m.p's toiling under him. His son, Ronnie, could now view close-up, what a pernicious effect his father's efforts had on the nation. Those efforts involved mending the badly bruised infrastructure, which had been so sorely neglected under the 12 years of Harding, Coolidge and Hoover.

Education, whether it was at the college level or vocational training, while of critical value to the welfare of the veterans and to the nation, was merely one aspect of the G.I. Bill.

Another, and doubtless one of equal value, was the provision for home ownership. Up until at least 1945, America had been a country of renters. Scarcely one-third of families owned their own homes.

Even among that rather select group, living conditions were by present day standards, disturbingly low. Far too many homes lacked any indoor plumbing. The family bathroom was an outhouse. For some the sole source of water was a hand-activated pump in the kitchen. Electricity, particularly in rural areas, either was not available, or was too expensive. That condition held true until well into the era of the Rural Electrification Administration. I can still easily recall from my childhood, how a few of my classmates from homes which relied on kerosene for illumination, had a distinct odor not altogether pleasant.

Now, the beguiling combination of education and home ownership radically uplifted the horizons of millions of newly formed families. By altering the society from one that was forced to rent, usually for an entire lifetime, into one that was predominately a nation of home owners, it utterly transformed these United States.

These two provisions forced open the doors to true middle-class status for millions of vets and their families. This was an elevated position in society which had been denied their hardworking parents. How could those parents climb out their wretched condition when they were forced to work 50-60 hours per week at what FDR called "dog's wages"? They never were able to put aside enough money for a down-payment even for a scruffy shack, much less a brand new home with a full-sized bathroom including a bath-tub and of course plenty of inexpensive electricity. This was what suddenly became available to veterans shortly after the war ended.

But before a house could be purchased the house first had to be constructed and previously few houses were at war's end. Then along came Bill, actually William Levitt, who had been a homebuilder in pre-war civilian life. The U.S. Navy put his talents to work by assigning him to their Construction Battalions, the famed Seabeas. It was there he learned how those individual battalions would construct an individual bridge. In combat, they frequently had to perform that chore under enemy fire. Completed sections of the bridge would be delivered to the site intact, rather than throwing together the unit one girder at a time. A modest sized bridge could be erected so that tanks and artillery could cross over a stream, all done in an amazingly short period of time.

All during the war, Bill Levitt would have these methods gestate in his mind. Back in civilian life his prolific imagination set to work to erect an entire suburban community – quickly, efficiently and inexpensively. First, he purchased an abandoned 1500 acre potato field in Nassau County, Long Island, New York. He began to design the entire lay-out that contained not dozens, nor hundreds, but thousands of nearly identical, compact homes, exclusively for veterans.

First streets had to be built, then street lighting erected. Next a crew would arrive that would lay the foundation for the house. They would move on and be followed by a new crew which would erect the flooring. Crew by crew would arrive until the house was finished and ready for a family. This assembly line construction process enabled the developer to complete houses at a sharply reduced cost.

I am normally unwilling to employ the term "genius" arbitrarily, but when the name William J. Levitt is introduced then genius can be applied. Several historians of the G.I. Bill period adorn him with that term and quickly compare him to an earlier American, Henry Ford.

Ford began to build his internationally known automobile, the Model T, in October, 1908. During the 19 years of its production run, around 15 and a half million of them flowed off the assembly line. (Ford invented the concept of the assembly line along which men were positioned and who then performed usually just one chore in finishing the product.) That staggering number of cars represented half of the entire production in the world. Henry Ford was an authentic genius who had only an eighth grade education and that in a one room school house. Of that unbelievable number of cars sold, customers were permitted to select any color they liked, provided it was black.

The Model T was directly responsible for what became the greatest sociological upheaval this country had ever witnessed. The horseless carriage, in a remarkably short span of time, caused the horse to nearly disappear from the American scene, both as the power to pull a carriage and as a farm animal for plows, and other agricultural implements.

That one auto model sparked the creation of numerous industries; industries in which each would create hundreds of thousands of new jobs; gasoline refineries; vastly expanded oil fields; filling stations to provide gas for these motorized carriages; service garages for repair; fancy auto sales agencies. The millions of new drivers would demand all-weather roads, so that a gridiron of paved roads would materialize.

The business districts of towns enlarged; stores became larger and fancier as farmers started to purchase these amazing vehicles. Home building expanded, lumber mills sprang up. Henry Ford was largely responsible for all of it. Henry Ford was in fact a creative genius.

So was Bill Levitt who single handedly created suburbs in America where none had existed before. His first development on that Long Island potato field was called Levittown.

Other developers quickly adopted this electrifying new method to sell homes, so Levittowns began to emerge across the country, like mushrooms in the spring. As soon as the original Levittown was filled to capacity, Bill Levitt began another.

Eventually 17,000 homes in the first Levittown were finished and sold just as quickly as they were ready for occupancy. The purchase terms were particularly enticing. Absolutely no down payment necessary since the loan was guaranteed by the Veterans Administration. There were several more incentives: no real estate costs or closing costs; finally an amazingly low interest rate, almost half what it would be for non-veterans. Under the G.I. Bill it was actually cheaper to purchase a sparkling new home in a pleasant neighborhood, than renting in the older parts of town.

It's difficult to fully understand that probably at least half of the pre-war housing ranged from inadequate to decrepit – and that was particularly so with rental properties. In some a bathroom didn't exist; the sanitary facility was an outhouse. Central heating consisted of a potbellied stove in the living room which used either coal or wood. In many of the older dwellings the electrical wiring posed a safety threat; it could readily overheat and cause a fatal fire.

All the new homes erected after the war were wired for electrical stoves and refrigerators, plus numerous wall outlets. The Levittown units included a very modern bathroom with a bathtub and shower. Many of the vets had never used a bathtub; certainly the military barracks had no such provision. Beyond that was an abundance of inexpensive hot water available.

It gets better – all of this was available for under $8,000 in the basic unit. More expansive models could be purchased. That amount of money delivered a dwelling of nearly 800 square feet, which is indeed diminutive by 2008 standards, but which, for returning veterans and their wives, proved to be an abundance of space, often times far in excess of what they were reared in.

Soon word raced across the land of this astonishingly new concept of an entire community springing up as if by magic from a forlorn potato patch. What made it even more entrancing for potential developers was the incomprehensible speed with which it occurred. Houses appearing in large clumps in only days accompanied, it would seem, by large aggragations of profit.

As these copy – cat Levittowns arose, from each home there would be an obvious need for a stove, a refrigerator and of course a washer. Soon appliance manufacturers were deluged with orders. With commendable speed they expanded their production potential and when that proved inadequate they erected new and enlarged facilities some distance removed.

Along with the new appliances, the married couple felt a need to purchase household furniture. So a similar explosion took place in that industry. Appearing in tandem was the demand for either wall-to-wall carpeting or individual area rugs. Here was a third industry that enjoyed monumental increases in size and profit.

But without question the most significant expansion occurred within the grocery and food industry. In 1940, when shopping for grocery items it was necessary to go into several separate and small shops. In the first could be found a few canned goods and a limited assortment of packaged items always at a high price. Often times the store owners lived above the business site.

From there you could proceed to the butcher shop where a modest array of freshly cut meats was on display. The butcher was invariably also the owner. This was the procedure for obtaining bakery goods and produce – small shops run by the owner who also waited on you. Since their unit cost was high and the sales volume low, the selling price was considerably raised. In addition these places of business were almost never adjacent to each other; instead they might be separated by one or more blocks.

One department that didn't exist was frozen foods. It's safe to say it wasn't even envisioned in that era. Packaged frozen foods wouldn't happen until a very entrepreneurial gentleman by the name of Clarence Birdseye made his appearance well after the war. In a standard supermarket of today the frozen food section is much, much larger than the typical grocery story of 1940.

Only in 1946 did the first expanded food stores make their appearance and while they were vastly expanded they would be absolutely dwarfed by the gigantic supermarkets of today. The 2,000 square feet unit of 1946 has now swelled to 60,000 feet and more.

Just as Henry Ford provided the spark which ignited a social and economic revolution in the early decades of the 20th century, so too did William Levitt provide an exhilarating impetus in mid century. As the new suburbs emerged with increasing speed, they spawned still more growth which radically altered the American landscape.

Accompanying the suburbs were shopping centers which introduced attractive, larger stores within easy access to the new homes. These centers invariably featured greatly enlarged grocery stores, now called supermarkets. Swank pharmacies were ever present containing many items not seen in the drab, old drug stores. All manner of sophisticated shops opened, catering to this youthful crowd.

General Eisenhower succeeded Harry Truman in the White House in January of 1953. He brought into office a keen desire to inaugurate a system of super highways spanning the nation. It was an old concept originally conceived by the top general in World War I, John Pershing. Eisenhower saw an application of it in Germany, where Adolph Hitler installed the Autobahn, the world's first superhighway. Hitler's sole motive in constructing it was to facilitate easy movement of troops and military equipment.

Eisenhower pressed Congress to pass this innovative program, so in 1956 construction could begin. This network of four lane, divided road ways inspired still more innovations. At every exit along the system, a handful or more of business places would sprout up – gas stations, restaurants, souvenir shops, and of course motels.

Possibly the first modern, comfortable motel in America was erected in 1952 in Memphis, Tennessee; it was called a Holiday Inn. An inspired entrepreneur named Kemmon W. Wilson conceived its striking concept, and in so doing begat several more industries.

Prior to his introduction to the overnight housing scene, the motels open for business quite often featured lumpy mattresses, a tiny shower stall with an inadequate supply of hot water, and a 40 watt bulb in the reading lamp. I am able to speak very knowledgeably on this subject.

Mr. Wilson could erect but one motel at a time, but with the arrival of the interstate of the new highway complex, the industry began its meteoric rise.

Now we can step back and witness the heroic efforts of Franklin Delano Roosevelt and how his benign, enlightened efforts created an entire chain of new industries. With his Presidency came a new deal for the wage earner; with it came an explosion of labor unions, an eight hour day, a 40 hour week. In one industry after another, the new labor codes produced daily wages that exceeded former weekly pay. In factories across the nation, the new codes also brought a two week paid vacation.

Yet it must be emphasized that while the President could do no wrong in the eyes of countless millions of workers, within the domain of the country club set he was an object of unalloyed antipathy. Two of their favorite and often expressed principles was that Roosevelt was striving to destroy their way of life. That was absolutely true, and by the time of his death he did in fact destroy the worst elements of the 1920's culture. It deserved obliteration.

Another of their maxims was "our children's children will still be paying for the New Deal debt." These favored few, the overdressed rich, were oft times seized with a near implacable frenzy at the thought of that man in the White House distributing government funds to the laboring classes, people who they regarded Raggedy –Assed Masses, the RAMS

Marquis Childs, one of the most widely celebrated columnists of the day, made a detailed study of the Roosevelt haters. He called the movement, "A phenomenon which social historians of the future will very likely record with perplexity if not with astonishment, the fanatical hatred of the President which today obsesses thousands of men and women of the American upper class."

Still, the total national debt in January 1981, when their darling Ronald Reagan assumed the office of the presidency, was under one trillion dollars. So from January 1789, to January 1981 a total of 202 years, all of our presidents combined had accumulated a debt burden of a thousand billion dollars. Yet in less than eight years their blessed savior would cause that debt to double while feeding the public a steady diet of "there's morning in America" and reminding us of "the shining city on the hill." Somehow the frenetic pace with which he maneuvered the nation into this intolerable burden didn't provoke any troubling doubt among them. Each of those lofty concepts cost the nation a trillion dollars.

Society's superior stratum would further degrade itself by wading through political sewage. They delighted in introducing the element of sexually transmitted diseases when discussing, the President, their bete noire. That Fellow's paralysis could only have been caused by syphilis, not the polio virus.

Not content with that slander they persisted in mocking him as a Jew. In doing so they resorted to the more demeaning synonyms, such as kike or sheeny. Decades later Richard Nixon was still spitting out that word kike on a routine basis, a fact faithfully recorded on Nixon's own White House tapes.

Mr. Childs summed up the feeling. "No other word than hatred will do. It is a passion, a fury that is unreasoning."

CHAPTER XXVII

President Roosevelt's agile and creative mine went into high gear following Japan's attack on Pearl Harbor and Hitler's declaration of war, four days later on December 11, 1941. Barely two more weeks would pass before the first infant steps were taken towards a monumental concept – the Declaration of the United Nations on January 1st. Signing the document were representatives from 26 nations now at war with the two new enemies.

FDR coined the term United Nations, and while not its sole creator, was its prime mover. By doing so he sketched out his imaginative vision for a postwar future. That organization would prove to be the most cooperative pact between nations in all of mankind's history.

It is entirely possible that a U.N. would have eventually formed, but without the incalculable aura of his world-wide prestige, would not have taken shape so quickly or with such a forceful impact.

Mr. Roosevelt was possessed of a zealous determination to avoid the snares which trapped President Woodrow Wilson in 1919-20. He would take steps to insure that there would be no treachery such as the machinations of Senator Henry Cabot Lodge and his Republican cohort of "bold reservationists" following WWI.

With this country now involved in a grim crusade of victory over world-wide fascism, he could sense that Republicans in Congress were likely to be carried along by a tidal wave of enthusiasm for a United Nations and its promise of enduring peace.

Already a Senator from Michigan, Arthur Vandenberg, newly freed from the bondage of Republican isolationism, would deliver this message to his colleagues. "I do not believe that any nation hereafter can immunize itself by its own exclusive action. I want a new dignity and a new authority for international law."

What a difference a second World War within a generation would make! The U.N. vision would motivate our country to conclude its sorry embrace of isolationism and in doing so provide the necessary direction for the world to pursue the dream of peace instead of chasing after the nightmare of war. This lofty concept had particular resonance in Europe which had been the breeding ground for war for a thousand years and more.

Constructing the enormous edifice that would become the Arsenal of Democracy occupied FDR for many months. Next maneuvering the G.I. Bill of Rights through a somewhat reluctant Congress would require high attention. On June 22, 1944 he signed that legislative triumph.

Weeks later in August the House passed a resolution introduced by a newly elected member from Arkansas, J. William Fulbright which requested, "the creation of appropriate international machinery with power adequate to establish and maintain a just and lasting peace among the nations of the world, and participation of the United States therein."

At this point the President contributed his vital message. "Peace like war can succeed only where there is a will to enforce it and where there is available power to enforce it. The Council of the United Nations must have the power to act quickly and decidedly to keep the peace by force, if necessary. A policeman would not be a very effective policeman if, when he saw a felon break into a house, he had to go to Town Hall and call a town meeting to issue a warrant before the felon could be arrested. So to my simple mind it is clear that, if the world organization is to have any reality at all, our American representative must be endowed in advance by the people themselves, by constitutional means through their representatives in Congress, with authority to act."

The final vote in Congress was conclusive; the bill that emerged contained no shackling amendments from Republicans. In the House, the count was 360 in favor, only 29 opposed. The Senate recorded 85 votes in favor.

The United States was now fully committed to involvement in maintaining peace around the world. Conrad Black, in his epochal biography, "Franklin Delano Roosevelt – Champion of Freedom", would weigh in on the subject. "Had the United States been constructively involved in the world in the previous 40 years, it is very unlikely that either world wars would have occurred. As a Wilsonian framework it provided American's permanent passport out of isolation, which produced a decisive and almost wholly positive influence on the future of the world.

That wholly positive influence found fertile ground in Europe where Germany, France and England, centuries old enemies, have not so much as fired a shot in anger at each other for over 60 years. On the contrary they have bonded together for mutual prosperity and are virtually wedded to each other.

But in this country, in barely a generation, two American presidents of different political parties, would see fit to plunge this nation into an insane war with a small country, half a globe away, and posing no security risk to us. The threat of a Chinese Communist take-over in South Vietnam was laughable. Yet intelligent advisors to those presidents insisted that we invade the country to protect it from the threat of international communism. Today that country beckons to us and longs for our friendship. Still, 58,000 of our armed forces lost their lives in that grotesque misadventure.

Once again, barely a generation later the current occupant of the White House has gathered about him a cabal of neocons suffering from a lack of conscience and pays heed to their counsel. This group shared one quality in common – none had participated in the Vietnamese venture to stop communism in its tracks. Each had displayed an impressive dexterity in evading the draft. None had come close to donning a uniform.

They invented all manner of fanciful tales about conditions in Baghdad, Iraq, where dwelt the evil monster, Saddam Hussein. It was his Weapons of Mass Destruction, the ominous WMD's. Once more this country was presented with a fearsome threat to its survival.

Condoleeza Rice and Dick Cheney dutifully trotted forward and outlined the ominous menace of mushroom clouds if the nation didn't act with dispatch. Next, Secretary of State Colin Powell, a former Army Chief of Staff, was permitted to address the United Nations' Security Council. General Powell, a black man of towering credibility, delivered a powerful speech urging the United States and the United Nations to remove this man Hussein and those threats immediately. The compelling nature of the speech, plus the continued exhortations of Condi and Dick, to say nothing of Wolfowitz and Rumsfeld, stampeded Congress into granting Bush the authorization to pursue war.

The current occupant of the White House didn't waste any time whisking our brave soldiers over to Iraq, and into a hornet's nest of ancient, poisonous tribal hatreds. After all the feverish tales spread by the neocons, one felt certain that the countryside would be littered with WMDs and lethal gases, or chemicals. Our lads scoured the land but alas, unearthed not a single one. After five, long years, all the agents of death had somehow vanished, as did the apocryphal tales.

Perhaps the outstanding book on the Iraq War was "Cobra II", jointly written in 2006 by Michael R. Gordon and Lt. General Bernard E. Trainer. It enjoyed a lengthy stay in the national best seller's list. The book summarized all the follies inherent in this application of the neocon's "global war on terror."

"But President Bush and his team committed five grievous errors. They underestimated their opponent and failed to understand the welter of ethnic groups and tribes that is Iraq. They did not bring the right tools to the fight and put too much confidence in technology. They failed to adapt to developments on the ground and remained wedded to their prewar analysis even after Iraq showed their penchant for guerilla tactics in the first days of the war. They presided over a system in which differing military and political prospectives were discouraged. Finally, they turned their back on the nation – building lessons from Balkan and other crisis zones and fashioned a plan that unrealistically sought to shift much of the burden onto a defeated and ethnically diverse population and allied nations that were enormously ambivalent about the invasion. Instead of making plans to fight a counterinsurgency, the President and his team drew up plans to bring the troops home and all but declared the war won."

The book manifests excellence throughout, and is a pleasure to read. However, when the authors suggest that Bush and his team committed five errors, they grievously underestimated the Bushies' proclivity for aberrance. Paul Wolfowitz, deputy to Donald Rumsfeld, the Secretary of Defense, probably sired five blunders merely in the first few weeks.

Eric Shinseki, the Army Chief of Staff, and Anthony Zinni, a top Marine general, both felt confident that policing Iraq after hostilities had terminated would require far more troops than would be needed to defeat the Iraqi Army. Their estimates varied between 350,000 and 400,000 men. Woeful Wolfowitz insisted that 150,000 men could do the job. When General Shinseki had the temerity to challenge Wolfowitz, his position as the head general in the Army was immediately terminated and Wolfie had him fired. With Shinseki went another general who abruptly resigned in protest.

Had the larger occupying force been in place after the war ended, most of the ensuing disaster would have been avoided. Both Rumsfeld and Wolfowitz were eased out of the Defense Department but far too late to prevent the disaster that now confronts the badly undermanned Army in Iraq today. Wolfie also was supremely confident that Iraqi oil would easily pay the cost of the occupation. The upfront costs of keeping our troops in that country exceed $10 billion dollars monthly. The ultimate price will doubtless exceed two trillion dollars. Some estimates insist it will be three trillion.

Our most venerated president, Franklin Delano Roosevelt, with his vision of a United Nations, delivered peace to Europe, and except for Russia and Serbia, no nation has engaged another in strife. He would have been sorely vexed to understand why, in less than 60 years, our country has chosen to invade two small, undistinguished nations, each thousands of miles removed from our shores. Neither of country could possibly have inflicted the tiniest harm to this land, but both of those countries, once invaded, did inflict ruinous damage to our armed forces, to our Treasury Department, and most especially to the super – abundance of good will we once enjoyed all over the globe.

Thankfully, most of the dealers of delusion have departed from positions of authority within the Bush Administration. George Tenet, the head of the CIA, assured Bush and the nation that the subjugation of Iraq would be "A slam dunk" and he is no longer heard from. Colin Powell, the only member of those orators who possessed even a dram of credibility, was thrown overboard following the 2004 election, and he too is engulfed in anonymity.

Not a murmur of apology was ever uttered by any of that gaggle. Bush and Cheney would sooner sever one of their limbs than admit they had erred – and that was for a two trillion dollar hopeless blunder.

President Roosevelt, as we have seen, committed the nation to a <u>two billion dollar</u>, gamble when he spirited money through defense budgets in order to fund the Manhattan Project, which ultimately produced the two bombs dropped on Japan.

Of course FDR was dealing with fanatically dedicated scientists, some of whom had previously been awarded Nobel Prizes in physics. Bush, Cheney and Rumsfeld were dealing with over – educated nitwits, who militarily speaking, didn't know enough to come in out of the rain.

A significant step in the development of the United Nations took place in this country over a seven week period starting on August 21, 1944. This was a meeting of what was called the Big Four – the United States, the Soviet Union, England and China. Amidst some wrangling much forward progress resulted. This was followed by a second conference held in San Francisco, beginning on April 25, 1945, only 13 days after FDR's death.

Even as his life was slowly ebbing away, the President once again revealed his mastery of politics, whether it was domestic or international. For this vital meeting he had selected an equal number of U.S. Republicans and Democrats to form this U.S. delegation.

The preliminary agreements reached in the 1944 conference served as an outline for the meeting the following year. The war in Europe ended in less than two weeks after the opening session, but the titanic struggle with Japan threatened to continue until well into 1946 and perhaps into the next year. Two months would pass before the charter was signed on June 26, and another four months were required to complete the binding regulations. That took place on October 24. At that point 51 nations comprised the initial membership.

By that time, the two bombs had been dropped on Hiroshima and Nagasaki and World War II had come to an end. It is extremely unlikely that anyone from the United States' delegation knew of the activities taking place in Los Alamos.

All subsequent meetings of this global organization would have interpreters and translators for the five official languages – English, French and Spanish of course, but now also Chinese and Russian. Any document issued or speech made is translated into the necessary language.

New nations could be added provided they were recommended by the Security Council; first the General Assembly would have to approve by a two-thirds vote. Only nations not at war, or not seeking war, could be considered.

The General Assembly is comprised of all the members in the UN. Its duty is to control all the individual units, or organs, of the body.

There is also a Security Council whose goal is to maintain peace around the world and promote security for threatened nations. It lacked the military power to do that when, in 1945, the Soviet Union established a bloc of Communist dictatorships in Central Europe called the Warsaw Pact Nations. That undistinguished group of countries began to break up in 1989 and finally shattered in the following months.

The Soviet Union suffered grave defections during this same period when a number of its constituent members broke free from the deadly embrace of the Kremlin in Moscow. The Soviet Union once more became Russia, only much smaller.

Except for the unpardonable depredations inflicted on the Warsaw Pact countries by Russia, no European nation has openly attacked another nation. Those Warsaw countries are for the most part now thriving and splendid examples of democracy in action.

After FDR's unfortunate death, President Harry S. Truman stepped forward to become the recognized authority in the organization. Only the United States with it's staggering wealth and prestige, could provide the powerful leadership necessary to make the UN a success.

The new President surprised nearly everybody in the country with his forceful guidance. "History has bestowed on us a solemn responsibility – we failed before to give a genuine peace – we must not fail this time. We must not repeat the blunders of the past."

With this bold statement, Harry Truman was reminding his countrymen of the treachery committed in 1919-20 by the Republicans in the Senate. Their presidential candidate, Warren Harding, ran on a platform openly hostile to the nascent League of Nations.

In July of 1945, at a meeting in Potsdam, Germany, Mr. Truman would declare to Winston Churchill and Josef Stalin that, "we are looking forward to a better world, a peaceful world, a world in which all the people will have an opportunity to enjoy the good things of life. We want peace and prosperity for the world as a whole. We want to see the time come when we can do the things in peace that we have been able to do in war. If we can put this tremendous machine of ours, which has made victory possible, we can look forward to the greatest age in the history of mankind. That is what we proposed to do."

Whatever its shortcomings the UN has performed heroically in numerous areas. In the realm of economic reconstruction its actions were particularly noteworthy. Planes, tanks and artillery had created huge zones in Europe where devastation was frightful. I personally witnessed many of these in France, Belgium and lastly Germany. U.N.R.R.A, the United Nations Relief and Rehabilitation Administration, performed superbly in delivering food, medicine and medical supplies. Temporary housing had to be constructed along with electrical power plants.

The World Bank evolved into an amazing gift to those areas as well as less developed countries in Latin America and Africa. Not only were gigantic loans made available, and at most favorable terms, but top-rate technical assistance often accompanied the money. Then too, trained supervisors were on had to oversee the distribution of the funds to minimize corruption and bribery.

If the UN had supervised our mortgage industry, it surely would have done a far better job than our enormous brokerage houses did.

Besides saving succeeding generations from war, one of the UN's greatest goal, it also established a large number of specialized agencies:

UNESCO – The United Nations Educational, Scientific and Cultural Organization.

WHO – World Health Organization, which alone has doubtless saved tens of millions of lives. Because of it, terrible scourges such as small pox have disappeared from earth. This disease was once one of the most virulent killers mankind had ever known. Today it exists only in a few test tubes in guarded laboratories.

Likewise poliomyelitis has vanished except for isolated groups who believe vaccination is not in accord with their religious principles.

One of my favorite UN projects is the Children's Fund, now known as UNICEF – the International Children's Emergency Fund. It feeds children where needed and also does exceptional work in preventing the spread of lethal diseases.

Once our troops had liberated France from Nazi bondage and the war in Europe came to an end, the newly formed French government began planning for the mammoth task of rebuilding the country's economy. It was indeed fortunate to have in charge two men who were possessed of courage and visionary ideas. This was in stark contrast to the craven politicians who led the country into disaster in 1938.

In Jean Monnet and Robert Schuman, it had a team who were boldly determined to prevent for all time any further hostilities between France and

Germany. The two also realized the futility of subjugating Germany and preventing its economy from blossoming.

This enlightened thought led to organizing an important segment of European economic activity and from it evolved the European Coal and Steel Community. This was a small but vital step toward the formation of today's 27 member, European Union, a United States of Europe. The original treaty was ratified by six members: France, West Germany, Italy, Belgium, the Netherlands and Luxembourg. Some years later Denmark, Ireland and England joined.

While these resolute actions in France provided a brightly lighted path toward eventual economic recovery, still the post war months continued to offer hardship and misery for unacceptably large numbers of citizens. Cold, disease and hunger prevailed over too much of Europe. Always lurking around the corner was the haunting specter of Soviet inspired Communism. All the western democracies were living on the ragged edge of destitution, yet by stubbornly clinging together they barely managed to survive.

Josef Stalin was unremitting in his zeal to subvert as many European counties as possible. He had already out lasted two of his comrades in arms from WWII; FDR, dead in April, 1945: Winston Churchill defeated for election in July of that year. He would even survive Harry Truman's near eight year term in the White House, living until March 5, 1953.

The appeal of Communist parties had already subverted a huge swath of Central Europe and was now threatening Greece and Turkey. They would be rescued by the emboldened efforts of our President in promulgating the Truman Doctrine. By convincing Congress to spend $250 million in Greece and $120 million in Turkey, both those countries stayed within the orbit of western democracies.

As had happened countless numbers of times, these two timely and courageous acts were met with stoical opposition from mean spirited Republicans in Congress. They lacked any program of their own – just blind contention to FDR's always brilliant concepts and now those of Harry Truman.

What almost inevitably evolved from the Truman Doctrine was the ERP – the European Recovery Program which shortly became know as the Marshall Plan. That Plan began its lengthy incubation period following a six week tour of Europe by Will Clayton, the Undersecretary of State. Committing his findings to paper, he wrote a memo to the President which he first handed to his boss, Dean Acheson, who in turned delivered it to Truman.

In the memo, Clayton emphasized how close to success were the Soviet Propaganda campaigns calculated to destroy a country's independence. "Feeding on hunger, economic misery, and frustration, these attacks have already been successful in some of the liberated countries."

Quickly, in a speech delivered to an American college audience, Acheson pointed out how Europe was clinging to survival by a tenuous rope. "It is one of the principal aims of foreign policy today to use our economic and financial resources to widen these margins. It is necessary if we are to preserve our own freedoms and our own democratic institutions. It is necessary for our national security. And it is our duty and privilege as human beings."

Only seven years earlier, as a consequence of Hitler's absurdly easy conquest of France and five other European countries, FDR had used a remarkably similar tone to describe the threat of German fascism.

Following that address in May, 1947, George Marshall delivered the Annual Commencement at Harvard on June 5th. I have read the 15 minute call to arms at the Marshall Library in Lexington, Virginia. I believe this short address to the Harvard students to be one of the most monumental of any post war speeches by an American.

In it he outlined in the starkest possible terms, the shattered state of the European economy. The remedy consisted of "breaking the vicious circle and restoring the confidence of the European people in the economic future of their own countries and of Europe as a whole."

The Truman Administration now acted quickly to pass the European Recovery Program. Soon it would be called The Marshall Plan. The Republicans fought it by introducing amendments to either delay the program or decrease its funding. In the House 75 of its members voted against the bill.

Over in Europe Foreign Minister Ernest Bevin of England and his French counterpart, Georges Bidault, arranged for a huge assembly of representatives of 15 more countries lining up to apply for desperately needed assistance, whether it be food, medicine, or transportation equipment. Most of the railroad structure in France was either destroyed or badly mauled by the Allied Air forces. So locomotives were needed almost as much as wheat.

Harry Truman and his astute aides estimated that the total aid package would reach $18 billion; its ultimate price tag was a more modest $12.5 billion.

In the early days of April, 1948, huge American freighters began leaving ports heading for Europe their holds filled to over flowing with what materials the Europeans needed the most. But the last thing Stalin wanted for Western Europe was democracy and prosperity, so he reacted in an outraged manner. His troops controlled all of Eastern Germany where Berlin is located. West Berlin had been allocated to the Allies – the U.S., France and England – but when he elected to shut down all entrances to the city, it appeared to be doomed to fall on June 24, 1948.

With the arrival of the freighters, hope found its way back to the beleaguered lands and with it renewed energy. Production soared in many of the Western

European countries. Farmers could anticipate bringing in abundant harvests once again, so that first hunger, then malnutrition ebbed away.

The Truman Administration, rather than allowing this blockade to become permanent, responded quickly and skillfully. West Berlin, the country's capitol, was a metropolis of two and a half million citizens, and at an absolute minimum, needed 400 tons of supplies everyday. The only avenue open to the Truman group was delivery by air. Never since airplanes had been invented was that idea even contemplated.

In the first weeks of this debacle all that was available for these flights was the C-47, a rather diminutive transport vehicle. But then from around the globe the American Air Force began to bring in the much larger C-54, and soon they had this craft in adequate numbers, then in formidable numbers. Two new airports opened. As cold weather descended upon the Berliners, so did coal in sufficient amounts. Along with it came medicine and other vital necessities.

Stalin and his stooges in the city came to realize that their game of threat and intimidation no longer worked, so early in May of 1949 they reopened all the blocked roads, railroads and bridges. The Berlin Airlift had been an enormous triumph for free men; for the Soviet Union and the Warsaw Pact countries it was a resounding defeat.

Returning to the Marshall Plan, we find that while Berlin had been under siege, the 16 countries benefiting from resuscitation with American aid were responding handsomely. The $12.5 billion already pouring out from the Treasury Department in Washington was purchasing untold decades of peace and prosperity for an entire continent.

Year by year following the first influx of American Aid, Europe would continue to flourish, always increasing in wealth and power. The Marshall Plan was working its healing balm. Within a bare four years the original ERP states would see their Gross National Product soar as much as 25%.

We have already seen how gifted, prescient, and unselfish leaders in France and West Germany fathered the European Coal and Steel Community which arrived on the scene with but six members.

From this slight but sturdy formation would evolve various mergers of early organizations – one large group was the European Community which took over the functions of both the coal and steel community and the important European Atomic Energy Community.

Next came the European Economic Community, formed to ease and even obliterate trade barriers. Immediately a much higher volume of goods started flowing across borders with less and less restriction. With each of these developments economic momentum increased and with it surplus capital for still more growth.

The Continent was progressing toward its ultimate goal of becoming the United States of Europe. Today there are 27 nations in the European Union – it excludes only the economically weak and the politically unstable countries. At least five more states are eagerly awaiting inclusion but no exact time table has been established for that event.

The most striking development is that no member of the EU has ever aimed a blow at any other. Numerous aspects of European society are truly noteworthy. They easily are the most civilized states in the world. None of its members are permitted to exact capital punishment. Think of that! The current occupant of the White House, the Preposterous Imposter, alone signed the death warrants for 152 *men and women* in the Texas penal system and hurried them to their rendezvous with death. And that in only six years as governor of Texas!

Isn't that what we should expect from a self-proclaimed compassionate conservative? In doing so he set the all time record for governors in this country, a record that will never again be approached. That number, 152, nearly approached the total number of prisoners executed in the other 49 states.

In healthcare the EU far out distances the United States. In nearly all of its member nations, universal health care reigns. It pursues the goal of the WHO, the World Health Organization, which strives for "a state of complete physical, mental and social well-being and not merely the absence of disease or infirmity."

Our nation has seen fit to ignore that lofty standard. Since the U.S. currently has nearly 50,000,000 citizens with a complete denial of health well-being, it is fair to state that as a nation we fall far short.

In the most advanced states of the continent, including all in Western Europe, their citizens enjoy a longer life span, with a superior level of health and achieve it at considerably reduced cost. Admittedly a high degree of health care is available in this country, but with each passing year fewer and fewer of our citizens can afford it.

In addition to the fifty million lacking any but emergency room treatment, there are far in excess of that number with only minimal care. Senior citizens on Medicare do have a high level and at rock bottom cost.

President Roosevelt attempted in vain to pass legislation for a single payer system in 1935, the same year as his Social Security Bill completed passage. The American Medical Association, by screaming about the dreadful effects of socialized medicine and doing it long and hard enough, was able to deny passage of the bill. That was an unrelieved tragedy for our people and 73 years later we are still suffering from that merciless lobbying.

Harry Truman tried again in the late 1940's with the same result. Lyndon Johnson, with two-to-one Democratic majorities in both houses of Congress, was able in 1965 to ramrod the Medicare Bill through that Congress, but it or course was available only to social security recipients.

I can easily recall with extreme distaste, listening to the debates of the 10 white male Republican aspirants for the presidential nomination and how they attempted to outshout each other in denouncing the evil effects of socialized medicine. But then consider how the 27 countries of the EU have happily embraced that evil and thrived because of it.

Of the tens of millions of my fellow senior citizens who have been on Medicare since 1965, how many do you suppose look upon it as an evil governmental affliction in their lives?

Because of the abject failure of the 74th Congress to pass FDR's Universal Health Care package in 1935, even with bulging three to one ratios of Democrats over Republicans, hundreds of millions of Americans have suffered needlessly from preventable illnesses and even deaths. That absence of a social conscience led to a tragedy of the highest order.

It is truly astounding how Franklin Roosevelt, a product of generations of wealth and privilege, should concern himself with raising the living standards of the farmer and the wage earner. From the moment he first occupied the New York governor's chain in 1929, that was his guiding philosophy. It would follow him into the White House in 1933.

Now contrast this with the Republicans who succeeded him: Dwight Eisenhower, Richard Nixon, or Ronald Reagan, all of who stemmed from lower middle class families. Not a one of them ever wasted a moment to raise the minimum wage, improve unsafe or even dangerous conditions in the work place, or ease the burden on indigent or handicapped people. Would eliminating child labor have taken up any of their time?

As indifferent as were Eisenhower and Nixon, Reagan was still worse. He devoted his time to cutting taxes on the rich and removing most of the burdens of governmental oversight on Big Business, just as Harding and Coolidge had done in the 1920s. That of course plus reminding us about the exalted status of the shining city on the hill!

With his $1400.00 tailor made suits, and his dyed black hair, he had erased all memories of life in Dixon, Illinois and how his father was barely eking out a living on a WPA relief project. Were the three Republican Presidents true Conservatives or were they merely a trio of sell-out artists?

For an even starker contrast, review the record of the four Democrats who strived to continue FDR's triumphant reign. They were Harry Truman, Lyndon Johnson, Jimmy Carter and Bill Clinton, all again products of straightened financial circumstances. (To be sure Jack Kennedy was president and he came from considerable wealth, but he too had liberal ideas.)

The Republicans have lacked any valid programs since Theodore Roosevelt left office in 1909, so their strategy is to attack Democrats, always invoking wicked equivocations. They have done this against every Democratic President or presidential candidate in my lifetime. We have seen the mountain of abuse they heaped upon our greatest President, Franklin Roosevelt, calumny that reached and even exceeded psychopathic levels.

No sooner had he been lowered into his grave than they directed their stream of falsehoods towards Harry Truman. For his benefit they coined the phrase "To err is Truman" and proclaimed him unworthy of this high office. In doing so they conveniently overlooked how they had elected three inferior duds to that office in the 1920s, including one that soon became our worst president.

These outrageous charges were a revolting example of chutzpah, a delectable Yiddish word meaning shameless gall. The newly inducted President had already initiated a series of courageous and highly intelligent decisions. I can think of no action undertaken by Harding, Coolidge or Hoover which merited terms like courageous or highly intelligent.

But Harry Truman quickly promulgated the Truman Doctrine which saved Greece and Turkey from the suffocating embrace of Communism. He was equally masterful in shepherding the infant United Nations through its first efforts. In the nick of time he and General Marshall launched the Plan which bore the general's name. While the Plan is named after Marshall, without vigorous promotion from the President, it would never have become law.

In spite of these wondrous accomplishments, when Harry Truman ran for reelection in 1948, he faced what appeared to be impossible barricades to his winning. The relentlessly reactionary Republicans never accorded him any tributes, only a barrage of partisan insults and lies.

Even among Democratic notables, enthusiasm for his candidacy was nearly nonexistent. His approval rating was around 36%, only marginally better than Bummy Bush's correct standing. On more than one occasion he was publicly snubbed by party notables, many of whom publicly demanded that he withdraw from the race.

Diminishing his chances even further, two independent parties soon formed. FDR's running mate in 1936 and 1940, Henry Wallace, started the Progressive

Party which inclined uncomfortably close to the American Communists. The worthless segregationists in the South, led by Strom Thurmond, started the Dixiecrat Party. Not since Abe Lincoln ran in 1860 were voters faced with so many factions.

Harry refused to surrender. He embarked on two lengthy train trips searching for votes and was soon finding them in heroic numbers. His advance team would line up outdoor sites in large cities, the election train would stop, Harry would address impressive crowds, and resume the crusade.

Meanwhile, Dewey was spending his time dealing with more important issues, such as selecting his cabinet, knowing beyond any doubt that his triumph was certain. Newspapers and magazines were proclaiming him the next president.

On Truman's second excursion, he had aboard 50 newsmen. A poll taken showed that every one of them thought Dewey would be the winner. Even Bess and Margaret Truman, the President's wife, and daughter who always accompanied him, began to doubt his chances.

Election night the Republican bigwigs, meeting in their favorite hotel in New York, were ecstatic, speculating at what hour they could expect the customary telegram from the detested Harry, conceding defeat. In Washington, the attitude in the Democrat's favorite hotel, was very reserved with no expectation of victory.

It is with extreme delight that I reveal the final piece de resistance. In Chicago, the Tribune editor was so certain of victory for the candidate his paper had endorsed, that his headline ran "Dewey Defeats Truman." This was the Chicago Tribune whose publisher, "Colonel" Robert McCormick had demonized FDR for 12 years.

The actual vote count showed that the President had been reelected by a rather decisive margin. He captured 303 electoral votes to Dewey's 189. His victory margin was over two million votes. Thurmond and Wallace combined, took almost the same number, most of which would have gone to Harry.

An enraged Senator Taft would give voice to this sentiment. "It defies all common sense to send that roughneck ward politician back to the White House." Now that's chutzpah of an immortal nature, this from the Taft who registered a long list of imbecilic votes for 14 long years. From the position of a Liberal all he ever did was pollute the Senate during those years, yet his reactionary, isolationist colleagues deemed him "Mr. Republican." He echoed the vacuous philosophy of Coolidge and Hoover, completely lacking any merit. In condemning President Truman he continued his pattern. He had earlier in his career condemned the 1940 Draft Bill plus the 1941 Lend-Lease to England

Russia. It is impossible to see how our Armed Forces could have vanquished Germany and Japan without those legislative measures.

The only legislation he is remembered for is the Taft-Hartley Labor Relations Bill of 1947, which placed onerous restrictions on organized labor. Truman vetoed the bill but it was passed over his veto. This indeed was Mr. Republican.

In the period leading up to the election, large numbers of the republican hierarchy began purchasing fancy homes in Washington having been informed they were either members of the Dewey Cabinet or would hold other high office in his Administration. On Wednesday, November 3, 1948, they were made aware of the revolting development that took place a day earlier, Election Day. With that a very brisk market was suddenly created in Washington real estate.

CHAPTER XXVIII

For a Liberal Democrat it is truly enlightening to review the records of the 18 Presidents elected in the 20th Century. Seven were Democrats, 11 were Republicans. In terms of years spent in the White House however, the total time is rather close – 48 years for the Liberal party and 52 for the other group.

Each of the Democrats enjoyed a sparkling intellect and a fully stocked brain. They brought into the White House, at the very minimum, a progressive philosophy. In turn they were hounded remorselessly and, in the case of Truman, virtually driven out of office.

The most abhorrent instance was in 1952 when the Republican nominee, General Dwight Eisenhower, dredged through the mud and picked out Richard Milhouse Nixon as his running mate. Milhouse has appeared in this humble effort at history repeatedly, and at some length – never, however with the tiniest degree of approval.

Soon he was racing around the land condemning the combined Roosevelt – Truman eras as "20 years of treason." No member of the Eisenhower campaign staff ever did anything to rein in this man. Georgie Patton, before his death, hoped that Eisenhower would make a better President than he did a general.

The first Republican President of the last century was William McKinley, originally elected in 1896. He was a man of passable merit, which for a number of Republicans who followed him into office, was a high rank. Six months into his second term he was assassinated and replaced by Theodore Roosevelt, a man worthy of the highest approbation. Teddy was, and may well remain, the second greatest Republican to hold that office. Roosevelt in turn guided William Taft into the White House in 1908. They had developed and especially close kinship but with each passing month in the office Taft lost most of Roosevelt's affection. Finally Teddy became so disenchanted that he even gave birth to the Bull Moose Party in a supreme effort to unseat his former friend. Both would lose decisively to the Democrat, Woodrow Wilson. Taft wasn't merely defeated, his candidacy was buried.

The next three Republicans to reside in the White House – Harding elected in 1920, Coolidge in 1924, and Hoover in 1928, were nor merely lamentable in office but proved to be inexcusable. All three were bewilderingly blind to the hideous plight of the farmer and the working class. The wage level, the long grueling hours and hazardous working conditions screamed for betterment. From those Presidents came not the slightest effort in that direction.

Nor could any mercy be expected from Cabinet members. The Republicans controlling Congress were largely creatures bought and paid for by Big Business, concerned mostly with their reelections. Not only were their hearts frozen into indifference, but what was even worse, these men (there were no women in Congress) were often openly antagonistic to the tens of suffering millions.

Following the 20 blessed years of FDR and Harry Truman, the White House would be in the control of Dwight David Eisenhower. With him arrived more of the hear no evil, see no evil attitude that characterized the 1920s. Smiling Ike was an acknowledged racist who was content to have the still deplorable level of civil rights to remain in place. Once Theodore Roosevelt vacated the Presidency in 1909 no Republican Chief of State has advanced the cause of Civil Rights by any measurable degree. On January 19, 2009 that will be an even hundred years, lacking about six weeks.

The three ciphers who followed Wilson into the Presidency starting in 1921, were not only ominously devoid of a social conscience, but continued to uphold and perpetuate segregation. Harding was inducted into the ranks of the Ku Klux Klan with a secret ceremony held in the White House. Coolidge was an agate-eyed WASP who shunned all non-WASPs. His administration held not a single woman, Jew or Catholic. Hoover perpetuated this fantasy that he was the President of all Americans.

When Franklin Roosevelt came into office he instantly flushed out much of this repugnant residue. With him came a small, but highly influential coterie of Jews who were his chief advisors as governor. As president he filled an even larger number of significant positions with Jews; shortly came the claim from fair minded Republicans that his was not a New Deal but a Jew Deal.

He also began filling high ranking federal judicial posts with Catholics, and in doing so finally acknowledging the large percentage of that religious affiliation in the country. For some odd reason all the Republican presidents had felt no pressing need to appoint Catholics to federal offices.

With his wife Eleanor continually prodding him, FDR resuscitated the dormant cause of Civil Rights by sprinkling a few black faces in the federal Bureaucracy. This was something no President had ever done and it instantly incited the wrath of the Southern Congressmen, all of whom then were Democrats, and who otherwise enthusiastically supported his New Deal programs. He needed to tread ever so carefully in this area. At the beginning of our entry into WWII, FDR directed the Army to begin the process of limited desegregation. Once our forces were in Normandy in June 1944, rather impressive numbers of Blacks could be seen driving the trucks bringing up supplies from the ships to the front lines. These truck convoys were called The Red Ball Express. I witnessed these black Army drivers by the hundreds. During the Battle of the

Bulge, when the Army was badly in need of front line replacements, Blacks by the thousands volunteered for combat. The Navy remained stoutly resistant to any influx of non-white personnel.

After he became President, Harry Truman gave a vigorous impetus to this movement, and succeeded brilliantly with the Army. By the conclusion of his term in office the AUS, the Army of the United States, was nearly free of any taint of segregation. With Eisenhower as President the movement continued but its momentum was far more tepid. Earlier we saw where Colin Powell would have ended his career as Colonel Powell, and not as Army Chief of Staff, a four star general were it not for the intervention of a Democratic President.

While Eisenhower was willing to allow more desegregation in the Army, he resisted its introduction into the general school system. Moreover he was embittered by what his appointee to Chief Justice of the Supreme Court was doing. The Court under Earl Warren declared segregation in public schools was unconstitutional on May 17, 1954.

The vote on the Warren Court was unanimous, 9-0. Of course on that court there was no Antonin Scalia, or a Clarence Thomas, or a William Rehnquist. It's safe to say they would have cast a nay vote.

On his appointment of Earl Warren, Eisenhower later grumbled, "The worst damn fool decision I ever made." With that pronouncement he solidified his position as both a racist and a bigot. His cabinet, by the way, nearly duplicated that of Hoover – mostly white male millionaires or prominent right wing Republicans. There was one lone exception that infiltrated these ranks, Oveta Culp Hobby. She served as Secretary of Health, Education and Welfare, a newly formed Board, for the first two years of its existence.

I find it extremely distasteful to elevate a racist and bigot to the high level of number seven, on the list of American Presidents. Understandably were he not inserted, there would be no Republican between number three, Theodore Roosevelt, and number 18, William McKinley, who annexed the Pacific Islands of Guam and Wake Island. (They cost this nation a number of thousands of American dead, both defending and recapturing them during WWII.) Perhaps the 168 historians who compiled the list felt compassion for the Republican Party and decided to toss in another name.

Returning to Earl Warren – today's Liberal Democrats look upon Earl Warren, a life-long Republican by the way, as perhaps the greatest Chief Justice in our history and the decisions of his Court as being among the most meritorious in Court history; a notable difference of opinion with the general.

Following the eight tedious years of Eisenhower's tenure, the nation was introduced to John Fitzgerald Kennedy. Handsome, debonair and exceedingly articulate, JFK in his tragically short term of office provided a delightful spark, a new vision for the future. The country was certainly ready for one.

As he proclaimed in his inaugural address, one that is still frequently quoted nearly a half century later, "The torch has been passed to a new generation," to that he would add, "And so my fellow Americans: Ask not what your country can do for you, ask what you can do for your country."

(Quick now – which lines are ever quoted from the nine inaugurals of Dwight Eisenhower, Richard Nixon, Ronald Reagan and the two Bushes?)

JFK would be shot in Dallas, Texas on November 22, 1963 barely 1000 days into office. His presidency did not achieve grandiose accomplishments, but it racked up a striking list of victories in a short time period. This in sharp contrast to the eight years of largely do – nothing government from General Ike.

John F. Kennedy's death on a Friday created one of the most sorrowful week-ends in our history. Just as it had only 18 years earlier when Franklin Roosevelt passed on. The nation was engulfed in another prolonged episode of intense grief. Truly, mourning in America. Again torrents of tears were shed for a gallant leader.

There have been seven Republican Presidents who have died in my lifetime. Only one died in Only one died in office. The cumulative volume of tears that fell from the eyes of grieving relatives and admirers for Warren Harding wouldn't have amounted to even a tiny trickle.

Jack Kennedy followed Eisenhower into the Oval Office and made determined, but not frenzied, efforts to advance the cause of Civil Rights in America. But it was with Lyndon Johnson that the minorities found a Chief Executive that would deliver great joy and inspiration. That came as a most pleasant surprise, given that until at least 1957, while a Senator from Texas, he voted with the Southern Segregationists but his racial orientation underwent a slow but inexorable progression toward liberalism.

As President, LBJ proclaimed in May 1964, "We have the opportunity to move not only toward the rich society, and the powerful society, but upwards to the Great Society. The Great Society rests on abundance and liberty for all. It demands an end to poverty and racial injustice. He thereby declared war "on poverty in America" and took the first of a notable number of giant strides towards ending "racial injustice."

Abe Lincoln had a Civil War thrust upon him the moment he took office, but still found time to issue the Emancipation Proclamation on January 1, 1863, which freed the slaves, although only in Union held territory. This was one of the most courageous and forceful acts in the entirety of presidential history.

Lyndon Johnson made a commitment to battle segregation and eliminate discrimination where ever it was in place. No other president before or since, has carried on this crusade with such intensity. FDR could not engage in energetic anti-segregation activity for fear of open revolt on the part of Southern Democrats in congress. At times they could be quote revolting.

LBJ's Civil Rights Act of 1964 represented a monumental forward stride in ending discrimination, whether it be in employment or in public places. He was certain that the Civil Rights Act of 1965 was of even greater import. It effectively ended nearly all resistance to voting rights for minorities in the South.

It's equally important to recall that in the Congress of 1964, two Republicans voted against the first Civil Rights Act – Barry Goldwater in the Senate and George Bush Senior in the House.

But as the President predicted with uncanny accuracy, the Republican Party, The Party of Abe Lincoln, would seize upon this long overdue action to create an extended period of political domination. He estimated a quarter of a century; realistically it has endured until at least 2006, more like 38 years.

Johnson of course helped pave the way because of his hopeless, hapless plan for destroying the Viet Cong in South Vietnam.

Before long the declining fortunes of the American military in Vietnam would not only destroy the future prospects of the Great Society, but bring an end to the war on poverty. It would also have another appalling consequence – it would help restore the political career of Richard Nixon, always lurking in the background.

Following his narrow defeat in 1960 at the hands of Jack Kennedy, and after the thumping he received when he tried to unseat Pat Brown, the popular governor of California, it appeared certain Nixon's political life was finished. In a press conference the following day, he rather conclusively admitted that fact.

His final words to a large assembly of the media were, "But as I leave you I want you to know – just think how much you're going to be missing. You won't have Nixon to kick around anymore, because gentlemen, this is my last conference." With that he turned and abruptly stode from the room.

I have in my modest library an even 25 books about Nixon - 23 biographies and two which he penned. And on this day to see his apparent exit from public life after he so mercilessly vilified Franklin Roosevelt and Harry Truman was an uncommonly satisfactory day. Another one, even more satisfactory was August 9, 1974, the day he was forced to resign from the Presidency.

Unfortunately for his long suffering wife, Patricia, and the 20 members of his Administration who collaborated in perpetrating or covering up the numerous

White House crimes, and who went to prison, Milhous had merely indulged in another of his predictable prevarications.

Tricky Dick's magical resurrection really began on the day President Kennedy was assassinated, a day of prolonged and bitter sorrow in America. The grotesque misadventure in Vietnam was for Nixon an unalloyed blessing. The ugly race riots which accompanied the murders of Martin Luther King and Robert Kennedy provided even more impetus to his prospects.

Herbert Humphrey, Nixon's rival in 1968, was far more deserving of victory, but his campaign suffered crippling blows largely inflicted by his fellow Democrats. The party has a well deserved reputation for self-immolation and has demonstrated that wondrous ability several times in my lifetime.

When he began his official run for the White House, at the conclusion of the National Convention in Chicago, a convention that had valiantly attempted to commit political suicide, Humphrey was confronted with a near impossible lead fashioned by Tricky Dick.

But late in the campaign Humphrey, a very forceful speaker, began to cut into that lead and the race tightened dramatically. It was widely believed by veteran political observers, that had the election been held three or four days later, Humphrey would have prevailed.

Nixon's ardent acceptance of the Southern Strategy, the thinly veiled code for racism, had dominated the contest. Originally deposited onto the national scene by Strom Thurmond, for his Dixiecrat Party in 1964, the Southern Strategy, beginning anew in 1968, produced seven presidential victories for the Republican Party: two each for Nixon and Reagan, one for George Bush Senior and two for his Imposter Son.

Of course The Party's employment of political consultants, in reality political assassins, of the caliber of Lee Atwater and Karl Rove aided tremendously.

It is almost entirely forgotten in contemporary America that before the advent of the Civil War in 1861, Southern Newspapers, politicians, and evangelical preachers spoke with great expectations of the prospect of extending the South's "peculiar institution, slavery, into the Northern states, by enslaving the millions of recent immigrants from Europe.

The Richmond Enquirer, in Virginia, presented this memorable editorial. "Northern free society is burdened with a servile class of mechanics and laborers with attributes of mechanics and laborers with the attributes of citizens. Master and slave is a relationship as natural and necessary as parent and child; and the Northern States will yet have to introduce it."

Of course, by 1858, all of Europe had totally renounced any semblance of slavery, save for the Muslim dominated areas in Greece and Yugoslavia. The moment a slave set foot on British soil, he became free. One of course has to wonder what it was that the editorial staff of the Richmond Enquirer ever inquired about.

When Reagan launched his presidential campaign in Philadelphia, Mississippi in 1980, an event already recounted in great length in this work, he very pointedly called for more leadership of the quality provided by Jefferson Davis and Robert E. Lee.

Davis was the highly controversial president of the Confederate States of America, a fierce advocate for Civil War, and a man who made a significant contribution to the defeat of its armies. At least two high ranking Confederate generals openly despised him for meddling in their military planning.

To illustrate how totally inept the Confederacy had become, increasing numbers of its troops leading up to the pivotal Battle of Gettysburg, July 1-3, 1863, were without shoes. You see, the servile class of mechanics and laborers in the North, which the Richmond Enquirer dismissed with excessive hauteur, could easily manufacture shoes in abundance.

Conversely, the arrogant Southerners were supremely confident in their ability to conduct war, but had a near inability to provide its foot soldiers with shoes.

The war was not only avoidable, but should never have occurred. It resulted in 608,000 fatalities, this in a population of 35,000,000. In World War II our forces suffered only 292,000 combat deaths in a population of 120,000,000.

After the war Robert E. Lee served as president of Washington and Lee College, a school with modest numbers located in Lexington, Virginia. I've driven past the campus many times. It doesn't take long to do so.

CHAPTER XXIX

The toothless American press, totally adrift from reality, almost completely ignored Reagan's speech to the friendly natives in Philadelphia, Mississippi (not to be confused with Philadelphia, Pennsylvania, the cradle of democracy.) In it he revealed his heartfelt acceptance of the Southern Strategy, with its implied adoption of racism. On Election Day in November, 1980, he rolled to an impressive victory over Jimmy Carter.

His first official act in the White House was to replace the official presidential portrait of Harry Truman, number seven in our list of great presidents, with that of Calvin Coolidge, number 36. Reagan insisted that Coolidge was his favorite president because he had removed the dead hand of governmental interference from the Nation's business activities. Many American historians believe it was because both Coolidge and Reagan were seized with an unnatural need for sleep. Coolidge spent 12 hours daily asleep about the same as did Reagan.

By all accounts the new President's next move was to remove all the solar panels which Jimmy Carter had installed on the White House roof. Reagan put a stop to all this nonsense about producing electricity from the sun's rays. Let electricity flow from its traditional and natural source – Saudi oil.

He next demanded from Congress a huge tax cut for his favorite Americans, the wealthy few. A complaint Congress obediently rolled over and did what it was told to do. The country was now on the road to eight years of fiscally imprudent deficits under Reagan, and even larger ones under Bush Senior.

As has been outlined, the trifling one trillion dollar dept piled up by all the previous presidents combined was now more than doubled by the Reagan Reign. *Fiscal prudence*, the Republican mantra for many years, was tossed out the window.

Once the federal income taxes for the very rich were reduced, so of course was federal revenue.

The 50 individual states were soon presented with growing deficits and an uncertain future. In order to stop some of hemorrhaging underway at the Federal Treasury, Reagan moved to slash at least $45 billion in payments from the national government to the states. With his goodness gland totally atrophied, he looked upon those programs as "waste and fraud," whereas the states saw them as highly beneficial in assisting Americans in need. These programs had been started in the early days of the FDR Administration and had been kept intact and even enlarged by the next seven presidents, three of them Republicans.

Reagan had served eight years as Governor of California, beginning in 1967. One of the first acts then was a bill to *raise taxes* in order to eliminate the deficit he inherited. That became law as did a bill to make abortion easily accessible – one of the most liberal in the land. He had no problem signing that into law.

As presidential nominee however, he easily was converted to the Republican ideological necessity to reduce income taxes rather drastically. The Republican Platform demanded *an end to all abortions*. In this sector, Reagan found that governmental interference into women's lives was absolutely necessary.

With the repeated and masterful use of patriotic phrases such as "the shining city on the hill" and "there's morning in America" and with his high degree of skill in reading prepared text, he soon became a father figure for the nation.

In a strange manner he was able to invoke affection for himself that no other president was able to approach, except for Franklin Delano Roosevelt. His charm and humor were particularly appealing to the electorate.

In his rare personal appearances, his staff under the leadership of Michael Deaver, prepared every word, every movement for him – all on index cards. One skill that Reagan possessed was an excellent memory.

All this worked to perfection during his first term. But ominous events were just over the horizon in the next few years. Then his ability to manufacture favorable public approval would desert him.

Running for reelection in 1984 he gave a new definition to the term landslide. His opponent was Fritz Mondale, Jimmy Carter's Vice President. Mondale barely pulled out a victory in his home state of Minnesota; Reagan swept the other 49.

Two extremely important members of his staff would now either change jobs within the Cabinet or leave the White House. James A. Baker III, an unusually skilled Chief of Staff, would weary of Nancy Reagan's constant hectoring and exchange positions with Donald T. Regan, the Secretary of the Treasury. Whereas Baker was dedicated to the Reagan mystique and provided invaluable counsel to him, Regan appeared more dedicated to the Regan mystique. What's worse he was possessed of a towering ego and often appeared to be playing the role of the president.

Michael Deaver, who could gauge Reagan's strengths and weaknesses far better than could Reagan himself, would also tire of the Porcelain Princess and her incessant interference in presidential affairs. He would start his own business but soon find himself indicted and convicted for influence peddling. He would serve no prison time, however.

As the Reagan Reign of Ruin neared its end, large numbers of Reagan biographies began pouring from printing presses. The tone varied only slightly – from unkind to downright uncharitable, even insulting. These were not partisan writers interested only in a fast buck. On the contrary, "some of them from the most unlikely sources: former officials in his own administration. The spate of memoires had begun a few years earlier with the publication of Alexander Haig's "Caveat" and David Stockman's "The Triumph of Politics." But both Haig and Stockman were generally perceived to be disgruntled men who had more loyalty to their own ambitions than they ever had to the President they served."

The quote was from "The Acting President" by Bob Schieffer and Gary Paul, published in 1989. Bob Schieffer has for many years presided over a highly respected Sunday morning talk show on CBS. Alexander Haig had been Nixon's last Chief of Staff and had guided the government through the final months of the turbulent Nixon presidency. He was accorded very high marks for that role. Haig was also Reagan's first Secretary of State. In that position his marks were not so high.

David Stockman was one of Reagan's chief economic advisors and often dominated discussions about Reaganomics, a venture into fantasyland.

From "The Acting President" we are further instructed. "In the early months of 1988, however, books were published by three men who had been high ranking members of the White House staff and therefore were in a position to reveal intimate accounts of Reagan's day-to-day performance. "Behind the scenes" by Michael Deaver, "Speaking Out" by Larry Speakes, and "For the Record" by Donald Regan. All three books drew portraits of Reagan as a pliant and disengaged President who was out of touch with his own government. They could have been read as companion pieces to the Tower Commission's report on the Iran-Contra scandal.

There are at minimum another 10 biographies of Reagan that view him in a highly unfavorable light. Typical of them is "Landslide" by Jane Mayer and Doyle McManus. The book's cover reveals that Ms. Mayer toiled for the Wall St. Journal for four years covering the White House. Mr. McManus similarly was engaged by the Los Angeles Times as a Washington correspondent. He still often appears on nation-wide TV talk shows.

On the opening page of their book we learn how Howard Baker, the former Senate majority leader when the Republicans controlled that body was about to be installed as Reagan's third Chief of Staff. Before venturing into this position which he knew would bring intense turmoil, he appointed Jim Cannon, "A wise and trusted aide to scout out the territory before taking over on Monday." Cannon was 69 and had been an aide to Vice-President Nelson Rockefeller, and advisor to Gerald Ford, and finally a counselor and confident to Baker. In neither of these men could be detected the faintest suggestion of Democratic Liberalism.

Cannon immediately "embarked on a series of exhaustive interviews with members of the White House staff, trying to determine what had gone wrong.

For six years, Reagan had been the most commanding presence in American politics, a president of apparently limitless popularity and success. He had been elected by a 49 state landslide only 27 months earlier, but the polls now showed that his popularity was plummeting. He had been praised for having restored the credibility of the office, but more than half the country thought he was not telling the whole truth about either the arms sales to Iran or the diversion of money to the Nicaraguan contras."

Reagan's aides spoke to Cannon in complete confidence. "They told stories about how inattentive and inept the president was. He was lazy; he wasn't interested in the job. They said he wouldn't come over to work – all he wanted to do was to watch movies and television in the residence."

Not long before that on the 100th anniversary of the dedication of the Statue of Liberty in 1986, the Reagan who made his appearance there confounded his partisan critics and elevated his stature to that of the president of all the peoples.

From "Landslide" we glean another nugget, this a quote from Time Magazine. "Ronald Reagan has found the American sweet spot. The 75 year old man is hitting home runs… Reagan is a sort of masterpiece of American magic – apparently one of the simplest, most uncomplicated creatures alive, and yet a character of rich meanings, of complexities that connect him with the myths and powers of his country in an unprecedented way."

One of the most celebrated presidential biographers is Robert Dallek, justifiably celebrated for his treatment of Lyndon Johnson. His comment on Reagan is unusually revealing. "Reagan saw Medicare as the advance wave of socialism, which would invade every area of freedom in this country. Reagan predicted that Medicare would compel Americans to spend their sunset years telling our children and our children's children what it was like in American when men were free."

A surprising number of my Senior Citizen friends do exactly that. On special occasions they gather their grandchildren around them and wistfully, even tearfully, relate how in the halcyon days back in 1933, free men were not yet shackled by social security checks nor had to put up with Medicare.

Without the wise guidance of Baker and Deaver, Reagan could no longer conduct the symphony of symbolism that enabled him to captivate the nation with the moonshine about the Shining City on the Hill. Unlike many of his age group, he was not growing wiser, just older. More and more he was falling victim to B.S. – Benign Senescence, a further state of Mild Cognitive Impairment.

His first child with wife Nancy was Patti, who refused to use the family name; instead she chose Davis, Nancy's adopted name. Nancy entered this world as Anne Frances Robbins, but in later life lopped off two years of age and changed her name.

In her very explicit autobiography, "The Way I See It," Patti tells of her fear and dislike of her mother and how her father was remote and uncaring.

She then relates how her father was utterly convinced that the newly elected President, John Fitzgerald Kennedy, was a Communist. In so doing he disclosed how far he had migrated from his earlier Liberal days, to where he was now a devoted John Birch Society member. The Birchers devoutly believed that the previous President, Dwight Eisenhower, and his Secretary of State, John Foster Dolles, were card-carrying Commies.

As shockingly senseless as that mind-set was, lets inject a measure of reality. On the day Jack Kennedy turned 21, his father, Joe Kennedy, gave him one million dollars. On the day Ronnie Reagan reached 21, in 1932, the cruelest year in this nation's history, his father, Jack Reagan, might have been unable to give his son even 21 cents.

Joe Kennedy was one of the nation's richest men, whereas Jack Reagan was one of the poorest. An extended reading of history strongly implies that upon inheriting a million dollars at age 21, a young man is exceedingly unlikely to turn Communist.

The current occupant of the White House informed the country that "Reagan leaves behind a nation he restored, and a world he helped save."

At total variance to that Republican view was a discordant vote from the Democrats in the house. They charged that Reagan "attempted to balance the budget on the backs of the poor." He manifested such a callous contempt for indigent children, in providing school meals, that it reached the level of depravity.

While his tax cuts for the wealthy were already in effect, so were his cuts for school lunches. The daily milk ration was reduced from six ounces to four. His attempt to have the tiny ration of ketchup be counted as a vegetable serving created such a revulsion among school personnel that it was abandoned.

Reagan refused to meet even once with the Black Caucus, a significantly large group of Black House members. They repeatedly declared that he was interested only "in making the poor hungrier, colder and sicker."

Franklin Roosevelt's determined effort to provide humanitarian measures in 1933, an attempt to alleviate homelessness and hunger, was met with contempt and fury by President Hoover. The new president, Hoover charged, was creating a generation of medacious parasites. At age 22 Ronald Reagan was the son of a prominent m.p. in Dixon, Illinois. Yet the dexterity with which son Ronald could totally erase that chapter in his life is astonishing.

Perhaps my favorite presidential advisor was Clark Clifford, counselor to both Kennedy and Johnson. He was considered by a large number of historians of the era as one of the shrewdest of that breed. He haughtily dismissed Reagan as "an amiable dunce."

Which is the most repellant charge? That of Clifford or the one by Reagan's biographer, Edmond Morris, who wrote him off as a "cultural yahoo"?

Abraham Lincoln, easily the greatest Republican President, most assuredly had more biographers than all other presidents *combined*. His closest rival in that category is Franklin Delano Roosevelt. But the president who has had *the most critical biographers* is easily Ronald Wilson Reagan. Reference had already been made to a significant number, scarcely any of which has anything resembling generosity towards the man. Included was the work by Patti Davis, his and Nancy's first child, in "The Way I See It."

Reagan and his first wife, the screen actress Jane Wyman, who had won an Oscar Award, had adopted a son, Michael. After the subsequent divorce he came to live with Reagan. Upon reaching adulthood, Michael wrote an autobiography entitled "Michael Reagan – On the Outside Looking In."

The book reveals he was "plunged into an abyss of despair, boarded out at school when he entered first grade, and seeing his parents on TV or in the movies more often than in person, and with nobody to talk to…"

Michael points out somewhat painfully that in high school he starred as the team's quarterback for two full seasons, yet never once did his father find the time to appear in the audience.

The way his two children saw it, the Reagan household was utterly dysfunctional, featuring an angry, cruel mother joined with a father incapable of loving parental care.

After Reagan was inaugurated as President, Michael discloses how far he was removed from the Ronald and Nancy household. Michael was ready to publish his autobiography. "It was about this time that he (Reagan) and Nancy invited my wife Colleen and our children to celebrate Palm Sunday and my daughter Ashley's fourth birthday at the Santa Barbara ranch. I'd had a stormy relationship with the first family for the past few years, and it was to be the first birthday either Ashley or eight year-old Cameron would spend with Grandma and Grandpa Reagan. It would be the first time we would be alone together as one family."

One of the foremost tenets of Republican thought for numerous decades has been the fervent advocacy of 'family values.' Here we see Ronnie Reagan embracing that platitude in a whole-hearted manner.

CHAPTER XXX

The President's pronounced proclivity for prevarication and his incredulous credulity would guide him into an infamous scenario called the Iran-Contra Scandal. He was unusually fortunate in not being tried for impeachment, as a result of his continuous involvement in this outrage.

Reagan's cast of characters conducting this affair were every bit as ill-prepared to deal with reality as were Nixon's notorious nitwits, the Plumbers, or George Bush's bewildered bumblers, the Neocons.

The initial phase of the Iran-Contra Scandal began when three Americans were taken hostage in Beirut, Lebanon, in 1984, by a previously unknown group calling itself the Islamic Jihad. Two more victims would be later kidnapped and held for ransom.

Reagan had repeatedly sworn to the American public that under no circumstances would he ever bargain with the outlaws involved.

The following year pressure increased on his Administration when a U.S. commercial plane, heading from Athens to Rome, was high jacked. Aboard were 135 Americans; the plane eventually landed in Beirut where the crew plus 39 additional Americans were held captive.

Before long, family members began a media campaign to effect release of their loved ones. Their voices became ever more strident, urging intervention on the President's part. While in public he was continually adamant about bargaining with the hostage-takers, in private he was determined that the victims be freed, no matter what the cost.

After all only months earlier he had engineered a 49 state election upheaval, trouncing his Democratic rival.

More terrorist activity involving Americans would take place, both in Germany and San Salvador. There, four marines were killed in an outdoor café explosion.

Reagan attended the funeral ceremony for the four victims and vowed the killers would be apprehended. "They will not evade justice on earth anymore than they can escape the judgment of God."

During his five years in the White House he continued to issue a stream of threats to terrorists would-wide but as yet had taken nothing in the way of action to bring any of them to justice.

In a vain, ill-advised effort to gain release of the original hostage in Beirut, a new cast of characters began to assert dominance. Americans would soon learn about Lt. Colonel Oliver North, Vice-Admiral John Poindexter and William

Casey, head of the CIA. All three were united in their determination to please the President and heed his direction – and he wanted the hostages returned.

Ollie North soon commenced negotiations between this country and the rogue nation of Iran, one of the most despised regimes on earth. Iranians convinced North they could obtain release of the hostages but in return they would need a significant supply of missiles.

Iran was fighting for its survival in a war which Saddam Hussein of Iraq had started. The Iranians had a dire need for TOW missiles to shoot down Iraqi bombers that were destroying Iran's cities, mostly Tehran. These were tube-launched, optically tracked, wire guided state of the art weapons developed by our Pentagon.

North, Poindexter and Casey tried hard to conceal the fact that the Reagan Administration was engaged in any weapons for hostage trade-off, so they enlisted the services of the Israelis who would fly the TOWs to Tehran. This country would then discretely re-supply the Israelis.

The first delivery of about 100 missiles was delivered, but alas, no hostages were released. A second shipment was made- this time one hostage was handed over to the Americans, but only after two weeks of waiting.

During this entire episode never once did the three adventurers realize that as hostages were freed, more could easily be captured. After all, there was an American University in Beirut. After thousands of TOWs had been delivered to Tehran, the Jihadists in Beirut had nine hostages more than when this lurch into lunacy started.

Meanwhile, when this matter of tradeoff for hostages first came up for discussion, two of Reagan's highest ranking Cabinet members expressed immediate and bitter opposition to the concept. George Schultz, Secretary of State, and Caspar Weinburger, Secretary of Defense, who rarely agreed on anything, made their disapproval known to Reagan. Reagan in turn was obviously displeased that they would not agree with this, his pet project. Accordingly, missiles for hostages would continue.

Later, Peter Rodman, an important aide to Schultz observed, "I thought it strategically crazy to make obsequious overtures to Iran. You don't go chasing after radical regimes."

At the beginning of the 20th century, President Theodore Roosevelt clearly enunciated American foreign policy. "Speak softly but carry a big stick." Reagan saw fit to slightly alter that unmistakable pronouncement. "Speak loudly but carry a wet noodle."

With Reagan's fierce hatred of Communism near the surface of his psyche, he soon developed a near love affair with the freedom fighters in Nicaragua.

These were the followers of the deposed fascist dictator, Anastasio Somoza, a brutal even murderous chieftain who had seized power of that country. His rule had been supplanted by the Sandanistas, a progressive legitimately elected party led by Daniel Ortega, whom Reagan believed to be a vile Commie. Freedom Fighters did most of their fighting with each other, endlessly striving to control supplies and cash. They were never able to capture and held even one town, much less a city, which was under the control of the government.

Ollie North, by handling the cash and supplies for the Freedom Fighters, was able in the process to liquidate his own monetary problems. A part of the cash filtering through his hands managed to stick to them.

The newly discovered method to raise funds for the Freedom Fighters was to sell TOWs by the thousands to the Iranians for cash. Ollie and his playmates would reimburse the U.S. Treasury for the cost of the TOWs, then remit the balance to the Freedom Fighters, less whatever dribbled away.

Congress meanwhile began to learn of these frenzied, illegal activities on the part of the Reaganites in Nicaragua. The CIA under its director, William Casey, had been planting mines in Nicaragua's harbors. In diplomatic circles this is an act of war. In the 1980 election Casey had been Reagan's Campaign Manager.

House member, Edward Boland of Massachusetts passed an Amendment cutting off all funding for the Contras. This became known as the Boland Amendment. The Democrats in Congress were now certain this legislation would stop this foolishness. Boland even declared that it "clearly ends United States support for the war in Nicaragua. There are no exceptions to the prohibition."

Secretary of State, George Schultz, even warned President Reagan and Casey that if any Administration members were to solicit money from foreign countries to continue funding the Contras, that might be considered grounds for impeachment.

Everybody involved ignored the warning and continued the illegal activities. William Casey would die of a malignant brain tumor on May 6, 1987. The campaign manager for George Bush in 1988 would be Lee Atwater. He too would die of a malignant brain tumor.

In Reagan's Second Inaugural address he bequeathed to the nation these imperishable words. "In this blessed land there is always a better tomorrow. Our nation is poised for greatness."

In the summer of 1928 Herbert Hoover reflected the same roseate optimism, when he delivered his acceptance speech to the Republican National Convention. "We in America today are nearer to the final triumph over poverty than ever before in the history of our fair land." Hoover, peering into the future, could actually visualize, "the poor house vanishing from among us. With the help of God poverty will be banished from this nation."

Not to be outdone by his successor, Calvin Coolidge bestowed these words to Congress on his final state of the Union delivered on December 4, 1928. "No Congress of the United States ever assembled, on surveying the State of Union, has met with a more pleasing prospect than which appears at the proper time… The main source of these unexampled blessings lies in the integrity and character of the American people."

In citing this statement earlier in the book, I commented on the aura of lunacy pervading the investment community. On September 3 of the following year the New York Stock Exchange would observe the first refusal of the stock market to rise any further. Instead it would begin its deathward plunge which ended on October 29. In that span of only eight weeks the net assets of the New York Stock Exchange shrank by $30 billion, an incalcuable sum of money in 1929. By March of 1930 the country was mired in the Depression and remained in a near perilous condition for nearly a decade. Adding to the tragedy was the complete collapse of the banking system before Hoover left office.

Republican Presidents or candidates for the office, manage to massage the multitudes with these messages of eternal optimism. It serves to gain the office desired.

CHAPTER XXXI

North, Casey and Poindexter would carry on this regrettable affair for some time, always with the solid approval of the President. Even though the Contras were provided with more than adequate funds to continue their insurgency, nothing of substance ever resulted.

Finally this deplorable misadventure came to an abrupt end. A CIA plane carrying weapons and supplies to the Contras was shot down by troops from the Nicaraguan government and the dirty secret was finally revealed.

Quickly Congress demanded a full investigation of this unprecedented scandal. Never before had an Administration showed such contempt for the will of this body. The Administration in turn was forced into forming an investigative agency, soon known as the Tower Commission.

The group was chaired by John Tower, a former Republican Senator from Texas, and one not known for any Liberal tendencies. A second member was Brent Scowcroft, Vice-President Gerald Ford's National Security Advisor. Ford had been Nixon's second V.P. following Spiro Agnew's departure. Scowcroft would become a principal policy advisor to the first President Bush. (He also warned the current occupant of the White House not to fool around with Saddam Hussein in Iraq) The third and last member was Edmund Muskie, Jimmy Carter's Secretary of State.

In appointing these three men, The Reaganites felt confident that this would be a rather toothless group. By denying the Commission subpoena power they were certain it would unearth little damaging evidence, especially with Tower as chairman.

Once the Iran Contra imbroglio became public Reagan was outraged. He considered the National media to be the real villain, because its members were printing stories and airing material that revealed how he and his hapless aides had been paying ransom for the Beirut hostages. Repeatedly he had been very emphatic in claiming he would never engage in that hypocrisy. Yet now it was obvious he had been doing just that.

"I have to say there is a bitter bile in my throat these days. I've never seen the sharks circling like they are now with blood in the water. The whole thing boils down to a great irresponsibility on the part of the press."

Reagan's first meeting with the Tower board took place on January 26, 1987. From "Landslide," written by Jane Mayer and Doyle McManus, we learn "that he told them he did not know important members of his National Security Council had been meeting with the Contras. That despite the fact he had been present at a number of briefings and even had met with Contra leaders and supporters."

From Bob Schieffer's "The Role of a Lifetime" comes this indictment. "In its report, the Tower Commission drew a portrait of a disengaged president who "did not seem to be aware of the way in which operation was implemented and the full consequences of the U.S. participation." John Tower issued his own statement. "The President clearly didn't understand the nature of this operation, who was involved, and what was happening."

From "President Reagan – The Role of a Lifetime," by Lou Cannon, who by general consensus is the most knowledgeable of the numerous Reagan biographers, having known him since 1965. "The Tower Board had been exposed to the real Reagan, as he was seen at close range everyday by the handful of aides with personal access to him. And neither Tower nor his colleagues Brent Scowcroft and Edmond Muskie knew what to make of Reagan's performance. They had not imagined that he would be devoid of any independent recollection *or so mentally confused*, and they thought it useless to question him further. Instead, Tower concluded the meeting and the board members retreated to their offices where Ed and Tower and Brent slumped on the couch or in their chairs just thunderstruck by what had happened." This was the observation by Rhett Dawson, The Tower Board's chief of Staff.

"Muskie was particularly appalled. As a former Senator and Secretary of State, he understood that presidents are busy people who cannot remember everything. But he had never seen such forgetful performances as the ones Reagan had given in his two appearances before the board." Muskie would be quoted making this observation." All the testimony we got from everybody was that the president was preoccupied with this goddamn problem every day. Every day in someone's presence he said, "What's new on the hostages? Here is a president who is agonizing over this thing every day, and yet he can't remember anything about it. My God."

This is the Reagan who, not many months earlier, was concerned only with freeing the hostages, even though it meant working through Iran, had this savage commentary about the country." An outlaw nation run by the strangest collection of misfits, loony tunes, and squalid criminals since the advent of the Third Reich."

Not to be forgotten in this troublesome venture were Lt. Col Oliver North and Vice-Admiral John Poindexter, both supreme patriots and proud members of the Armed Forces. When called before the Tower Commission they both refused to testify, invoking the Fifth Amendment.

Mark Green and Gail MacColl had this dismissive note about their subject in their book, Reagan's Reign of Error" and on the very first page, "From day one his standard operating procedure, as illustrated by his initial answer on arms to Iran, was a blend of ignorance, amnesia and dissembling."

Before he was twice summoned to testify at the Tower Commission, Reagan had held a press conference during which he issued a continuous stream of statements strongly suggesting he habitually misused the truth.

Once these inexcusable deceptions were uncovered, the media found it distasteful to pursue the matter too far. The leader of the free world had to be either an egregious liar or an amiable dunce.

Quoting at some length from "The Reagan Reign of Error," we find this satisfactory explanation. "There are three favored interpretations for all his misstatements: habit, ignorance and deceit…Reagan often elevates ideology over evidence. Thus errors appear to be the result of not only ignorance, but also strategy. So if a good anecdote advances a right-wing cause, he won't let facts get in the way. It is this powerful combination of personal and ideological habits that makes Reagan so incorrigible. He is simply incapable of entertaining information that conflicts with his ideology. When facts differ from his beliefs, he changes the facts, not his beliefs. He has sunk to a point where he can't make a major statement without making a major misstatement."

Two glaring examples of this – In his press conference he insisted that his Administration hadn't traded missiles to Iran for hostages held in Beirut. Next he asserted that all the TOWs sent to Iran could easily be tucked into one cargo plane.

Actually a total of 2004 TOWs were dispatched to Iran and they required eight separate shipments in the holds of large aircraft.

Soon a joke was making its rounds in the more civilized circles of the country – what did Reagan forget and when did he forget it?

One of the many hundreds of comments stemming from his lips: The trouble with our Liberal friends is not they're ignorant; it's just that they know so much that just isn't so."

The trouble with Reagan was that he was ignorant. He also knew an unbelievable amount that just wasn't so. Undoubtedly one of the most outrageous facts he knew was his famous assertion that trees cause pollution. That would be the equivalent of believing that rain causes drought.

The promoter of Reaganomics doubled the national debt within eight years, a debt that took 192 years to amass; yet he felt no sense of responsibility for that feat.

His manic desire to deregulate otherwise stable industries caused the near self-destruction of the Saving and Loan offices. Soon the Federal Reserve was forced to sell about $600,000,000 worth of bonds to cover the horrendous deficits rung up by the members. And much of that was caused by outrageous fraud, corruption and bribery that permeated the industry because of lax governmental oversight.

Since the nation's standard banking system still retained the regulatory supervision established by the New Deal in 1933, no similar upheaval took place within it.

In Reagan's Second Inaugural Address to Congress in 1985, he boasted that Americans could look forward to years "when our economy was finally free from government's grip."

Just look at the enchanting results that accrue to a country when the dead hand of government control is finally released and business is free to run its own affairs in an entrepreneurial manner.

Reagan was not long into office when the country was first introduced to the terrifying results of a brand-new disease called AIDS. His reaction was complete indifference towards the victims of this often fatal disease; further he had an abhorrence for the life style that produced the malady. Even worse, that lack of concern was reflected throughout his Administration.

Throughout Hollywood and wherever movies were crafted, the disease struck with a frequency that was shocking. The victims of the AIDS virus watched their immune system become completely compromised and they soon went into a death spiral.

The Broadway Theater district in Manhattan underwent similar devastation. Deaths in both arts and entertainment centers climbed into the hundreds. Across the nation those fatalities mounted into the thousands.

But in the White House, Reagan and his principal aids maintained a detached aloofness that was a companion to their sociopathic lack of compassion for the underdogs in life - the poor and the handicapped -The Raggedy - Assed-Masses. Displaying compassion for the RAMs was viewed by The Reaganites as a form of sentimentality, an emotion shared by people of weak character.

One of the many pompous pronouncements Reagan gave vent to during his long political career was, "The nearest thing we have to eternal life we will ever see on this earth, is a government program."

Beginning in March, 1933, at the bottom of the Great Depression, a number of these government programs became embodied into law, and are still viewed fondly today.

On his first full day in office, Sunday, March 5, FDR acted as the Nation's Chief Executive should – forcefully and knowledgably – by shutting down the entire banking system in America. Few banks were solvent enough to remain open.

Under his exceptionally capable guidance the newly installed President solved the banking problem. Working feverishly and with little rest, his Administration, which included Hoover's Secretary of the Treasury plus the Under Secretary, presented Congress with an inspired banking bill.

They did this in only four days and it represented the first Congressional regulation of the banking industry. Self regulation, dearly beloved by laissez-faire Republicans, had completely destroyed the banking system in America. Only the Federal Deposit Insurance Corporation saved the industry from its self inflicted greed and corruption.

On March 9, only five days after the new congress had convened, it was presented with this revolutionary form of legislation. The bill was read to its anxiously awaiting members. Time did not permit the normal process of having the bill presented in printed form. Both houses shouted out unanimous approval and the President signed it that same day.

The following evening, a Sunday, FDR delivered the first of this 20 fireside chats to America. Many Roosevelt historians consider that chat to be the most comforting speech ever delivered by a President to a morose, frightened public.

In it he told his fellow Americans it was now safe to deposit their money in any banks that reopened. The next morning long lines of customers eagerly waited for banks to open their doors. The horrific banking crisis was over.

That was only the first of numerous governmental programs sprung to life under FDR's Liberal policies that appear to have "eternal life."

Simultaneous with the banking crisis, another presented itself with a sickening impact. In "The Defining Moment – FDR's Hundred Days and the Triumph of Hope," Jonathan Alter presents an inspiring account of the President's war to save democracy.

This was the scene FDR viewed as he assumed office. "The American economic system had gone into a state of shock, its vital organs shutting down as the weekend began. On Friday, the New York Stock Exchange suspended trading indefinitely and the Chicago Board of Trade bolted its doors for the first time since its founding in 1848." Mr. Alter then quotes a prominent journalist who declared, "Capitalism itself was at the point of dissolution."

Once FDR disposed of the banking crisis, he turned his attention to the securities problem. The Securities Act was presented to Congress on March 29. It did nothing more than administer a mild spanking to the crooks and con artists who had flourished on Wall Street.

Enlisting the services once more of Mr. Alter we find - "But the Securities Act of 1933 did require any company selling securities to the public to disclose its financial condition and register with the federal government."

The President, in his message to Congress had written: "This proposal adds to the ancient rule of 'caveat emptor' the further doctrine of 'let the seller beware.' It puts the burden of telling the whole truth upon the seller."

Mr. Alter picks up the narrative. "Without directly saying so FDR was beginning to redraft the American Social Contract, adding a claus in which the U.S. government acknowledged a duty at least to try to protect investors from ruin at the hands of unscrupulous players in the market."

The next year the Securities Exchange Commission (the SEC) was formed and it would add some long, sharp teeth to the original legislation.

Here we find another glittering example of a government program assuming eternal life. Adding to them would be a continuing stream of revolutionary legislation all designed to bury the dead corpse of laissez-faire doctrine.

The President was keenly aware of a long idled program, a project created during World War I, called Muscle Shoals, on the banks of the Tennessee River. With his wide ranging imagination in play he began thought about starting "the widest experiment ever undertaken by a government."

Congress had twice passed a Muscle Shoals Bill, designed to produce cheap electricity and with it, nitrogen fertilizer. Twice, blind unthinking Presidents named Coolidge and Hoover had vetoed the legislation.

Jonathon Alter continues the chronicle. "Why not use the Tennessee Valley as a pilot project to see if government planning could remake a whole region? The project could include dams, power plants, soil-conservation, reforestation, navigational improvements. The cheap power could lure industry to the area kicking off a boom for the desperately poor people in the valley."

One considerable enterprise it lured to the area was the Manhattan Project. Without the inordinate abundance of cheap, easily obtainable electricity the atomic bomb project might not have been completed.

One other consequence – the descendants of those desperately poor people, having been ministered to lavishly by the federal government, now vote Republican and find intrusion by that same federal government quite repellant.

Both Coolidge and Hoover, if made aware of this devilishly socialistic endeavor, would have twirled around in their graves at a feverish rate. This demonic concept violated every tenet of their economic principles.

The TVA legislation was signed by FDR on May, 18. Its immediate and overwhelming success in the South prompted the President and his triumphant New Dealers to enlarge its application nationwide. (The program increased the pathetically low income in that area by a factor of ten or more. Large numbers of its citizens even began paying income taxes.)

The Rural Electrification Administration was conceived to do for the entire country what the TVA had done for its region. The REA would quickly transform life in America. Before electric power was delivered to farming communities and directly to the farm house and barn, farmers might as well have been European peasants living in the 19th century.

Once the REA became law non-profit co-operatives, first by the hundreds, and then the thousands were born, financed by large, low cost loans from the government. With power brought to the barn a farmer could enlarge his dairy herd by using electric milking machines, a far swifter method than milking each cow by hand.

It is also important to realize how these new co-ops enriched lives in small communities. Cheap electricity increased productively in many ways and in so doing enhanced earnings and the ability to pay income taxes.

Once more we see a government program nearing eternal life while having vastly benefited many millions of lives.

Earlier in this work we discussed at considerable length FDR's First Hundred Days. During that span between March 9 and Jun 18, 1933 he presented 15 bills to Congress.

In that year these legislative measures were condemned by Republicans as abhorrent Socialism or even a witch's brew of Communism.

All 15 were passed by a Democratic Congress and, at the very minimum each one provided some measure of relief to an anguished public. None did any harm. Portions of most of them still linger on the books 75 years later. That's close to eternal life for legislation.

CHAPTER XXXII

Reaganomics was an effort to repudiate FDR's New Deal and reintroduce us to the Roaring Twenties and with it the sickening greed, the corruption and incompetence that always accompanied that decade of debauch! During Reagan's eight years in the White House, the nation tumbled off its pinnacle as the greatest creditor counting in the world, to the ignoble role as the greatest debtor.

The huge annual deficits caused the national debt to double in the eight years Reaganomics was in play. Interest paid to service that debt soared from $117 to $264 billion annually.

Dedicated to delusion and freed of any memory of the Great Depression, Reagan silently observed the entire Savings and Loan Industry collapse. Here was an inordinately successful enterprise that enabled millions of that enabled millions of Americans to purchase homes posting only a minimal down payment and featuring a 2.5% interest rate on a 30 year mortgage.

Waving his magic wand, Reagan allowed the entire industry to disappear after a profitable life span of over 50 years. This cost the tax payers another $600,000,000,000.

On one calamitous day, October 27, 1987, the Dow Jones Industrial Averages plummeted 554 points, representing a 25% decline of its value. Never in the history of the securities industry had anything of that magnitude ever happened in this country. Not even on October 29, 1929 had the percentage drop been so ruinous. This is a fact well worth repeating.

At the conclusion of that marketing day, the New York Stock Exchange was bankrupt. Alan Greenspan, the chairman of the Federal Reserve Board, found the means to bail out the venerable institution.

Reagan tried repeatedly to strangle Social Security. No program in the U.S. today is as universally loved by Senior Citizens as Social Security, and with complete justification. Until the project was fully funded years after its inception in 1935, retirees were some of the most vulnerable Americans. Today they're some of the most affluent.

These are all indisputable facts, completely divorced from any hokum about 'There's morning in America' or 'the shining city on the hill.' Perhaps even more disheartening is the fact that Reagan passed this economic philosophy to the Preposterous Imposter who has ardently adopted it.

Yet in the face of this incontestable mountain of evidence that Reaganomics is inherently fraudulent, all 10 contestants for the Republican Presidential nomination professed a deep yearning to continue the Reagan Legacy.

Three of them considered Evolution a false doctrine; none expressed any warmth for the concept of Global Warming. All 10 were fiercely opposed to Universal Health Care. We have already seen how the 27 countries which comprise The European Union all tenderly embraced complete health care for its citizens and none are the least bit likely to revoke its benefits.

As opposed as the 10 were for health care for all Americans, they were in complete accord for a continuation of Reagan's tax cuts for wealthy Americans.

In so doing they adopted another characteristic used frequently by Reagan – total loss of memory when unpleasant facts arise.

Only four years after amnesiac Reagan left office, Bill Clinton came to power. He and his brainiacs advanced a plan running counter to Reaganomics – a tax increase, but only for the upper 1 ½% of American tax payers.

Congressional Republicans could scarcely contain their wrath. Aging Bob Dole, the Senate Majority Leader, insisted it was the greatest tax raise in history. Uttering such a statement revealed that Dole was either unpardonably misinformed about taxation in the U.S. or else an unacceptable liar.

Dick Armey of Texas could always be depended upon for a vaccous pronouncement. If President Clinton's tax proposal became law, he bragged, weeds would flourish on many American streets.

Similar cries of outrage from lying Republican Reactionaries could be heard. When the tax bill came up for vote every Republican in Congress voted against its passage. This proved there wasn't a single Republican in either house that was capable of mature thought.

Armey's idiotic utterance simply echoed Herbert Hoover's prediction in 1932 that if his opponent, Franklin Roosevelt, were elected weeds would sprout and other bad things would happen. From 1932 until 1993, a span of 61 years, the Republicans hadn't learned a damn thing!

Instead of Americans seeing weeds growing in the street, investors in stocks pleasingly observed the DJI vault heavenward. Whereas Reagan's huffing and puffing produced a puny rise of 1000 points in eight years, the Bill Clinton market streaked into the wild blue yonder and didn't stop until it reached 11,722 on the DJI, a momentous gain of 8300 points in eight years. In one record breaking month the market shot up 1000 points, roughly 96 times faster than Reagan's.

Since so much enthusiasm exists within this hierarchy of Republican talent for a return to the Reagan Legacy, it seems reasonable to inquire which attribute of Reagan's stands out.

Could it be his determination at times to act the role of the amiable dunce? A fair amount of evidence points in that direction. Then again he sometimes could be seen as a cultural yahoo. That attitude certainly has more than a little merit.

Perhaps a vote or two should be cast for Reagan as chronic liar, unable to distinguish fact from fantasy. Certainly the fact must be considered that he possessed a sieve-like memory.

In appearances before the Tower Commission, various witnesses swore under oath that he had presided at meetings with important figures in the Iran-Contra Affair. Yet due to the extreme porosity of his memory, Reagan testified he simply could not recall any of those events.

As humiliating as were his two abrasive encounters with the Tower Commission, both televised on national TV, and his unpleasant skirmish with the press also shown on TV, what followed after he and Nancy left the White House was even more humbling.

Word soon drifted back to him in retirement in California, that members of his staff still retained by Bush Senior, were mocking him in the cruelest, most unforgiving manner.

With that Nancy insisted he call President Bush and demand that this conduct be halted. He did and Bush Senior commanded his staff to cease their merriment at Reagan's expense.

The exquisite irony of that situation was that as President, Reagan never once invited the Bushes to visit the presidential living quarters on the third floor. Neither did the Eisenhower's invite the Nixons.

This seems an appropriate point to bring this chronicle to an end.

The End

EPILOGUE

Every Democrat in America today should seriously consider engaging some portion of his or her resources to delivering Barack Obama to the White House and with an over powering plurality of votes. They should calculate which ingredient they are best able to contribute: money, materials, or time.

A minimum goal of 370 electoral votes should be established – that is the exact amount Bill Clinton received in 1992. Only 268 are needed for victory.

President Obama will need a plentiful number of new faces in the House of Representatives to insure easy passage of desired legislation. Securing 32 more Democratic seats would bring the Democratic total to 268, leaving the other party with but 167, a net difference of 101.

In the Senate a pick-up of eight seats is realistic giving the President 57 Democrats, plus two Independents. These efforts will create much consternation within the ranks of the sullen opposition.

With fond expectations Democrats can next look forward to a scene of immensely elevated drama when our first black President addresses the 111th Congress with its full contingent of lily-white Republicans. Numbers of them will be acutely uncomfortable as the reality of a new order sinks in.

As an act rich in symbolism, I would like to see President Obama, as one of his first official decrees, order solar panels to be reinstalled on the roof of the White House. This was one of the first acts by Jimmy Carter in 1977.

Four years later another President, Ronald Reagan, had them torn off. This was an act totally lacking in common sense, with nothing to commend it except an appeal to a group of likeminded fools.

This might be followed up with another act of even more heightened symbolism, plus suitability. Appoint a Czar pledged to declare war against the more pernicious effects of Global Warming. Who could be more highly recommended than Al Gore, doubtless the only man in history to have been awarded both a Nobel Prize and a Hollywood Emmy for meritorious work in that area?

Working in tandem with President Obama and a sympathetic Congress, the new Czar might consider a move to apply solar panels to the roofs of every federal building in greater Washington, D.C. This would be followed up with legislation to cover every roof of every federal building in the United States. The next step would be to grant generous subsidies to state legislatures to adorn every state building with solarization. Completing the cycle would be providing subsidies for city and county buildings nationwide.

Paying for these costly solar additions would require a very considerable outlay of federal funds. Where would Congress and the President find that kind of money? Actually huge piles could be extracted with very little effort and no new tax legislation.

Simply hire hundreds of auditors for the IRS to pursue the legions of tax cheats who have been notably laggard in paying what they owe the government. Then subject these delinquent types to the thorough scrutiny of a tax audit which could bring frightening fines or something worse, a prison sentence.

Huge amounts of revenue are lost annually because of phony tax havens like Bermuda or the Caymen Islands. Large businesses purport to have their company headquarters in these places whereas the alleged place of business is nothing more than a post office box.

These simple, inexpensive measures would produce a revenue stream amounting to several hundred billion dollars annually according to knowledgeable sources. Considering the vast number of buildings throughout the nation that would require solar installations, it is easy to see where a need for thousands of small companies would arise. Each of them would require new workers needing training for the task.

Judicious use of subsidies would bring about a demand for individual homes, office buildings and factories to be blessed with a solar roof. Methods are already available to use solar to heat water for families. All of this feverish activity would soon stimulate the natural inventiveness of Americans to produce more effective uses of renewable energy while continuing to lower costs.

Already impressive design innovations are in play utilizing the sun to manufacture electricity without using any form of solar panels. Installations now in use, involving several hundred acres, employ concave glass mirrors which heat water which then spin turbines and produce electricity. These mirrors automatically adjust to the angle of the sun to capture its maximum intensity.

White the initial outlay is of necessity very large, once in operation it costs very little to operate. It of course produces zero carbon emissions, the nasty stuff that pollutes the atmosphere and is a major contributor to Global Warming. Fossil fuels like coal and oil, by contrast produce tons of it.

Finally we can turn to wind production, another method of generating electricity. This country has been tragically slow in putting to work this clean, inexpensive way to create a product each of us uses in abundance. Individual windmills can tower several hundred feet above the ground with arms extending another 100 feet. While they are undeniably majestic they are also guilty of killing birds who fly into them. This is a problem that can be overcome.

They have another drawback. In Regions where the wind is frequent and strong is also where the concentration of people is the slightest. The Rocky Mountain states have a near continuous supply of wind but contain the fewest people. The electricity so easily produced must be transmitted over wires for long stretches before reaching cities and towns.

Once again power manufactured from wind is exceedingly clean and lacks any trace of carbon emissions. As more and more electricity is produced by these renewable sources, less and less imported oil is needed. We should view the outrageous upsurge of oil prices as a long term blessing. At every point less demand for electricity produced by fossil fuels, coal and oil will exist. Both of these are notorious creators of carbon emissions.

Another area which requires an immediate and huge improvement is public transportation. Bus lines will need to be extended to cover larger areas and the buses need to arrive more frequently. As more bus routes are opened, more buses will need to be constructed. Bus manufacturers will be forced to open second and even third shifts. Workers in growing numbers will need to be trained.

Accompanying this necessity will be an ever increasing demand for more drivers with still more employees required for maintenance and repair. As service improves even more auto drivers will elect to leave the car in the garage and use the bus.

Another area that begs for improvement is passenger rail service. That industry has been starved for funds altogether too long. The federal government instead has lavished enormous sums on the Interstate Highway

Systems plus the Airline Industry.

In this area our country lags pathetically behind when compared to countries in Western Europe like France, Germany, Spain and others. Actually it has fallen to the very bottom amongst the developed countries.

France, which many reactionary Republicans love to revile, probably has the most efficient, fastest and safest trains in the world. From Paris they glide across the nation at speeds we can only wonder at. If our aging trains attempted to reach even half the velocities of French trains, they would quickly part company with the tracks.

My father was a locomotive engineer for 38 years and I have tried to keep well informed about the industry. I feel confident I know whereof I speak. The entire French railroad system is government owned, by the way.

We in this country need to do for short and long distance passenger rail service what should be done in the realm of renewable energy.

Steel tracks would need to laid down by the thousands of miles and soon by multiples of that number. They would need to be set in place with infinitely more care than for our ponderous freight trains. They would need to be welded together to form a continuous, solid span. This would require steel mills in this country to hire more men and even start second and third shifts. Quite literally the industry would be in need of hundreds of new, high quality locomotives and passenger cars.

Before the completion of President Obama's first term many thousands of new jobs would be created, and these would be for skilled workers and jobs which couldn't be exported to China and India.

When I was a lad back in 1930s, I rode on the elegant New York Central Line from Chicago to New York each summer. The distance was 960 miles and the NYC proudly boasted that it made the 960 miles in 960 minutes. That's an average of a mile a minute or 60 miles an hour. Today, French and Japanese trains speed along at 275 miles per hour.

Passenger trains in the U.S. haven't improved their slow speed significantly in the last 75 years. Perhaps in a few highly selective areas between Boston and New York and then on to Washington, service has been improved but nothing remotely comparable to Europe.

Of course it must be pointed out that the French owe their fast rail service to the accuracy of the Army Air Corps bombers in 1944-5. Our flyboys did an amazing job in laying waste to the pre-war railroad system.

It was almost entirely rebuilt with the aid of American tax dollars and administered through the United Nations as early as 1945 and then the Marshall Plan beginning in 1948. Very fortunately for the French Nation there were no Republican presidents in that epoch.

In closing, Barack Obama has indicated in several different speeches that he intends to launch a concerted program to extend healthcare to the entire nation. He was careful however to state that even by the end of his first term it will by no means be universal.

The American Medical Association and the hospitalization insurance industry will spend billions of dollars to prevent further extension of free medical care such as is provided for Senior Citizens with Medicare.

Recall that some of our greatest Democratic Presidents attempted and failed to reach that goal. The wondrous Franklin Delano Roosevelt in 1935 was unable to overcome the might of that barrier to progress.

Harry Truman renewed the quest in his second term and was equally unsuccessful. Lyndon Johnson reached the goal but only for those on Social Security.

Hillary Clinton's plan was destroyed by a monstrous avalanche of TV lies and distortions. In 2009 we can expect even worse, as soon as legislation is introduced by the Obama Administration.

Once again we Democrats will have to counter those ads with our own. Under the leadership of President Barack and the Democratic Party I feel confident we will.

INDEX

1702518